ESTHER SIMPSON

ESTHER SIMPSON

The True Story of Her Mission to
Save Scholars from Hitler's Persecution

JOHN EIDINOW

ROBINSON

ROBINSON

First published in Great Britain in 2023 by Robinson

1 3 5 7 9 10 8 6 4 2

A CIP catalogue record for this book is
available from the British Library

ISBN: 978-1-47214-322-8 (hardback)
ISBN: 978-1-47214-323-5 (trade paperback)

Typeset in Dante MT Std by SX Composing DTP Ltd, Rayleigh, Essex
Printed and bound in Great Britain by Clays Ltd, Elcograf S.p.A.

Papers used by Robinson are from well-managed forests
and other responsible sources

Robinson
An imprint of
Little, Brown Book Group
Carmelite House
50 Victoria Embankment
London EC4Y 0DZ

An Hachette UK Company
www.hachette.co.uk

www.littlebrown.co.uk

For Elisabeth

CONTENTS

Prologue

Your Royal Highness and Chancellor, I present to you Miss Esther Simpson. Esther Simpson's name does not appear in Who's Who. *Considering her profound influence on our intellectual life, it leads one indeed to question who is not in* Who's Who.

– Professor Lesley Rees, London University Public Orator, on awarding an Honorary LL.D. *h.c.* 1984

If you had any capacity for vanity (which you haven't) you would be immensely proud as you look back on your imperishable achievement in these past thirty years or so. Seldom can so many have owed so much to one person working with such few material resources. Yours was a wholly personal success, the giving of yourself and your friendship unstintingly in a way that literally changed the cultural history of the world.

– Sir Walter Adams, general secretary of the Academic Assistance Council/ Society for the Protection of Science and Learning 1933–1938, on the occasion of Esther Simpson's retirement presentation 9 June 1966.

Join us to honour the memory of Esther Simpson and the values that she stood for, which included inclusivity, community and support for marginalised groups, the global role of academia in benefiting society, progressing human rights, and a love for music and the arts.

– from the invitation to the Grand Opening of the Esther Simpson Building at Leeds University and the unveiling of a Leeds Civic Trust blue plaque on 8 March 2022, each signalling her iconic status as a twentieth-century heroine saint.

In a report anticipating the Grand Opening, the *Guardian* newspaper quoted Martin Hamilton, the director of Leeds Civic Trust responsible for the plaque:

> It is no exaggeration to say that without Esther's work . . . the way the world has changed, it would have changed in a different way.

Drawing on an interview with Hamilton, the *Guardian* report by the paper's North of England correspondent Mark Brown described Esther as,

> An unsung heroine who helped save the lives of hundreds of scholars seeking refuge from Nazi-occupied Europe . . . She was not the head of the charity, but she was the one who did the work.

And,

> 'She was the engine behind the whole thing,' said Hamilton. 'She was responsible for dealing with all the applications for people to go to safety and she made the decisions. Esther Simpson was making life or death decisions every day of the week, working very long hours. Simpson said the work she did was the academic equivalent of the kindertransport [*sic*] programme.'

The *Kindertransport* programme brought 10,000 unaccompanied Jewish children to Britain from Germany and Austria on an emergency basis, and then about 700 from Czech lands (after annexation in March 1939 of the Protectorate of Bohemia and Moravia). The first arrivals in Britain were on 2 December 1938 at the port of Harwich.

The plaque itself reads:

Esther Simpson OBE
This graduate of the University of Leeds was born in nearby
Little London to immigrant parents
She was appointed Assistant Secretary to the
Academic Assistance Council in 1933
Through her work in the decades that followed
the hundreds of refugee scholars she saved
from persecution and death included
sixteen future Nobel Laureates
1903–1996

After the opening, an Esther Simpson memorial concert was held, including 'pieces linked to her Jewish heritage'.

1

The Desk Saviour

From July 1933, when she was thirty years old, Esther Simpson's whole working life was principally committed to one cause and one organisation.

The cause was support for displaced refugee academics, initially from Hitler's Germany, in their search for a renewed academic life abroad. The organisation was named the Academic Assistance Council (AAC), established in London in May 1933 to offer that support. In 1936 the AAC took on a wider social mandate, becoming the Society for the Protection of Science and Learning (SPSL).

It continues today, having returned to its roots as, first in 1999, the Council for Assisting Refugee Academics (CARA), and in 2014 preserving the acronym but widening the remit by becoming the Council for At-Risk Academics.

'Principally committed' because from 1944 to 1966 she was in practice manager and hostess of The Society for Visiting Scientists, a club in the West End of London for foreign scientists visiting or working in Britain.

In the AAC/SPSL's heyday, she was assistant secretary. Later she became secretary, and on official retirement a Council member, and finally an honorary consultant. But the point is that, as memorialised, Esther Simpson in effect became the AAC/SPSL and the heroine and saint of displaced academics.

A summary of her role at the AAC/SPSL in Sybil Oldfield's riveting study of the Gestapo's plans for a post-invasion Britain, *The Black Book: The Britons on the Nazi Hit List*, catches exactly Esther Simpson's public memory.

The Society for the Protection of Science and Learning was targeted in the Black Book, and having noted 'the council's most influential backers, the Nobel prize winners Lord Rutherford and Professor A. V. Hill, and Sir William Beveridge at the LSE', Sybil Oldfield continues,

> However, the one person really running the show at the Academic Assistance Council was Esther (Tess) Simpson (1903–1996). She became a one-woman reception centre, accommodation bureau and specialist academic re-employment exchange for around 2,600 refugee German and Austrian Jewish intellectuals between 1933 and 1940. Tess Simpson started work in 1933 and did not stop for sixty years, still helping persecuted intellectuals from all races and from all over the world. Being the only person manning the Academic Assistance Council's offices at Clement's Inn, she would certainly have been arrested there after a Nazi invasion.

In her book *Doers of the Word: British Women Humanitarians 1900–1950*, Sybil Oldfield writes further:

> They [refugee intellectuals] arrived in Britain rejected, nearly destitute, traumatized by humiliation and hatred, with apparently no prospects. She greeted them with warmth, sympathy, a highly cultured intelligence, and immense practical help, and set them 'on the stairway to survival and success' [obituary Hampstead and Highgate Express Nov/Dec 1996]. For many she found sanctuary and employment in Britain. For others she found a new life, first of all in small colleges in the United States or in universities in the British Commonwealth. For almost all of them, their broken lives were mended.

The encomium for her London University Honorary Doctorate, written and delivered by the Public Orator (Professor Lesley Rees) from a previous consultation with the graduand, sums up the work involved in rescuing the displaced academic. We can take it as Esther's own account:

> She started securing residential and labour permits and constructing Curricula Vitae of academics seeking help, and helping them re-establish existing contacts and obtaining support from referees.

The data were sent to specialist panels who advised on career prospects and the SPSL awarded grants to tide them over until they built a home, mastered the language, and obtained suitable employment.

The Public Orator then took up the theme of what made Esther's work with the refugees so distinctive:

Your graduand became the friend of all those who passed through the SPSL and a family grew with her at the centre and the intellectual life of this country gained immeasurably by this activity, infinitely more than it gave.

The Public Orator then took the concept of Esther's family to its limit:

As I said before, Esther Simpson regards all those she has helped as her family . . . She still follows the progress of her children, grandchildren, and now great-grandchildren, rejoicing in their successes and caring and sharing in their griefs. Hundreds of scholars have looked to her for help, and her kindness, efficiency, and phenomenal memory have created an atmosphere of warmth and affection.

Esther was an active Quaker and the journal of the Society of Friends, *The Friend*, for 23 November 1984 carried an account of the award: 'Tess Simpson among Family and Friends (a great deal of academic ceremony and some very funny hats).'

The story is her 'family':

She became the friend of all those who passed through the SPSL and they in turn became her 'family' – and a very distinguished family it has turned out to be. (The full register of the SPSL has produced at least fifteen Nobel laureates, seventy Fellows of the Royal Society, forty Fellows of the British Academy, and fourteen Knights of the Realm!)

Doers of the Word also describes Esther's role in the release of interned 'enemy alien' scholars in 1940, putting her at the head of the release campaign:

. . . it was to take a year of non-stop day-and-night lobbying, letter-writing and interviews, all backed by the most meticulous

documentation attesting to the integrity of each individual 'case',
before Tess Simpson, aided by Professor A. V. Hill, Vice-President of
the Executive Committee of the Society and MP for Cambridge
University, and Eleanor Rathbone,[1] succeeded in having all the
interned intellectuals released.

That Esther Simpson played a significant part in the release process for
interned 'enemy alien' scholars in 1940 is beyond question: cometh the
hour, cometh the woman.

Where she actually fitted in that process is for later. But the tenor of the
description – it was Tess Simpson who succeeded in having the internees
released – is absolutely in line with heroic accounts of Esther Simpson's life
and work, for the realities of which she was in fact justly celebrated in her
lifetime. In his 1955 letter to the then prime minister, Sir Anthony Eden,
seeking an OBE for Esther, A. V. Hill included this passage:

> During the war I was MP for Cambridge University and also Secretary
> of the Royal Society. In both capacities I had the opportunity of helping
> to get the services of able refugees better utilized for the war effort.
> In this Miss Simpson's knowledge, critical judgement and experience
> were invaluable. By what she did then not only did she build up a fund
> of goodwill towards this country when it was most needed but she
> made a substantial contribution to the national cause.

---

1 Independent MP for the Combined English Universities

2

Sung

No heroine is so appealing as one declared unsung. But at the risk of lessening her appeal, it has to be acknowledged that far from being 'an unsung heroine', by the end of her long life Esther Simpson (1903–1996) had been the subject of an international paean, outstripping other champions of refugees, say, Bertha Bracey or Eleanor Rathbone.

She had been awarded the French *Ordre des Palmes Académiques* and *Officier D'Académie Ministère d l'Education Nationale*, the OBE, honorary doctorates from the universities of London and Leeds, Honorary Membership of the Royal College of Physicians, and in 1996 the Austrian *Ehrenkreuz für Wissenschaft und Kunst* first class for services to 'Austrian scientists compelled to emigrate 1933 to 1945'. The order was presented to her in London by the then Austrian ambassador, Dr Georg Hennig.

Though not a scientist, she also enjoyed – precisely the right term – recognition by The Royal Society in London, the world's oldest national scientific academy. It was founded in 1660 to form a permanent learned society with the aim of bringing together the brightest scientific minds of the day. To be elected a Fellow is to receive the highest recognition from fellow scientists. As of November 2020, more than 280 Nobel Prize winners were numbered among its Fellows and Foreign Members.

The Royal Society gave her the right to lunch there, which she did regularly, taking guests. She was an invitee to its main events. In 1990, at the annual meeting of the Royal Society, the retiring president George Porter had saluted Esther by inviting her to stand for applause.

Her life and work is the subject of a 1992 book, *Refugee Scholars: Conversations with Tess Simpson*, edited by Ray Cooper, of which we will hear much more. In May 2017, BBC Radio 4 broadcast a deservedly highly praised documentary by David Edmonds, *Miss Simpson's Children*; a compelling programme which rediscovered her, and from which this book sprang. David Edmonds also wrote an article on her for the *Jewish Chronicle*:

> Esther Simpson – the unknown heroine. The extraordinary story of how one woman offered refuge to philosophers, scientists and musicians fleeing from the Nazis, and in doing so reshaped the cultural and intellectual landscape of the Western World.

Why then 'unsung'? Perhaps the tribute 'heroine' was felt to be incomplete without it.

The invitation's recitation of 'the values that she stood for, which included inclusivity, community and support for marginalised groups . . .' also has an iconic feel to it.

Esther's commitment from July 1933 on was precisely to the succour of previously comfortably-off academics of the highest calibre who had been displaced as 'non-Aryans' or political opponents in Hitler's Germany, then in Austria, Czechoslovakia, and in Mussolini's Italy. Yes, as a fact of history Hitler's regime excluded and marginalised them, together with other 'non-Aryans' and political opponents. But in the years from 1933 to her death in 1996, fighting for the 2022 contemporary values of *inclusivity, community and support for marginalised groups* was never, visibly at least, part of her social or political outlook. Nor, it must be said, was she on her own in succouring the displaced academics, much as she may have wanted it to seem so.

She had not been in at the creation of the AAC in May 1933: that lay with a group of established British academics and their reaction to Hitler's policies towards German academics after he took power in January 1933.

In his 1959 account of the Academic Assistance Council/Society for the Protection of Science and Learning [AAC/SPSL], *A Defence of Free Learning*, the AAC's founding prime-mover Sir William Beveridge wrote that his book was concerned only with the help needed by and given to a special class – university teachers and scholars. They were an insignificant proportion of refugees, 2,600 against hundreds of thousands. 'Individually they are of outstanding importance . . . World famous scientists and scholars whom we saved.'

As the French Committee *Association Universelle pour les Exilés Allemands* put it:

> The Academic Assistance Council of England . . . was formed to give immediate succour to the refugee scholars and to investigate every possibility of placement. No praise can be too high to give this distinguished body of British scholars and men of affairs for their unceasing efforts on behalf of the displaced German professors.

In December 2008 a two-day conference was held at the British Academy in London to celebrate what was expressed as the seventy-fifth anniversary of the founding of the Council for Assisting Refugee Academics (CARA), successor to the AAC/SPSL. The contributions were published by the British Academy as Proceedings 169 in September 2011 under the title *In Defence of Learning: The Plight, Persecution, and Placement of Academic Refugees 1933–1980s*.

In her comprehensive introduction to the volume, Professor Shula Marks, former SPSL/CARA Council chair, writes:

> Nevertheless, this 'heroic' story – which is part of the social capital of CARA and one it therefore likes to repeat – is somewhat misleading about CARA's past and even more so about its current work. As Lord Moser (himself a child refugee who came to Britain with his parents in 1936) remarked in his 1992 Zweig lecture:
>
> 'It is all too easy to list refugees who have reached fame and influence, though even with them one needs to ask whether they have made lasting contributions . . . One also has to remember that often their distinction or contribution did not . . . come with their luggage but was brought to fruition here. Then one has to remember the many who made contributions which didn't hit the headlines; and even more the perhaps tens of thousands who have lived unglossy and ordinary lives, perhaps happy, perhaps dominated by illness, poverty and loneliness.'

George Eliot's lines from *Middlemarch* immediately come to mind:

> . . . for the growing good of the world is partly dependent on unhistoric
> acts; and that things are not so ill with you and me as they might have
> been is half owing to the number who lived faithfully a hidden life,
> and rest in unvisited tombs.

The version of the AAC/SPSL's history that has Esther Simpson single-
handedly rescuing mainly Jewish (future) Nobel Prize winners from Nazi
oppression and British internment might be termed super-heroic. The
common attribution is that she saved sixteen future Nobel Prize winners.

How far this presents the realities of the woman herself and her long and
devoted commitment to the succour of academic refugees is the subject
of what follows.

3
Hitler's Apples

Walter Cook, founding director of New York University's Institute of Fine Arts, famously quipped:

> Hitler is my best friend. He shakes the tree and I collect the apples.

At the core of this story, then, lie the malign workings of the Hitler regime, racial and political, as they affected scholars. In consequence, in Peter Gay's much-quoted observation in *Weimar Culture: The Outsider as Insider*:

> The exiles that Hitler made were the greatest collection of transplanted intellect, talent and scholarship the world has ever seen.

The plight of refugees generally has not been better summed up than by Hannah Arendt in *The Origins of Totalitarianism*. Of the civil wars that erupted at the end of the First World War, she remarked,

> They were followed by migrations of groups who, unlike their happier predecessors in the religious wars, were welcomed nowhere and could be assimilated nowhere. Once they left their homeland they remained homeless; once they left their state they became stateless; once they were deprived of their human rights, they were rightless, the scum of the earth.

Herself a veteran of the Vichy regime's 1940 Gurs internment camp, she wrote,

> After the Germans invaded the country the French government had
> only to change the name of the firm. Having been jailed because we
> were Germans, we were not freed because we were Jews.

But it must be recognised that the scholars Hitler displaced from their seats
of learning and who became enforced migrants were, potentially at least,
among the more fortunate of the exiles.

Whether from science, philosophy, philology, history or archaeology,
they belonged to an elite, an international fellowship of learning whose
other members far and wide could recognise their worth and offer them a
new home, or who were possibly already acquainted with and respectful
of their academic work.

They were a world apart from a refugee example Hannah Arendt gives
in her 1943 essay *We Refugees*, with its plaintive and probably hopeless claim
for respect,

> You don't know to whom you speak. I was section manager at Karstadt
> [a major Berlin department store].

The Nobel laureate and driving force of the AAC/SPSL from its foundation
[also Member of Parliament, war-time government scientific adviser, orna-
ment of the Royal Society], Professor A. V. Hill identified this when he asked,

> Why a special Society of Scientists? There are two reasons – and we
> needn't be too modest about it. First it must be recognised that science
> has come to play a decisive role in human society. Secondly, science
> provides an international fellowship whose members have a common
> language and a relationship of esteem and appreciation with colleagues
> elsewhere. No other occupation has comparable world-wide
> interconnections of interest, knowledge, respect and understanding.
> [A.V. Hill 1956]

In his 1959 account of the AAC/SPSL, *A Defence of Free Learning*, Lord
Beveridge, an economist, makes a similar point about his colleagues from
the natural sciences:

> Not only were they ready to give an indefinite amount of time to the
> task of considering cases for assistance, but they began by knowing

all about the work and worth of their fellow scientists in all countries. They showed themselves to be truly international.

As a champion of academic refugees, Sir William Beveridge was already a national figure as director of the London School of Economics from 1919 to 1937, when he went as Master to University College Oxford. But he was known and respected for his work in the public service from before the First World War when he had already organised the new national labour exchanges and system of National Insurance. During that war he had worked on manpower control; after the war he was briefly permanent secretary in the Ministry of Food. He was chairman of the Unemployment Insurance Statutory Committee in 1934 and chairman of the committee to plan food rationing in 1936. The epochal Beveridge Report, the blueprint for the post-war welfare state, lay ahead in 1942.

In his obituary of Beveridge for the *New Statesman*,[2] the editor Kingsley Martin, who had worked under Beveridge at the London School of Economics, described him as

> ... by nature lonely, a despot who resented criticism, could not tolerate opposition, did not hide his view that the people whose welfare he gave his life to securing were fools who deserved no such consideration ...

But Martin also wrote of his being

> ... entirely disinterested in his desire to do good to his fellow men ... No one I think ever had as voracious an appetite for facts, as swift a capacity for marshalling them, or a more creative gift for seeing how a beneficial policy could be advised from them. He was a superb planner, but a bad administrator because administration involves individuals.

Access to the highest levels of government was his for the lifting of a telephone. He wrote of,

---

2   https://www.newstatesman.com/politics/2013/04/
    kingsley-martins-obituary-william-beveridge-1879-1963

> All the contacts which my varied life had given me with the Press and
> BBC, with ministers and civil servants and businessmen, with the
> Foundations that might give us money.

So, for instance,

> With the government we had friendly contact through Sir John Simon
> [Home Secretary 1935–1937; Chancellor 1937–1940] – he accepted AAC
> suggestions made to him that landing conditions should be relaxed . . .
> Our list of such people included some very distinguished names
> indeed, among the most valued additions today that the free world
> owes to Hitler.

And with the press, he had the best of all contacts – the editor of *The Times*,
Geoffrey Dawson.

> We never failed to tell him in advance when we wanted special
> publicity and we never failed to get it.

To note these elite characteristics attaching to the refugees' academic
champions is not to devalue the individual pain of exile, which springs
from its unfortunate subjects' uprooting, the sense of loss and deprivation
of what was and what might have been. But it is essential to understanding
the circumstances of the story of Esther 'Tess' Simpson that follows.

Before embarking on her life, we should also mark the centrality of
Germany and German to the creation of the modern Jewish experience,
whether in terms of religious reform, emancipation, assimilation or the
pathways into secular culture. Historic Germany is inescapably at the heart.

It lingers there still in the attachment to their German cultural heritage
of the second and third generation of the original German-speaking Jewish
refugees, enforced migrants, exiles – the uprooted – and realised in well-
attended cultural, historical, subject groups. (Internment in 1940 remains
a topic of prime interest.)

As Hannah Arendt wrote in the preface to her 1957 edition of *Rahel
Varnhagen: the life of a Jewish Woman*, originally completed in 1933:

> The German-speaking Jews and their history are an altogether unique
> phenomenon; nothing comparable to it is to be found even in the other

areas of Jewish assimilation. To investigate this phenomenon, which among other things found expression in a literally astonishing wealth of talent and of scientific and intellectual productivity, constitutes a historical task of the first rank, and one which, of course, can be attacked only now, after the history of the German Jews has come to an end.

Bound into that is German pre-eminence in science at the start of the twentieth century. As A. V. Hill put it in a 1933 lecture,

A country unexcelled in its contribution to science in the last hundred years.

The German Empire was the undisputed hub of the scientific universe. From 1901, when the Nobel Prizes were established, to 1932, Germans won almost a third of all the Nobels awarded to scientists – thirty-one in total. American scientists, in contrast, won five during the same period. This impressive German record was fuelled, in part, by Jewish researchers who just decades earlier would have been excluded from prominent academic positions – a quarter of German laureates were of Jewish descent, despite the fact that less than 1 per cent of the German population was Jewish.

At the time the Nazis seized power on 30 January 1933, it was not unusual for German major scientific institutes to be led by Nobel laureates with Jewish roots: Albert Einstein and Otto Meyerhof, both Jewish, ran prestigious centres of physics and medical research; Fritz Haber, who had converted from Judaism in the late nineteenth century, ran a chemistry institute; and Otto Warburg, who was raised as a Protestant but had two Jewish grandparents, was the director of a recently opened centre for cell physiology.

Of course, 'Jewish' does not mean necessarily observant. As the novelist Jakob Wassermann put it in *Mein Weg als Deutscher und Jude* (*My Life as German and Jew*):

I am a German and I am a Jew, one as much and as fully as the other, both simultaneously and irrevocably.

The Nobel Prize-winning physicist Max Born wrote to his fellow-physicist Paul Ehrenfest:

I have never felt myself to be particularly Jewish. [His family] (and I also) have absolutely no emotional ties to true Judaism, to its ways and laws. I am – or believe myself to be – basically a liberal Western European with a heavy streak of German culture. I am as little nationalistically inclined toward Juda as I am towards Germania, but actually less so, since I know neither Hebrew nor Jewish literature and have come to love the German language, poetry and art.[3]

We must also contemplate the word *refugee*. In this account of Esther Simpson it is inescapable. Her own account of her life and work, as narrated to R. M. Cooper, is entitled *Refugee Scholars: Conversations with Tess Simpson*.

Yet as Hannah Arendt points out in her illuminating 1943 essay *We Refugees*,

A refugee used to be a person driven to seek refuge because of some act committed or some political opinion held. Well, it is true we have had to seek refuge; but we have committed no acts and most of us never dreamt of having any radical opinions.

They are 'refugees' because they have to seek assistance from refugee committees, she says. But starting again required optimism and so they were optimists even though,

We lost our home, which means the familiarity of daily life. We lost our occupation, which means the confidence that we are of some use in this world. We lost our language, which means the naturalness of reactions, the simplicity of gestures, the unaffected expression of feelings. We left our relatives in the Polish ghettoes and our best friends have been killed in concentration camps, and that means the rupture of our private lives.

Now they are required to forget the past and so they learn to make no allusion to it:

Apparently nobody wants to know that contemporary history has created a new kind of human beings – the kind that are put into

3 Ehrenfest scientific microfilm No. 535, DMM; cf. also Wolff 11993, p. 268.

concentration camps by their foes and into internment camps by their friends.

As Bernard Schweizer writes in 'Rebecca West and the Meaning of Exile',[4]

The view of exile as deprivation, struggle, and homesickness is arguably the common experience among the majority of displaced people throughout the world.

Rebecca West spoke at SPSL fundraising meetings before the Second World War. Schweizer quotes her vivid metaphor,

. . . all over England and France and America so many Jews were mourning for the fatherland in a grief visible as jaundice.

4 'Rebecca West and the Meaning of Exile', *Partial Answers: Journal of Literature and the History of Ideas*, Volume 8, Number 2, June 2010, pp. 389–407, published by Johns Hopkins University Press.

4

Her Children

Famously, Esther Simpson called them her children, the mainly Jewish academics whose careers she helped to restart after they had been displaced from their universities and research institutes under Hitler's government.

So, for instance, in 1953 she wrote to an Austrian friend and former SPSL grantee, the leading scientist Engelbert Broda, now back in Vienna,

> . . . Another of 'my' children has got the Nobel Prize – [Sir Hans] Krebs (Biochemistry); his colleague [Sir Ernst] Chain was in the Society for Visiting Scientists [which she was then running] the other day.

The claim of kinship extended to the descendants of the original displaced scholars. A letter to Engelbert Broda in 1971 informs him,

> I now have another FRS [Fellow of the Royal Society] of the second generation – John Polanyi, son of Michael, Professor of Chemistry in Toronto.

And in 1972,

> In spite of the horrible news all round, I am feeling happy today. Yesterday was the annual election of Fellows of the Royal Society, and 'I' have three, as well as two others in whom I am interested. 'Mine' are Herman [sic] Lehmann, Gustave [sic] Born, and Fritz Ursell; the two latter are 'my' second generation, of whom 'I' now have three

(the other is Walter Honigmann). Did you know Ellis Cosslett, husband of Ann [sic] Wischin, who died not very long ago, and former friend of Kätl Schiff (Dornberger)? He is now FRS . . . So I continue to be a proud grandmama [referring to her 'children'], having well over 50 FRSs by now . . .

[Walter Honigmann may be a mistaken reference to the zoologist Hans Honigmann, though he is not listed as FRS. Katharina Boll-Dornberger. Anna Wischin was a chemist.]

What was the significance of the inverted commas? We might suppose they are intended to signal that she was writing not literally but speaking as the SPSL, though where she and the Society in effect were one and the same.

In 1972, after a visit to Cambridge she wrote again about Hermann Lehmann:

> . . . my newest FRS. Last night I told Kürti (He gave the vote of thanks) that 'I' had three more FRSs, and he said he was not at all surprised, as there was no stopping me. I wonder which of the next generation I will be congratulating in the future?

[Professor Nicholas Kürti, a low temperature physicist, one of a group brought to Oxford by Professor Lindemann. Professor Lehmann, Professor of Biochemistry at Cambridge.]

Those of her 'children' who could not attend Esther Simpson's 9 June 1966 SPSL retirement party in person (the retirement was more nominal than real) sent tributes to her and her work giving succour to them as politically displaced academics.

Sir Walter Adams, formerly Director of the London School of Economics and Principal of the University College of Rhodesia, had been in at the beginning as the AAC's initial general secretary. He was among those writing for her retirement, with the most striking – if somewhat bizarre in its magnitude – of the tributes, partly quoted above. Perhaps we should see him as playing on his memories of Esther at work:

> Seldom can so many have owed so much to one person working with such few material resources. Yours was a wholly personal success, the

giving of yourself and of your friendship unstintingly, in a way that
literally changed the cultural history of the world. I do not know what
your present score of Barons, Knights, Fellows of the Royal, and so on
is, but your family – of which you are mother and sister – is without
doubt the most talented and distinguished in the world.

In that score would be numbered sixteen Nobel Prize winners, eighteen
Knights, seventy-four Fellows of the Royal Society, thirty-four Fellows of
the British Academy, two Companions of Honour, two Members of the
Order of Merit. But just as important to mention is the range of learning
the enforced migrants had brought to British academic life, subjects then
almost unknown to Britain: art history, psychology and sociology; a new
depth of analysis to philology and musicology. Child psychiatry also made
the journey.

With the retirement tributes came a cheque for £3,500 [some £56,000 in
today's money] intended for the purchase of a retirement flat. In her long
years of service to stricken academics, Miss Simpson had moved from one
rented room to another in the Hampstead area of north-west London, most
recently in 1960, where at 28 Steele's Road she had found, she told Broda,

> a room at the top – 89 steps – a nice big room with a high ceiling, large
> bay windows that don't fit and a door with hiatuses all round making
> it impossible to heat.

Until the 1970s it was impossible for a single working woman to find a
mortgage in her own right, but anyway Miss Simpson had seemed content
to rent on her meagre salary. Surprisingly for an established charity, the
AAC/SPSL never had a settled office, eventually residing with Esther.
Equally, she had never had a settled home, taking the Society with her when
she moved. Whither she lodged, it lodged. She and the Society became as
one, inseparable.

Now her 'children' had determined that she should have a place of
her own and had come up with the cash. Her choice was a flat in the
Swiss Cottage area of north-west London, at 3 Buckland Crescent, a white
stuccoed Victorian terrace house, then home to six people and requiring
substantial maintenance, which dominated her first months there. A short

walk from Steele's Road, it now became home to the SPSL and was left to the Society in her will (to the surprise of Council members). From the age of thirty, the work to support displaced academics had been her life; she continued that support in death.

When she died, obituaries appeared in the *Daily Telegraph*, *The Times*, the *Guardian*, the *Independent* and the *Jewish Chronicle*. The grandest salute of all has been the posthumous naming after her of a building at Leeds University Business School in 2022. Helen Greaves, Divisional Assistant at the School, said she had suggested the building be named after Esther Simpson as she found her 'a real inspiration'.

Albie Sachs, the anti-apartheid South African lawyer seriously injured in an assassination attempt, whom Esther helped when he came to London, saw her as combining the ethereal and practical, though not necessarily a hero,

> I regard her as an exemplary person of loveliness and kindness and efficient support. I don't think we need heroes in the world. We need courage and solidarity.[5]

It was not only her administrative work for the would-be refugees that brought praise. Engelbert Broda could not come to London to attend her 1966 retirement party and presentation. From Vienna he wrote in terms that bring to life what she offered her refugees beyond form-filling. The letter is quoted here as it appears in *Scientist Spies: A Memoir of My Three Parents and the Atom Bomb* by Engelbert's son Paul, a compelling narrative of why he could not have returned to Britain, to which we will return:

> Many people have grounds for delight on this day when you will be honoured by the large number of former refugees who have every reason to be grateful to you . . . It has not only been your power of discrimination between genuine and phoney and your sheer efficiency and tenacity that made this achievement possible. (An efficiency that I initially took, in my ignorance, as being the inheritance of generations of North English nonconformists . . .) The other pillar has been your

---

5 Quoted in *Esther Simpson – The unknown heroine* by David Edmonds, *Jewish Chronicle*, 11 May 2017.

human approach, your interest in the individual, your readiness to act for real persons, not numbers. Never in my life I have found that particular combination again, and I think that this combination has dominated the feeling of everybody in your sphere . . . I remember the first visit to your office – there was tea. I had been pressed by friends for a long time, and had been hesitant to call. I dreaded the inevitable question of my official status at Vienna University; how could I expect an Englishwoman to understand that in the 'thirties there could be no official status for a left-winger in Austria – even if he were far better as a scientist than I? But you inspired confidence. There was also the moment when – again with hesitations – I asked you whether you would like to see the baby. Through you I obtained my first real job in England – in fact the first real job as a scientist at all, in the sense there was official status and payment (£15) every first of the month. That work (visual purple) is still the work to which I most like to think back; quiet, concentrated work by myself in a most interesting field.

Esther herself struck a humble note after receiving the honorary doctorate from London University in 1984, as she reflected in what passes for her autobiography, *Refugee Scholars: Conversations with Tess Simpson*. 'I can't have done too badly.'

In the typescript she has handwritten underneath, 'What more is there to say?'

Whether she meant in that particular ceremony or in life, either seems appropriate.

5
Refugee Scholars

Some who worked with Esther Simpson put her elevation into the pantheon of refugee saviours down to the 1992 book *Refugee Scholars*, edited by R. M. Cooper. More than edited. He tape-recorded Esther's recollections and had them transcribed, organised the text, and self-published it as a paperback in 1992 as from 'Moorland Books' at his home address in Leeds. (Moorland Books in 2022 is a bookshop; the proprietor patiently fields enquiries after the now non-existent publisher.)

Cooper and his wife Kay lived in a Victorian house in the leafy suburb of Roundhay in north-east Leeds, where Esther visited them, writing to congratulate Kay on the size of the peonies in her large garden.

It is a book of eight chapters. The first is Cooper's summary of Esther's account of the years 1903 to 1925, what she has told him of her childhood and education in Leeds up to her first-class degree in French and German at Leeds University. Then:

And now for the next five chapters let Esther speak for herself.

Cooper lets the transcribed tapes take over the story in chapters on her post-graduate years working in Breslau, Paris, Vienna and Geneva, where she heard the call to rescue displaced scholars and set out for London; on the SPSL; on The Society for Visiting Scientists (and the British Association for the Advancement of Science); on refugee scholars she had known, organised by the distinctions they received; and, the last chapter from the tapes, looking back at her love of playing chamber music.

Cooper added a chapter on the part played by the SPSL and by Esther in securing the release of some 500 refugee scholars from internment in 1940; this he compiled from the Society's archives as Esther 'did not enlarge' on it. He also added an illuminating account by Paul Jacobsthal, a leading authority on Celtic art, of his internment in the notorious Warth Mill and in Hutchinson Camp on the Isle of Man. An Epilogue recites some of the tributes paid to Esther by the 320 contributors to the cheque presented at her retirement party on 9 June 1966. Cooper also lists the globe-encircling cities from which the contributions and tributes came, from Ann Arbor to Zürich via Sydney.

His personal tribute comes in his introduction to the book:

> What stood out from our conversations was Esther's total commitment to the refugee cause and her instinctive ability to involve herself completely in each and every one of the hundreds of refugee scholars who appealed to the Society for help.

Of her interlocutor, and initiator of the book, Ray [short for Raymund] Cooper, no sound is to be heard or presence felt in the 'conversations' – more interaction-free monologues covering her life and its full realisation through her friendships with the best and the brightest of German-speaking, mainly Jewish refugee scholars, and their children, and their children's children, and with fellow musicians. Perhaps that is explained by the book's original sub-title, 'Personal Recollections of Refugee Scholars'.

For a sense of contact with Cooper, we must go to his subsequent 1996 work, *Retrospective Sympathetic Affection: A tribute to the academic community*, also self-published from Leeds. In the preface he writes that the more he discovered about the SPSL and the Society for Visiting Scientists [where Esther worked from 1944 to 1966], the more he came to realise how much we owed to the small group of scholars and scientists who founded these societies.

Ray Cooper. Reproduced by kind permission of Hugh, Martin and Frances Cooper

Assiduously researched, this second book's unstated purpose seems to have been to revisit some of the narrative in *Refugee Scholars*, and to cure its errors and omissions, particularly to reweight the AAC/SPSL story towards the senior academics, such as A. V. Hill, whose importance in its history cannot be overstated.

Hugh Cooper recalled to me his father's determination to ensure that Tess was given the credit for what he regarded as a significant role in the development of academic life in this country. But though it played a major part in shaping public perceptions of Esther Simpson, *Refugees Scholars* was not the book Cooper had envisaged. The more personal account of Esther's life he had urged on her, her anecdotes of the well-known, the development of her musical tastes, remained out of reach.

6
Esther's Version

The story of *Refugee Scholars* starts with a letter in *The Times* on 24 August 1987 that caught the eye of Ray Cooper. It was from a Francis Steiner and advocated a study of the contribution to Britain made by the refugees of the 1930s.

Steiner came from a Viennese Jewish family, and had arrived in London on the first *Kindertransport* from Vienna in 1938. He had been prompted into writing by two recent *Times* obituaries of refugees, Hans Motz, Professor of Engineering at Oxford, and Peter Schidlof, the Amadeus String Quartet viola player. Steiner likened the influx of refugees from central Europe to that of the Huguenots in 1685, and the impact of the skills they brought with them. He also wrote an article for the *AJR* (Association of Jewish Refugees) *Information* in December 1987, 'The Case for a History of Refugee Achievement', which roused more interest among former refugees.

A dozen or so people responded to Steiner's letter and attended a meeting to discuss how his proposal could be taken further, among them Ray Cooper.

Having volunteered for and served in the Royal Artillery throughout the Second World War, Raymund Michael Cooper took a war degree at Oxford in 1946, where he was a noted sportsman. He then was employed in government service in Sudan for several years before going into business. Having retired, he took an MA in British history at Leeds University in 1987 and was indeed looking for a research project when the letter in *The Times* from Francis Steiner aroused his interest.

At the meeting he sat next to Joan Stiebel (1911–2007), who had worked for the World Jewish Relief organisation and had been involved in bringing Nazi concentration camp orphans to Britain after the war. She was recognised by the British Government as a British Hero of the Holocaust in 2019. If he was interested in following up Steiner's idea, she advised Cooper, he should get in touch with Esther Simpson.

In fact, in collaboration with Steiner and the interested group he assembled, Ray Cooper initially looked at a broad range of contributions made to Britain by German Jewish refugees of the 1930s and '40s. In the course of this he telephoned the SPSL at 3 Buckland Crescent and Esther Simpson sent him three documents about its origin, aims and refugee scholars. She also directed him to recordings at the Imperial War Museum of people who had contributed to the war effort, including her own. They met for the first time in December 1987.

From the correspondence, the relationship takes time to warm. In March 1988 it is still 'Dear Miss Simpson' and 'Dear Mr Cooper'; 'Dear Esther' comes in June 1988; 'Dear Tess' has to wait until May 1989, though she is signing herself 'Esther' in 1993. She invited him to lunch at the Royal Society; he invited her to stay in Leeds, which she had not visited for twenty years.

Cooper told her how the Steiner group were casting about for an area or category of refugees to research with a book in mind: *A History of Refugee Achievement*. But discovery in early 1988 of plans for a wide-ranging academic conference on German Jewish immigration to the UK to be held at Cambridge under the auspices of the Leo Baeck Institute was a red light. Cooper wrote to Esther that they were contemplating how to proceed, if proceed at all. The whole subject of refugees had been extensively researched and there was little point in repeating this effort.

Esther's response was briskly to dismiss the Leo Baeck Institute conference as concerned with German-speaking Jews, not necessarily refugees, and adequate only within narrow limits. It was not enough that certain sections had done well as individuals. The emphasis should be on the intellectual, practical and indeed spiritual contributions made to the life of this country and through the achievements of refugees to the world in general. It would be a great pity if he gave up at this stage.

Another suggestion that came Cooper's way if he wanted to research 1930s refugee scholars was to start with the SPSL papers in the Bodleian Library in Oxford. Or he could pick on particular refugees. Or he could look at the origins of the British Academy 'Thank Offering to Britain' Fellowships (from the central European Jewish refugees' 'Thank You Britain' fund established in 1963).

While Cooper was pointed to the SPSL papers in the Bodleian, that was in general terms. At this point, 'Esther Simpson' is not seen as a public figure, a possible topic for research, either as the moving spirit of the AAC/ SPSL or as the supreme protagonist of refugees. That remained the case for Cooper's next move, which was to draft a book proposal for Francis Steiner and his group: 'A Tribute to refugee endeavours 1933–53'.

On 23 March 1988, he wrote about the 'vast' Steiner project, the funding for which still had to be settled, and the danger it could run into the sand as everywhere they turned an academic was already working.

He himself was still finding it difficult to settle on his own topic for research: would it concern the educationist Kurt Hahn (already well-researched)? The founder of the Camphill Movement, Karl Koenig? Sir Ludwig Guttmann and his work with the disabled? All three were refugees so they would work as a thesis.

Then he came to what is in retrospect a historic question: had Miss Simpson ever thought about recording her experiences on tape?

Evidently this would not be with a research project or publication in mind; simply to make a historical record, for posterity. Esther replied ('Dear Mr Cooper') non-committedly that she would need to be asked questions as she could not ad lib into a recorder.

Cooper warmed to his idea of recording, writing again in May 1988. He did hope she would agree to his attempting to record her experiences. They had been so interesting they should certainly be recorded in as much detail as possible for posterity. He had in mind, he told her, an anecdotal approach to the interesting and important people she had met.

But then Esther offered a different approach, to which, she told Cooper, she had given much thought. A quite different approach, inspired by the idea of the tapes going to the Brotherton Library. She would talk about scholars divided into groups based on their receipt of recognised distinctions – Nobel laureates (16), Companions of Honour (2), Orders of Merit (2), Knights (16), Fellows of the Royal Society and of the British Association, Oxbridge heads of house (3). She would pick individual Royal Society and British Association Fellows for a one- or two-sentence mention. After that she'd talk about Louis Rapkine. Then on to the SPSL officers (A. V. Hill, Sir William Beveridge, and Walter Adams) and non-refugees such as Ludwig Wittgenstein. Within these categories she would discuss the new fields the refugee scholars had opened up. These would include art history (especially Gombrich and Pevsner), atomic energy (Fermi, Frisch, Lise Meitner, Peierls, Szilard), biochemistry, musicology (Gal, Gerhard, Rostal, Wachsmann, Wellesz), medicine (Guttmann, Rothschild, Trueta), philology (Simon). She ended by reassuring Cooper that if he thoroughly disapproved, he should unhesitatingly say so. The tapes were his baby.

Inclusion by distinctions received governed the structure and reach of the eventual *Refugee Scholars*. It meant the exclusion of scholars she assisted post-war from such countries as Hungary, Czechoslovakia, South Africa, Ghana, Biafra, Bangladesh, Chile. It also seems to have meant Esther's opening sentences of the eventual Chapter 5, 'Refugee Scholars and Others':

> It has been my privilege to have known and had as friends people of outstanding quality. Many are refugee scholars, others have come my way through the Society for Visiting Scientists and, of course, there are all those connected with the Society for the Protection of Science and Learning. The eminence achieved by so many refugee scholars has been a source of great pride and it is about them that I shall speak in the first place.

First place or last, her gaze did not venture from the cohort of mainly Jewish German-speaking academic titans to the emerging scholars of the decolonised developing world beyond Europe.

This organisation was far from what Cooper had had in mind, but he started recording in that framework, and he declared the first tapes, in which Esther reached the FRSs, valuable for future historians.

However, he had not abandoned the idea of her sharing her more personal and anecdotal memories of these distinguished and interesting people. Furthermore, with most of the refugees covered, Cooper suggested Esther go on to talk about other well-known people with whom her work had brought her into contact and about whom she knew things of interest – civil servants, people from other refugee organisations, and so on. These would be her own recollections, which probably didn't appear in official biographies.

He proposed a similar approach to her music, which would have a separate tape broken up into different periods and covering musical details that would interest fellow musicians – composers played, preferences, how her tastes changed over the years, the musical idiosyncrasies of fellow musicians, and so on. This would be fascinating, he suggested – in vain, as it turned out – as would the British Association meetings she went to and a record of the successive generations of refugee families and their contribution to the country.

The recording process stretched on into autumn 1988, with Esther working hard on her diaries to keep track of her musical activity. Vienna, Geneva and London (before the SPSL's wartime move to Cambridge) lay ahead.[6]

What memories her diaries must awaken, Cooper wrote, hopefully; their next session would indicate how her repertoire and musical approach broadened and developed from her Austrian experiences. Esther did not take up his suggestion.

His daughter-in-law Lucy was transcribing the tapes on an IBM business computer (why not a typewriter? asked Esther rhetorically) and was willing to do them all. The transcribing actually took place in Dubai where Lucy's husband Martin was working.

Cooper also wrote to Esther towards the end of November with news that she was to be awarded an honorary degree by her alma mater, Leeds University. The Honours Committee had accepted his suggestion – that of a part-time MA student, he noted, supported by three of the most eminent scholars in their fields. It was really a great tribute to her. Esther responded that she had a great feeling of unworthiness and so was ambivalent about

---

6   While the tapes Cooper recorded were said to be destined for the Brotherton Library in Leeds, where Esther's personal papers are held, they are not listed there. The diaries, apparently mostly recording chamber music sessions, are also not listed.

his initiative. [She already had an LL.D. from London University that she owed to Sir Rudolf Peierls.]

By January 1989 they had covered internment and dealings with HMG. Work was still to be done, Cooper pointed out, on the SPSL and the SVS, which was not in what he termed Beveridge's excellent book. Esther had gone through the typed transcripts so far 'with a fine toothcomb' – her memory was phenomenal, said Cooper – and Lucy would retype.

Cooper was still thinking about a project of his own and was going to talk to the Leeds historian Professor David Dilks, the official biographer of Harold Macmillan, about a possible Ph.D. on a tripartite proposal encompassing 'The refugees who escaped from central Europe during the 1930s and 1940s and affected this country in unexpected ways. This study assesses three very different aspects.' These included the Camphill Project, already mentioned; the East Anglian Refugee Committee's Children's Committee 1938–1946;[7] the assistance given to academic refugees by the SPSL, of which Dr Esther Simpson was the secretary from 1933–1978 [sic]. Based on the reminiscences of Dr Simpson, the study would investigate how the SPSL and Dr Simpson helped to secure the release of academic refugees from internment.

Cooper sent a copy of this proposal to Esther, who replied at once to correct him: she had been assistant secretary to Walter Adams. She had done all the normal donkey work; Adams had had all the organising to do, the dealing with official bodies, the general strategy. She became secretary only in 1951 when the office moved back to London from Cambridge, continuing until retirement in 1975, when she became honorary consultant.

Cooper's error over her title and role might also have prompted Esther into pointing out that she was not the sole member of AAC/SPSL staff beside Adams. But no. It went unmentioned that a Percy Gent and a secretary were at work in Burlington House when Esther first arrived in July 1933, and Gent was still active in that October, managing the case of Betty Heimann, a professor of Indian philology, specialising in Sanskrit. He left in 1934:

---

7 The Children's Committee was based in Cambridge and the secretary, Greta Burkill, a close friend of Esther's.

[The Council] wishes to record its appreciation of the work of the office
staff and in particular of the Assistant Secretary, Mr. Percy Gent, who
has recently left the Council's office.

At this stage their correspondence also reflects the changing world in which
the SPSL's services were called upon. In early 1989, Esther told Cooper that
their latest application was from a Ghanaian scholar. She found it sad, she
wrote, when the developing countries suppressed free thought instead of
setting an example of better government.

In Dubai Lucy was ploughing on, edging closer to the eventual book.
Ray initially suggested breaking the text down into four sections: Esther's
childhood, education and career; refugee scholars and others; music;
supplementary aspects (if any). This misses out Esther's time with the
SVS and the post-war refugee world.

Ray collaborated closely with Esther on every chapter, plainly experiencing some difficulty over how her family life should be dealt with and
her unwillingness to flesh out the narrative with colourful detail.

As the work went along, with Ray sending Esther transcripts and draft
chapters, with suggestions (pleas really) for enlarging certain areas, such as
more on famous people she remembered; more on Beveridge, Adams, Hill,
and other contributors to the SPSL; more on the less well-known refugees
not yet mentioned; more on social life in Vienna, where she had worked for
the International Fellowship of Reconciliation (IFOR) in the late 1920s and
early 1930s, embellishing the European way of life; more on the SVS; more on
interesting cases she dealt with.

Esther's response was to agree how much more she could have said
had she included the political situation in general. She added that when
she was back in London she found Hugh Gaitskell, future leader of the
Labour Party, occupying her former room, and met the future Labour
Lord Chancellor Elwyn Jones, and the writer Naomi Mitchison, and Dora
Frost, later to become Dora Gaitskell.[8]

---

8 Like Esther, Anna Dora Frost (*née* Creditor) had a connection to Latvia. She was born
   in Riga, Latvia, in 1901, coming to London with her family in 1903. She and Hugh
   Gaitskell were married in 1937. In 1964, a year after his death, she was appointed to
   the House of Lords as Baroness Gaitskell. Again, like Esther, Dora Gaitskell would
   have an honorary degree from the University of Leeds [1966]. She died in 1989.

Gaitskell and Mitchison had been in Vienna, where they were part of an intellectual circle that included the economic anthropologist Karl Polanyi and the philosopher John Macmurray. John and his wife Betty were friends of Donald Grant, Esther's boss at the International Fellowship of Reconciliation in Vienna, and his wife Irene stayed in their Vienna apartment, presumably meeting Esther. However, she ignored or resisted Ray's invitation to enlarge or embellish: she had told him about refugees of whom she could say something special.

Ray also wrote to her as to how the content should be ordered. What the outcome would be, and who would pay for it, remained uncertain as work on the text went along.

A few bound photocopied copies was one suggestion of Cooper's. His attempt to interest Weidenfeld in a book came to nothing. Finally, a self-published book was arrived at under the title *Refugee Scholars: Conversations with Tess Simpson* edited by R. M. Cooper, on the front cover a striking portrait of Esther from her Vienna days.

Portrait of Esther Simpson from the cover of
Refugee Scholars. © Hanna Schiff, Vienna 1933

7
Launching Esther

Refugee Scholars was launched on 2 July 1992 at a reception held in London at the Ciba Foundation,[9] in its elegant Adam-designed Portland Place headquarters, a leading venue for scientific symposia.

The proceedings were introduced by Sir Gordon Wolstenholme, the first director of the Foundation, who had opened the premises to SPSL Council meetings. In the printed record of the *Reception at the Ciba Foundation on July 2nd 1992 to launch REFUGEE SCHOLARS*, he hailed the assembled 'Dear Friends of Esther Simpson' as,

> Surely, if I may say so, a unique collection of friends for any person in this world, wonderfully represented by all of you who have come today.

It was the third occasion when they had celebrated 'some aspect of Tess Simpson's wonderful and fruitful life'. One was a 'great party' for her 'so-called retirement'; a little later, another party 'on one of her more youthful birthdays'. The great warmth towards Esther rises unmissably out of the printed record of the launch.

Sir Gordon called on two refugee scholars to speak, both members of the Order of Merit: the molecular biologist Max Perutz, a Nobel Chemistry laureate, and the art historian Sir Ernst Gombrich.

---

9 CIBA foundation for the Promotion of International Cooperation in Medical and Chemical Research.

We are very well aware that they have, immeasurably, between them enriched the intellectual life of our world, and that they have been able to do this in this country.

The contributions by Gombrich and Perutz make very interesting reading over a broad and personal front. Naturally, they present their view of the subject of the book.

Gombrich taxes Esther with showing,

> ... extraordinary skill in what the Bible describes as putting her light under a bushel ... In any case you have to read between the lines to grasp how much the organizations and societies she served owe to her initiative and self-denying efforts ... She has always embodied the ethos of secretaries, that unsung army of heroines who prevent our world from going to pieces.

He also praises the AAC/SPSL as 'unique even in the glorious annals of British charities'. And he locates in her devotion to chamber music the seeds of Esther's ease in taking up the academic cause. 'For in chamber music you cannot and need not always play the first fiddle.' Whether, in the circumstances of the book launch, Esther appreciated that is another matter. He is led on to reflect on the portrait of Esther on the book's cover, drawn in Vienna in 1933 by Hanna Schiff, whom he knew very well, frequenting the evenings of chamber music in the house of her father Artur Schiff, mentioned by Esther in the context of her acquaintance with Sir Karl Popper FRS, FBA, CH.

In what must have been an intensely moving moment, Sir Ernst concluded,

> Hanna was a cousin of Karl Popper who tells me that she was arrested in Berlin, having been released from an Austrian prison and that she was presumably deported and killed. The testimony to her gifts as a portraitist that now graces the cover of Esther's book thus also serves as a stark reminder of the darkness that would have engulfed so many more of us, had it not been for the beacon lit in this country that Esther was to tend throughout the years with exemplary dedication. We thank her.

Hanna Schiff is not mentioned in Esther's Vienna reminiscences. This deeply felt recollection of the dark fate she shared with so many was Sir Ernst's to bring up, not Esther's. Is there the sense of a rebuke for the omission of Hanna Schiff and her fate?

In the book, Esther recounts how she made music with members of the Schiff family in Vienna, but nothing of their varied destinies, involving emigration, deportation, death, under the Nazis.

She tells us she wanted to work with the AAC as the people losing their academic jobs were the same sort she had played chamber music with in Vienna, but shows no concern with what life had in store for those who could not fit the AAC criteria. Esther's recollections are all of the exceptional and successful.

Whether of the rise in Austrian Nazi violence in Vienna, or pre-war repression and concentration camps in Germany and Austria, or the emerging news of the murder of Jews in Wehrmacht-occupied eastern countries,[10] or the revelation of the final attempt at annihilation, or the release and help offered to the survivors of the camps (so often led by Quakers as with the Windermere boys), or the 1945–6 Nuremberg trials of the major Nazi war criminals or the Eichmann trial April to December 1961 – in the book's recollections or her letters to Broda no mention of these is to be found. This seems the more remarkable when we remember that her life from 1933 to 1945 had been centred on victims of what the British press then termed 'Nazi frightfulness'.

As remarked earlier, Hanna's cousin, the philosopher Karl Popper, is there, in the book:

> Sir Karl Popper, who is both a Fellow of the Royal Society and of the British Academy and, also, a Companion of Honour, is a world-famous philosopher of great influence. His intellectual biography, Unended Quest, mentions the Academic Assistance Council and Walter Adams.

---

10 On 17 December 1942 the foreign secretary, Anthony Eden, told the Commons that 'the German authorities, not content with denying to persons of Jewish race in all the territories over which their barbarous rule has been extended the most elementary human rights, are now carrying into effect Hitler's oft repeated intention to exterminate the Jewish people in Europe'. At the end of the statement the House stood in silence for one minute. HC Deb, 17 December 1942, Vol 385 cc2082–7.

It does, though making it clear that he, a schoolmaster in Vienna in 1936, albeit with a growing international reputation as a philosopher and looking for an academic post as a teacher of philosophy, did not become a refugee.

In November 1936 Popper calculatedly resigned his teaching post and declared his intention of leaving Austria. This change in his circumstances was sufficient to satisfy the AAC as to his eligibility for assistance: Popper received an offer of 'academic hospitality' from Cambridge 'together with a letter of support from Walter Adams of the Academic Assistance Council'. He would be delivering eight lectures in the spring of 1937. He preferred to take up the offer of a lectureship in philosophy at Canterbury University College New Zealand, where he had put in for a post. The philosopher John Macmurray, Esther's and Karl Polanyi's friend from Vienna, was chair of the Canterbury appointment committee in London.

These are highly idiosyncratic circumstances, but they have not prevented Karl Popper regularly appearing in lists of the great refugee scholars saved by Esther and the AAC.

In his contribution to the launch, Max Perutz places Esther in a historical context.

> Tess Simpson personifies the great tradition of British liberalism that values the individual for his or her intrinsic worth, for the value that Schopenhauer defined when he wrote that a person should be judged not by what he has, wealth or power, or by what he represents, social position, nationality, and so on, but only by what he is, by his character and abilities. She also represents the Quaker tradition of pacifism, tolerance and Christian aid to all people in need.

And as for her work,

> The foundation of the Academic Assistance Council was a victory for Christian charity and the liberal ideal. Tess devoted the rest of her life to that ideal and helped thousands of scholars to mend their broken careers . . . If Tess had not taken the job, would someone else have done it equally well? She or he might have done it as conscientiously, but I cannot think of anyone else with the same combination of warm affection for the individual scholars and iron toughness in the face of officialdom.

Interestingly, Perutz asks, would he have done as well if he had stayed at home? And gave a resounding no:

> Had I stayed in Vienna I would never have done the research that won
> me the Nobel Prize. Cambridge made me what I am. The people
> around me taught me how to do research, and the great papers by
> Rutherford, Bragg and others taught me how to present it.

(Though at its foundation the AAC had declared: 'We ask for means to prevent the waste of exceptional abilities exceptionally trained.')

Persons of Tess Simpson's faith in Christian values and liberal ideals, with her dedication and courage, said Perutz, were needed then [1992] as much as fifty years ago when she started on her selfless career. (Was this a reference to Esther as a Quaker? Or a generalisation, as with Christian charity earlier, in ignorance of her Jewish origins?)

> She has set a shining example for others to follow, but you know, even
> she is not a saint. She has been seen doing The Times crossword in
> office hours while displaced scholars still pined in exile.

Ray Cooper gave a tactfully edited version of the origins and production of the book. [It could not have been further from the collection of personal recollections he had originally hoped for.] He thanked the Trust Funds, Learned Societies and other bodies that contributed to the publication costs.

> That they should have done so, so readily and generously in these hard
> times when approached out of the blue by a total stranger, seems to
> me to be a very great tribute to Esther herself.

Then it is Esther's time. She is not going to make a speech, she says, having jotted down what she wants to say so as to be brief.

She mentions only four people, Sir Gordon Wolstenholme, naturally. Her successor in the secretaryship, Liz Fraser, noting that she, Esther, has remained involved as the only survivor of the pre-war period who knew how the Society functioned then.

> I'm in constant touch with Liz. I hasten to add that I'm in no way a
> back seat driver; Liz is, thank heaven, very much her own woman.
> She has brought her own insights to deal with present day problems,

and she takes a keen personal interest in our grantees, for which I am very grateful.

After Liz Fraser she turns to Ray Cooper, making it clear that the book is,

> . . . entirely his own conception. I didn't know what he was up to till I saw his final version.

And,

> . . . the selections from the tapes he recorded, and from our records in the Bodleian are entirely his own.

And that was entirely her acknowledgement of his initiative, interest and work.

Was it a pleasure to work with him? Was she grateful for his four years of researching, recording, editing, arranging publication? Was she grateful to his daughter-in-law for transcribing and retyping the tapes and to his wife Kay for her hospitality in Leeds? Was she grateful for the result?

She is delighted, though, that Lord Ashby agreed to write a Foreword, before moving on to mention Sir Gordon a second time:

> To me personally he and Lady Wolstenholme were – and have always remained – immensely helpful and generous.

Finally, she is very grateful to Sir Ernst Gombrich and to Max Perutz for their contributions to the launch.

> They represent the great number of distinguished refugee scholars, their children and grandchildren, who enrich the intellectual life now of the whole world. Knowing them makes me immensely proud and very, very humble.

A listener who knew of Esther's humble origins, about which she was so reticent, might have thought she had every cause to feel proud.

8
Arks and Stoats

It is important to note that the AAC/SPSL was not the only agency through which displaced German-speaking scholars could find refuge and a renewed career.

To have an Oxford professor as a contact and mentor was to have a lifeline, as the 2017 comprehensive study *Ark of Civilization: Refugee Scholars and Oxford University 1930–1945*, edited by Sally Crawford, Katharina Ulmschneider and Jas Elsner demonstrates.

To be part of the international network of Olympian scholarship meant you were likely to have what mattered to your survival: both what you knew and whom you knew. Given the right contacts, the SPSL's insistence that its chosen scholars (of exceptional abilities exceptionally trained) must not exceed the prime of [intellectual] life could be by-passed.

The Oxford University Press also played a part, with book advances enabling the Home Office requirement for an income of £200 a year [£14,000 in 2023's value] for two years to be fulfilled. The Rockefeller Foundation's support for OUP and lecture series worked similarly.

The list of Oxford academics involved with the SPSL as recited in *Ark of Civilization* could not have been more formidable. Hugh Last, Camden Professor of Roman History; Gilbert Murray, Regius Professor of Greek and a signatory of the letter to *The Times* launching the AAC on 24 May(of which more later); John Beazley, Professor of Classical Archaeology and Art; Maurice Bowra, classical scholar, dean and later warden of Wadham

College; James Brierly, Chichele Professor of International Law and Diplomacy, on the council of the SPSL; David Ross of Oriel, philosopher and Provost of Oriel College and president of the British Academy from 1936 to 1940; A. D. Lindsay, Master of Balliol and vice-chancellor of Oxford University 1935–1938.

The Oriel webpage[11] for David Ross recites that his period as British Academy president involved,

> ... officially and otherwise helping scholars seeking refuge from Europe. Some of his admirable efforts involved persuading his colleagues at Oriel to extend fellowship to refugees such as, among others, Otto Pächt [Austrian art historian], Lorenzo Minio-Paluello [Italian linguist], and Richard Walzer [a German scholar of Greek and Arabic philosophy].

And as *Ark of Civilization* points out,

> Their knowledge of the Society meant that, by 1939, a collaboration between individual Oxford academics and the SPSL could work with breathtaking efficiency to negotiate political and economic business and to pull academics out of danger.

For example, Arnaldo Momigliano's contact was Hugh Last. An Italian historian of classical antiquity and Professor of Roman History at Turin, his plea for assistance was made on 4 September 1938. Within three weeks the SPSL gathered all necessary references and paperwork and had agreed to support him. He arrived in Oxford on 31 March 1939 and his family followed. He had little English and no obvious place, but after spending time in Oxford, he became a professor at University College London. He was made an honorary KBE in 1974, though he does not appear in Esther's list of 'her' honoured children.

Another pleasing example who found refuge in Oxford is Felix Jacoby, a German classical philologist, renowned for his collection of text fragments of Ancient Greek historians and his work on Herodotus. He had been a pupil of the giant of German classical philology Ulrich von Wilamowitz-Moellendorff, of whom Gilbert Murray was a close friend.

---

11 https://www.oriel.ox.ac.uk/our-history/historical-figures-and-alumni/

The SPSL had been unwilling to take Jacoby on as it would have been 'contrary to the usual practice of securing re-establishment for scholars in the prime of life'. Jacoby, Jewish by birth but a baptised Christian, had been professor of Classical Philosophy at Kiel University. He is also said to have voted for Hitler.

When the prospect of working on a life of Esther Simpson first appeared on my horizon, serendipity produced a letter to the *London Review of Books* [27 July 2017] from the then chair of CARA, Anne Lonsdale. Her letter had been prompted by the *Review*'s earlier article on *Ark of Civilization* by Stefan Collini, Professor of Intellectual History and English Literature at Cambridge. The letter was headed 'Rabbits Addressed by a Stoat' and began,

> Stefan Collini's essay on scholars displaced by the Second World War mentions that Eduard Fraenkel's seminar on Aeschylus' Agamemnon was described in one account as 'a circle of rabbits addressed by a stoat' (LRB 13 July). I was one of Professor Fraenkel's 'rabbits' from my first week in Oxford.

Eduard Fraenkel's reputation places him among the greatest classical scholars of the twentieth century. An assimilated Jew, in 1933 he was displaced from a professorship at Freiburg and found a place at Corpus Christi, Oxford, where his seminars redefined the teaching of classical scholarship.

Anne Lonsdale's letter continued:

> Unusually, for Oxford in the 1950s, Fraenkel treated young women as equals, and savaged us equally, which was refreshing at a time when lectures often started with 'Good morning, gentlemen.' We progressed at a rate of between ten and twenty lines in two hours. Each session was the responsibility of a single student, who would establish each word of text from a variety of manuscripts and then its meaning with the help of any and every tool known to literature, history, art and scholarship. The bit one 'did' was engraved on the brain for months . . .

Fraenkel, who had retired in 1953 but continued to hold seminars, died in 1970, committing suicide shortly after the death of his wife Ruth.

In his honour, the college named his college office the Fraenkel Room. In 2017 allegations of unwanted touching of female students by Fraenkel resulted in demands by Corpus undergraduates for the removal of this memorial, that the Fraenkel Room should be renamed 'to spare the feelings of college members who might be offended by it'.

Widening the horizon, the enforced migrants also had a major cultural presence, including popular entertainment, in opera, dance, film, theatre, radio and, of course, music; 420 playwrights and 4,000 actors and directors fled to upwards of forty countries worldwide.

9

Haim, Haimisch

Esther Simpson was born Esther Sinovitch on 31 July 1903 in the industrial city of Leeds in the north-east of England. She was the youngest of the four living children of Ilya and Sora Liba Sinovitch, Jewish immigrants from Dvinsk (Dünaberg until 1893, Daugavpils from 1920) in the south-east of the then Imperial Russian Grand Duchy of Latvia. They changed their first names to Ellis and Sarah, but retained their Russian surname.

Ahead of her in the family were her three brothers, Joseph, Isaac and Israel. The 1911 census[12] shows the family living at 22 Crawford Street in the area known as Little London, now long slum-cleared, though judging by the names of their neighbours it might have been called Little Russia. Returning to Leeds in 1988 after a gap of twenty years, Esther confessed herself unable to find her way.

The children had been born in nearby Lower Brunswick Street, but the 1911 census return provides a snapshot of the family and its living conditions. It shows their small terrace house had six rooms, including the kitchen but not counting any scullery, bathroom or closet.

Nine people shared those six rooms. Seven years earlier when the Sinovitch family was living in 33 Lower Brunswick Street, two young boarders lived with them, Phillip Samuel, aged twenty-one at the time, and Israel Abrams, twenty. Phillip Samuel seems to have been something of a fixture; he was still shown as a boarder in Crawford Street, together

---

12 Accessed here through The National Archives partner Findmypast [findmypast.co.uk]

1911 census. 22 Crawford Street.

First name(s)	Last name	Relationship	Marital status	Sex	Age	Birth year	Occupation	Birth place
Ellis	Sinovitch	Head	Married	Male	41	1870	Tailor's Machinist	Dwinsk Russia
Sarah	Sinovitch	Wife	Married	Female	43	1868	-	Dwinsk Russia
Joseph	Sinovitch	Son	Single	Male	17	1894	Shorthand Typist	Yorks Leeds
Isaac	Sinovitch	Son	Single	Male	15	1896	Trimming Shop Salesman	Yorks Leeds
Israel	Sinovitch	Son	-	Male	13	1897[8]	School	Yorks Leeds
Esther	Sinovitch	Daughter	-Brunswic	Female	7	1903[4]	School	Yorks Leeds
Phillip	Samuel	Boarder	Single	Male	28	1883	Tailor Coathand	Covna Russia
Jack	Miller	Boarder	Single	Male	23	1888	Tailor's Machinist	Baske Kourland
Israel	Vurl	Boarder	Single	Male	20	1891	Trousers Machinist	Plotsk Pollan

with Jack Miller, twenty-three, and Israel Vurl, twenty. Of Esther's father Ilya and his Latvian family nothing personal seems to have been recorded or handed down. His first name, Ilya, appears to be Slav but Ilya is a Slavic form of the Hebrew Eliyahu or Elijah. His choice of English first name, Ellis, is a derivative of this.

He was born in 1870 and worked as a tailor's machinist, according to the census. He was two years younger than Sora Liba (Sarah); by 1911 they had been married for nineteen years. They had seven children, of whom three had died in infancy. Ellis was naturalised in 1897, and it looks as if Sarah became British at the same time. Shown as British by parentage, their two elder sons were already at work: Joseph, seventeen, as a shorthand typist; Isaac, fifteen, as a trimming shop salesman. Israel, thirteen, and Esther, seven, were at school.

The boarders were all in the clothing industry, for which Leeds was famous: Phillip Samuel, twenty-eight, a tailor's coat hand; Jack Miller, twenty-three, a tailor's machinist; and Israel Vurl, twenty, a trousers machinist. The three boarders portrayed Jewish eastern Europe, coming respectively from Russia, Courland and Poland. Phillip Samuel had been naturalised. The nationality of Miller and Vurl is shown as 'Jew'.

Additional information presented with the 1911 census shows that 153 local people had the same occupation – tailor's machinist – as Ellis. Of these, forty-three had been born in Russia or Russian Poland.

Of Sora Liba's family, by contrast, everything is known thanks to forty years' worth of genealogical work by Esther's Canadian second cousin Morty Wellen. His *Outline Descendant Tree of Meyer Perevosnik* (his great grandfather) that he generously shared with the present author extends over six closely typed pages with entries ranging from 1859 to 1993 and shows that Meyer Perevosnik had three sons, Male, Joshua and Zalman Hillel, and five daughters, Aida [Morty's grandmother], Raizel, Sora Liba, Essie and Dora. We can see how Aida, Sora Liba, Essie and Dora all married and emigrated from Dvinsk with their husbands: Aida, Essie, and Dora across the Atlantic, to eastern Canada and the United States; Sora Liba and Ilya to Leeds.

These roots in Jewish Dvinsk are profoundly significant for our understanding of Esther's sense of herself and outlook.

Jewish Gen Jewish Families of Dvinsk offers a vivid portrait of Ilya's and Sora's background,[13]

> Dvinsk (now Daugavpils, Latvia) was one of the leading Jewish cities of the Russian Empire and a centre of high Jewish culture and debate. At the time of the lists forming this database, it was part of the Russian Gubernia (province) of Vitebsk, and its commercial importance was well established. Jewish gravestones found in the area date from the 17th century are evidence of an early Jewish presence.
>
> In 1910 the city numbered 111,000 of which 50,000 were Jews. Unlike its immediate neighbour Courland, Dvinsk was within the Pale of Settlement. Its ethos derived more from Russian, Lithuanian and Polish influences than from the Courland region which was broadly German in character and cultural background as a result of nearly 700 years of de facto domination by the Baltic Germans.
>
> According to the *Jewish Encyclopedia* (Funk & Wagnalls), commerce and manufacturing in Dvinsk were largely in Jewish hands. The 1893 census showed 330 industrial establishments owned by Jews and 99 owned by non-Jews. The census records only 741 Jewish artisans, but this figure has been challenged by Herman Rosenthal in his article on Dvinsk published in the *Jewish Encyclopaedia* (1916), citing 'private investigations' as the source for the claim that in 1898 there were 4,862 Jewish artisans including 2,193 Masters, 1,700 journeymen and 909 apprentices.
>
> The poverty of the Pale was a feature of Dvinsk Jewish life and it is estimated that 30 percent of Jewish families applied for aid from the community in 1898. There were numerous Jewish aid societies recorded, including a Mutual Aid, founded in 1900 and with more than 1,200 members by 1901. A loan fund was established in memory of the Merchant M. Vitenberg. Loans, secured by personal property, were advanced without interest. Other charitable institutions included a society for aiding the poor founded by the Jewish governor, with an income in 1899 of some 8,917 Roubles, soup kitchens, a charitable dining hall, a *bikkur holim* [referring to the duty to visit and aid the sick],

---

13   https://www.jewishgen.org/databases/Latvia/DvinskFamilies.htm

a dispensary and a lying-in hospital all organised and run by the community. These testify to the traditions of self help and community organisation that reflect the high value placed on charity to those less fortunate.

Dvinsk was an important centre of Jewish thought and culture and nurtured a number of Rabbis known and respected throughout the Jewish world. Ashkenazi Chief Rabbi Kuk [Kook] of Palestine was a pupil of Reb Reuvele Dunaburger. Meier Simcha HaKohen, Rabbi of Mitnagdim [orthodox opponents of Hasidism] for 39 years, while Rabbi Yosef Rosen served as the Chassidic rabbi for 50 years. Both were formidable Talmudic scholars and vivid personalities.

Other accounts of Dvinsk tell of its being a centre of the tailoring trade.

Esther sedulously recorded nothing about her childhood or religious upbringing – apart from saying that her parents never assimilated – but her Canadian relatives have family stories that suggest a strictly observant household in Leeds, one that followed east European Ashkenazic practice. Apropos, her mother's names Sora Liba are Yiddish, as is her mother's sister Raizel's name – Yiddish for rose.

The idea of Esther's being brought up in a culture of *Yiddishkeit* and contentment with a meagre lot in a religiously correct life is important to our understanding of her, and we must return to it later.

Although she gives no hint of it, let alone reflecting on how it felt or its influence, Esther's childhood was passed in what must have been a close and vibrant east European Jewish culture, the house resonating to chatter in Yiddish and Russian and blessings and curses in Hebrew, a home where Sarah was the *balehboosteh* (boss) and Israel the *boychik* (the lad).

Esther remarks in a letter of December 1950 to her long-time friend and constant correspondent the Austrian scientist Engelbert Broda that,

> My parents were immigrants to this country, and they never assimilated. I was born here. By virtue of my background I was able to have a more objective view of the country than others, and this was strengthened by my living in other countries. England is full of faults, and these hurt me because I feel part of England, in spite of my parents' origin . . .

Nonetheless, in constructing our picture of Esther, we have to note her claim or outlook that as a child of unassimilated parents her background enabled her to have a more objective view of her country than others [with native-born parents?]. And the phrase 'I feel part of England' is not a phrase someone who was unthinkingly part of England would feel called on to use.

We could take the observation that her parents never assimilated as meaning her growing up amid her parents' and the boarders' household chatter in that mix of Yiddish, Russian, Hebrew and English, and living a home life infused with the idioms, customs and practices of east European *Yiddishkeit* as a way of life. (In a 1959 letter to Engelbert Broda's son Paul she described her home as 'cosmopolitan', not the best chosen of phrases.) In Crawford Street they were not alone. This was a heavily Jewish area; for instance home to ritual baths for Jewish women.

An official account reads:

> Crawford Street 1956.
>
> Leeds Terrace is on the left and Albert Grove to the right. On the junction is the Jewish Women's Public Baths and two Mikvah baths. These resembled wide mouthed wells and were used for ritual cleansing observance. They were later leased by the Jewish community who took responsibility for them. The cost of the land and building was £2,400 and the baths opened in October 1905. In 1909/10 there were on average 800 attendances a month; by 1957 it was less than 40 a month. By then the building was in a poor state of repair and the area had generally deteriorated. The Jewish population had on the whole moved to areas in North Leeds.

The playground at her local elementary school, Lovell Road, must also have echoed the *Yiddishkeit* of the many Jewish pupils' family lives.

Leeds was a home to thriving Jewish communities, with their own synagogues and cemeteries. The clothworkers had their own. Esther's mother, who died in October 1930, when Esther was in Vienna, is buried in the New Farnley Jewish cemetery. Sarah Sinovitch's traditionally wrought headstone celebrates her as wife, mother and grandmother.

Ellis Sinovitch died in Leeds in February 1943 at the age of seventy-two. Cemetery data shows him as buried in the same cemetery as his wife, New Farnley, but in an unidentified grave: he has no headstone. In 1943 Esther was in Cambridge and Israel in Newcastle-on-Tyne (Heaton School where he taught French had been evacuated to Whitehaven early in the war but only for a brief period).

In wartime circumstances, it might have been difficult for Israel and Esther to return to Leeds to see their father buried as rapidly as Jewish burial customs required. But the setting of a headstone traditionally takes place a year after death. And if Isaac and Joseph could not cross the wartime Atlantic from Canada where they were living, what was it that held Israel and Esther back from marking their father's decease? Then or later. Had there been a catastrophic breakdown in relations?

Esther exhibited a decided reluctance to talk about her family. In her 1979 interview for the Imperial War Museum Second World War archive,[14] the interviewer is challenged when she asks about Esther's parents:

> *What did you father do?*
>
> Well, he was in the clothing industry in Leeds.
>
> *Yes. And your mother?.*
>
> But why is this relevant?
>
> *I think it puts your story in context a bit.*
>
> Yes but I don't' really see the point. However,
>   I'll answer your questions.

The tone is noticeably sharp. The interviewer leaves family background there.

That this instinct to hold back on her family was deeply rooted is also shown by her encounter with a Canadian academic, Father John [Jack] Costello SJ. He got in touch with Esther when researching his biography of the philosopher John Macmurray, [*John Macmurray: A biography*] whom Esther had first met when she was working in Vienna for the International

---

14 https://www.iwm.org.uk/collections/item/object/80004429

Fellowship of Reconciliation at the end of the 1920s. Macmurray later became an advisor to the SPSL. Esther invited Father Costello to lunch at the Royal Society.

Jack Costello lives and works in Toronto, the largest city in Canada, where Esther's elder brothers Joseph and Isaac had settled. She had a vast network of Canadian relatives, some of whom she entertained in London.

Had Esther ever mentioned to Father Costello that she had brothers living in his home city? Relatives in Canada? No, she had not.

10

A-tailoring They Will Go

The Dvinsk connection was inescapably part of Esther's upbringing.

With the Latvian city known for its tailoring, it comes as no surprise that numbers of its Jewish emigrants arriving at the north-eastern port of Hull, and perhaps intending to head to the US via the north-western port of Liverpool, should have stopped off in Leeds, then the epitome of the Victorian northern manufacturing city, in this case making cloth and clothing. 'Leeds' was said to be the only word of English some Russian and east European emigrants knew on arriving at Hull.

In his vivid study *Victorian Things*, Asa Briggs writes of Leeds being

> transformed after 1855 as a result of the introduction of sewing machines, hand-knives and ready-made clothes . . . In 1871, 1,523 men and 483 women were employed in the clothing trade, including hat and cap making . . . By the end of Queen Victoria's reign the number of men had multiplied tenfold and the number of women thirtyfold. Some workers had been diverted from other older local textile industries. More were migrants . . . By 1901 more people in Leeds were employed in the clothing industry, including footwear, than in engineering. It was only during the last decades of the century that Leeds forged ahead not only of London but of Manchester, Birmingham, and Glasgow . . . There were scores of Leeds workshops, many of them Jewish.

By 1891 the Leeds Jewish community already numbered 8,000, primarily concentrated in an area north of the city centre and known as The Leylands, a dense concentration of back-to-back slum housing.

The city was home, for instance, to Montague Burton, the founder of the popular high-street chain Burton Menswear, who was born Meshe Osinski in Kurkliai Lithuania. Marks and Spencer set up their first stall in Leeds market. Esther recalled to Ray Cooper that her father talked about Montague Burton and took her to the Marks and Spencer Penny Bazaar.

Leeds itself at the turn of the nineteenth century was an archetypal industrial city, described by one of its most famous citizens, the art critic Herbert Read, as 'a wilderness of stone and brick, with soot falling like black snow'.

Crawford Street was in a cluster of red-brick terraces adjacent to The Leylands. A former resident remembered a house with a front room and a 'fairly large' kitchen with a door from which a staircase led up to the three bedrooms. Another door led to the only lavatory down in the 'spooky' cellar with the coal hole next to it: coal was dropped in from a grating in the street. [At least it was in the house: The Leylands had communal lavatories or even middens.] The kitchen had a black leaded range and a large sink where the household washing was done in a metal tub. The front doorstep had to be scrubbed and rubbed with a dolly stone (a scouring block). The street was cobbled. A lamp-post with a rope thrown over it was used as a swing by children. There was a pub and a cinema, one of two in the area.

Esther lost her two elder brothers to emigration before the Great War. First Isaac, at sixteen, sailed for Quebec from Liverpool in 1912, followed by nineteen-years-old Joseph in 1913, both emigrating to Canada to join their mother's family there.

Crawford Street was far from a permanent home for Ellis, Sarah and their two remaining children. Records show Ellis and Sarah living at nearby 5 Patti Street between 1918 and 1927. The 1921 Census presents a teaser, with both Ellis and Sarah recorded as having been born in Vilnius, Lithuania, rather than Dvinsk, Latvia, as in their 1911 Census return.

Why he and Sarah might have altered their birthplace ten years later can only be guessed at. While the local Jewish records for Dvinsk and Vilnius show that the surnames Sinovitch and Perevosnik[15] are not uncommon, Ilya and Sora Liba themselves have proved elusive. (The present author's guess is Dvinsk.)

Again, *Findmypast* has offered some pertinent additional information to this Census record. In 1921 Ellis, then fifty-one, was working as a tailor's machinist at 'A Wyman Clothiers' in nearby Brunswick Terrace. Twelve people worked there. But 1,543 people living nearby had the same occupation, tailor's machinist, as Ellis. The impact of the Great War can be seen in the balance between males and females. Women outnumbered men in all age groups except 0–9 and 10–19.

Between 1923 and 1924 Israel was again living with his parents in Patti Street. They then moved to 4 Hayes Street (Alfred Cross St). Esther is not recorded as living with them. Ellis took ship for Quebec in August 1925, presumably to see Isaac and Joseph, returning to Liverpool on the Canadian Pacific *Montroyal*, but he went alone, and was back registered as a machinist at 4 Hayes Street between 1927 and 1936, on his own from 1930.

Esther mirrored this itinerant existence when she came to London to work for the AAC, moving from one set of furnished rooms to another, always in north London.

Her brother Isaac, who changed his name to Ian Simpson, she seems never to have seen again after he emigrated from Leeds to Canada. He seems not to have returned to England. For her part, she never accepted her brother Joseph's frequent invitations to visit Canada – all expenses paid and even a job found if she wanted to stay there.

Joseph had returned to Leeds in 1915, recrossing the Atlantic during the war to marry Florrie Collins (a Leeds girl: let's presume his childhood sweetheart). Later, in December 1951, when he was working for a Canadian chemical company owned by ICI, Joseph paid a visit to England with Florrie. He'd written to Esther that the idea of their coming to England was very hard to grasp, but it really was happening.

He described the trip as a holiday with courtesy business calls on ICI. He would stay with 'Srol' [the childhood abbreviation for Israel] in Heaton. Esther he planned to meet in London. It would be their first meeting since

---

15   Perevoznik in some genealogies.

he had emigrated. He told Esther she couldn't imagine how thrilled they were at seeing all of them after so many years. Ian he did not see very often, but certainly would before the trip. He had been in touch with Srol, sending food parcels to Heaton for Srol, his wife Eva, and son Francis Vivian.

Joseph and Esther had been in touch, and Joseph had both congratulated her on her French award of the *Ordre des Palmes Académiques* and *Officier D'Académie Ministère à l'Education Nationale* and commiserated over the financial woes of the Society for Visiting Scientists [where she had been working since 1944] that she had shared with him. Was there anything he could bring her?

If things didn't turn out well, he'd reassured her, it would not be difficult to have her placed in Canada, in a suitable job which would fit in with her experiences, and he could not imagine anything that would give him more pleasure than to have her on that side. If she paid a visit, the only expense she would have to worry about would be the fare. He'd also thanked her for a subscription to the *New Statesman*.

On Boxing Day 1951, Esther wrote a long letter to Broda from Newcastle-upon-Tyne where she was having 'the weirdest reunion': she was with her brother Israel and sister-in-law and nephew, and with them were her oldest brother [Joseph], whom she hadn't seen since she was a little girl, and his wife.

Esther saw Joseph's milieu and orientation as utterly different from hers and Israel's – she explained that Joseph was in business, a buyer for Canadian Industries Ltd, a chemical company – and yet the family feeling was tremendously strong. She was hearing about their numerous relatives in Canada, whom she didn't know and felt she didn't ever want to know. She had been terribly apprehensive of the meeting, as she knew how utterly different their outlooks were, but her brother had seemed anxious to understand them, and although the one criterion in his circle was the possession of money he seemed to realise that where Srol and Esther were concerned other criteria existed. He and his wife were very generous in a nice way.

She never visited her relatives in Canada or the United States, but a number of her Canadian and American cousins came to London over the years, and universally retained happy memories of meeting her. She told

Broda she had masses of Canadian relatives whom she did not know and
many whom she did.

Rochelle Sherreff (whose husband Jesse was the grandson of Meyer
Perevosnik's daughter Essie) remembered how they bought Esther cheese
from Fortnum & Mason:

> Esther was a tough and wonderful woman. She loved Stilton cheese
> and double Gloucester cheese, which we always brought her from
> Fortnum and Mason. She told us the stories of helping the academics
> find new employment in other countries. For her kindnesses, a group
> of scientists bought her a bedsitter in Swiss Cottage. She lived very
> frugally, but had a very interesting and wonderful life.

It is interesting to speculate on the clear divide between Sarah's and Ellis's
two elder and two younger children, with the two elder already in work
in their teens, re-emigrating to Canada, and going on to lead prosperous
business lives; the two younger continuing at school, going on to university,
and then settling into a working lifetime of public service, each attached to
one institution. Israel as a grammar-school teacher; Esther as a saviour of
displaced academics. The Canadian siblings retained contact with Jewish
religious practice. The English brother and sister not at all.

Israel and Esther were both fortunate in that Leeds offered an exceptional
secondary education, of which they took full advantage. On 9 August 1915
the *Leeds Mercury* recorded:

University Scholarships

The following entrance scholarships have been awarded . . . Israel
Sinovitch Leeds Central High School.

And he went on to study French and German at Leeds University, but not
without a serious interruption because of the First World War.

In 1917, Israel was sent to prison. He served two terms, one in Pentonville,
one in Wormwood Scrubs. Esther nowhere mentions this.

If his sentences had been for, say, theft, Esther's ignoring or suppressing
them might be understandable. But in Israel's case his imprisonment was

for refusing to be conscripted into the Duke of Wellington's Regiment and for assaulting a sergeant sent to take him to barracks to be conscripted.

For the detail of what follows I am indebted to retired University of Leeds lecturer Cyril Pearce and his research into conscientious objectors in which he collated eighteen stories from 278 Leeds men who refused to fight.

Israel is listed in the *Jewry Book of Honour* for his service in the Duke of Wellington's (West Riding) Regiment from 1915: 'I Sinovitch Jewry Book of Honour 205010 4th Bn'.

Service is a misnomer. Cyril Pearce's research has established that Israel refused to serve:

> Forces War Records: I Sinovitch / British / listed in the Jewry Book of Honour / Private / 205010 / Service: deemed enlisted in D of W's (West Riding) Reg 4th bn 205010. Refused medical. Charged with insubordination, Disobedience. 'The accused was charged with an offence against a Sergeant.' 4th (Reserve) Bn Secondary Unit. District court martial 1917 April 2 – May 23 205010 WO86/75

When the Military Service Tribunal refused Israel's claim to be recognised as a conscientious objector he was deemed to be conscripted and given an army number, which he refused to accept. He was sentenced to prison for two years hard labour for refusing the order to take a medical and for assaulting a sergeant who, presumably, was attempting to enforce his conscription.

His military record described him as an 'absolutist' in his refusal of military service. This distinction meant that 'he not only refused to accept or cooperate with military service, but also refused to accept or cooperate with any alternative, non-military, compulsory service'. (Objectors who were willing to undertake an alternative were called alternativists.) That might have been working on the land at home or driving an ambulance at the front. Esther's future employer, patron and friend Donald Grant had been an alternativist conscientious objector, working on a Home Office scheme in Dartmoor Prison.

Israel was released and discharged from the Army on 8 April 1919. How did his sister Esther react to her brother's resolute refusal to be conscripted? Admiration for his standing on his own two feet? Shame at his not serving his country when so many died for it? She makes no mention of his stand even when relating her own formative experiences in private letters.

Having served two sentences and almost two years in civil prisons seems not to have presented any difficulties back in civilian life. He took up his place and scholarship at Leeds, where he won a first-class degree in French and German.

On 29 November 1922 Israel changed his name by deed poll to Israel Simpson. Was that prompted by a wish to distance himself from the conscientious objector and jailbird Israel Sinovitch as he contemplated a career in teaching, with teachers' common rooms filled with ex-officers swapping experiences of life in the trenches? Esther did not follow suit until 27 September 1933, after she returned from Switzerland to work for the AAC.

His time in prison seems not to have affected Israel's progress into teaching. He gained a Board of Education Certificate and began teaching in 1923 as Assistant Master in a series of well-known boys' schools – Bedales (twice), Macclesfield Grammar School, Beverley Grammar School – before becoming Senior Modern Languages Master at Heaton Secondary School for Boys in Newcastle-upon-Tyne in 1930. He became a registered teacher – on the Teachers Registration Council Register – in 1931.

In 1925 he had married Ivy Honor King, sister of a university friend and daughter of a Methodist minister, and settled in Newcastle-on-Tyne, where he passed the rest of his career teaching French and German at Heaton School, one of three French teachers. In a 1970 letter to Broda, Esther described how her brother had great concern for the general ignorance of schoolboys:

> . . . (and masters) and he initiated courses which he ran himself for the sixth form in international affairs, civics, philosophy – subjects to broaden their minds and improve them as citizens.

He and Ivy both died in 1969.

Esther wrote to Broda that for her it was the end of an epoch when Israel died.

> My brother was something of a saint, and his widow has been overwhelmed by the tributes paid to him by so many friends and former pupils – she had no idea herself how widely he was esteemed.

Really? No idea?

Their son, Francis Vivian, became a doctor and was also a noted musician.

Esther was also fortunate in her educational opportunities – initially at her local elementary school, Lovell Road, under its longstanding headteacher Thomas Hawley Bentley.

In *Identity, Migration and Belonging: The Jewish Community of Leeds, 1890–1920*, Aaron M. Kent praises the efforts of Bentley, with other Leeds headteachers, to offer their Jewish pupils, from 'the ghetto', a culturally integrated education that accommodated Jewish traditions and culture, including holidays for the major Jewish festivals. On his retirement in 1937, after thirty-six years, three-quarters of his staff were Jewish. Kent quotes a Louis Teeman:

> . . . the best headmaster one could possibly hope for. The whole school was Jewish and the teachers and he were absolutely super. He himself was kind and strict. He inculcated into us patriotism, love of country, cleanliness and discipline.

Kent writes,

> This kindly man opted to combine discipline with understanding and teach the children in a way that would bring out their best qualities. His methods were also implemented in such a way as to bring England into the classroom.
>
> Every child in his school paid him a penny a week. With this money he introduced violin lessons and bought the school a lantern projector.
>
> Along with his staff, Bentley worked to help the children assimilate quickly (in language, custom and ability) and move forward to secondary education if possible.

Thomas Hawley Bentley died in 1941.

Ray Cooper sent Esther a cutting from the *Yorkshire Evening Post*, a letter in which Mr Bentley was recollected as

> a good friend and mentor, especially to the children of Jewish immigrants in whom he took a keen interest and produced some of the most intellectual men and women . . . even a Lord Mayor.

In her reply to Cooper, Esther did not acknowledge her first head teacher's work with the children of Jewish immigrants nor any personal debt to him or to his school. Instead, she shared a recollection of her form-teacher's personal relationship with him.

Esther told Ray how she was in her last year at Lovell Road and was form monitor. She was alone in her classroom, tidying it, and her form mistress, a Miss Hardy, came in, delighted-looking, glowing, and licking her lips. She was like a cat at the cream. Miss Hardy and Mr Bentley were married not long after. Esther still saw that classroom, she said.

Crucially for her future, when she was nine years old, she was among the pupils Mr Bentley encouraged to take up the violin.

Ray Cooper writes in *Refugee Scholars* that,

> She was provided with a half-size violin and bow in a case, a music stand and a tutor at a cost of fourteen shillings, to be paid off at a shilling a week.

Of course, the First World War was the background to these years of childhood and adolescence.

Curtains Drawn: The Experience of Leeds in World War One (2014) by Stephanie Webb of Leeds Museums and Art Galleries describes how no part of Leeds was untouched by the conflict.

Tailoring switched from suits to uniforms; women found sometimes lethal jobs in munitions factories. In the fighting, the 'Leeds Pals' battalion, formed at the outbreak of war, lost 750 of its 900 officers and men on the first day of the Somme in July 1916. It was said every street in the city had at least one house with curtains drawn. Belgian refugees – 800 had arrived by October 1914 – came to work in the city. Several military hospitals opened; in one, a teacher training college at Beckett's Park, 57,200 injured soldiers had been treated by 1918.

Ray Cooper recorded how he asked Esther about being at school during the First World War – but other than the lack of sweets and sugar she didn't remember a great deal. In fact, as we have seen, the war had touched the Sinovitch family a great deal more closely and personally than a shortage of sugar on the breakfast table.

During the war, Esther had the great good fortune to move up to an outstanding girls' secondary school, Leeds Girls Modern, where she studied from 1915 to 1921.

It taught Latin by the direct method, she recalled, though no teaching was available for higher mathematics, which she might have taken. But she also records in a letter to Broda that her whole outlook on life was changed by a lecture given at the school on Ibsen's *Brand*, to which we will return.

Leeds Girls Modern is long since amalgamated with Lawnswood High School, but in the Modern School's Centenary Souvenir (1854–1954), p. 32, we find:

> Esther Simpson (Sinovitch) 1915–1921 writes of her schooldays with affection and gratitude. She comments on the capacity for independent work which was fostered by the staff, and which stood her in good stead when she went to the University; and remarks on the happiness and serenity of the atmosphere so unlike that experienced at school by most of her fellow students.

The following paragraphs recall what the twelve-year-old Esther Sinovitch from the Crawford Street ghetto encountered on moving to her secondary school.

Houses had been created in 1907 for games and given colours as names: Pale Blue, Dark Blue, Pale Green and Light Green. There were three tennis courts, a hockey ground, and a cricket pitch. (Further research is needed to discover if the teenage Esther wielded a cricket bat.)

> Uniform had also crept in, at least on gymnasium days, 'when a special costume consisting of a box-pleated skirt of navy serge' had to be worn with navy-blue knickers, and a bright red woollen blouse of the right shade of red, obtainable at Edmondson's warehouse. Every girl had to have her hair tied back and wear the school hatband.

The ethos of the school under its gifted headmistress Miss Garbutt is also shown by an account of *A Midsummer Night's Dream*, staged in 1916. 'The accent appears to be on authentic Greek costumes with hair fillets and key pattern designs on the robes.'

Esther's family found the extra money for the uniform and for supplementary fees for the upper school. The money was also found for violin lessons.

Esther had been born with two gifts: in Edith Wharton's phrase, 'a gift for friendship', and a gift for music that was to play a major part in the future pattern of her life.

While still at the Girls Modern she went for lessons to the Leeds Conservatoire, and played in public while at school and university, as the local press recorded,

Leeds Mercury, Thursday 30 January 1919:

'College of Music Successes'
Violin examiner Pte Louis Pecskai
Pass cert. Esther Sinovitch

Yorkshire Post and Leeds Intelligencer, Saturday 29 November 1919:

Leeds College of Music 8th Free Thursday Concert at 7:15
. . . Solo violin Miss Esther Sinovitch. At the piano Mr Cyril Hampshire

Yorkshire Evening Post, Saturday 19 June 1920:

Leeds College of Music Concerts – at the Albert Hall.
Miss Esther Sinovitch played violin solos with pleasant tone and certainty.

The same edition also paraded the picture of an addition to British naval might:

HMS Eagle the new 30,000-ton aeroplane ship, popularly known as 'The Ugly Duckling'. Note the unusual situation of the funnel which is built at the side to give a clear roof-deck for aircraft.

Yorkshire Post and Leeds Intelligencer, Saturday 12 February 1921:

Leeds YMCA Albion Place
Tuesday February 15th 1921 at 7:30 pm

High class concert under the direction of Mr Edgar Haddock. Artistes – Mrs Mabel Salter Contralto. Mr W E Smith Tenor. Miss Tilly

Goldberg Elocutionist. Miss Esther Sinovitch Violinist. Mr Cyril
Hampshire Solo Piano.

On the same day at 7:30 a Public Lecture by Capt. P. T. Kettlewell MC 'With
British Forces in Northern Russia'.

Yorkshire Post and Leeds Intelligencer, Tuesday 2 December 1924:

Leeds University Dramatic Society – Great Hall of University
6 of Maurice Baring's 'Diminutive Dramas'

During the proceedings Miss Sinovitch and Mr Wightman gave some
admirable music.

Then readers of the *Leeds Mercury*, 10 August 1921, could note:

Leeds Scholarships – Higher School Certificate –
  Leeds City Council Senior Scholarship awarded . . . Sinovitch
Esther Girls Modern

So Esther too went on to Leeds University to read French with German as
a supplementary subject; she hadn't learned German at school, but perhaps
the echoes of childhood Yiddish helped.

Her French course offered a year in France, at Caen University, but there
is no mention of university time spent in Germany. As Cooper recounts,
she was secretary of the university debating society and on the Committee
of Social Sciences. A harbinger, she was also secretary of Leeds University
Imperial War Relief Fund (IWRF), set up to relieve food shortages in war-
stricken formerly enemy countries of Europe. 'I had my collectors in all
the faculties,' she recorded.

When she joined the AAC, the name Beveridge could have rung a bell
as he had been shown on the IWRF's letterhead as vice-chairman of its
Universities Committee, together with a list of representatives for each
of the University Relief Committees. She had also to correspond with the
IWRF HQ in Vienna, whose secretary was one Donald Grant, then field
director of the European Student Relief Committee of the World Student
Christian Federation.

Esther was evidently comfortable at Leeds University. When she was
working on *Refugee Scholars* in 1989–1991, she compared Cambridge, where

she lived and worked during the Second World War, unfavourably with her alma mater:

> It had never occurred to me before to be thankful that I had been to a red-brick university rather than Oxbridge, but when I saw the women's colleges in Cambridge I knew I wouldn't have been able to tolerate being a student there. The lack of freedom seemed to me like a glorified boarding school, even during the war. They have certainly changed since but then they definitely lacked the freedom that we had as students at Leeds University.

In 1924 she too was awarded a first class degree and in 1925 embarked on a teacher-training course. Here the parallel with brother Israel breaks down. Teaching was not for Esther.

> I didn't really want to be a teacher, but no-one at school or university ever told us that any other profession was open to us. Because of my scholarship I was able to get the extra year for the diploma free, so I took a teaching diploma like everybody else.

Esther was awarded her Diploma in Education in 1925, but any prospect of her following a teaching career (and vacancies were very few, she says) crashed with the teaching practice that followed.

This was in a large girls' school in Leeds, Thoresby High School, where the modern teaching principles of her diploma were rejected in favour of the traditional methods that had served the school well and matched the exam syllabus.

Put to teach French in the lower forms where '[m]y pupils were often girls who didn't speak their own language properly and whose last wish was to learn a foreign language', she also faced a problem with keeping discipline. 'I was not capable of keeping discipline. I was just not interested in that sort of thing.'

We must wonder at her lack of sympathy for, 'girls who didn't speak their own language properly' – a curious comment from the child of Crawford Street. And whether that lack had something to do with her not being 'interested' in keeping discipline. Later, of course, she was not short of sympathy for her refugee academics who needed to learn English.

But what was the alternative to the classroom? She took advice from the teacher who was responsible for business studies, telling her that she would like to go in for secretarial work; her aim eventually would be to do international work in some form. With the teacher's advice to learn the American Gregg system of shorthand, Esther set about teaching herself secretarial skills.

In Leeds, Esther became acquainted with Roger Soltau, a friend of her brother Israel's, who was to have a significant influence on her future. Soltau was a lecturer in French, a historian, an alternativist conscientious objector who had served in France in 1917 with the Friends Ambulance Service.

Soltau, who came from a family of Plymouth Brethren, became a Quaker in Leeds in July 1920, transferring his meeting to Westminster in November 1927, when he left the university and joined the International Fellowship of Reconciliation (IFOR).

He had a connection to the Quaker Swarthmore college in Leeds and through him Esther became friends with a German teacher there, Martha Steinitz, who had been very active in the German pacifist movement. According to Esther, this made it very difficult for her to continue living in Germany. And so in 1925 a new phase began in Esther's life.

As recounted in *Refugee Scholars*, seeing Esther at a loose end, Martha suggested she take the opportunity to become a governess in a very well-to-do family in her hometown of Breslau (since 1945 the Polish city of Wroclaw) in north-east Germany.

11

Breslau Briefly

Then the largest city east of Berlin, with some half a million inhabitants, Breslau was twelve hours by train from Dvinsk, though Esther seems not to have taken the chance to make a visit. The idea was an appointment for ten months, teaching English to the twelve-year-old daughter of the house.

But if teaching the badly spoken impoverished pupils at Thoresby High School had not been to Esther's taste, it turned out that neither was living and working with Herr Weiss's well-to-do Breslau family. He was in the leather business and had, says Esther, done well out of the war.

It seems the appointment lasted a bare ten weeks of the projected ten months. Esther tells us Herr Weiss had been to the US for two years and returned with his version of American ideals.

> One was that you worked hard but your women-folk didn't lift a
> finger . . . Another of these American ideals was that you had to have
> a mistress and that was something which did not make his wife very
> happy.

(Esther does not record the source of her knowledge of Herr Weiss's American ideals.)

Frau Weiss spent all her time in bed on the telephone – they had eight telephones in the house – sharing her unhappiness with her friends. The daughter wasn't interested in learning English or anything else; this did not disturb her father as she was an heiress.

Living in what she pictures in *Refugee Scholars* as Herr Weiss's beautiful, architect-designed, book-free mansion, in which all the beautiful fixtures and fittings had, she notes, been chosen by the architect, and enduring Herr Weiss's stuffy formality was apparently not at all to the taste of the young woman from Leeds' Little London. But, as in her accounts of Thoresby High School, we have no suggestion of Esther's attempting sympathetically to engage with Frau Weiss or her daughter. We are not even told their first names, let alone whether they and Esther had any sort of social contact.

At first glance, Breslau in 1925 would have seemed an ideal resort for a gifted, musical, young Jewish woman. It was a thriving and culturally lively city, with a strong Jewish community. Esther was particularly taken by the *Konditorei*, the bread and cake shops quite unlike anything to be found in Leeds.

Musically, this was a city as rich as any in Germany, with an orchestra society and a choral society, visited by pre-eminent performers of the day, including Artur Schnabel, Wilhelm Kempff, Vladimir Horowitz, Fritz Kreisler, Rudolf Serkin. Esther records hearing the violinist Adolf Busch play.

As well as sampling the cakes, she took advantage of the city's musical life, joining an orchestra and playing chamber music with Martha Steinitz's brother.

Culturally, too, Breslau was rich. A historian of German-Jewish history and of antisemitism, Dr Barbara Suchy noted to me,

> . . . so many many most outstanding Jewish scientists, artists, politicians, philosophers, entrepreneurs, architects, scholars were 'Breslauers'. Three historians and a musician immediately come to my mind: Joseph Walk, Walter Laqueur, Fritz Stern, and the cellist Anita Lasker-Wallfisch, a survivor of the Auschwitz Women's Orchestra.

Given Breslau's toothsome *Konditorei*, its musical life, the opportunity to practise her German, hone her shorthand skills, live in luxury, Esther's decision to leave when she had no alternative arranged seems to have come in very short order. Was something else in the Weiss household a problem for her?

Tracking down Esther's Herr Weiss is not simple in a city the records
of which show Weiss to be a quite frequent name, particularly among the
city's Jewish community. Delving into the records, Barbara Suchy identified
two possibilities:

> In a most beautiful book *Breslauer Juden 1850–1944* (based on an exhibition
> of the Historical Wroclaw Museum 1996) I found an announcement:
> Wahlen zum Verband preußischer Synagogengemeinden, Dez. 1924.
> Edited by: Der Konservative Wahlausschuss der Synagogengemeinde
> Breslau. Signed by more than 50 most honourable men and women.
> Among them: Elkan Weiss and Siegm. (Siegmund) Weiss.

[The reference is to a call to vote in Elections to the Association of
Synagogue Associations by the Conservative election committee of the
Breslau Synagogue Council.]

The city's Jewish character comes to mind:

> Thinking of Breslau means also thinking of the Jüdisch-Theologisches
> Seminar. The 'Jüdisch-Theologisches Seminar Fraenckel'sche Stiftung'
> (1854–1938) attracted rabbinical students from all over Europe and the
> US. Its orientation was Orthodoxy with a certain liberal openness.
> This attitude is also evident from the appeal for the elections by the
> 'conservatives' which I mentioned to you earlier.

Was Esther's Herr Weiss a pillar of the Breslauer conservative Jewish
community? If so, was the Jewish practice of his household such that it
was too trying for Esther to remain more than ten weeks? Suchy does not
scorn the possibility:

> I believe that you are right: your heroine probably disliked the
> outspoken 'Jewishness' of that family – constricting this young woman
> on her way into the life outside.

Or had Esther already turned her back on her inherited Jewishness,
separated herself from her family's east European religious practice?

Esther records knowing the Steinitz family when they came to Britain.
Given her later commitment to German-Jewish refugees, did she ever
wonder if Herr and Frau Weiss and their heiress daughter survived the war?

One of the pre-eminent Jewish diaries of life under Nazi rule would be written in Breslau, later published as *No Justice in Germany: The Breslau Diaries 1933–1941*, by Willy Cohn, a historian, recipient of a First World War Iron Cross for bravery, anti-assimilationist, Zionist, observant Jew. He became an admirer of some of Hitler's policies, but rigorously penned his observation of the steady marginalisation of his fellow Breslau Jews under Hitler from 1933.

> Troubled times in any case, especially for us Jews. We're sitting in a mouse trap.

A Gymnasium teacher, he lost his post in 1933. He observed,

> We Jews get a very strange feeling whenever we walk out in the open these days. On the one hand, this is the land in which we were born, whose development we have pursued over the decades; on the other, we have been excluded from it and been made alien. We are completely isolated.

But also, his love for Germany could not be shaken

> . . . by the unpleasantness that we are now experiencing. It is the country whose language we speak and whose good days we have also experienced! We have to be loyal enough to submit even to a government that comes from an entirely different camp.

In 1941, with his wife and two young daughters, he and the remaining Jewish community were sent to Lithuania to be slaughtered.

12
Saturdays in Auteuil

Putting Breslau and the distastefully luxurious Weiss mansion behind her, Esther took herself to Paris. By now short of money, she found a secretarial job with a British-owned company manufacturing road-building equipment. Situated in the north-western working-class suburb of Asnières, Machines Millars made tarmac and asphalt layers, steam rollers, and concrete mixers.

Esther was living in a house with other Leeds graduates, with one of whom, Brian Woledge, she played Bach sonatas for violin and piano. He had been at Leeds Boys Modern School and was at the University of Paris studying for a doctorate in mediaeval French.

Esther records compiling

> a dictionary for Machines Millars in four languages for the parts of their asphalt plants and concrete mixers and so on based on their technical literature. They thought this was marvellous and were extremely kind to me.

It is easy to be left with the impression of Millars as a small company. But this would be far from the case.

With the expansion of motor traffic in the industrialised world, the demand for better roads had led to demand for better road-building machinery and, according to *Grace's Guide*, Millars had won themselves the

position of which they may be justifiably proud as the leading manu-
facturers of road-making plant and contracting machinery, and to them
practically the whole contracting world looks for its equipment.

They were, for instance, the originators of the tilting cement mixer. The
French letterhead shows a reach across Europe. It also has a list of products
in French.

She was with them, Esther says, for about a year, leaving on 31 May 1927
(though she is also recorded by then as working at her next Paris job).

> Then I was offered a most extraordinary job, which was not going to
> be a permanent one either.

She was to work for an English aristocrat who, Esther says, acted as liaison
between the French Socialist Party and the British Labour Party.

But the reach of the Hon. Elinor Frances Bethell (1869–1943) extended
much beyond that.

She was also a Yorkshire woman, though her birthplace was not Leeds
but Nidd Hall near Harrogate. She was to be found in *Kelly's Handbook*,
Debrett's Illustrated Peerage and *Who Was Who*, being the eldest child and
elder daughter of Henry Butler the 14th Viscount Mountgarret and the half-
sister of the 16th. She had been married twice, at twenty to Yorkshireman
Andrew Lawson of Aldborough Manor, who died in 1914, with whom she
had two daughters, and to Alfred Bethell who died in 1920 after only two
years of marriage.

Esther says that he had been a Labour MP, but this is not the case for
either husband. In his portrait by Sir Leslie Ward, published in *Vanity Fair* in
1895 under the heading 'Men of the Day No.625' with the caption 'Go, Gas
& Gold', Alfred is noted as being a landowner. He was also the author of
Notes on South African Hunting: Ride to the Victoria Falls by the Zambesi (1887).

In the mid-1920s, Elinor moved to Paris to live in the west of the city
at 21 rue Leconte-de-Lisle in fashionable Auteuil, in the wealthy 16th
arrondissement, birthplace of Proust and verging on the Bois de Boulogne.
She had a butler, Esther noted, though she does not give his name, George.
The post involved secretarial help with the production of a journal Elinor
was starting, *The Green Leaf*.

Someone recommended the young English secretary to whom Elinor wrote 'in great haste' in her sprawling hand from 21 rue Leconte-de-Lisle to 'suggest' that she came and worked at *The Green Leaf* 'as secretary/typist etc.'. Plainly Elinor had not met her but she believed her to be a good French correspondent and that she typed and did shorthand in French as well as English. Elinor would insist on 3,000 francs per month [£42 then or some £2,700 today] and wanted Esther to come and talk things over that very evening if possible.

Elinor's expectations were not disappointed. When she went to stay in Baveno, Switzerland, she left Esther in charge, sending instructions by post for the running of *The Green Leaf.*

Elinor had become secretary of the Paris Group of the British Labour Party and the Paris Group of the Union of Democratic Control. Her Auteuil apartment was the official address for both. It was also the meeting place for the study circle of the British Labour Party, Paris Group, getting together on alternate Wednesdays at 9 p.m. A lending library of books on social and political subjects was also available to members of the Labour Group through the Auteuil apartment, at a charge of 50 centimes per week per volume.

The Announcements page of the first edition of *The Green Leaf* (*La Feuille Verte* in its subtitle) in December 1926 shows Ramsay MacDonald, leader of the Labour Party since 1922 and briefly Prime Minister in 1924, as president of the Labour Party Group. It had a committee of six, including Esther Sinovitch, the only woman; it was not a position she recorded in *Refugee Scholars.*

Among the articles on the Senatorial Election, the Molinella Affair, and Art and Drama, is a translation by Esther, 'Pan-Europa and the Working Class' (*Pan-Europa et la Classe Ouvrière*) by Georges Michon *Docteur ès-Lettres.*

On the page opposite, the Editorial sets out *The Green Leaf*'s mission. Baldly stated, it was propaganda. The (unsigned) editorial ends:

> As Britishers in a foreign country our opinions on Home politics are necessarily uninformed, and we may find ourselves at a disadvantage in writing about matters of which we have no first hand know ledge [*sic*]. Yet there is a saving clause. Most of our contributors are young

and tireless in their enthusiasm for a reorganised society. From them therefore will come the new ideas on old subjects, the inspiration and vitality which the Green Leaf will require if it is to develop into an effectual instrument for propaganda.

Elinor regarded the provision of translated articles as central to the existence of *The Green Leaf.* Esther's role was French to English, and subsequent editions credited her with the translation of such pieces as 'From War to Peace by Truth', 'Socialism and Democracy in France', 'The Position in France after the Senatorial Elections' and 'The Socialist Press in France'.

21 rue Leconte-de-Lisle was also home to Elinor's weekly salon, held on a *jour fixe*: she was 'at home' on Saturdays at 3.30 p.m.

In *Refugee Scholars* Esther references the *Manchester Guardian* correspondent Robert M. Dell, as well as Italian and German exiles as regular attendees. But in fact, according to an engaging contribution to *The Wellsian: The Journal of the H. G. Wells Society* (2002):[16] 'Wells in Paris: The Impressions of an Australian Student' by Kenneth R. Dutton, the salon was held for young people from across the Empire, principally post-graduate students at Paris University, who were sympathetic to international cooperation and would enjoy the conversation in Elinor's, broadly, Fabian atmosphere, with occasional prominent guests.

One such is featured in 'Wells in Paris'.

Given her resolute refusal to include any personal memories in Cooper's book, it is included here to give a sense of what the twenty-three-year-old Esther might have experienced:

> One of the students who attended a number of these receptions, throughout 1928 and in early 1929, was Ian Henning (1905–1975), a brilliant graduate of the University of Sydney who had won the University Medal for both French and German. Henning had subsequently been awarded a French Government Scholarship which took him to Paris to undertake a doctoral thesis on the influence of the nineteenth-century author Mme de Staël on French perceptions of Germany.

16 https://thewellsian.awh.durham.ac.uk/ojs/index.php/Wellsian/issue/view/14

Henning wrote weekly letters to his family in Australia. In November 1928, a letter recounted how

> George, Mrs Bethell's butler, rushed round to see Alan yesterday afternoon and told us to turn up at half-past three today and meet: H. G. Wells! So I can tell you we didn't need asking twice. Mrs Bethell had mentioned that we might meet him as he was passing through Paris, but we thought it might all blow over as some of her things do. But it didn't. At half-past three this afternoon [I] was ushered in to the little drawing-room [I know] so well and was immediately introduced to Wells himself.

The letter goes on to narrate what amounted to a political seminar held by Wells.

A year before the Wells salon, Esther had left Elinor and Paris to work for Roger Soltau and the International Fellowship of Reconciliation, IFOR (or the FOR as its members called it). But when in Paris she was no more than three years out of university, with time as a student in Caen and a governess in Breslau giving her experience of cities other than Leeds. This was Paris of the so-called 'lost generation'; the Paris of which Hemingway wrote, 'If you are lucky enough to have lived in Paris as a young man, then wherever you go for the rest of your life, it stays with you, for Paris is a moveable feast.'

Inevitably the question arises, why the academically gifted students of Elinor's salon and why Paris itself in the twenties apparently made so little impression on Esther Sinovitch, or at least not for her memoirs. The answer may lie in the pull of her next move – to Vienna. But it is also plausible that though her first-class degree was in French, she did not feel any harmony with the French themselves – particularly intellectuals.

A letter to Broda in 1952 provides some evidence for this. It contains a vigorous (albeit highly conventional) defence of Britain's saying 'No' in 1940 when seemingly at the desperate point of capitulation – and succeeding in 'No'.

> 1940 when clever continental intellectuals [she can only mean the French] thought all was up with Britain, the stupid British weren't clever enough to see it and the extraordinary thing is that they were right. That is only one instance . . . With primitive peoples the logic

of the intellectuals breaks down and so it does with the British – perhaps not because they are primitive but because they have a national character which gives them something that – say – the clever and rational and logical French haven't got when it comes to community feeling?

In 1927, Esther, twenty-four, left Paris, Elinor and *The Green Leaf* to act as an interpreter at the International Fellowship of Reconciliation (IFOR) annual conference held in Switzerland in the former municipality of Vaumarcus on Lake Neuchâtel. The invitation came from her brother Israel's friend Roger Soltau, who had left Leeds University to join IFOR's management.

IFOR, set up as a response to the horrors of war in Europe to promote understanding between formerly hostile nations, had its roots in an ecumenical conference held in Switzerland in 1914 by Christians seeking to prevent the outbreak of war in Europe. The outbreak of war put paid to their going further but a Christian gathering in Cambridge to keep the flame alive set up the Fellowship of Reconciliation (FOR). In the US, the Fellowship of Reconciliation was founded by Christian pacifists in 1915. An organisation of conscience, it was riven by disagreements over such issues as the meaning of pacifism in action, which were alive at this time.

Today the International Fellowship of Reconciliation organisation has as its aim 'to apply principles of peace and social justice and non-violent social change to issues such as disarmament, conscription, race relations, economic justice, and civil liberties'.

An invitation to spend her holiday with Roger Soltau and his family on Lake Lugano followed the Vaumarcus conference. And an offer to be Soltau's secretary in London was made while there. She said she would love to.

Esther says she knew the job with *The Green Leaf* was coming to an end, though why she does not say. She went back to Paris 'and finished that off', then went to London and the IFOR.

The Green Leaf had undergone a decisive change of tone. In the December 1927 edition, the last in Esther's archived collection given to her by Elinor on her leaving, all mention of the Labour Party has gone. Instead, the review is said to be 'Of interest for all to whom the reconstruction of society is of deep interest'. The management is no longer listed, nor translators. The content is much less directly political. But it is in the language and viewpoint of the editorial that change stands out, suffused as it is with a pacifist religiosity. A decision the previous month to cease publication of the bilingual edition is not to be put into effect, along with what looks like a shift to publishing short stories of a suitably elevated nature: 'Imagination is the Universal Nature without which we are as sounding brass and tinkling cymbals.'

At this point, Esther had travelled in post-war Europe and worked up her bilingual secretarial skills, but she had shown no signs of settling into a vocation or calling. The next turn in her life seemed a continuation of that: Roger Soltau was about to move with IFOR to Vienna and suggested to Esther she come too.

Esther records how at first she was unsure; her musical gift prompted her to agree. A conversation with a musical friend from Vienna, Lisl Kallberg, about the matchless opportunities for making music in the Austrian capital decided her. If she had sympathy for the IFOR's ambitions, she does not say so.

13

Vienna – Paradise

On 4 September 1928, after holidaying in the Cevennes, Esther took a train from Venice to Vienna, where she gave as her address Döblergasse 2/26 in the Vllth district, the IFOR address, the seat of IFOR's eight-member International Executive Committee, of which Roger Soltau was chair from 1929 to 1936.

The VIIth district or Neubau, one of the districts ringing the inner city, with popular but not ultra-fashionable shops and cafés, a resort for students and intellectuals, would have been a good place to begin acquaintance with Viennese life.

Esther's time in Vienna between 1928 and 1933 was one that saw growing political turmoil, always with the potential for violence, in the rump republic that had been washed out of the former Austro-Hungarian Empire at the end of the Great War by the forces of national sovereignty that it unleashed.

Article 10 of US President Woodrow Wilson's Fourteen Points of 8 January 1918 stated:

> The peoples of Austria-Hungary, whose place among the nations we wish to see safeguarded and assured, should be accorded the freest opportunity of autonomous development.

In Austria between 1926 and 1934, the division between 'Red' Vienna and the deeply conservative and Catholic countryside was the governing impetus of political activity, the division intensified by the growth of paramilitary forces on either side. On the right, the *Heimwehr*, 107,000 strong, opposed to parliamentary democracy. On the left, the *Schutzbund*, the Socialist Republic Defence League, 100,000 strong. By 1929, their membership had trebled. Unemployment was rising; the world economic crisis hit in 1930. The National Socialists, following the strategy its German counterpart had utilised, were emerging as a political force in local associations and regional elections. In 1932, the Christian Social Engelbert Dollfuß became Chancellor and brought into being the Fatherland Front, a corporatist amalgam of right-wing forces, populist, conservative, Catholic, statist.

In March 1933, the Austrian parliament was suspended and Dollfuß ruled by decree, establishing a corporate state with the support of the Christian Social Party, the *Heimwehr* and the *Landbund* (Rural Union). He was assassinated by Nazis in July 1934 and succeeded by Kurt Schuschnigg, who governed until the forced union with Germany, the *Anschluss*, in 1938.

Esther had a Vienna University student card, apparently attended lectures, and so would have been affected by the university's closures on account of Nazi student violence, although she left no references to such happenings. Altogether in the 1930s, she was in Vienna with the FOR, then in Geneva at the Disarmament Conference, then in London for displaced scholars but travelling regularly to the Austrian capital until 1937 to visit friends for her summer holiday. But in *Refugee Scholars* or writing to Engelbert Broda at Vienna University after the war and reminiscing very occasionally about her time in Vienna, she makes no comment on the fall of Austrian democracy at the hands of corporate Catholicism, or the rise of Nazism, or the horrors of Austrian antisemitism, neither remembrance nor reflection.

Roger Soltau soon left the FOR to take up a post at the American University in Beirut, and Esther was assigned to Donald Grant, the FOR secretary-general from 1929 to 1936, a Scottish cleric who was prominent in the Student Christian Movement.

Grant was a veteran of Vienna, having been Field Representative of the European Student Relief Committee in 1922 for Austria and Hungary, and also a member of Innsbruck University. He and his wife Irene and their daughter Wendy [in later life, Dr Helen Grant, the neuropathologist who warned the British public in the 1980s about BSE or mad cow disease] became true friends of Esther's, with a sense of their taking her under their wing.

As it happened, Grant was in New Zealand for the SCM when Soltau left: he and Irene would remain there for another year. In his absence, Esther worked for the acting secretary Kaspar Mayr, as well as for the French Christian pacifist pastor and future resistance hero Henri Roser who was secretary-general for Europe.

Roger Soltau wrote to 'Tess' in August 1929 hoping she would enjoy working with Grant; he should suit her temperament better than Mayr. A Scotsman was not unlike a Yorkshireman [sic], he wrote.

Vienna entranced Esther. In February 1950, writing from London to Engelbert Broda in Vienna, she remarked that she had just been to see Carol Reed's 1949 film set in post-war Vienna, The Third Man. She found it sad

> . . . and it made my heart ache to see the excellent Austrian actors I have seen so often given such small parts in the film, especially Ernst Deutsch.

Deutsch, who played the memorably sinister Baron Kurtz in the film, was a Jewish actor born in Prague in 1890. In post-war, four-power Vienna he was probably glad enough to have the work in a British feature film with such stars as Orson Welles and Joseph Cotten.

He had risen to stage and film stardom in Germany and Austria before being forced to emigrate in 1933. He had then restarted a successful career in other European cities, including performing on the London stage in 1936, when Esther might have seen him, before emigrating to the United States and Hollywood. After the war he returned to Vienna and Berlin and to rebuilding an award-winning film and stage career. He died in 1969.

The music and the contacts were all Lisl Kallberg had promised. People played chamber music there, Esther pronounced, as naturally as cleaning their teeth – repeated in Refugee Scholars, a claim that caught Gombrich's doubtful eye.

She found musical partners in the Schiff family, maternal relatives of Karl Popper's through his mother, and mentioned earlier in reference to

Refugee Scholars' launch. She had the student card for the university. A 1948 letter contains a reference to a probable member of the,

> Carnap-Schlick-Wittgenstein school as far as philosophy goes. They
> all seem to, from Vienna, and it doesn't always lead in a happy direction
> (I'm thinking of Karl Popper) . . .

But no suggestion can be found that she attended Professor Schlick's lectures or meetings of the Vienna Circle of logical-positivist philosophers/ believers, then in its heyday. The not always 'happy direction' remark about the unquestionably eminent Karl Popper, with whom she maintained a correspondence, presents a challenge. Members of the Circle she helped later when they sought refuge in England included Friedrich Waismann, Otto Neurath and Rose Rand.

In *Refugee Scholars* Esther records herself as playing chamber music non-stop with a variety of partners. One charitable commitment was, it seems, playing to Austrian children who had been sent to England after the First World War to escape the famine.

> These children in due course returned home. The Friends in London
> had a concern about these children; they were anxious that links should
> be maintained and that the children should not forget the English they
> had learned. So every evening at the Friends Centre in Vienna there
> was something special put on for these children: drama, readings, and
> sometimes music, which is where Trevor [Fisher] and I came in.

She was living and working in the Vienna of legend, of frontier-breaking modern culture and traditional coffee houses, though whether she frequented those is unknown. She seems to have gone to the theatre, if the reference to seeing Ernst Deutsch is indicative. She went walking in the countryside around the city.

One circle with which she did have some sort of connection was that around the Austro-Hungarian economist Karl Polanyi. This would have come through the man for whom she finally worked in the FOR, Donald Grant. Through him she also met the personalist philosopher John

Macmurray and his wife Betty, who became dear friends of Tess, again with a hint of taking her under their wing.

The FOR, Donald and Irene Grant, were on close terms with the Quaker mission in Vienna, The English-American Mission of the Society of Friends at 16 Singerstraße, and its formidable American head, Emma Cadbury.

To the non-Quaker, the term 'Quaker' might conjure up from school history lessons one of the Society's founding spirits, George Fox, who in 1650 was brought before magistrates on a charge of heresy and made them tremble – or quake – with his defence. It might also conjure up Quakers using 'thee' and 'thou' to address each other, and sitting in silence at their meetings (not services). Or, perhaps, if none of the foregoing, the superlative humanitarian work that brought Friends in Britain and the US the 1947 Nobel Peace Prize.

Lisa McQuillan, archivist and librarian at the Society of Friends Library in London, writes on the Quaker.org website,

> At the time of the award in 1947, Quakers in Britain, the USA and other countries were still heavily involved with relief work for one of the worst humanitarian crises of the twentieth century: the hundreds of thousands of 'displaced persons' in the aftermath of World War II.
>
> Friends had been equally involved during the war itself. Their far-reaching humanitarian activities include ambulance and medical work, assisting refugees to escape from Nazi Europe and establish new lives, and providing aid to prisoners and internees.
>
> As well as all this, the Nobel committee made clear that the prize was also being awarded to recognise the Quaker commitment to non-violence – something that had been present since the faith's inception in the 17th century.

Under the heading Our Faith, the website records that,

> Quaker faith is a search for truth, not an arrival.
>
> We don't offer neat creeds or doctrine. Instead, we try to help each other work out how we should live. All people are welcome and accepted at a Quaker meeting.
>
> Quakerism is almost 400 years old. It's the common name for the Religious Society of Friends. It grew out of Christianity and today we

also find meaning and value in other faiths and traditions. We
recognise that there's something transcendent and precious in every
person. Different Quakers use different words to describe this, but we
all believe we can be in contact with it and encounter something
beyond our individual selves.

And under the heading Our History, the website declares:

The key beliefs of Quakerism were formed at this time. They include
the idea that each individual can experience inner light, or the voice
of God, without needing a priest, or the Bible. This belief has evolved
to mean that Quakers don't have strict set rules governing their
Church – how each individual chooses to act, if it is driven by this inner
light, is valid. It also means that Quakers believe there is that of God
in everyone, they seek to 'meet' this in all people and see all humans
as equal and deserving of equal treatment and respect.

Early Quakers also preached there was no need for churches,
rituals, holy days, or sacraments, to practice [sic] religion. Rather
religion should be something one lived and acted out every day.

These ideas were radical in a period where the established church
held great political power, and many early Quakers were imprisoned
and oppressed for these beliefs.

Through history, these beliefs have led Quakers to act in ways they
are now well known for; campaigning for the rights of prisoners, refusing
to fight in wars, mediating in conflicts, and becoming the first religious
organisation in Britain to officially recognise same-sex marriage.

The Quaker Vienna mission had been established after the First World War
to aid the defeated and starving population. It set up training and cultural
activities – Donald Grant was among its lecturers – and sought to ward off
violence between the country's warring political factions of right and left.

The monthly eyewitness political reports one of the Centre's full-time
members, Headley Horsnaill, sent to London are extraordinarily insightful as the country turned to clerical-fascism and Austrian Nazis were on
the rise.

In her October 1928 report to the American Friends Service Committee
in Philadelphia, Emma Cadbury recorded the opening in Vienna of the

FOR with Kaspar Mayr as secretary *pro tem* (Esther has him as deputy head). Donald Grant had been appointed general secretary, she wrote, but would not take up his post until the next summer. And in her October 1929 report, Emma Cadbury duly affirmed that Donald Grant had arrived and had spent a fortnight with them at the Friends Centre while starting work and looking for a home for his family. She recorded how much she was enjoying having Grant in the hostel. He would be a great help in their activities, religious and educational.

Donald Grant became a regular lecturer at the Centre, talking to its English discussion group on 'Is the Peace Ideal Practicable Today?' and on a recent visit to Belgrade, Sofia, and Salonika for the FOR. The FOR also held a meeting on disarmament.

Meanwhile, the autumn reports also recorded the seriousness of the economic depression in Austria, with 300,000 unemployed and threatened clashes between the right- and left-wing militias, the *Heimwehr* and the *Schutzbund*, which the Quakers pleaded with the government to take steps to avoid.

At the turn of the year 1931–1932, the political atmosphere was thought so threatening that the Centre was contemplating sending personal possessions to England – 'We feel we should be safer not to have so many things which we value here.'

By the onset of 1932, reports from the Centre noted that while the shops in the city centre were brightly lit, there were long queues for food and clothing from the Winter Assistance charity, *Winterhilfe*. One consequence of the crisis, they noted wryly, was that street musicians were better than elsewhere – they were all young men.

The reports from Singerstraße in October, November and December 1932 also chart the descent of Austria into political turmoil. One [from Rikki Teller] notes disturbances at the university accompanied by the students' feeling of hopelessness.

> Lies were at the bottom of racial hate against the Jewish race, a hate which is used by political elements and which led, after some pandemonium, to an attack on the Jewish students on October 15th and 16th and to the closing of the university on the 17th. At reopening on the 20th some more disturbances made the Rector close it again

until November 3rd. But at the end of November it came to serious
disturbances between the National and Catholic students which made
the university close so early as December 9th for Xmas holidays.
A Bulgarian student told me he had been able to study only 12 days at
the university this term.

In building a picture of Esther's time in this great European city, we look
to her in vain for any observation of or reaction to its political or economic
turmoil. Equally, we look in vain for any record of her participation in the
Friends Centre's social activities, its young people's club, its University
Women's Club. Possibly she was too engaged with music outside her office
duties to be aware of the darkening world around her.

One letter of Emma Cadbury's is significant. She notes,

> Esther Sinowitsch [sic], Donald Grant's young English secretary, asked
> for a meeting with Bernard Walton.

Presumably, this would have been to discuss her becoming a Quaker. The
wording also indicates that Esther was not closely involved at the Centre.
Then, on 27 January 1932, Emma reported to Philadelphia,

> I have told the English lady who has been corresponding with Bernard
> Walton that she should try to see the Hulls [William and Hannah Hull]
> in Geneva and I hope she can also be in close touch with the Quaker
> group there. She is a secretary in the international office of the FOR and
> is going to help in the centre of the FOR which is set up in Geneva for
> the duration of the Disarmament Conference. Donald Grant is leaving
> this week to be in charge of the Centre there. The address is Pension, 3
> Ave Calas Geneva. Donald Grant thinks that the daily conference by W
> Arnold Forster arranged by the Joint Disarmament Conference of the
> Christian International Organizations would be very valuable.

As well as Esther's next move, to Geneva with Donald Grant, this gives
us the timing, if not the motivation, for her becoming a Quaker. In fact,
she applied not to the Vienna meeting, to Geneva, or to the Friends'
London headquarters but to Swarthmore in Pennsylvania to become a
corresponding member of the meeting there. On the application form she
gives the FOR office in Döblergasse as her address in Vienna.

Strangely, she also gives her mother's maiden name as Steingold not Perevosnik.

('Steingold' does appear in Morty Wellen's Perevosnik family tree, but at some distance from Esther's mother.)

In April 1932 Irene Soltau wrote to Tess from Beirut saying how glad she was Tess had joined the Friends: she had always felt the kind of religion the Friends stood for, and from time to time attained, was a real force in their lives.

However, Tess's Jewishness was integral to their image of her, with Irene writing in 1930 from Beirut that she had some nice Jewesses in her class, one of whom especially reminded her of Tess.

As the introduction to Hannah Arendt's *Rahel Varnhagen* puts it, speaking of assimilation in Germany around 1800, 'It meant being forced to assimilate with a people who only accepted Jewish individuals who had left their roots behind. Jews were supposed to forget who they were, and yet in return the Gentiles never forgot that they were Jews.' Nor, of course, did other Jews.

If, with the joys of non-stop music and becoming a Quaker, Esther felt she had landed in a personal paradise in Vienna, working at the FOR was not part of it. Discord was rife in the Döblergasse, and Esther became part of it.

Roger Soltau had told her in his August 1929 letter how the organisation was under the financial lash – a promised American donation had been substantially reduced – and jobs were being cut. Not Esther's, he told her: everyone agreed she was indispensable. In fact she would benefit from the cuts, with an office of her own.

In September 1932 Headley Horsnaill wrote that he had heard from Kaspar Mayr of the International FOR

> ... that they may have to give up the whole of the flat which they are occupying in the Dobling before long. They want if possible to let the part of the flat which has been used as a dwelling at once and to retain their office rooms until February. KM asks if there is any chance of our letting them have two rooms at a reasonable rent till latest September 33 ... In this case there are difficulties also particularly till February when Donald Grant and Esther Sinowitsch are leaving. They

would still have to be housed. After that when KM and his secretary only will be here it would be much easier to manage.

The FOR stand closer to us than any of the other Peace Organizations.

Finance was not the only, or even the greatest, difficulty the FOR faced, one which the move to Vienna had been made to ameliorate. It was riven by structural questions – was it a Christian organisation? was it anti-war? – that put the leadership at odds.

Esther did not like what she was seeing and wrote to Roger and Irene Soltau to share her concerns from early on.

In her 1930 letter, Irene had written to sympathise with Tess over the death of her mother and her father's being left all alone.

(Sarah died in Leeds on 30 October 1930 at the age of sixty-one. Ellis on 14 February 1943 at seventy-two. Esther makes no mention of them in *Refugee Scholars*, though in a letter to Ray Cooper she has a brief reference to her father's taking her to concerts when a child.)

She was so sorry too, Irene continued, that things in the FOR were not more settled. She blamed unsound work by the leadership over the years, which might still be having an effect on the organisation.

And so it proved. In her letter of April 1932, Irene takes up what Tess has been writing to them about the state of the FOR in Vienna.

In a surprisingly unsparing tone, she refers to Tess's implying a senior colleague had been acting in a way quite dishonest and unchristian. Reprovingly, Irene in effect tells Tess she should say what she means or leave it. She and Roger had their disagreements with that colleague but had never doubted him. Then – and remember Roger had brought Esther to Vienna – Irene straightforwardly advises her that Donald Grant might get on better with the colleague if she, Tess, were not there.

The sense of Irene's unease is strengthened when she goes on to advise that if Tess felt as she did, it would be best to make a change. They had enquired for work for her in Beirut and good secretaries were in demand in Jerusalem, though a grasp of Hebrew or Arabic was required.

Roger added a page in support of Irene, noting there were differences between the English and International FOR. He also challenged what

Esther must have written about lies in the FOR's past history. He wondered if she was not exaggerating a bit!

While we are far from having the whole story of the discord in the Döblergasse, plainly Esther was not a passive onlooker. Her friends and previous supporters did not conceal their dismay, to the point where they thought the FOR would be better off without her, at both how she represented to them the personal difficulties at the FOR and her part in them, her actions in support of her boss. But, as we will see, Donald Grant seems to have been grateful.

14

The Quaker

Esther was accepted as a corresponding member of the Pennsylvania Swarthmore Meeting. That this meant something to her is shown by her wanting to keep that membership when applying to join the north-west London Hampstead Meeting in September 1945. Such dual membership was unusual and Hampstead were resistant to the idea, insisting on Swarthmore Meeting's agreement, but finally accepted it in October 1945.

Lisa McQuillan of the Friends Library wrote:

> The minutes certainly suggest themselves that this was an odd arrangement, and one Hampstead were initially reluctant to accept – that of joint membership of two meetings – and I can't remember coming across joint membership arrangements elsewhere, although I wouldn't rule them out as occasionally occurring. Friends usually either transferred membership if they moved to a new area (even for a short period) or had temporary permission to travel to other meetings from their meeting . . . There was a lot of transatlantic travel between Friends in this periods; it would not be uncommon for British Quakers to go to meetings in Swarthmore and visit or study at Swarthmore college. I would say that the minutes suggest it was an arrangement Esther was keen on particularly rather than either meeting pushing for it, for whatever reason.

Esther certainly had no intention of crossing the Atlantic.

Why Swarthmore? Why Steingold? Why wait for twelve years before seeking membership, even on a temporary basis, of a meeting where she could be present, actively participate? The Cambridge Meeting has a history going back to the seventeenth century and a meeting house in the heart of the university that dates to the eighteenth. They would surely have welcomed a visitor, guest or new member so actively involved with refugee scholars. (It may be that she joined meetings in London or Cambridge as a guest, but no suggestion of this has turned up.)

These point to the larger question, what drew Esther to the Quakers in the first place, in Vienna? Given the closeness between the Vienna Centre and the FOR, was she drawn to the Quakers through contact with the humanitarian work of the Centre and the spirit in which it was carried out?

If she had broken with the strict Orthodox Judaism of Crawford Street, of which more later, to stand on her own two feet, as an individual and a woman, was a gap still to be filled in her life that basic Quaker tenets satisfied?

> This belief has evolved to mean that Quakers don't have strict set rules governing their Church – how each individual chooses to act, if it is driven by this inner light, is valid. It also means that Quakers believe there is that of God in everyone, they seek to 'meet' this in all people and see all humans as equal and deserving of equal treatment and respect.

What Swarthmore, Penn and Steingold then suggest is the idea of separation, putting distance between her inherited and her novel Quaker selves.

She went on to play an active and respected part in the Hampstead Meeting, appointed to two important posts: overseer in 1952 and elder in 1964. She also served on the Quaker refugee council after the war.

Rod Harper of the Hampstead Meeting told me:

> My records of membership of Hampstead Meeting only go back as far as 1952. Esther is listed as being a member at this date, she remained a member of the Society until her death, attending Hampstead meeting on a regular basis. She was [a] highly respected member and served the Meeting both as an overseer – concerned with the welfare of members – and as an elder – concerned with the spiritual well-being of the

Meeting. We remember her as a highly intelligent warm and friendly person who had an unswerving commitment to academics all over the world that for a variety of reasons found themselves in isolated persecuted positions . . . I do know she had a vast correspondence and said to me on one occasion that she could not possibly be unwell as there were urgent matters to which she needed to attend. I remember once meeting her on the tube at about 11.30 at night, she was in full evening dress having been at a dinner at the Royal Society.

Perhaps that was the opening of the Royal Society Tercentenary celebrations in May 1960 to which the president of the SPSL, Lord Beveridge, invited her to go as 'his lady'. Or, as she put it in a letter to Engelbert Broda, ' . . . he asked me to go as his girlfriend. It should be quite interesting.' As we have seen with her elementary school headteacher Thomas Bentley, Esther did not do private expressions of gratitude. When Lord Beveridge died in 1963, all she commented to Broda was that she 'was quite fond of him' – the man who had founded and presided over the AAC/SPSL.

In the same letter she told Broda that she had been to the Israeli Embassy for the twelfth anniversary of independence. As for dress, others recall her as the soul of modesty, wearing the same classic dress summer and winter, with sensible shoes. Period pieces, was a phrase used.

On her appointments as overseer and elder, Rod Harper explained further,

Elders and overseers are appointed by the Area Meeting, not the local Meeting. The Area Meetings are groups of about 3–8 local Meetings and are superior meetings. The area meeting appoints a nominations committee whose job it is to discern who would be suitable for the various jobs that need doing to enable the Society to function effectively. Appointments are for three years and are usually renewed for another three. I think one could assume that she held the offices for 6 years each.

The Hampstead meeting house is towards the top of Hampstead High Street, a short distance from the top of the Heath and the White Stone pond. If she were feeling energetic, Esther could walk there in, say, half an hour from the Buckland Crescent flat she bought with 'her' children's fund.

A less than ten-minute walk from the flat in the opposite direction is what was originally known as the German Synagogue (now the Belsize Square Synagogue), established originally for refugees from Germany, Austria and Czechoslovakia, and offering Liberal German rites and practices. Some of 'her' children were among its first congregants. She refers to it in a letter, but whether she ever set foot in there is unknown.

In May 1944 Esther also became a member of the Friends Committee for Refugees and Aliens, of which the remarkable Bertha Bracey – a principal instigator of the *Kindertransport* and saviour of the 600 so-called Windermere Children from the Theresienstadt concentration camp in 1945, among many other heroic works – was general secretary.

The FCRA demonstrates the Friends' long concern with relief for the starving and impoverished by war. It had its roots in the post-1919 German and Holland Committee that in 1933 became the Germany Emergency Committee. By 1939 it occupied twenty-five rooms in Bloomsbury House, with eighty staff and 14,000 case files. By the end of summer 1939, the figures were 119 staff and 22,000 case files. In the first six months alone of 1939, 1,795 visas had been issued on GEC applications.

The Quakers' long and committed service in relieving poverty and famine in Germany and Austria gave them the experience and official standing to take on the political oppression that came with the Hitler regime.

At the Vienna Centre, Emma Cadbury noted in October 1935 of arrivals at the Centre:

> . . . a number calling themselves refugees who have left for other reasons. Fugitives from civil justice. Also no doubt a few spies. Recently an influx of Jews for whom it seems to be getting increasingly difficult to live in Germany, whether because their business is taken away or because dealers refuse to sell them food, especially in small towns.

As a contemporary report after *Kristallnacht* (the night of broken glass) in November 1938 stated:

> The Jews expect no quarter from the present German government. The policy they say is to get rid of them at all costs, through suicide,

sickness, despair, emigration. There is no future for them in Germany
and no temporary relief which Friends might be able to give can alter
that fact.

The position of so-called 'non-Aryan' refugees (those with a Jewish
background but not part of a Jewish community) was worse than that of
Jews as such. The Quakers tended to look after the 'non-Aryans'; Jewish
Relief was concerned with observant Jews.

By 1945 the FCRA, which also had representatives of the major Christian
denominations, had moved on from German refugees. Its agenda included
children from concentration camps, prisoners of war, displaced persons,
clothing, the treatment of Germany, non-fraternisation orders, parcels
to relatives of German POWs, repatriation of refugees, foreign domestic
workers.

The committee was wound up in 1949. Esther's attendance had been
patchy, unsurprisingly as she was constantly complaining how she was
run off her feet at the SVS. That this nuts-and-bolts agenda was not of any
great interest to her is also likely.

15

Disarmament in Geneva 1932

Esther's Vienna idyll did not last long. The FOR could not afford to keep its offices at Döblergasse. Emma Cadbury recorded its request to use one of the mission's spare rooms. Donald and Esther went to Geneva, where he was to report on the International Disarmament Conference. The arrangement also removed them both from Vienna and Kaspar Mayr (acting secretary/ secretary 1929–1936).

Esther's contemptuous recollection of the Geneva proceedings appears in *Refugee Scholars*, 'We saw how the cynicism of our delegate helped to sabotage the Conference. He was Sir John Simon.'

Esther was very depressed, she recalled in a letter to Broda, at the waffling; the only person worth hearing was Einstein.

The *New York Times* had a different reaction, reporting with incredulity on 23 May 1932 on the suggestion that the Disarmament Conference needed a Gandhi and Dr Einstein agreed, stressing that complete war-resisting pacifism was the only cure. 'A more preposterous suggestion you can't imagine.'

Donald Grant acted as interpreter for Einstein.

The Conference ended in November 1934, but Donald Grant's reporting from Geneva did not go beyond 1932. Esther found – she makes much of the contacts she made in Geneva – or was found a new employer, with the international World Alliance of YMCAs in Geneva.

In her brief account in *Refugee Scholars* of working there, we have her only mention of feeling outraged as Jewish.

> We used to have little religious services at the end of Thursday morning, and I remember being very shocked when, on one occasion soon after I joined, the French parson said that while rather awkward happenings were taking place in Germany, we had to ask ourselves what was the will of God. Quoting from Isaiah, he proved to his own satisfaction that it was the will of God that the Jews should be persecuted until they all became Christians. That was a little much for me. I mentioned this to my friend, Frank Willis, who ran their institution for training YMCA leaders, and who hadn't been present on this occasion. When I told him about it, he was quite furious. Later Frank Willis became Sir Frank Willis, head of the YMCA in this country.

Esther does not comment on the phrase 'rather awkward happenings taking place in Germany'. Hitler took power on 30 January 1933 and Esther left Geneva in July that year. We have no indication of what 'rather awkward' would have covered or what Esther would have known of it.

That was a little much for me. A reader who knew Esther only from *Refugee Scholars* might well assume Esther's outrage stemmed from a principled opposition to such antisemitism. At no point does she mention being born into and brought up in a Jewish family or that her birth-name was Sinovitch and her parents had emigrated from Latvia. Nor does Ray Cooper refer to this in his introduction, though Esther's coming from a refugee family might have been thought relevant. Of course, he may not have known.

The incident as recalled in *Refugee Scholars* seemed significant to a reviewer, Dr Anthony Joseph, Emeritus President of the Jewish Genealogical Society of Great Britain, writing to the *Jewish Chronicle* on 19 May 2017.

> I was asked by Joan Stiebel to review the book and my review was published in the Birmingham Jewish Recorder in January 1993. Although Tess rarely admitted to any influence from her Jewish background, I was impressed by her comment about when she moved to Geneva in 1933.

'We used to have little religious services at the end of Thursday morning, and I remember being very shocked when, on one occasion soon after I joined [the World Alliance of YMCA's] . . . That was a little much for me'.

I think this may have had a profound influence on Tess's subsequent devotion to her attempts to help the persecuted peoples under Hitler's regime.

Esther had now had five jobs in four different countries in eight years since the end of her teacher training, all abroad, none offering anything approaching a calling or career or even a future, though four of the jobs demonstrated her considerable abilities.

At this time, Roger Soltau was looking for a new post for her. He wrote to a contact in Tel Aviv to ask about possible employment there or in Jerusalem. A post with the Palestine government would best be found in Britain, the contact replied, but a new newspaper would shortly be starting that might have possibilities. Soltau's picturing of Esther can be seen in his contact's response, understanding that she was not content to be a mechanical clerk, and wanting a position to be found in which she could demonstrate her abilities among congenial colleagues.

But from that YMCA office in Geneva, she would leave for London and the calling that would occupy her for almost literally the rest of her life and bring personal acclaim from the brightest academic minds of her time.

In reflecting on her story, we should remember how, as this next chapter in her life begins, it is still the story of an educated single Jewish working woman making her way in the 1930s.

16

Germany Turns the Page

For this turning point she could have thanked the accession to the leadership of Germany of the then newly installed *Reichskanzler*, Adolf Hitler, leader of the National Socialist German Workers Party, the *NSDAP*.

Hitler was sworn in as chancellor by the eighty-six-year-old President Paul von Hindenburg on 30 January 1933. That night, watching a torchlight parade by Nazi stormtroopers from a window in the Reich Chancellery, Hindenburg is said to have turned to an aide and asked, 'Are they all Russian prisoners?'[17] Hindenburg died in August the following year, clearing the way for Hitler to assume the title of *Führer und Reichskanzler*.

Fundamental to the success of his radical constitutional and cultural drive to mould Germany and Germans in the Nazi way was the tradition of faith in authorities – *Obrigkeitsgläubigkeit* – reinforcing the popular view that something needed to be done to see Germany out of its deep economic woes following the 1929 Wall Street Crash and that Hitler both knew what it was and had the will to do it. His bid for office as leader of the largest party in the Reichstag, though without a majority, had been banked by established conservative politicians who believed they would be able to control him.

Some Jews also thought that he might bring order to their divided nation.

---

17 That was told to me when at school by my European History teacher, Dr Alex Natan. He was a German Jew – an athlete once known as 'the fastest Jew in Germany' – and had been among the last enemy aliens to be released from internment.

On 21 March 1933, Professor Lise Meitner of the Kaiser Wilhelm Institute for Chemistry listened to the broadcast opening ceremony of the newly elected Reichstag, held in the Garrison Church Potsdam, following the destruction by arson of the Reichstag building in Berlin.

As quoted in Klaus and Ann Hentschel's *Physics and National Socialism*, she wrote to Professor Otto Hahn that it had been thoroughly amicable and dignified. President Hindenburg had said a few short sentences and then allowed the new Chancellor Adolf Hitler to speak, who spoke very moderately, tactfully and personally. Hopefully things would continue in this vein. If the level-headed leaders could prevail, among whom von Papen could be counted on primarily, then there was hope for things turning out well in the end. Periods of transition inevitably produced all kinds of blunders, of course. Everything now depended on rational moderation.

Lise Meitner also told Hahn that the Kaiser Wilhelm Institute had ordered the swastika flag to be flown alongside the black-white-red imperial flag. Raising the swastika had created a difficulty for the Jewish director Fritz Haber, known as the father of First World War gas warfare, but he surmounted it by giving the building superintendent directions to hoist the new flag, which was so much more dignified for him. Haber resigned not long after.

Hitler's rise to power in the politically splintered Weimar Republic is well documented and analysed – Wikipedia simply says thousands of books have been published on Hitler. What might be helpful as background to Esther's involvement with the scholar-victims of his taking power is a view of his initial approach to power: it was simple in intention – the political takeover of every aspect of German life – but fraught with legal difficulty over, for example, definitions of 'Jew'.

The point for Hitler's newly installed German government went beyond the seizure of power to the creation of a state corporately subservient to the will and vision of the party, meaning its leader, and dedicated to expressing that vision. Fundamental to that, the structural basis of the new state was to be the *Volksgemeinschaft*, the pure 'Aryan' racial community. Not only Jews were excluded but also Slavs, Sinti, Roma and *Fremdvölkische* [foreign people/races/non-Germans].

The roots of this and of the measures excluding Jews from German society could be seen in the Nazi Party programme of 1920, part authored by Hitler and reissued in 1933. This called for laws to reduce Jews' rights of citizenship, including their right to vote or hold public office; prohibit Jews from publishing or editing German newspapers; and deal with unemployment by expelling Jews from Germany.

We should also note that already from the late nineteenth century the so-called 'Aryan paragraph' [*Arierparagraph*] had been a fact of German public life, though not based on the constitution, and also not the case during the Weimar Republic. This limited positions in a corporation, membership of an organisation, tenancies, to 'Aryan'.

Such clauses were to be found at every level, from nationwide societies to local choirs. (And not only in Germany, of course. Far from it.)

In Cambridge in 1940 Esther sought help for a friend from an exiled German Lutheran pastor, Franz Hildebrandt, who had resigned from his Berlin church in June 1933 in protest against the introduction of such a provision in some of the regional Protestant churches (his mother was 'non-Aryan').

This veining of antisemitism in public life now became state policy. In his personal account of Hitler's taking power, *Defying Hitler*, the journalist and historian Sebastian Haffner recollects being out for a walk with his Jewish girlfriend in Berlin's Grunewald in late March 1933. The Nazi organised boycott of Jewish businesses is approaching. As they sat on the grass under a clear sky,

> The world was full of the peace of springtime. We sat there for about two hours and every ten minutes or so a group of young people would go past. It seemed to be a day for school outings. They were all fresh-faced adolescents, accompanied and supervised by their teachers, who often wore a pince-nez or a little beard, as one expects of a teacher faithfully watching over his little flock. Every one of these classes, as they passed, shouted 'Juda verrecke!' [Jews perish!] in their bright young voices, as though it was a sort of hiker's greeting.

The policy of control was carried out through the Enabling Act *Ermächtigungsgesetz* passed in the aftermath of the burning of the

Reichstag on 27 February 1933. The government falsely portrayed this as a communist plot to overthrow the state and on 28 February the Reichstag Fire Decree was passed 'for the protection of people and state'. On that day the *Reichspräsident* issued a decree (*Reichstagsbrandverordnung*) which suspended all articles of the constitution related to the citizens' rights. Together with the law of 24 March 1933 – the *Ermächtigungsgesetz* – for the 'elimination of hardship of people and state', it became the 'legal' base of the NS-dictatorship. It gave the government power to issue emergency decrees under the previously well-used Article 48 of the Weimar constitution – the legal underpinning for Hitler's rule by decree. In effect, the police could arrest anyone they believed presented a threat to the Nazi Party.

The last free speech made in the Reichstag is said to have been made on 23 March 1933 in opposition to the *Ermächtigungsgesetz* by the Social Democrat leader Otto Wels, who died in exile.

Decrees to put the Nazified state and society in place emerged in a steady flow. And the takeover was not only by decree; political pressure, administrative action and ever-present violence all had a role. Speed and certainty brushed away any opposition.

The guiding principle was summed up in the phrase coined by the Minister for Propaganda and Enlightenment Dr Joseph Goebbels: *Gleichschaltung*, usually rendered 'coordination'. (Barbara Suchy observes of *Gleichschaltung*, 'One of the countless obscuring euphemisms for destruction of all social diversity, for the elimination of all opposition.')

'A quarter past 11 [the hour when the conservative parties sealed their fatal deal with Hitler] led, in only 100 days, to the Thousand Year Reich,' the historian Peter Fritzsche writes in *Hitler's First Hundred Days*.

'Coordination' touched every aspect of life. On 15 May 1933, *Time* magazine reported on the 'Nazification' of labour and capital:

> Catholic unions announced complete allegiance and subservience
> to the Hitlerites and were accepted as good converts. Socialist
> unions with a total membership of over 4,000,000 were not given a
> chance . . . Storm Troopers raided their headquarters throughout

the Reich and marched 50 union leaders off to jail . . . With the disappearance of the Socialist unions, the Social Democrat Party will be permanently deprived of the soil in which it lived . . . [Robert Ley] will have the full direction of the labour front, which is to be newly constructed . . .

Nazification did not stop with the seizure of the unions. At the other end of the economic scale it was announced that the powerful Federation of German Industries had been Nazified too. It was not necessary to send Storm Troopers to call on the tycoons. After a brief conference in the Chancellery it was announced that none the less than Gustav Krupp von Bohlen und Halbach, head of the great Krupp works, had been given a power of attorney to reform the Federation, to bring it into line with the government . . .

The management of sports, cycling, football, athletics, gardening and music clubs was taken over by Nazi Party members or sympathisers. Doctors, dentists and lawyers were grouped into compulsory organisations.

A recollection of Goebbels in action by the former chief of the Berlin bureau of the Associated Press, Louis P. Lochner, in his introduction to *The Goebbels Diaries* illustrates well the extra-legal means employed to bring all aspects of life under Nazi rule.

Goebbels had been Reich Propaganda Leader of the Nazi Party. In power, in June 1933, Hitler made him Reich Minister for Public Enlightenment and Propaganda, with a major role in the coordination of German life with Nazi policies and outlook, hence a key figure in fostering antisemitism. On 22 September 1933 he brought all intellectual and cultural life under the Reich Culture Chamber, with sub-chambers for literature, press, radio, theatre, music, the arts. A Journalists' Law in October 1933 (*Schriftleitergesetz*) abolished freedom of the press and banned all 'non-Aryan' journalists from the profession.

Dr Lochner narrates how in November 1936 the Associated Press bureau received an invitation to attend a meeting of the Reich Chamber of Culture in the Philharmonic Hall. Goebbels was to speak and the Berlin Philharmonic was to perform. Principally to hear the orchestra, Lochner decided to attend. He records how:

Goebbels arose and in cold, biting language, and without his usual effort to ingratiate himself with his listeners, calmly announced that musical, theatrical, literary and artistic criticism was hereafter forbidden. The professional press and radio critics were ordered to limit themselves to Betrachtungen (reflections or contemplation) . . . But nothing to indicate a critical attitude toward either the performer or his work.

The representatives of every sector of German art present looked at one another in amazement. The newspaper critics bit their lips angrily. The last vestiges of relative freedom of the press was thus eliminated by the dictum of the Propaganda Minister.

Legally, this had already been done in October 1933.

(An American employee of a major international news agency, Louis Lochner experienced a brief internment in the American embassy when Germany and Italy declared war on the United States on 11 December 1941.)

The governing principle was that membership of these state-approved groups was open only to those qualified to be members of the *Volksgemeinschaft*. By definition, this excluded anyone with Jewish blood. How much Jewish blood was a question that caused problems for Nazi racial geneticists.

But sheer violence or the use of the forces of law and order were just as common.

Early in 1933 the management of the *Münchner Illustrierte Presse*, a non-political illustrated paper with the largest circulation in south Germany, was taken over by Nazi sympathisers. To assist the process, Stefan Lorant, the Hungarian picture editor, was arrested and imprisoned. His release came only after the Hungarian consul intervened. In 1935, having found his way to London, Lorant published his experience of the paper's being taken over under the title *I Was Hitler's Prisoner*; it went through four editions between April and August. Lorant went on to transform British photo-journalism as editor of Hulton's *Picture Post*.

The opening words of *I Was Hitler's Prisoner* read:

Munich Police Prison 19th March 1933 I have been in prison a week today. Why? I don't know. When shall I be let out? I don't know. What will happen to me? I don't know.

Lorant had been taken into so-called 'protective custody', a device used against tens of thousands of Jews and political opponents (which quite often coincided, as with Lorant) in those opening weeks of the Hitler period. In his case it was while a battle was fought over the ownership and political direction of his paper. *I Was Hitler's Prisoner* is the diary he managed to keep while in prison. In its preface he records:

> For six and a half months I was shut up in Hitler's prisons – in 'protective custody' as a political offender. To this day I do not know the real reason. I was never informed of it. My case never came up for hearing. No legal proceedings were ever instituted against me.

The existing managers of his newspaper's publishing firm were also taken into protective custody, and in early April Lorant heard how the National Socialists had appointed two commissioners to run it. Both he knew as hostile to him; one had actually denounced him. It did not bode well for his release. But on 25 September, Lorant was released through the efforts of the Hungarian government.

His experiences were typical, he reflected,

> . . . of what happened to tens of thousands of others in the Third Reich . . . living behind prison walls – thousands of innocent people, kept in a state of constant uncertainty from one day to another, without hope of being released, without rights or protection, completely at the mercy of those in political power. Thousands of innocent people, even today, are in 'protective custody' on political grounds. DO NOT FORGET THEM! DO NOT FORGET THEM! There is no change in my affection for Germany. I love the country and I love the German people. It is not their fault that things have come to such a pass. They are living in a dream. Their awakening will be a terrible one.

When Lorant reached Budapest, his son Andi was waiting to greet him. Three-year-old Andi had been living in Berlin during his father's – and mother's – imprisonment and at first failed to recognise his father:

> 'Aren't you going to greet me?'
> 'All right.' He raised his hand in the 'German salute' and yelled at the top of his voice, 'Heil Hitler!' . . .

'What's next?' I asked. I was thinking of a kiss of greeting.

'Next? Next the band plays and they bang the big drum.'

He had given the best and most succinct description of Hitler's Germany.

17
Exclusion by Law

With the Reichstag Fire Decree and the Enabling Act as the legal basis for its controlling measures, and with widespread violence and arrests at the heart of its exercise of power, the Nazi state aimed to bring all aspects of German life within its grip.

A fortnight after the Enabling Act came the first such, on 7 April 1933, the law at the heart of this book, and of Esther Simpson's future life: the Law for the Restoration of the Professional Civil Service [*Gesetz zur Wiederherstellung des Berufsbeamtentums*]. This excluded Jews and political opponents from the Civil Service. Exempted from the operation of the law were First World War front-line veterans; those in the civil service continuously since 1 August 1914; those who had lost a father or son in combat in the First World War.

A cascade of measures followed targeting 'non-Aryans' and political opponents: by 1939 more than 400 would affect every aspect of a Jew's life.

What follows are the major elements of the Nazi scheme:

7 April 1933: Law regarding admission to the Bar: 'Non-Aryans' lost their admission; exempted were those who had been admitted since 1 August 1914 and/or those who had been front-line veterans.

11 April 1933: Decree requiring civil servants who acquired their positions after 1 August 1914 to prove their 'Aryan' ancestry or their status as front-line veterans of the First World War – involving about 37,000 Jews.

25 April 1933: Law against the overcrowding of German schools and

institutions of higher learning. A *numerus clausus* was introduced. New admissions should not exceed 1.5 per cent, in the case of 'overcrowding' 5 per cent. Enforcement depended on individual heads of institutions: many schools did not allow even 1.5 per cent, while a few allowed pupils to remain until 1938.

25 April 1933: 'Non-Aryans' banned from youth and gymnastic clubs and forbidden to use athletic facilities.

30 June 1933: The Civil Service Law was extended to exclude those married to 'non-Aryans'.

14 July 1933: Law against the founding of parties (*Gesetz gegen die Neubildung von Parteien*). The National Socialist German Workers Party became the only legal political party in Germany.

4 October 1933: The Reich Press Law silenced Jewish journalists.

November 1933: Theatres came under the *Reichskulturkammer*, of which Jews could not be members, and agriculture was similarly controlled by a *Reichserbhofgesetz*.

The *Reichskulturkammer* had seven sub-chambers, including writing, film, music, theatre, the press, broadcasting and fine arts, all excluding Jews. Jews, however, could and did work inside the Jewish realm, the 'Jüdischer Kulturbund': culture by Jews for Jews.

15 September 1935 saw a definitional moment for the place of Jews in Hitler's Germany: the Nuremberg Race Laws [*Nürnberger Gesetze*) so called, as passed by a special sitting of the Reichstag at the Nazi Party annual rally at the ancient city of Nuremberg in southern Germany.

The Reich Citizens Act – *Reichsbürgergesetz* – aimed at a legal separation of Jewry from the German *Volk*. This did not remove citizenship as such; it affected civic rights not passports. In effect only people of pure German blood could be full German citizens (*Reichsbürger*), enjoying all the rights of citizens; all others – principally Jews – became so-called 'subjects of the state', with a deliberately narrowed legal personality. However, the Reich Citizenship Law of 1913 (*Reichs-und-Staatsangehörigkeitsgesetz*) remained in force, regulating who was a German citizen until a decree of 25 November 1941 that finally removed citizenship from Jews who had taken permanent residence beyond the borders of the Reich, in other words those who were deported into the ghettoes and concentration camps in the occupied countries. (The reason for this was to have a 'legal' basis for seizure of their belongings. It was argued that someone who left the Reich declared by this act opposition to the Reich and therefore lost his or her *Staatsbürgerschaft*.)

Jews who emigrated travelled on German passports and when interned were interned as enemy aliens, i.e. Germans. And in a deeply tragic irony, Jews who perished in death camps on German territory perished as Germans; those who died in camps in, say, Poland, were stateless.

For Nazis and their supporters, the most essential part of the 'Nuremberg Laws' of September 1935 was the Law for the Protection of German Blood and German Honour, the purpose of which was to 'maintain the purity of German blood' by forbidding marriages and extra-marital relations between Germans and Jews. It also forbade the employment of German females under forty-five in Jewish households. On 14 November 1935, with a supplementary decree, the so-called *Mischlinge* were added as a racial category subject to these laws – those with two Jewish grandparents who did not adhere to the Jewish religion and/or were not married to Jews. *Mischlinge* with one Jewish grandparent were forbidden to marry a Jew.

Jews were also forbidden to stand for election or vote or show the flag.

Many historians see these so-called Nuremberg laws as legally paving the way to the Wannsee Conference in 1942 and the Final Solution. But the roll-out continued.

26 April 1938: Decree for the Registration of Jewish Property.

18 August 1938: Naming regulations required Jews who were German citizens to have forenames from an approved list or add Israel or Sarah to their existing names.

In *I Shall Bear Witness*, Victor Klemperer's diaries for 1933–1941, in his entry for 24 August 1938, Klemperer (1881–1960) noted that most of the new names were not Old Testament but 'curious-sounding Yiddish or ghetto ones'. He became Victor-Israel.

25 July 1938: Decree prohibiting Jewish doctors from treating 'Aryan' patients.

The last four months of 1938 saw a string of decrees excluding Jews from the everyday German life they had enjoyed before 1933, including the closure and forced sale of Jewish-owned businesses. Freedom of residence and of movement was drastically limited.

Particularly after the November pogrom, named by Goebbels *Kristallnacht*, the government-inspired nights of savage rioting against Jews on 9 and 10 November 1938 that put an end to any remaining Jewish hopes of a new *modus vivendi*, delivery of such regulations steadily gathered pace and intensified.

Among other measures of social exclusion over the years between 1933 and 1942, Jews could not own cars, could not use public libraries; were banned from parks, public swimming pools and restaurants; were forbidden to own bicycles or typewriters or pets, to attend public schools and universities; were shut out of cinemas, theatres and concerts, and public beaches; could ride only on the front platform of trams; had to add a red 'J' to their passports; were banned from owning radios; were forced to sell their homes and to move into designated Jews' houses.

Without needing to discuss how far this sequence of measures fits the intentionalist or functionalist analysis of Nazi policy on the road to the Holocaust, what we are shown here is how it steadily narrowed German Jewry's existential space, political, economic, social, cultural, physical.

On 18 September 1941 Klemperer recorded:

> The 'Jewish star' black on yellow cloth at the centre in Hebrew-like lettering 'Jew', to be worn on the left breast, large as the palm of a hand, issued to us yesterday for 10 pfennigs, to be worn from tomorrow. The omnibus may no longer be used, only the front platform of the tram – For the time being at least Eva [his non-Jewish wife] will take over all the shopping. I shall breathe in a little fresh air under shelter of darkness. Today we were outside together in daylight for the last time . . .

A Jew became a *Sternträger*, a 'star bearer', whose presence could constantly be circumscribed and tracked.

By September 1939, some 185,000 Jews still resided in Germany and Austria. But all hope of a legal exit was ended in October 1941 with a ban on emigration – leaving 163,000 Jews remaining.

At this point, a glance at the numbers involved in Germany's Jewish population and in the emigration figures (including, of course, the political exiles – liberals, pacifists, socialists, communists – and cultural opponents) will be helpful. In terms of enforced migration the numbers of 'Jews' would depend on the mutable definitions of the Nazi racial genealogists.

Barbara Suchy supplied the following detailed figures based on Herbert Strauss' article on Jewish emigration from Germany in *The Leo Baeck Institute Year Book,* Volume XXV, Issue 1, January 1980, pages 313–61.

German Jewry had been in decline since 1925, when the census listed 564,379 Jews (defined by religion). In January 1933 a number of 525,000 was estimated (0.7 per cent of the German population). The census of June 1933 listed 499,682 (all defined by religion/self-designation; at that time the registration papers could be filled in as religion 'Jewish' even if not a member of a *Gemeinde*.) The actual number of persons threatened by the 'racial laws' exceeded the numbers before the census of 1939.

The census of May 1939 showed 213,390 Jews (defined by race in the official census). September 1939: 185,000 (defined by race). In October 1941, when the deportations started, the estimate is 164,000. 1942: 139,000; 1 January 1943: 51,257; April 1943: 31,910; 1 September 1944: 14,574.

At the end of the war, 25,000 Jews had survived in Germany, some in hiding, most in 'mixed marriages'.

The persecution of political opponents, as well as the introduction of anti-Jewish measures was followed by a wave of flight and emigration, particularly of liberal and leftist journalists, artists, writers and publishers whose living had been taken away and who were threatened with imprisonment. (Academics we shall, of course, come to.)

In 1933 up to 38,000 left for bordering states, principally the Saar (under French occupation until March 1935), France, Czechoslovakia and the Low Countries, to sit out what was hoped would be a short period before another change of government, Weimar-style.

Emigration became the Nazi regime's initial preferred solution to what it insisted was Germany's 'Jewish question'. But it came at a price. In Vienna in 1938 – the year of the *Anschluss* with Austria, the Munich Agreement and the *Kristallnacht* (also known as *Pogromnacht*) violence against Jews and Jewish property – Field Marshal-General Hermann Goering put it differently: 'The Jew must clearly understand one thing at once, he must get out!'

This was not emigration *simpliciter*, but also aimed at enriching the impoverished German exchequer by stripping the emigrating Jews of their assets. The emigration 'flight' tax (*Reichsfluchtsteuer*), which originated in the Weimar Republic, levied on capital, the restrictions on taking property out of the Reich, the exchange rates offered by the Reichsbank to buy foreign currencies – all were designed to strip the enforced migrants of their assets.

And a strategic benefit was also contemplated from a policy of increasing antisemitism in other, receiving countries by forcing waves of impoverished Jews across their borders.

As a German Foreign Ministry circular of 25 January 1939 put it:

> The poorer the Jewish immigrant is and the greater the burden he constitutes for the country into which he has immigrated, the stronger the reaction will be in the host country, and the more desirable the effect in support of German propaganda.

Herbert Strauss writes in the Leo Baeck Institute Year Book XXV and XXVI 1980/1981: *Jewish emigration from Germany,*

> The total number of Jewish émigrés can be estimated from German census data, Jewish sources and the reports periodically submitted to Nazi authorities by the Reichsvereinigung . . . an estimate of between 270,000 and 300,000 Jewish émigrés appears a reasonable approximation. About 30,000 of these are estimated to have been interned in their country of refuge in occupied Europe during WWII and to have perished . . . About three-fifths of German Jews succeeded in leaving the country.

An initial wave in 1933 was followed by a quieter two years, with the Jewish population attempting to settle down under the new dispensation. Strikingly, emigration did not increase after the passage of the Nuremberg Laws in 1935, defining and distinguishing Jews ('non-Aryans') from the non-Jewish population and effectively removing much of their civil standing. While Jews were angered and frightened by the Laws, many saw them as ultimately providing a secure, if separate, place for the future.

Of Germany's Jewish population of 523,000 in 1933, 37,000 emigrated in 1933 and 40,000 in 1938. In the years between, the numbers leaving did not rise above 25,000. In the first half of 1939, 78,000 left.

All in all at least 278,500 Jews fled Germany from 1933 until 1943. From 1933 to the end of 1935 some 80,000 Jews fled, many among them for political reasons.

Emigration then flattened until the watershed year of 1938, which saw the annexation of Austria in March and later, on 9 –10 November, in Germany/ Austria *Kristallnacht*, the violence of which was not confined to the street but reached into the homes of private Jewish citizens, demonstrating that any hopes of a decent life for Jews in National Socialist Germany were illusory. From the November Pogrom in 1938 until September 1939, nearly as many Jews left Germany as in the previous five and a half years: by October 1939, 400,000 had managed to leave; in addition, 140,000 from Austria and Bohemia. 40,000 managed to leave Germany in 1938 and 78,000 between May 1939 and December 1939. By September 1939 the number of German Jews had gone down to 185,000.

Jewish refugees constituted the vast majority of the 500,000 German-speaking enforced migrants. After the *Anschluss*, 150,000 Austrian Jews out of 190,000 left the country. 25,000 fled the Sudetenland on the German occupation. Only some 6 per cent were non-Jewish political refugees, such as communists, socialists, liberals.

In the general picture of enforced emigration, Italy must not be forgotten. In November 1938 wide-ranging decrees restricting the civil liberties of Jews included the expulsion of all Jews who had arrived in the country after January 1919 and the forced resignation of all academic staff of Jewish origin. Ninety-six university professors and lecturers, 133 assistants and research fellows, and 279 high school teachers had to leave their posts. By 1941, 6,000 had left, just 27 per cent of the country's Jewish population.

After Germany closed its frontiers to emigration in 1941, 135,000 German Jews were later deported. Between 1942 and 1943 a quarter of all deaths of Jews in Berlin were suicides.

Of the impact on Britain of this enforced emigration, self-exiles arriving as refugees, the figures showed a considerable flow and ebb.

In 1933, 300 to 400 reached Britain each month; by 1934 this had reduced to a trickle – only about 100 per month, among them relatives, friends, academics with university contacts, businesspeople with new enterprises. Between two and three thousand refugees had reached Britain, and in 1935 the figures did not increase markedly.

In 1936 the Home Office noted:

> Several thousand desirable, industrious, intelligent and acceptable persons have been added to the population. They have brought with them considerable capital, and established industries that have already given employment to more British subjects than the total number of refugees who are now living in the UK.

Industrialists were directed to Special Areas in the north and north-west of England, to Scotland and Northern Ireland.

In December of the watershed year 1938 the Home Secretary Sir Samuel Hoare told the House of Commons that 11,000 refugees had been settled in Britain and as a result 15,000 British workers had been employed who would otherwise not have been.

In the House of Commons on 6 April 1939, the Paymaster-General Earl Winterton gave the following figures:

> Between March 1933 and March 1938 4,325 men and 3,310 women arrived in Britain from Germany classed as refugees. On 28 February that year [1939] there were in Great Britain 4,674 German men, 3,663 women, 3,340 Austrian men and 2,446 women, 357 Czech men and 169 former Czech women subjects. At that time there was, in addition, a total of 4,404 children in this country.

Some 40,000 of the 100–150,000 who left Germany at that time were allowed to remain in Britain. Many entered with the intention of moving on but were caught by the outbreak of war in September 1939.

In the UK by April 1939, 20,000 adults and more than 4,500 children were admitted; altogether between 1933 and the beginning of the Second World War in September 1939 46,458 refugees had entered the country; about 9,000 of them were under the age of eighteen.

The largest group of immigrants were women admitted as domestic servants: more than 20,000. About 1,000 unaccompanied children (on the *Kindertransport*) escaped to the UK between December 1938 and September 1939. (Looking ahead to 1945, almost 8,000 orphans from concentration camps were admitted at the initiative of the Quakers.)

During the war Britain then sheltered some 80,000 refugees from Germany, Austria and Czechoslovakia; 50,000 refugees from Central Europe were still in the UK in 1946.

With reference only to displaced scholars, by February 1939 appointments had been found in Britain for 128 academic refugees, twenty-seven in Oxford, with support but no post for as many again.

With war declared between Britain and Germany in September 1939, scholars who could went directly to the United States and the numbers entering up to 1941 rose until they surpassed those placed in Britain.

In 1946, 601 of 2,541 registered scholars were living in Britain; 307 were German. The great majority had gone to the US.

18

Coordination for Professors

The dire hand of 'coordination' (aka submission) reached out to bring education under control. Universities, technical colleges and schools naturally fell to be 'coordinated'. Academics and teachers were already under pressure from Nazi-orientated students. Higher education teachers of Jewish descent, many of them in universities, had already experienced organised disruption from Nazi-inspired student groups aimed at forcing them out. Nazi student movement leaders denounced their professors and also any member of their teaching staffs who tried to assist them as 'Jewish sympathisers'. Students declared themselves 'for the state and against the professors'.

On 31 March 1933 Victor Klemperer, who since 1920 had been Professor of Romance Languages at Dresden Technical University, recorded the statement by Dresden students that the honour of German students forbade them to come into contact with Jews. They were not allowed to enter the Student House, which had substantially been paid for by Jewish money.

These recipients of the German *Bildung*, the finest and most thorough education in Europe, were also the 'bibliomaniacs' who scoured their libraries for books by authors they determined were 'unGerman', and then heaved them on to the notorious book-burning bonfires of 10 May 1933 – at least seventeen had taken place already in various cities.

At midnight, before a crowd estimated at 70,000 in the centre of Berlin, the Minister for Propaganda and Public Enlightenment Dr Joseph Goebbels gave political meaning to the book pyre:

Jewish intellectualism is dead! National Socialism has hewn the way.
The German folk soul can again express itself! . . . These flames do
not only illuminate the final end of the old era, they also light up the
new. Never before have the young men had so good a right to clean
up the debris of the past . . . The old goes up in flames, the new shall
be fashioned from the flame in our hearts . . . As you had the right to
destroy the books, you had the duty to support the government.
The fire signals to the entire world that the November revolutionaries
have sunk to earth and a new spirit has arisen!

Later they took that experience with them into the SS, the SD and Death's
Head units, where up to one quarter of the officers had Ph.D.s.

Germany's great universities had a proud tradition of self-management,
but their staffs were civil servants and thus made subject to the law
promulgated on day 67 of Hitler's first hundred days, The Law for the
Restoration of the Professional Civil Service [*Gesetz zur Wiederherstellung
des Berufsbeamtentums*].

As to numbers of academics, the basis taken from the winter term 1931
is a rollcall of 6,744 university teachers: 2,741 full professors, 1,741 assistant
professors, 1,799 non-tenured lecturers, together with 10,584 academic
researchers. Under the Third Reich 2,000 university post-holders and
research workers lost their posts in Germany and Austria.

In his short 1953 book on the SPSL, *The Rescue and Achievement of Refugee
Scholars*, Norman Bentwich remarks that it was intolerable for the Nazi mind
that Jews – barely 1 per cent of the German population – filled an eighth of
German professorial chairs and won a quarter of Nobel Prizes awarded
to Germans. And when petitioned by Professor Max Planck stressing the
importance of the physical sciences for the national welfare, Hitler retorted,
pace Bentwich,

Our national policies will not be revoked or modified even for scientists.
If the dismissal of Jewish scientists means the annihilation of contemporary German science, we will do without science for a few years.

And, says Bentwich, 1933–1934 saw 4,650 scientists emigrating from Germany,
including six Nobel Prize winners, scientists of international reputation,

professors of every discipline, large numbers of *Privatdozenten* [an unsalaried but fully qualified university teacher en route to a full-time post]. 1,200 were immediately dismissed: medicine 412; social sciences 173; law 132; physics 106; philology 95; chemistry 86; technology 85.

The government also radically changed the university management system to give the government control over appointments.

Presided over by the Minister of Science, Art and Education for Prussia, Dr Bernhard Rust (after a power struggle with Goebbels), the Law for the Restoration of the Professional Civil Service excluded two classes of person from the civil service: those holding political views incompatible with the ruling party, and 'non-Aryans'.

Signed by Hitler, the Interior Minister Wilhelm Frick and the Finance Minister Schwerin von Krosigk, the Civil Service Law did not apply to officials who had been in service since 1 August 1914 or who had fought in the war at the front for the German Reich or for its allies, or whose fathers or sons had been casualties in the war. This was the so-called Hindenburg clause, which expired with the Nuremberg Laws in September 1935 redefining German citizenship.

Some scientists, notably Fritz Haber, refused to take advantage of the derogation and stepped down at once.

In his diary Victor Klemperer notes anxious hours securing evidence of his having been at the front – from November 1915 to March 1916, when he was transferred to the Book Examination Office of the Military Government of Lithuania. In late August 1933 he notes with relief the arrival of his 'Front-line service certificate'. 'It attests one engagement and trench warfare in Flanders from 19.11.15 to 19.2.16.' That is not quite correct, but it will do, he decides.

Clause 2a of the Law for the Restoration of the Professional Civil Service was directed against communists: civil servants who, based on their previous political activities, cannot guarantee that they have always unreservedly supported the national state, can be dismissed from service. [They would receive three-fourths of their pension.]

Clause 3 covered Jewish descent – accounting for nearly three-quarters of all dismissals.

Clause 4 covered other politically unreliable persons.

Clause 6 related to so-called administrative convenience but was aimed at removing opponents of the regime not clearly falling within the other clauses: to simplify administration, civil servants might be placed in retirement even when they were not yet unfit for service.

The first Ordinance implementing the Law was published on 11 April 1933. It required the dismissal of any civil servant who was or had been a member of the Communist Party. And it defined as 'non-Aryan' anyone descended from 'non-Aryan', and in particular Jewish, parents or grandparents. One 'non-Aryan' grandparent sufficed, especially if the parent or grandparent had practised the Jewish faith. After the Nuremberg Laws in 1935, the Civil Service Law *Deutsches Beamtengesetz* of 1937 demanded that civil servants' spouses should also not be 'non-Aryan'.

In Vienna after the *Anschluss*, 24,000 Austrians who did not adhere to religious Judaism were still classified as Jewish and nearly 5,000 who were members of the *Kultusgemeinde* [Jewish Community Vienna] were forced to leave it as not being Jewish.

In the first wave of displacements under the April law, 15 per cent of all university teachers were suspended; by 1940, up to 15 per cent of university teachers – some 1,500 people – had emigrated. In another estimate, that becomes 15–17 per cent. In brief, some 25 per cent of academic staff in universities and research institutes had to leave their posts, of whom some 70 per cent, or 2,000, emigrated.

In terms of specialisations, 950 were physicists (200–300), mathematicians, chemists or biochemists. Two-thirds of all physicists had the *venia legendi* (permission to teach); 209 out of 322 were employed at only fifteen of Germany's thirty-five universities, Göttingen and Berlin leading the field. Of course, certain specialities, nuclear physics for one, lost a much higher proportion of their practitioners.

Help for displaced academics is our subject. (For all his years as a civil servant, Beveridge was not minded to set up a Civil Servants Assistance Council.) But we should be clear that the *Law for the Restoration/Re-establishment of the Civil Service* was not solely or even mainly concerned with teachers and academics.

Sebastian Haffner describes its individual paragraphs allowing:

> . . . civil servants to be demoted, involuntarily retired, laid off with a
> lump sum or sacked without any lump sum or pension. Every clause
> contained a destiny. 'Clause 4' [politically unreliable] was a devastating
> blow. 'Clause 6' [administrative convenience] was demotion and
> humiliation.

Haffner tells how his father, a retired senior civil servant, received former
associates from his old department and would ask about a colleague, speaking his name: 'The visitor's answer was a laconic "Clause 4" or "Clause 6".'

Although long retired, Haffner's father too received an official letter.
Under the Law, he was required to answer a questionnaire 'truthfully and
in full' on pain of losing his pension, the fruit of forty-five years' devoted
service.

> My father had to state which political parties, organisations and
> associations he had ever belonged to in his life, he had to list his
> services to the nation, explain this and excuse that, and finally to sign
> a printed declaration that he 'stood behind the government of national
> uprising without reservations'. In short, having served the state for
> forty-five years, he was required to humble himself again in order to
> continue to receive his well-earned pension.

Haffner recounts how the stress this brought so affected his father's health
that he died within two years.

A little later that year, Haffner, who was in the final stage of taking his
judicial qualifications, read in the press that all those lawyers at his stage
would be required to

> go to training camps where they would take part in military and
> sporting exercises and ideological indoctrination sessions to prepare
> them for their great task as German people's judges . . . There followed
> an editorial comment, full of praise and 'Heil': 'Every young German
> lawyer will be grateful to the Minister of Justice . . .'

By this time, all Jewish lawyers had been excluded from the courts, expelled
in the first instance by Brownshirts storming the court buildings.

How was the Civil Service Law received in the academic world itself? Expressions of sympathy for dispossessed colleagues were generally kept private. Einstein's resignation from the Prussian Academy of Sciences is well known.

> Under present circumstances I consider my position's inherent dependence upon the Prussian government intolerable.

He was not in Germany at the time and had also been threatened with assassination. A more instructive example is to be found, along with its further consequences, in Klaus and Ann Hentschel's *Physics and National Socialism*: the resignation of the 1925 Nobel laureate physicist James Franck (among eight Nobel laureates) from his directorship of the Second Physical Institute at Göttingen University on 17 April; he held the Iron Cross first class and so was not liable for immediate displacement.

News of his resignation letter, addressed to the Prussian Minister of Education Bernhard Rust, appeared simultaneously in the *Göttinger Zeitung* and the Ullstein-owned *Vossische Zeitung*:

> Voluntary Resignation of Prof James Franck Requested Release from his official duties.

The paper quoted a line of his letter:

> This decision is an inner necessity for me because of the attitude of the government towards German Jewry.

The government-supporting *Tägliche Rundschau* was demanding that the thirteen Jewish and three Marxist university professors 'who were ousted last Friday' should be forbidden to leave the country.

> It is indispensable that these gentlemen might presently be settled in London, Oxford or Paris and from professorships there agitate against Germany . . . some of these professors, especially Bonn, Lederer and Kelsen enjoy the most excellent foreign connections.

Minister Rust, meanwhile, made it clear, as reported in the *New York Times*, that the 'recent retirement of sixteen university instructors on "enforced leave" would be followed by further "oustings".'

The Göttingen science and mathematics department would lose some 30 per cent of its faculty, including world-class scholars like Max Born.

Edith Hahn, the physicist Otto Hahn's wife, wrote privately to Franck and his wife Ingrid:

> If I didn't like you so much I could envy you for being Jews . . . and thus for having justice completely on your side and we for ever and ever the humiliation and inextinguishable shame which never can be made good again. You both did something, this is what is so marvellous, and it has certainly made a big impression.

Her private sentiments were not publicly shared by forty-three of Franck's Göttingen colleagues, who issued a statement denouncing his move as an act of sabotage of the government's domestic and foreign policy activities of national renewal, and calling on the government to carry out the necessary purging measures.

It must also be said that his very public resignation did not have the wholehearted backing of the Jewish editors of *Berliner Tageblatt*, who respected his action but thought he would have served his cause better had he stayed at his post.

Similarly, when Otto Hahn proposed a public declaration of solidarity by thirty non-Jewish professors with those caught by the Law for the Restoration of the Professional Civil Service, Max Planck resisted it, stating it would only bring denunciations from 150 who wanted to take their places.

It's also easy to have the impression that all 'non-Aryan' teachers were dismissed immediately, but the universities had a high degree of independence and the implementation of the new law varied.

Some academics were dismissed at once, some later, some offered early retirement, some removed from teaching for a period before being retired or dismissed. Where still in post, 'non-Aryans' were, for instance, not allowed to sit on committees or conduct examinations. Proclaiming, 'When the Jew writes in German, he lies', students produced indexes of books by Jewish authors that should no longer be read.

But it was far from 'non-Aryans' only who lost their posts. Socialists and other political opponents of the new regime were in the firing line just as much. Alongside the Law for the Restoration of the Professional Civil Service, a second was promulgated for 'Loss of Duties', giving the authorities a choice on how to rid themselves of the unwanted academics.

Victor Klemperer noted on 7 April 1933 that a friend at Frankfurt am Main, Albert Hirsch, had been put on 'leave of absence' after thirteen years' service and, 'unsure what to live on', was moving with his wife and two children to his parents-in-law.

> Perhaps at best he'll receive a few pennies for a pension, but certainly not anywhere near enough to live on. One case out of thousands . . .

And on 12 April 1933, having gone to the local council office to talk about drains to two [municipal] officials in SA uniform, but both very polite, he reflected:

> But here I saw for the first time with my own eyes that we really are entirely at the mercy of the Party dictatorship, of the 'Third Reich', that the Party no longer makes any secret of its absolute power.

Nonetheless those who were deemed Jewish by 'race', observant or not, baptised or not, married to an 'Aryan' or not – Klemperer, the son of a rabbi, was both baptised and married to an 'Aryan' – saw their careers brought to an end, with 'Aryan' former pupils, friends and colleagues stepping up to take their places in seminars, lecture halls, examination boards, learned journals.

Access to lectures and libraries was forbidden; the prospect of learned work being published in German peer journals nil.

On 28 November 1937 the *New York Times* reviewed *German Universities and National Socialism*, a study by Harvard sociologist Edward Yarnall Hartshorne of the changes wrought in German universities by the law of 7 April 1933.

Hartshorne, who would be in charge of the revival of the universities in the American zone of occupied Germany after the war, had spent 1935 to 1936 in Germany. The study noted that up to the end of 1936, 1,145 professors of various ranks and 539 assistants and other scientists had been dismissed. Berlin and Frankfurt had lost one third of their faculties and Heidelberg a quarter. In half the cases, reasons for dismissal were unknown; in most cases pretexts were given. 'The humanist tradition that had made German universities great had vanished.' Admissions and the selection of professors were now governed by non-intellectual criteria: physical, political and racial fitness. 'All for the Fatherland!'

Hartshorne also queried figures issued by the AAC of 1,300 'university teachers' displaced. His alternative was 1,150 but including 232 assistants, 133 workers at non-university scientific institutes, 105 recent graduates who had held no academic posts and 69 miscellaneous intellectuals (writers, school teachers, government officials, even musicians).

The *New York Times'* reviewer Boris Edrich Nelson noted from the study that Germany could no longer be referred to as the world's greatest intellectual training ground. Instead, the country was rapidly falling into a quagmire of intellectual provincialism. Least forgivable of all, they (the Nazis) had submerged 'all the fine free play of human intellect under the dull stupefying vapor of ideological conformity'. And what, asked Nelson, was the Nazification of Germany's culture and civilisation but the complete collapse of every form and motivating flux of human progress. The author (Hartshorne) mentioned 'the hidden burden of self-deception, hypocrisy, compromise, petty revenge, heartless oppression'. To which the reviewer added,

> the complete suppression of free discussion on principle, the prescription of an officially benign dogma (Weltanschauung [world outlook]), the politico-militarization of campus and classroom, research for national advancement only, state-political control and creation of a pattern curriculum, pattern-student and a pattern-human, the obsession on physical fitness and Wehrsport [military] sports.

What next for someone whose entire career had been built on following the *cursus honorum* of the German university system, its dignity, recognition and certainty? On achieving the god-like status, remote and authoritarian, of professor?

In London, from May 1933, the Academic Assistance Council stood ready with support for academics who 'on grounds of religion, political opinion or race, were unable to carry on their work in their own country'.

19

Tea and Sympathy

The tale of the AAC's founding has been well told in a number of varying versions, but the crucial moment is over a tea table in the luxury Hotel Bristol in Vienna – described as an art deco gem adjacent to the state opera – probably on 13 April 1933.

Esther Sinovitch is in Geneva working for the International YMCA, but she might well have recognised the name of the central protagonist, William Beveridge, from the letterhead of the Imperial War Relief Fund, for which she worked as a collector when at university.

Then Director of the London School of Economics, Beveridge is in Vienna from 10 to 18 April for his research on unemployment. He's having tea with an Austrian economist Ludwig von Mises. Also present at the tea table is another British economist Lionel Robbins, who had been Beveridge's research assistant at the LSE, later Lord Robbins.

An evening newspaper is brought to their table and von Mises takes it and (probably) translates one of the stories for his companions. It reports the names of some of the latest German academics displaced under the newly passed Law for the Restoration of a Professional Civil Service.

The international press has been regularly reporting events in Germany under its new regime, including the displacement of academics.

On 1 April the *New York Times* reported how an American college girl who had been doing postgraduate work at Berlin University went to pay a farewell visit to a Jewish faculty member. She found him haggard and dejected.

. . . He slowly pulled out a drawer of his desk and took from it an Iron
Cross. 'I got this in the war but I doubt I shall ever lecture again at any
German university.'

The Times reported the first displacements made by the Law for the
Restoration of a Professional Civil Service (Baden and Freiburg: 'indefinite
leave') on 10 and 14 April. The *New York Times* headlined on 15 April '10,000
Jews Flee Nazi Persecution' and on 17 April 'New Curb Urged for Ousted
Jews'. And in its edition of 14 April it had the then latest list of the displaced,
making publication likely in Vienna on 12 or 13 April in the newspaper
brought into the Hotel Bristol and read/translated to Beveridge over the
tea table by von Mises. This (the probable) list includes four professors
of public law, four economists, two zoologists, two law professors, two
Bonn medical faculty members, two geologists. The universities include
Frankfurt am Main, Cologne, Breslau, Berlin, Bonn, Halle.

Among them is one name that will have been familiar to Beveridge: the
Berlin economist Moritz Bonn, who had lectured in Britain and had, said
the *New York Times*, 'done great service in conciliating world opinion toward
the German view on reparations'. He had also spoken in England at Liberal
Party meetings. (As remarked earlier, the pro-regime *Tägliche Rundschau*
had accused Bonn of enjoying 'the most excellent foreign connections'.)

Bernhard Rust was reported as saying that the professors' suspensions
were ordered because of a most profound conviction to meet the desires not
only of the student body but of nationally minded circles. 'We regard the
coordination of the institutions of higher learning an imperative necessity.'

In his 1959 account *A Defence of Free Learning*, Beveridge wrote:

> As Mises read out the names to our growing indignation, Robbins and
> I decided we would take action in the LSE to help scholars in our
> subjects who should come under Hitler's ban. I posted the newspaper
> cutting at once to the Secretary of the School so she might prepare for
> what was afoot.

Beveridge's reaction will be the imperative of setting up the Academic
Assistance Council for those displaced academics, based on his profound
conviction of the necessity of the freedom of higher education.

In his 1971 *Autobiography of an Economist*, Lionel Robbins notably characterised Beveridge's reaction as one of his great moments ' . . . Slumped in a chair, with his great head characteristically cupped in his fists, thinking aloud, he then and there outlined the basic plan of what became the famous AAC', though in his introduction to Norman Bentwich's *The Rescue and Achievement of Refugee Scholars*, Beveridge states that,

> The AAC was invented during a weekend in May 1933 which I spent
> at Cambridge with George Trevelyan, later Master of Trinity . . . At
> Cambridge I found many gravely concerned and anxious for action . . .
> From the beginning the Council depended on and could obtain
> untiring service from distinguished men of science and learning.

It seems unlikely that Beveridge and his British colleagues were anyway unaware of the Nazi onslaught on universities: in London two of Beveridge's colleagues were already at work drafting an appeal.

The idea of bringing German professors in need of help to Britain was not new to Beveridge. As an officer of the Imperial War Relief Fund he had helped to organise just such relief missions in 1919. Also with Oxbridge Colleges hosting Viennese academics and men of learning in 1922.

David Zimmerman devotes his contribution to *In Defence of Learning*, '"Protests Butter No Parsnips": Lord Beveridge and the Rescue of Refugee Academics from Europe, 1933–1939', to Beveridge's role in initiating the AAC:

> From 1933 to 1938, Beveridge was the heart and soul of the British effort
> to rescue academics. By examining his work we can come to an
> understanding of how the AAC, and its successor, the Society for the
> Protection of Science and Learning, became the most important of all
> the many organizations established throughout the free world to aid
> academic refugees . . . Beveridge devoted more of his time and energy
> to the organization than the others perhaps because of his passionate
> belief that even freedom of thought was at stake . . . His commitment
> to the cause of assisting academic refugees . . . directly helped to make
> possible the rescue of over 1,000 scholars from Germany, Austria,
> Spain, Portugal, the Soviet Union, and Czechoslovakia in the years

leading up to the Second World War. Beveridge was the principal general in what he would later call 'the spontaneous uprising of British Universities against learning directed by Hitler and his imitators'.

Incidentally, the German Consul-General in Cleveland was reported as responding to anti-German protests there,

> You say there is a complaint against the removal of Jews from public positions in Germany. May I remind you there has been an even greater removal of Gentiles. It is a political fact that when one party goes out, the succeeding party holds the right of appointment.

On his return to London the ever-practical Beveridge put two projects in hand. One was centred on the LSE, to encourage the staff to contribute a percentage of their salaries to a fund to assist displaced academics and to invite displaced teachers of especial distinction to the School to strengthen its postgraduate teaching.

The other project was to gather support for and lay the foundations of what would become the Academic Assistance Council, involving the highest levels of British academic society. An Academic Assistance Fund would fund research fellowships for the most distinguished of the refugee scholars under the auspices of the Archbishop of Canterbury, the presidents of the Royal Society and the British Association, Lord Horder and the Hon. R. H. Brand [a businessman and civil servant].

Beveridge's own account details how, fortuitously, he was due to spend the weekend of 6 May with the eminent historian George Macaulay Trevelyan and two Nobel laureates, the doyen of British science, the nuclear physicist Ernest Rutherford (1871–1937) and the biochemist Frederick Gowland Hopkins (1861–1947). The AAC of the future was conceived. Rutherford was persuaded to become president, which made the nascent AAC an unstoppable force. Treasurer and secretary already presented themselves: Professor C. S. Gibson (1884–1950) of Guys Chemistry Department as honorary secretary, and Professor Major [first name, not military rank] Greenwood (1880–1949) of the London School of Hygiene and Tropical Medicine as honorary treasurer.

A Memorandum and an Appeal for establishing an Academic Assistance Council was polished and sent to the Royal Society. The team began collecting sponsors. By 18 May Beveridge came down to discussing names of honorary secretaries to be.

On 24 May the birth of the AAC was announced. Deliberately a-political, the founding statement, aimed at British universities and politicians, focused on practicalities: support for academics who 'on grounds of religion, political opinion or race, were unable to carry on their work in their own country'.

> Our action implies no unfriendly feelings to the people of any country; it implies no judgment on forms of government or on any political issue between countries. Our only aims are the relief of suffering and the defence of learning and science.

Of course, the underlying principle being asserted was the right of academics to work freely without political interference.

Beveridge had recruited a forty-one-member Council including the brightest stars in the British scientific firmament. As well as Lord Rutherford, the first president, they included J. B. S. Haldane (1892–1964), Sir Frederick Gowland Hopkins (1861–1947), A. V. Hill (1886–1977), and Sir William Bragg (1862–1942).

A close relationship with the senior associations, the Royal Society and the British Academy, both at arm's length from government, promoted the AAC as having the highest academic credentials. Later, exploring the AAC's history when editing *Refugee Scholars*, Ray Cooper was particularly struck by the closeness of the relationship and the cooperation between the AAC/SPSL and the Royal Society. Sir William Bragg was president of the Royal Society from 1935 to 1940. The secretary of the Royal Society was always a member of the SPSL council. And so it had appeared with the AAC being launched in a letter to *The Times* dated 22 May and printed on 24 May appealing for funds: it was signed by forty-one of the most eminent academics in Britain, including John Maynard Keynes; Gilbert Murray, the presidents of the Royal Society and the British Academy; nine chancellors or vice-chancellors of universities and seven heads or directors of colleges. Two of the signatories were women. Besides Lord Rutherford, among the forty-one who signed the original appeal for the AAC, seven either were or would become Nobel laureates and seventeen were Fellows of the Royal Society, including A. V. Hill, its Nobel laureate biological secretary from 1935 to 1945.

It announced the setting up of the AAC, detailing its aims and structure:

> To raise a fund, to be used primarily, though not exclusively, in providing maintenance for displaced teachers and investigators, and finding them work in universities and scientific institutions.

It called for support, and included the defining ambition that distinguished it from all other rescue agencies:

> We ask for means to prevent the waste of exceptional abilities exceptionally trained.

It was an interesting comment on the contemporary social culture that although the displaced academics were largely Jewish, the AAC's founders were anxious that it should not appear to present itself as Jewish-centred.

> The issue raised at the moment is not a Jewish one alone; many who have suffered or are threatened have no Jewish connection.

Before the AAC's letter went to *The Times* the names of the proposed supporters were scrutinised for evident Jewishness and one agreed his be removed – Professor Charles Singer (1876 –1960), a historian of science and medicine who had served as a doctor in the British Army.

Beveridge's confidence in his close relationship with the editor of *The Times* Geoffrey Dawson was more than justified. The paper offered the AAC its backing in the form of a second leader on 24 May under the heading 'Academic Assistance', though it cast its net wider than Nazi Germany alone:

> Under the name of the Academic Assistance Council a number of men and women of high distinction have banded themselves together in the interests of those university teachers on the Continent of Europe who have lately been deprived, on political grounds, of their posts and their livelihoods. The appeal addresses itself to an ancient and justly cherished English tradition of tolerance . . . Bolshevist, Fascist, Nazi

– all alike have sent professors into exile . . . The Byzantine scholars displaced by the Turks in 1453 sowed the seeds of the Renaissance in Western Europe, and thus repaid a hundredfold the patrons who befriended them. In some such manner we may expect value to be returned for the money which it is now proposed to collect.

An AAC news story also appeared under the headings 'The Security of Learning / Displaced German Professors / An Assistance Council':

An appeal issued yesterday addressed to all those 'concerned for academic freedom and the security of learning' states: 'We ask for the means to prevent the waste of exceptional abilities exceptionally trained.' 'Our only aims are the relief of suffering and the defence of learning and science.' 'The names are given of 164 teachers who have all been named in German newspapers as having been given leave of absence, or dismissed, or as having resigned in protest against other dismissals or action of students between April 4th and May 15th 1933.'

A further short paragraph headed 'Displaced German Teachers' ended by telling readers, 'The appeal appears on page 10'.

Elsewhere in the same edition a single short paragraph told readers of a 'British Fund for German Jewry . . . Places for Refugees and Transmigrants'.

A crowded Anglo-Jewish Conference under the chairmanship of Anthony de Rothschild had been held for the purpose of launching a British Fund for German Jewry . . .

On 16 June a letter went out to university vice-chancellors, signed by Beveridge and Gibson as honorary secretaries. It summarised the aims of the AAC and asked the vice-chancellors if they were in a position to find openings for any of the displaced.

The first meeting of the AAC Council took place on 1 June at the then home of the Royal Society in Burlington House, a neo-Palladian mansion, the courtyard of which opens on to Piccadilly.

Originally a private house, after 1854 and its purchase by the British government it housed the Royal Society (until 1968) together with a number of learned societies and (from 1867) the Royal Academy.

The accommodation offered to the fledgling AAC by the Royal Society was a bedroom and a bathroom at the top of its headquarters. Initially this was staffed by a Percy Gent and a secretary, 'in the attic of these august premises', says Bentwich. 'But later it ascended in dignity and descended in space.'

The AAC's/SPSL's office was always a movable feast: starting in those two rooms in Burlington House, moving to an annexe of the LSE in Clements Inn, Clare Market, for a couple of years, then from 1937 into 6 Gordon Square in Bloomsbury, before removing to Cambridge on the outbreak of war where the story of constant moves, as required by their temporary hosts, is the same. That the officers never seem to have contemplated a permanent base before the war is a tribute to their belief that the need for the Society's work was essentially short term. After the war, the Society resided with the secretary – the officers' meetings were generally hosted by the Royal Society – reinforcing the view that the SPSL and Tess Simpson were as one.

Rather like the exiles it served, wandering seems to have been a characteristic of the SPSL. Liz Fraser, Esther's successor after her ultimate retirement as secretary, noted to me that the SPSL was 'in the wilderness for quite a while, perching in several places'.

The founding officers all had national eminence in common. Lord Rutherford was the first president and William Temple, Archbishop of Canterbury, the second. Sir Frederic Kenyon and Professor A. V. Hill became vice-presidents of the Council, Kenyon chairing the executive committee in the early days and Hill becoming chair of the executive committee in 1946. Professor Major Greenwood was honorary treasurer until 1949. Professor C. S. Gibson was honorary secretary from the first meeting until 1945. And, Beveridge recorded, 'We lured Walter Adams from University College London to be our full-time secretary – to work harder for the same salary without pension or prospects.'

Adams (1906–1975), a lecturer in history, served until 1938, when the post of secretary fell vacant at the LSE and he was appointed, though becoming an honorary secretary of the SPSL and, says Beveridge, 'almost unfairly attendant at all executive meetings until his departure in 1955 for [the then British Protectorate of] Nyasaland [now Malawi]'. He had made a practical reality of the AAC's mission in those tumultuous days when the unprecedented flood of displaced academics seeking a new life surged over the two rooms at the top of Burlington House.

When war came, Adams was recruited into the Political Intelligence Department of the Foreign Office, moving to Washington as deputy head of the British Political Warfare Mission to the United States. He returned to London in 1945 as assistant deputy director-general of the Political Intelligence Department, when he resigned from the LSE.

In his reference for Adams, A. V. Hill wrote:

> His sympathy for the exiles, his willingness to shoulder the burdens of others, and his wisdom in dealing with difficult personal and admin-istrative problems, are combined with a critical and unsentimental judgment, and have made his services of quite exceptional value.

Archibald Vivian Hill CH OBE FRS became vice-president of the AAC in June 1933, then served as vice-chair of the SPSL executive committee from 1937 to 1945 and its chair from 1946 to 1956, and then served as chair of the SPSL Council from 1960 to 1963 and president in 1963. Beveridge wrote of him that he ' .... was never absent from our councils or failed to undertake any exceptional task that came along'. This he combined this with a life of outstanding service, academic and public.

Hill had personal experience of German universities, having researched in Jena and Tübingen before the First World War, and of German scientists, who flocked to work in his laboratories. And he had personal experience of working as a scientist with government, on anti-aircraft gunnery technique in the First World War and on the mobilisation of science and scientists in the Second.

He was a passionate believer in the necessary political and intellectual independence of science and scientists, a belief he pressed to be reflected in the AAC's name change in 1936 to the Society for the Protection of Science and Learning.

> Scientists should remain aloof and detached not from any sense of superiority, not from any indifference to the common welfare, but as a condition of complete intellectual honesty.

And after the passing of the Nuremberg Laws in 1935, Beveridge saw that
the AAC's apolitical stance could not be sustained. The 1935 AAC executive
committee memorandum recommending the formation of the SPSL also
noted that

> ... dismissal of scholars and scientists on political or other grounds
> irrelevantly to their work is not confined to Germany. In Russia and
> Italy freedom of study and teaching in large portions of the field of
> learning has long been proscribed. Within the past year in Portugal a
> number of university teachers in various faculties have been retired
> on grounds of political opinion.

Following an informal International Meeting in Oxford that November,
it also added corresponding members to its Council from eight other
European countries. Beveridge wrote that the Oxford meeting

> brought home to me more clearly than anything else the exceptionally
> favourable conditions in which the SPSL could do its work, through
> the solid support of our universities.

In his introduction to Bentwich's short book, Beveridge listed four points
about the AAC:

The AAC was brought into being by Nazi persecution in Germany, but
the AAC had helped displaced scholars from many countries including
Austria, Czechoslovakia, Hungary, Italy, Poland, Portugal and Spain.

The AAC found the bulk of those from Germany were in need because
they had Jewish blood in them.

The AAC raised and administered funds from which grants could be
made to displaced academics but the making of these grants was the least
part of the Council's work. The Council became a specialised employment
exchange for displaced academics.

The AAC was a spontaneous growth of British individualism not created
by any existing organisations. But for all it did in practice it depended
on the help of existing organisations, in particular on the universities
and the learned societies, with the Royal Society at their head. It also
depended on the goodwill of successive Home Secretaries, Sir John Simon,
Sir Samuel Hoare, Sir John Anderson, and of key officials, the Permanent

Under-Secretary Sir Alexander Maxwell, and the head of the Aliens Department Mr E. N. Cooper.

Highly specialised as it was, the AAC was part of a mosaic of refugee agencies that interacted with each other: domestic, such as the Jewish Professional Committee (first called the Jewish Academic Committee), formed in Britain to help doctors, lawyers, teachers, social workers, and the British Federation of University Women; and international, such as, in France in May 1933, the *Comite pour l'Acceuil et Organisation du Travail des Savants Etrangers*, and in Switzerland the *Comité International pour le Placement des Intellectuels Refugiés*.

In the United States, in New York in 1933, two American academics, Stephen Duggan and Betty Drury, set up the Emergency Committee in Aid of Displaced Foreign Scholars [its executive officer was Ed Murrow, the future iconic anchorman]. Grants made by the American Rockefeller Foundation were also crucial to the rescue and resettlement of academic refugees.

Of course, whatever the goodwill and commonality among refugee organisations, what counted for the emigrant arriving at a British port was the attitude in Westminster and Whitehall, and in the universities and professional organisations beyond.

20
It Takes Two to Tango

The British government's starting position was that those fleeing Nazi Germany could be granted asylum provided they did not enter into direct competition in the labour market with British subjects. Applications from well-established displaced professors for posts in this country would be looked at sympathetically if funded by organisations dedicated to that purpose. No political controversy was the unspoken condition of the relationship.

The official policy could be summed up as pragmatism for the national interest. For the most comprehensive and penetrating study, Louise London's *Whitehall and the Jews 1933–1948: British Immigration Policy, Jewish Refugees and the Holocaust* is unsurpassable.

No specific legislation was passed to meet the change in circumstances with the advent of Hitler. Immigration control had been introduced with the Aliens Act 1905, brought in to answer anti-immigrant campaigning against the numbers of Russian Jews coming to Britain from the west of the Russian empire to escape pogroms and conscription into the Russian army. Conscription could mean forced conversion.

The Act both introduced controls – the immigrants had to be able to support themselves and be in good health – and set up novel mechanisms to enforce them at ports of entry. The legislation also clearly affirmed the right to asylum on religious and political grounds: 'Leave to land shall not be refused'.

Then came the Aliens Restriction Act 1914 and the Aliens Restriction (Amendment) Act 1919 which, with subsequent Aliens Orders such as 1920, made all aliens subject to entry controls, and which remained the legislative authority. The 1905 Act's provision on asylum was suspended in 1914: that remained a tradition and a matter of discretion.

The practical working out of an immigration policy stayed with the Home Secretary of the day and what he (as it then was) thought was politically desirable and possible within a generally restrictive framework, always with one eye on the Treasury. As Louise London says, 'British policy towards the refugees revolved around the issue of finance.'

This was rooted in the concept of Britain's not being a country of immigration. Of temporary refuge, yes; of immigration, not really. Reinforcing this posture was the article of faith for the administration that an increase in Jewish immigration on any scale was a threat to British stability, as it would stimulate antisemitism – a view shared by the established Anglo-Jewish communities.

Economic arguments in further support of the posture said the level of unemployment (at some 2.2 million in 1933 as a consequence of the Great Depression) could not bear any addition, and that the taxpayer could not be asked to support jobless and destitute immigrants.

So while some humanitarian immigration was unavoidable – the enforced migration of Jews was seen as a refugee question by the recipient country – the immigrant was not to see this as at all permanent but should expect to move on within a year, unless of course remaining was in the national interest.

Those given permission to land had to undertake not to take a job without the consent of the Ministry of Labour. In fact, most refugee scholars had their eyes on the US; the UK was only a gateway.

By the end of the war, according to Lord Beveridge, the SPSL had 2,541 scholars on its register: 624 were in the US, 612 in Britain, 80 in Central and South America, 74 in the Dominions, and 66 in Palestine.

The already famous and notable were welcomed with open arms, as were business owners who could set up their businesses afresh (and offer jobs in deprived areas). The filling of domestic service posts – particularly by women – was welcome so otherwise unwelcome male

German professionals found themselves retraining as butlers and footmen; 20,000 entered by this means, the vast majority women. 14,000 alone came after 1938.

In her 1983 memoir of the time, *The Ninth of November*, Hannele Zürndorfer, who left her home city of Düsseldorf on 3 May 1939 on one of the last *Kindertransport* trains, recalled how after *Kristallnacht*,

> The family must prepare to leave. My mother started to go to evening classes run by the Jewish community. These were an attempt to prepare women, most of them not used to earning a living, for a penniless fresh start. She went to courses in English and pastry baking. [18]

By September 1939, 80,000 people from Germany, Austria and Czechoslovakia had been admitted; 10,000 had come and gone; 70,000 were Jewish.

Hannah Arendt, who had applied unsuccessfully to the AAC from Paris in November 1934, records a refugee joke:

> A forlorn émigré dachshund, in his grief, begins to speak: 'Once when I was a St Bernard . . .'

She herself settled down and into great intellectual eminence in the United States, even if her major works in English had to be 'Englished'. She also settled into elevated social status. In Janet Malcolm's study of the poet Sylvia Plath, *The Silent Woman*, she quotes the critic Alec Alvarez referring to John Berryman's poem 'New Year's Eve',

> . . . which, I suspect, was about one of Hannah Arendt's New Year's Eve parties. They were marvellous parties . . . I went to a couple. I always saw Berryman there. His poem has a marvellous line: 'Somebody slapped somebody's second wife somewhere.'

With the flight of German Jews a desperately increasing reality, the Board of Deputies of British Jews came to a crucial agreement with Ramsay MacDonald's national government. In return for the stricken Jews being

---

18 Zürndorfer, Hannele: *The Ninth of November.*

allowed to come to Britain, the Board undertook that no cost would fall on public finances.

Here the leading figure was Otto Schiff (1875–1952), president of the Temporary Jewish Shelter since 1922, a German-born businessman who had organised relief for Belgian Jews in the First World War and now put his life into organising relief for the German Jews seeking refuge in Britain.

He set up the Jewish Refugees Committee in March 1933. Funds were provided through the Central British Fund for German Jewry, which became the Council for German Jewry in 1936, the Central Council for Jewish Refugees in 1939, and then reverted to the Central British Fund for Jewish Relief and Rehabilitation in 1944. Schiff undertook most negotiations with the Home Office on refugee matters on behalf of the Jewish community.

He established the Children's Refugee Movement (set up by the JRC and the Inter-Aid Committee) and the 1943 Jewish Committee for Relief Abroad, which was financed by the Central Council for Jewish Refugees. He was responsible for making the organisational arrangements to bring Jews out of Germany and Austria to Britain, for supporting them financially once here, and for helping them to find accommodation and employment.

The JRC's reach extended across Britain into local assistance committees, and it offered a helping hand to all those who, though now safe from Hitler's depredations, lacked the basic necessities of life.

In the House of Lords on 5 July 1939 the Earl of Lytton 'rose to call attention to the nature and magnitude of the refugee problem' and urge government action in meeting it:

> Never had a single catastrophe created such a volume of human misery and suffering as that which is involved in the problem of either the actual or the potential refugees in Europe.

He listed the various voluntary organisations that had undertaken the task of relief: The Council for German Jewry, the German Jewish Aid Committee, the Society for the Protection of Science and Learning, the Arts and Letters Refugee Committee, the International Student Service, the International Hebrew Christian Alliance, the International Christian Committee for German Refugees, the International Solidarity Fund, the

Save the Children Fund, the Germany Emergency Committee of the Society of Friends, the British Committee for Refugees from Spain, the British Committee for Refugees from Czechoslovakia, and the Co-ordinating Committee for Refugees. He went on to mention some of the financial appeals. The Baldwin Fund alone had produced £500,000 [some £35 million in 2022]. The Mansion House Fund had exceeded £350,000. The Council for German Jewry – 'they are quite a small Jewish community' – had raised since 1933 no less than £3,000,000. £1,000,000 had been subscribed for sufferers from the Spanish Civil War. 'Altogether, in a few years, £5,000,000 has been raised through private charity in this country.' But the problem was far larger than could be dealt with by private charity or voluntary effort. He referred to the wholesale persecution of the Jews, but also of Communists, Social Democrats, even persons of mildly Liberal views.

> I myself, I have no doubt, would be a victim of such persecution if I lived in Germany . . . All these people are forced to choose between the probability of a living death in a concentration camp or exile from their country.

But the Anglo-Jewish community could not continue with its original undertaking to fund the (steadily increasing) cost, and turned to the government for help. In 1940 the government contributed £533,000 to the Central Council for Jewish Refugees, and in 1941 £264,000, and by the end of the war the entire cost.

Not all emigrants were welcome, even by the reception organisations. In 1938, after the enforced union of Germany and Austria, the *Anschluss*, had brought a fresh wave of enforced emigrants, Schiff worried about too many of the shopkeeper class being difficult to immigrate, and endorsed the need for visas. The tightening included refugees being admitted on three-month time limits.

The government introduced a grading system. Entry might be granted to 'distinguished persons, i.e. those of international repute in the field of science, medicine, research or art' along with certain 'industrialists with a well-established business'. But small shopkeepers, artisans, minor musicians, commercial artists, and rank-and-file lawyers, doctors and dentists were consigned to the back of the queue. Teachers, actors,

academics, tourists able to show they would support themselves or had
sponsors could be given temporary visits for three months. In practice, the
majority of those allowed to work had entered as visitors.

A high degree of selectivity was part of the AAC's/SPSL's DNA. The
initial concept of 'exceptional abilities exceptionally trained' remained the
key to its selection process.

Only likely winners were given grants. One of the main principles of this
admissions policy had been to avoid friction with their British academic
colleagues. British universities in the 1930s were generally small, not well
funded, and had queues of well-qualified graduates eager for appointments.

The ideal applicant was an established scientific scholar from a leading
German university, aged between thirty and fifty, with some international
recognition in the international fellowship of science or humanities. This
was not exceptional. A French selection statement of eligibility spoke of
'those of lesser quality or who were beyond the age of high intellectual
productivity'.

How Esther Simpson saw it was set out in an article in *The Times* of
1 July 1992, to coincide with the publication of *Refugee Scholars*, where Esther
defended the AAC against the charge of elitism:

> We could not give grants promiscuously. We knew that academics
> would have to be first class if they were going to be easily absorbed
> into the country either in academic research, industry or teaching.

Under-thirties faced too much competition from young post-seeking local
academics; over fifty was seen as having peaked. Applicants falling into
those categories, though, could be sent on lecture tours of non-Ivy League
American universities that might offer them a post. Classical philology was
suitably international. But historians and particularly lawyers faced a steep
uphill battle to find places.

One way of seeing the AAC/SPSL is as a quasi-official mechanism
through which the well-being of Britain and the humanitarian duty to
the enforced migrants could be brought into balance – as Professor David
Zimmerman of the University of Victoria shows in *In Defence of Learning*,
('Protests Butter No Parsnips'),

With a low profile, the AAC and other organizations found limited bureaucratic obstacles. Gradually, restrictions on employing the refugee scholars were relaxed. In return, the AAC became a quasi-government agent, acting as the direct intermediary between all refugee scholars and the Ministry of Labour, the Foreign Office, and the Home Office. All applications for work permits etc were handled through the Council. The AAC was designated as employer of record for all exiled academics working in Britain.

For the academic refugees, Esther Simpson would become the human face of the AAC's quasi-governmental role.

21
Two Small Rooms,
A Universe of Learning

By summer 1933, the Academic Assistance Council, the AAC, was in full operation helping displaced scholars at its Burlington House office in Mayfair. Cash was not a problem. By 1 August it had raised £9,690 [£740,000 in 2022 money] including £2,500 for the Central Jewish Fund. Over the next ten years, £2 million would be raised by 2,000 voluntary contributors.

By the end of the first year, all its funds had been allocated to assist forty-two displaced, enforced migrant scholars. Within two years the AAC had placed sixty-two such professors in tenured professorial positions and 148 in temporary teaching positions: fifty-four in London, thirty-one in Cambridge, thirteen in Oxford. (An alternative version of the figures gives them as London sixty-seven, Cambridge thirty-one, Oxford seventeen.) Where British university lecturers were paid between £400 and £500, the AAC made grants of £250 for applicants with families, and £182 for those single. Imperial Chemical Industries (ICI) offered eighteen Fellowships. By 1939 the SPSL had placed 1,000 scholars. (See also *Ark of Civilization*.)

Individual British academics were also looking to help – and profit by the upheaval. Germany's pre-eminence in low-temperature physics was unchallenged. And at Easter, mid-April, 1933, Professor Lindemann [as Lord Cherwell, Churchill's war-time scientific adviser] set off for Germany from Oxford's Clarendon Laboratory, some accounts say in his Rolls-Royce, intent on rivalling Rutherford's Cavendish Laboratory in Cambridge by recruiting Professor Franz Simon from Breslau University. Close contacts already existed and Professor Simon's colleague in Breslau, and cousin, Kurt Mendelssohn had set up a helium liquefier in Oxford. Lindemann secured funding from ICI for Simon and Mendelssohn at what was the beginning of new, stellar academic careers in Oxford.

However, displaced German scholars were not passive bystanders of their Nazi-instigated plight.

A German-rooted organisation was set up, the *Notgemeinschaft deutscher Wissenschaftler im Ausland* [the Emergency Association for German Academics Abroad], based on an earlier German Research Association that had been Nazified. Its purpose was to assist displaced scholars to migrate by making their names and qualifications available in a directory.

The progenitor was a displaced academic from the University of Frankfurt am Main, Philipp Schwartz (1894–1977), a Hungarian by birth, Professor of General Pathology. He had moved to Zurich on 23 March 1933 where he announced the setting up of the *Notgemeinschaft* on the 16 May. Enquiries flowed in.

The point was to assemble the directory of displaced and at-risk scholars in science and the humanities rather than to find or help them find new positions. Unlike the AAC, the *Notgemeinschaft* was wholly dependent on contributions from the displaced scholars. Its efforts saw 2,000 emigres placed mainly in the US and England.

The Turkish government also commissioned Schwartz to assist in recruiting scholars for its new Istanbul and Ankara Universities. In 1936, publication of the directory was paid for by the Rockefeller Foundation. (Between 1933 and 1939, the Rockefeller Foundation amassed $775,000 [some £12 million in today's money] as a Special Research Aid Fund for Deposed Scholars. Post-1939, $730,000 was allocated worldwide.)

Beveridge described the *Notgemeinschaft* as 'one of the two rescue organizations with which the AAC/SPSL collaborated most often'. The collaboration started early: in June 1933 two senior AAC figures, Walter Adams and Professor C. S. Gibson went to Zurich. The idea was to invite the *Notgemeinschaft* with its unique index to London, but that had to wait until December 1935. Schwartz himself went to Istanbul as head of its Pathological Institute and had Fritz Demuth (1876–1965), a jurist, take over from him.

On 8 October 1935 a proposal to transfer the offices of the *Notgemeinschaft* to London was on the agenda for the twenty-first meeting of the AAC executive committee, noting its headquarters were then in Zurich:

> Its chairman is Dr. Demuth. (Catholic: formerly state-administrator of the Berlin Technische Hochschule; and secretary of the Berlin Chamber of Commerce). In the immediate future there will be intricate negotiations with South American states and with countries in the Near East. For this the intimate collaboration of the Academic Assistance Council and the Notgemeinschaft is essential and can best be achieved by moving the central office of the Notgemeinschaft to London.

The 'Suggested Plan' was that:

> Office accommodation for Dr. Demuth and one secretary-typist could, although with some difficulty, be provided in the new offices of the Academic Assistance Council.

The 'Advantages of moving the *Notgemeinschaft* to London' were 'Daily contact on case work' and 'Joint elaboration of plans for finding openings'.

The *Notgemeinschaft* enjoys only a fleeting mention in *Refugee Scholars*. Given the closeness of working between the two organisations, a major feat of forgetfulness must have been required by Esther in 1989–1990 not to include the AAC's (her own) close, daily, collaboration with the *Notgemeinschaft* in writing about the AAC/SPSL, as had been noted in the 1937 Annual Report.

> The Society receives indispensable assistance from the German scholars themselves, organised in the Notgemeinschaft Deutscher Wissenschaftler im Ausland, under the chairmanship of Dr. Fritz Demuth . . . The officers of the Society work in daily contact with Dr. Demuth and the other officers of the Notgemeinschaft, and are grateful for this extremely valuable collaboration.

Demuth became an advisory member of the SPSL executive committee in 1937. 'The *Notgemeinschaft* had no financial resources to compare with those of the SPSL', wrote Beveridge, 'But by its personal knowledge of the scholars themselves and by using its contacts with universities everywhere, it rendered invaluable service.'

And in January 1938 minutes recorded,

> The Council agreed that the provisional executive committee [of a new international body] should consist of: Professor Gibson, Professor Demuth, Dr Louis Rankine, Dr Walter Adams.

The US was the final destination of choice, though antisemitism was rife, a quota system governed numbers, and recovery from the Great Depression meant Americans first for jobs.

Later, on the US entering the war, the huge sums – rising from $48 million before the war to $500 million during it – poured into research under the war budgets meant opportunities for the talented European scientist at Los Alamos, Oak Ridge. 48 per cent of all forced migrant scientists ended their journey in the United States, compared with 8 per cent in Britain. Only half the 139 refugee physicists and mathematicians stayed permanently in Britain.

The AAC executive had noted the *Notgemeinschaft*'s contacts in the Near East. The new Turkish universities, set up under Ataturk's westernising initiatives, were among those looking to take advantage of the upheaval in German universities and recruit displaced staff. Among the forty scholars who found a refuge in Istanbul was the leading romance philologist Erich Auerbach, who composed his great literary critical work *Mimesis: the Representation of Reality in Western Literature* (1946) there.

He was Professor of Romance Philology at Marburg University, and extracts from his correspondence between 1933 and 1946 with such friends and colleagues as the critical theorist Walter Benjamin and Fritz Saxl of the Warburg Library [the private research Warburg Library for the Science of Culture], as published in *Scholarship in Times of Extremes*, will give a sustained picture of the increasing turmoil and the stress on Jewish scholars – 'the denial of the right to be German' – that flowed from the April 1933 civil service law:

May 1933 – Our new *Kurator* emphasized in several ways that it is only a matter of temporary measures and interim solutions; suspensions have merely been spoken of as leaves. Now that the minister has the student body in hand, one could hope for an easing of tension.

September 1935 – [Auerbach, who had served at the front and been awarded an Iron Cross, was still in office] I believe that my family and I (I have a wife and child of 12) cannot endure it much longer in Germany . . . Retirement, which I can take if necessary, would not improve the situation . . . To be sure, I am still in my official position, colleagues and students and other friends behave decently, many superbly – but it cannot continue much longer like this . . . On the contrary. So I must try, as difficult as it is, to find something suitable abroad . . . But that must be done carefully, for it would be unnecessary for German officials to learn of my departure prematurely . . . Incidentally the AAC in London invited my application in December 1934, and at the time I answered that I planned to stay in Germany for the time being – do you think it makes sense to contact this institution?

September 1935 – I am always in my office, but I make very little use of it; my *privatdozent* reads the lectures, holds the seminars and examines. It seems questionable whether I will still be giving lectures in the winter.

October 1935 – . . . Incidentally, the day before yesterday I was suspended and relieved of whatever stock of responsibilities was still left me.

December 1936 – In Istanbul (since the middle of September). Furniture and books in transit. I am the only cultural historian among the newly hired Europeans.

January 1937 – As far as research goes, my work is entirely primitive, but personally, politically, and administratively it is extremely interesting. [This solution] was not easy to arrange because at least seven comrades-in-fate and several European ministers of culture, particularly the German and the French, did not look kindly on my candidacy . . . I am more and more convinced that the contemporary world situation is nothing other than the cunning of providence to lead us along a bloody and circuitous route to the Internationale of Triviality and Esperanto culture. I thought this already in Germany and Italy, especially in the horrifying inauthenticity of 'Blubopropaganda' [blood and soil propaganda] but here for the first time it has become a certainty for me.

October 1938 – The challenge is not to grasp and digest all the evil that is happening – that is not difficult – but much more to find a point of departure for those historical forces that can be set against it . . . The old forces of resistance – churches, democracies, education, economic laws – are useful and effective only if they are renewed and activated though a new force not yet visible to me.

May 1939 – Life is for the time enchanting here – only books, that is a useable university library, are lacking and travel is impossible.

June 1946 – No passport, no money [to return to Germany]. I hear Marburgers want to call me back. I believe one must have patience with the viscosity of the Germans and their tenacity in holding on to the appearance of bourgeois orderliness . . . Things are not bad for us, only that we have become rather poor. I could not bring my money out and wages are very low.

Erich Auerbach moved to the United States in 1947 and became Professor of Romance Philology at Yale University in 1950, in which position he died in 1957.

22

View from the Dark Side

Understandably, studies of refugee scholars' emigration tend to concentrate on the success stories: displaced scholars of the first rank, or potentially so, successfully reinstated and going on to further achievements to their glory and the cultural or scientific benefit of their host country. The AAC's aim – 'to prevent the waste of exceptional abilities exceptionally trained' – loaded the dice in that direction.

But what of those academics whose distinguishing characteristic was their sheer academic ordinariness, or age, their best work far behind them, or both? Such a one was Victor Klemperer, professor of Romance Languages at Dresden Technical University for thirteen years. He had become an academic rather late in life – working as a journalist in Berlin after his university studies for seven years before returning to academia.

In his diary entry for 30 March 1933, published in *I Will Bear Witness 1933–1941*, Victor Klemperer recorded:

> I feel shame more than fear, shame for Germany. I have truly always felt a German.

Four days later he writes:

> Everything I considered ungerman, brutality, injustice, hypocrisy, mass suggestion to the point of intoxication, all of it flourishes here.

His proven front-line service had kept Klemperer in his post at the Dresden

Technical University until 1935, when he received a letter terminating his service. The reason given was his being surplus to requirements – no students to attend his lectures.

2nd May, Thursday

> On Tuesday morning, without any previous notification – two sheets delivered by post: a) On the basis of para 6 of the Law for the Restoration of the Professional Civil Service I have . . . recommended your dismissal. Notice of dismissal enclosed. The Commissary Director of the Ministry for Popular Education, b) 'In the name of the Reich' the notice itself signed in a child's hand: Martin Mutschmann . . . At first I felt alternatively numb and slightly romantic; now there is only bitterness and wretchedness. My situation will be very difficult. I shall still receive my salary, 800 M, until the end of July, and after that a pension, which will amount to approximately 400 M.

Surviving the bombing of Dresden in February 1945 and the final threat of deportation to the east, he was reinstated in 1945 and went on to hold chairs at the Universities of Greifswald, Berlin and Halle. He published his famous study of the corruption of the German language by the Nazi regime in 1957, *LTI Notizbuch eines Philologen* [*Language of the Third Reich (Lingua Tertii Imperii)*[19] – *A Philologist's Notebook*].

He records writing letters immediately on being dismissed seeking assistance in leaving Germany. He compared his chance of finding a decent living abroad with that of winning first prize in the lottery. And it was sadly true that a fifty-two-year-old Romance Language professor from a technical university would not seem a suitable prospect to an allocation committee looking out for promise a university department or laboratory would consider too good to miss. As Klemperer himself assessed his position on 7 February:

> I am so agonisingly helpless. Because I am a modern philologist who cannot speak any foreign languages. My French is completely rusty, I am afraid to write or speak even a single sentence. My Italian never counted for much. And as for my Spanish, I can do nothing useful.

---

19 *Lingua Tertii Imperii* – Klemperer's cover name for the Third Reich.

Nonetheless he took urgent steps to find a haven:

> It was snowing on Wednesday, the 'Day of Celebration of National
> Labour'. I wrote correspondence for hours. Three identical letters to
> the 'Notgemeinschaft deutscher Wissenschaftler im Ausland', Zurich,
> to the 'Academic Assistance Council', London, to the 'Emergency
> Committee in Aid of German Scholars', New York City . . . I
> emphasised everywhere that I can lecture both in German and
> comparative literature, that I can lecture in French and Italian
> immediately(!), in Spanish within a short time(!), that I 'read' English
> and if necessary would also speak it in a couple of months.

On 7 May, he recorded that:

> In response to my many letters I have so far received an application
> form from England, which applies to the whole world of the
> unemployed and offers me no chance at all.

On 15 May, the AAC responded:

> Dear Sir,
>   We thank you for your questionnaire received to-day. We have
> registered the information you give us and will let you know should we
> hear of any suitable opening.
>   Yours very truly,
>   p.p. Secretary

The sound of a door closing must have echoed in Klemperer's ears as he
read this pro forma response.

A more personal opening then came his way. A day or two after
Christmas 1937, a friend who was leaving Germany gave Klemperer the
address of a London banker, Felix Bacharach, who might be interested in
helping him, though Klemperer felt he would not get away; ' . . . we are
digging ourselves in here and shall perish here.' Nonetheless, Klemperer
wrote to Bacharach – and on 8 January 1938 recorded that the letter

> had fairly embarrassing consequences; instead of giving a private reply
> to a private letter, the man passed it on to the Warburg Institute (what

is it?); there a Fräulein Dr Gertrud Bing made two copies and sent them to my old friend Demuth [of the Notgemeinschaft Deutscher Wissenschaftler im Ausland sharing the SPSL office] and a Society for the Protection of Science and Learning. Now today a letter comes from Demuth again: Send three curriculum vitae etc. to us once again, we shall go on looking. Just scribblings, waste of time, annoyance, hopelessness. However Fräulein Dr Bing also wrote to me, she will try to arrange a lecture for me in London . . . But what is the point of it all? It is not only that there are no prospects, but that I am afraid of the prospects. Eva and house and garden and I myself without knowledge of the languages – how could it work out? But what is going to happen here?

Nonetheless, he writes a new curriculum vitae and publications list and sends them off.

Gertrud Bing, meanwhile, has written to Esther passing on Klemperer's letter to Bacharach. She is sure the SPSL have his papers but she has asked him to send his CV and list of publications. She adds:

> At the same time I am forwarding a copy of his letter to Dr Demuth, because the obvious thing would be to try to find professor [sic] Klemperer a post in South America. He is certainly a very good scholar, and it would seem a great pity if nothing could be done for him.

The personal touch can go no further. Her in-tray no doubt overflowing with the exceptionally able, Esther's reply to Dr Bing returns Klemperer to the holding pen of his pro forma status:

> Many thanks for your letter of December 30th enclosing a copy of the letter you have received from Professor Victor Klemperer. We already have full papers concerning Professor Klemperer and regret that till now no suitable openings for him have occurred. I hope it will not be long before a position offers itself in one of the South American States.

With the war less than a year ahead, that is the last Klemperer hears from the SPSL until October 1946. Esther's successor as secretary, Ilse Ursell [m. Eton], is closing the remaining open files. The United Kingdom Search Bureau for German Austrian and Stateless Persons from Central Europe has supplied her with Klemperer's address. As he recounts in his diaries, the fire-bombing of Dresden in February 1945 had saved him from deportation to the East.

> Dear Professor Klemperer,
>
> You may remember that you registered with this Society upon your dismissal by the Nazis. We were very glad to receive the news that you have survived the war and are still living in Dresden, and should like to send you our greetings and best wishes.
>
> Yours sincerely,
> Ilse J. Ursel
> Secretary

By this time, Esther had been working for the Society for Visiting Scientists for two years, though she had not severed her connections with the organisation to which she had been called in 1933. 'Well, you could say it was a call.' [*Refugee Scholars*]

23
London Calling

In putting *Refugee Scholars* together, Cooper himself had become interested in and worked hard on two topics that Esther simply ignored when he tried to interest her in them.

One was the October 1933 Albert Hall joint fundraising rally, mounted by the Joint Refugee Committee of five refugee charities including the Academic Assistance Council; a rally at which, famously, Einstein spoke.

When Beveridge recounted the steps taken to bring the AAC into fully functioning life, he identified two nodal points: the letter to *The Times* in May announcing its presence in the field of refugee organisations, and the four-charity joint fundraising meeting at the Albert Hall on 3 October 1933 held by the German Refugees Assistance Fund (Academic and Professional), the AAC, the International Student Service, the Refugee Professionals Committee, the Friends Germany Emergency Committee.

The heroic version of Esther and the AAC conflates Tess, the AAC, the Albert Hall meeting, and Einstein's speaking. But Esther had nothing to do with the meeting, as she told Ray Cooper, and Einstein was not there for the AAC alone.

As engagingly told in Andrew Robinson's *Einstein on the Run*, having fled Germany, Einstein was taking refuge in Cromer as the guest of a Conservative MP, the characterful Commander Oliver Locker-Lampson CMG, whose gamekeepers, armed with shotguns, acted as the professor's bodyguards. In July 1933 Locker-Lampson had introduced a private member's bill to give British citizenship to Jewish refugees – unsuccessfully and, in the light of the internment crisis, unfortunately.

Beveridge was among the speakers at the Albert Hall and also gave an interview to the BBC.

After the meeting, a problem had arisen with the Joint Refugee Committee failing to produce accounts of the funds raised. Cooper set out to untangle it. Though he felt he had got to the bottom of the accounting problem – just a muddle, with Walter Adams seconded to be secretary of the German Refugee Assistance Fund for six months – nothing came of that part of Cooper's work.

The second topic was a question dangerously close to Esther's personal interests: why in his account of the setting up of the AAC in *A Defence of Free Learning* did Lord Beveridge not mention the Hungarian-born physicist Leo Szilard and the role he played in its founding, described by others as central, and in Esther's being offered and taking a job with the nascent AAC?

In some accounts of the AAC's origins, Szilard is credited as co-founder with Beveridge, even as the sole *fons et origo*, with Esther cited in support. In correspondence she described Szilard as 'one of the founders' of the AAC, though she was in Geneva at the time and could have had no first-hand knowledge – or any knowledge other than what Szilard told her.

Leo Szilard was the polymathic scientific Hungarian genius, who entered histories of the Second World War when he joined with Einstein in August 1939 in writing to President Roosevelt to alert him to the prospect of a German A-bomb, a letter that led to the setting up of the Manhattan Project, in which Szilard took part. He was among the Chicago University team of exceptional scientists who brought about the world's first nuclear chain reaction in 1942.

He is also widely, and it seems eagerly, credited with the initiation and setting up of the AAC.

That Szilard had a founding role in the creation of the AAC has become part of Esther's public story. Esther's own account, admittedly dictated for *Refugee Scholars* nearly sixty years after the events she describes, differs substantially in detail from that in William Lanouette's Szilard biography, *Genius in the Shadows*, though the leading role allocated to Szilard in the

AAC's founding narrative remains the same in the end. Accounts may vary; the narrative is much as follows.

When Hitler rose to power, Szilard had been studying and working in Berlin at the famous Kaiser Wilhelm Institute, where he had taken a brilliant doctorate on Maxwell's Demon – a puzzle in thermal and statistical physics – under the supervision of the great Max von Laue. (Later, in the United States, Szilard was included among the so-called Martians, a group of brilliant Hungarian scientists.) However, this had not yet led to a university post and in 1932–1933 he was lecturing once a week – on current developments – at the Institute. But, as his story is told, he was also exceptionally attuned to the potential for danger Hitler posed, advising his Hungarian friends to take their money out of Germany and to leave. He left for Vienna, with his money, just after the Reichstag was set ablaze on 27 February 1933 and before the Jewish boycott began on 1 April, having kept two suitcases packed and ready by his front door. To survive, he said, you don't have to be cleverer, only a day earlier. Or perhaps be travelling on a Hungarian passport.

However, if about anything beyond getting money out of Germany, this boast appears problematic when Nazi policy on passports and crossing the frontiers is taken into account. After all, 25,000 German exiles fled to France by the summer of 1933, the majority Jewish.

Barbara Suchy writes:

One needed a passport to cross the border. And Jews crossed the border. Not all who did, emigrated. However:

To get a passport you had to get an OK from the local police, also from the tax authorities. In case of emigration you had to pay *Reichsfluchtsteuer* (introduced in 1931).

From October 1937 those émigrés, who returned (Jewish and also non-Jewish) were arrested by the Gestapo and brought into a *Schulungslager* [re-education camp]. Exempted from this were those who declared their intention to leave Germany 'at once' i.e. as soon as possible. This was seen as necessary in order to reduce the number of – mostly – Jewish – *Rückwanderer*: re-migrants.

After the November Pogrom about 30,000 men were sent to concentration camps. Those who could prove that they had realistic plans to emigrate were released . . .

With other words: Why should the Nazis refuse Jewish citizens to cross the border? Not at all. On the contrary. They wanted to get rid of them. And because the tempo of flight and emigration did not meet their expectation, the November Pogrom was staged.

In the Szilard-as-AAC-founder version, the start of the academic displacements under the Law for the Restoration of the Professional Civil Service prompted him into thinking up plans for some sort of international university where the displaced could resume their careers. Safeguarding his and his brother's money took him to Switzerland, to Zurich and then to Geneva, there to call on a young English secretary, Esther Sinovitch, who, this version claims, wrongly, was working for the International Student Service, to ask her to type some letters for him. His fellow Hungarian, the economist Karl Polanyi had suggested this: he knew Esther from Vienna through his scientist brother Michael with whom she played quartets. Michael was part of a group interested in social reform that included Donald Grant and John Macmurray.

She would type Szilard's letters. And so she did.

Back in Vienna, Szilard got in touch with Beveridge and discussed with him the setting up of an organisation to assist the displaced scholars. Beveridge was thinking about it too and agreed Szilard should come to London and prod him about it.

Szilard went to London and more than prodded. He helped to set up the AAC in its office in Burlington House, including sending for the secretary who had typed some letters for him in Geneva.

Another version of this narrative, with some interesting differences, appeared in the December 1964 edition of *Encounter*, in a memoir of Szilard by Edward Shils, Professor of Social Thought and Sociology at Chicago University.

In this account, Shils pictures Szilard for the reader:

> He was short and plump; he had a large head, a high, broad, somewhat sloping brow, and small, fine, neatly curving features . . . It was the face of a benign, sad, gentle, mischievous cherub. The whole formed a picture of unresting sensitivity and intelligence, immensely energetic

and controlled, and yet with great ease and gentleness of manner. He had sparkling eyes, a beautiful melancholic twinkle of a smile, and spoke in a low musical voice, which had a slight touch of a sob in it.

No mention is made of Szilard's meeting Esther in Geneva. Shils's memoir has him in Vienna after the *Reichstag* fire, having already decided 'something must be done to save German scientists and scholars after the expulsions which he saw were inevitable. He thought first of an "international university" and gave up the idea.' Through contacts with an econometrician Jacob Marschak and Gottfried Kuhnwald – 'the old, hunchback Jewish adviser of the Christian Social Party' – Szilard was directed to Beveridge, who was staying in Szilard's hotel, the Regina Hotel.

So Kuhnwald, Beveridge and Szilard met for tea. Beveridge agreed that as soon as he got back to England and had got through the most important things on his agenda, he would try to form a committee to find places for the academic victims of Nazism; and he suggested that Szilard should come to London and occasionally prod him. If he prodded him long and hard enough and frequently enough he would probably be able to do something. Very shortly after Beveridge's departure, Szilard went to London. Beveridge was at once ready, and with his customary decisiveness, he set about the details of raising funds. In a relatively short time the Academic Assistance Council was established. Szilard took a great interest in its working: he came regularly to the office to help out, provided contacts in Germany for the general secretary and arranged for the recruitment of Miss Esther Simpson, who remained its secretary throughout its existence.

In a footnote, Shils adds:

. . . Szilard himself, in his conversations with me, never claimed credit for [his role] . . . It was absolutely characteristic of Szilard to do a thing like this, to be so foresighted, so selfless, so inquisitive, so imaginative, so unsparing of his own energy and time, and so undemanding of benefit or acknowledgment for himself.

Assiduous researcher that he was, Cooper went into all the circumstances of the AAC's origins, wrote them out in detail for Esther, and summed up his findings in a letter of December 1989 to her, that while Szilard had fostered the AAC, he had not been (in capitals) NOT an AAC founder.

He was confident he had answered the question, 'Why did Beveridge not mention Szilard's part in setting up the AAC?', and he hoped Esther would agree with him when he had the final version typed. Not so, and his Szilard research became Appendix A of *Refugee Scholars*:

> As Szilard figures so prominently in Esther Simpson's account I thought it would be valuable to find out a little more about how he helped the AAC while such evidence can still be traced.

He gave the story a truly original opening:

> As far as I know Leo Szilard is the only one of Esther Simpson's friends who has had a crater on the moon named after him.

Crucial to Cooper's accuracy is that he was working from Esther's diaries of the period – diaries that are not among her papers in the Leeds archive but to which she refers in her letters to Cooper, noting they are filled with musical engagements.

In a letter to her of 10 April 1989, Cooper recounts in detail (someone has added amendments in red ink) how Szilard and she had dinner in Geneva at the Restaurant Yvonne on 23 May after which Esther went to her office and was there until 12.50 typing letters for Szilard. (Cooper comments that in future years this would not be infrequent.)

The letters were to Professor Gilbert Murray, Sir William Beveridge, Sir Philip Hartog, Chaim Weizmann, John Macmurray and Roger Soltau, then at the American University in Beirut. Presumably they explained Szilard's ambitious plans for an international university for displaced academics, says Cooper.

On 24 May 1933 – the day the AAC's founding appeal appeared in *The Times* – Szilard lunched with Esther at the Café du Nord before catching the 2.27 train to Paris.

Cooper has not left us details of the meals, but Shils records that Szilard's great favourite for lunch was:

. . . a glass of buttermilk into which he poured the entire contents of
the sugar bowl, followed by sherbet. If one lunched with him, he might
be silent for a long time and then come up with a scheme for improving
the selection of librarians.

In her version in *Refugee Scholars* Esther makes no mention of typing letters
for Szilard. According to her account, what Szilard wanted from her was
an introduction to the secretary of the International Student Service, the
Reverend James Parkes. That she gave him.

A letter of Esther's in the Brotherton Library archive offers a
contemporary account of her meeting Szilard and his version of events.
Written on 24 May, this is from Esther to her friend and mentor Roger
Soltau.

She is writing to him, she says, at the behest of Dr Szilard, a friend
of Michael Polanyi, the eminent chemico-physicist at the Kaiser
Wilhelminstitut [*sic*] in Berlin and brother of their dear friend Karl Polanyi
in Vienna, with whom she had played quartets. Michael had resigned
his Berlin post in protest at the expulsion of so many of his assistants
in the Institute; Szilard had also resigned his post as a *privatdozent* at
Berlin University.

Szilard had visited her that week with an introduction from the Grants
and Polanyis. While in Vienna, about 1 April, he had had the idea of an
organisation for the placement of scholars who could no longer work in
Germany, at first in terms of international fellowships for international
research.

A banker and economist in Vienna, Dr Schlesinger, had promised to
raise funds in Austria, Czechoslovakia and Hungary. Esther then recounts
how Sir William Beveridge was staying in the same hotel. After Schlesinger
and Szilard had interviewed him, Beveridge had promised to create an
English academic group for this purpose. That this had been done he
would see from copies of the letters enclosed, and an appeal would shortly
be made through this English non-Jewish group for the raising of money.
If Dr Szilard succeeded in creating an international framework for his
scheme, according to Esther's account, with the funds raised in England
and America awards could be made to scientists and scholars for them

to work for three to five years as guest researchers or lecturers in some less developed countries where there would be some hope of their being eventually permanently settled.

The letter continues with three questions about the readiness of the American University to participate in Szilard's scheme that Szilard has asked Esther to put to Soltau on his behalf. (Presumably Esther had mentioned her friend in Beirut to Szilard.) She will pass on Roger's reply to Szilard, who will keep her informed of his movements. As she writes, he is chasing round Europe seeing all the people he can; he will be most of the time in London, where something really active was being established.

Esther then went on to tell Roger how she was troubled by an even more complicated problem than the Jewish one. It related to her wanting to help a young colleague, a Russian of German descent, who had escaped the revolution and had travelled on a so-called 'Nansen passport'. He had been sacked, could not get other work in Geneva, but could not travel elsewhere.

This letter is a near-contemporary account of Esther's encounter with Szilard in Geneva, and this account is at odds with her recollection in *Refugee Scholars* of meeting him. What she reported of Szilard's activities was necessarily at second-hand, but close to the events he told her about.

Historically, we should note the misapprehensions in this letter about the state of affairs in Germany. The letter states that Szilard first had the idea of fellowships for the displaced when in Vienna about 1 April. This would have been a remarkable premonition as the Law for the Restoration of the Professional Civil Service was not passed until 7 April. Its supplementary requirement that civil servants prove their Aryan ancestry or status as front-line veterans was decreed on 11 April.

Then, Esther says that if a proper distribution of scholars and students could be effected, the whole problem could easily be solved. Tentative figures were of about 400 research workers and lecturers to be placed. The number of students could not yet be estimated as the German Minister for Education did not seem to be lending wholehearted approval to the current evacuation of Jewish students – not on the present scale anyway.

(That is not a description of his attitude that the Prussian Minister for Education Bernhard Rust would have recognised.)

Given the international press coverage of German professors being displaced, as read by or to Beveridge in his Vienna hotel, it looks as if Esther had not taken any prior interest in the German displacement of Jewish and politically opposed scholars over the previous six weeks. All this is on the basis of one conversation with Szilard. Yet it tells us that Esther had learned in May about the start-up in London and the forthcoming appeal, while Szilard was still actively pursuing his idea of an international foundation.

More intriguingly, no hint of any personal interest in what was going on, was 'active', in London, or of a 'call' is to be found in her letter to Soltau. And yet on or about 9 June, little over a fortnight later, she is assuring the newly established AAC that she was with their work heart and soul.

According to *Refugee Scholars*, she had realised that a job there was the kind of thing she wanted to do, call it a 'call', and that the people who were losing their jobs were the same sort as she had played chamber music with in Vienna.

Among Cooper's documents is a letter written by Szilard to a Dr Alexander Sachs in November 1939 about his membership of a committee involved with uranium chain reaction, and quoted in *Szilard: His Version of the Facts*:

> When the German government started to dismiss German scholars
> I persuaded Sir William Beveridge to form a committee and create an
> organization for assisting placing these scholars.

Cooper annotated:

> helped to persuade??

Why should Beveridge have needed persuading at all?

He had returned from Vienna to a London where proposals for a programme to assist academic refugees were already being outlined by Professor Major Greenwood and Professor Charles Singer, with the draft of a public appeal. The same Charles Singer whose name was too Jewish-sounding to appear among the signatories of the May letter or for the Royal Society to agree his appointment as AAC joint honorary secretary. Sir William had immediately set about securing backing for the future AAC, starting at his weekend visit to the historian George Macaulay Trevelyan in Cambridge.

A draft public circular secured support from the doyen of British science Ernest Rutherford and six other Nobel laureates in science. Beveridge would be AAC honorary secretary 1933–1938; SPSL vice-president 1938–1944; SPSL president 1944–1963.

In the initial formative stage of the AAC's creation, what part any 'prodding' by Szilard could have played is unclear. (If at all, most likely a tea-table politeness by Beveridge.) The privileging of Szilard in the founding of the AAC – anyway not the international university he continued to tout – is not of itself a part of the Esther Simpson story. What is of interest is her backing the Szilard-as-AAC-co-founder claim when she, in Geneva, could have had no personal knowledge of what occurred.

In the correspondence between Esther and Ray Cooper over Szilard's role in the AAC's origin and Beveridge's alleged forgetfulness or blanking of it, the location of that role moves from Vienna to Burlington House, where Szilard worked voluntarily in the AAC office from May to December. [How that squares with accounts of Szilard's habit of spending mornings cogitating in his hotel bath is another matter.]

Esther expresses her surprise that Beveridge failed to acknowledge this contribution, one that made him effectively a co-founder. To her mind, Szilard's early conversations were of the utmost importance.

Cooper responded by saying that Beveridge's apparent forgetfulness could be accounted for by his not having visited the AAC's small office. Could Esther remember Beveridge visiting? Esther couldn't believe Beveridge didn't know of Szilard's contribution, but did not respond to the question. It was all a long time ago.

In April 1975 Esther wrote to Engelbert Broda that she was involved in the preparation of Beveridge's history of 'our Society'. It was hard going as Beveridge did not want to give credit to anyone else. [On reading those words, 'pot' and 'kettle' inevitably come to mind.] Beveridge had ignored A. V. Hill's part, especially at the time of internment, but she had insisted that as A. V. was on the spot, Beveridge should get his own account from him. On the question of Szilard's role in setting up the AAC, she said she had protested vigorously about omitting Szilard, but had come to the conclusion that Beveridge had really completely forgotten him: he just would not listen . . . There was not the slightest doubt of Szilard's part in getting Beveridge to act. Her only basis for this assertion, however, was what Szilard himself must have told her in 1933.

Given the variations in the Szilard version, taken together with Lionel Robbins's eye-witness account of Beveridge's tea-table inspiration and his having previously aided academics, the idea that Beveridge needed 'prodding' to set up the AAC impresses only by its sheer implausibility.

Meanwhile, in Geneva on 2 June 1933, Karl Polanyi met Esther and told her the action in England had grown enormously and that a man and a typist had been installed in the rooms of the Royal Society in Burlington House. And on 8 June Esther wrote to tell Szilard that Roger Soltau saw no prospect of setting up his international university at the American University in Beirut. At the same time, Cooper says, Esther asked Szilard to find out if there would be room for her in the new office in London as that was the kind of work she wanted and was competent to do.

Beveridge recorded an additional member of the initial staff as one of the AAC's three pillars. Together with A. V. Hill and Walter Adams,

> Miss Esther Simpson, coming to us as Assistant Secretary in 1933, became Secretary in 1939, and in her present post of Assistant Secretary at the Society for Visiting Scientists she continues as an indispensable Secretary also.

He also wrote,

> One other name, that of Esther Simpson, starting from near the beginning in the modest role of Assistant Secretary, proved to be of lasting and growing importance.

In 1953, Bentwich wrote of Esther Simpson's 'tireless devotion' to the refugee scholars collectively and individually for twelve years.

24
Esther Comes to Town

The AAC required an assistant secretary for its Burlington House office.

For such a post in central London, in a Piccadilly office, recruitment should have presented little problem. Curiously, the invitation to take the post without previous interview was sent by telegram from London to Geneva, to a young woman secretary with no background in academic administration or immigration.

This life-changing telegram was among Esther's papers on her death:

SINOVITCH CHEZ BELMENT 5 RUE PIERRE FATIO GENEVA

ACADEMIC COUNCIL HELPING GERMAN SCIENTISTS NAMELY SZILARDS [sic] WORK WANTS SECRETARY STOP IMPORTANT START MONDAY NEXT BUT TEN DAYS DELAY POSSIBLE STOP TERM AT LEAST ONE YEAR BEGINNING FIFTY SHILLINGS WEEKLY LATER RISE PROBABLE. I AM WIRING INFORMATION AND OFFER TO YOU

Esther records in *Refugee Scholars* that she was working in Geneva as personal assistant to the director of the World Alliance of YMCAs. She had a note from Karl Polanyi in Vienna introducing Szilard. As noted earlier, she records how he was looking for an introduction to the secretary of the International Student Service [now the World University Service], the Reverend James 'Jimmy' Parkes. It's not clear why he should have looked for an introduction from Esther rather than contacting his quarry directly, as he did with countless others. It is also unclear how Polanyi in Vienna might have known Esther in Geneva was in a position to introduce Szilard to Parkes. Szilard wanted to – and according to Esther did – discuss with Parkes his idea for a displaced scholars' university in Switzerland. They agreed it wasn't feasible, and Szilard returned to Vienna.

An additional question concerns Szilard's apparently not getting in touch with the *Notgemeinschaft*, then established in Zurich, a city which he visited. With its comprehensive directory of displaced scholars and wide experience of contacting them, the *Notgemeinschaft* would have seemed the ideal starting point for discussions of a possible international university of the displaced. It's hard to believe that Szilard would not have been aware of its existence. Perhaps we should assume its leadership and working could not have suited his purpose.

Esther recollected that Szilard was

> an extraordinary person, quite brilliant, but not everyone found him easy to get on with. He had a sense of humour some didn't understand. I understood him and we got on very well and remained friends until he died [in 1964].

Esther then narrates in her *Refugee Scholars* account how Szilard, back in Vienna, checking his hotel register, saw that Beveridge was staying in the same hotel: either the register recorded his position as Director of the LSE or Szilard knew this anyway, either way he decided Sir William would be a good person to talk to. Esther couldn't have had first-hand knowledge of what followed, so presumably her account is Szilard's, according to which Sir William promised to get something done on his return to London. She also records that 'at that moment it was Jews who were being sacked', which was not the case: political opponents were also being displaced.

As for Esther herself, she narrates how the month after Szilard returned to Vienna she was

> told that something had got started in London: there were two rooms, in the Rooms of the Royal Society at the top of Burlington House where a man and a typist were established. I inquired whether Szilard was going to London as I wanted him to see if there would be a job there for me because it was the kind of thing I wanted to do.

The people who were losing their jobs were the same sort as those I had played chamber music with in Vienna. I had the language and I had the interest. As it happened, at the same time as Szilard went to London, Donald Grant went there too, and they both together called on the Honorary Secretary of this new organization, Professor C. S. Gibson. They told him about me. As a result I received a cable offering me a job for no longer than some months, because they had no idea whether they would be getting funds, at a salary of £2-10s-0d a week [£153 in today's money]. That was about a third of what I was getting in Geneva, but that didn't bother me, because I knew I could get a job abroad again if necessary. I was still young at the time. But this was something I could do – well, you could say it was a *call* [author's italics]– and so I accepted . . . I started my job with the Academic Assistance Council on 17 July 1933 in the office at the top of Burlington House, where I found Leo Szilard already installed.

She found a room in a semi-detached house in the Muswell Hill area of north London, and, two months later, she changed her surname by deed poll from Sinovitch to Simpson:

I ESTHER SIMPSON, of 6, Halliwick Road, London, N.10, Spinster, a natural-born British subject, heretofore called and known by the name of Esther Sinovitch, hereby give notice that I have renounced and abandoned the name of Esther Sinovitch and that I have assumed and intend henceforth on all occasions whatsoever and at all times to sign and use and to be called and known by the name of Esther Simpson, in lieu of and in substitution for my former name of Esther Sinovitch. And I also hereby give notice that such change of name is formally declared and evidenced by a deed poll under my hand and seal dated the 21st day of August, one thousand nine hundred and thirty-three, duly executed and attested, and that such deed poll was enrolled in the Central Office of the Supreme Court of Judicature on the 26th day of September, one thousand nine hundred and thirty-three.—Dated this 27th day of September, 1933. ESTHER SIMPSON, formerly Esther Sinovitch.

Some have been tempted to assume the change must have stemmed from the impact on her of the Nazi takeover in Germany. But as we have seen, her brother Israel had already changed his to Simpson, and well before him his older brothers in Canada had already changed theirs. It was a well-trodden path. A fellow inhabitant of Crawford Street changed his name from Cohen to Crawford before going to medical school. Perhaps we should see the change simply as one step further in assimilation, with Esther Sinovitch becoming Tess Simpson. But, remembering Charles Singer, it is tempting to ask if Sinovitch was considered to be too Jewish-sounding when the AAC's assistant secretary picked up the telephone.

Miss Simpson had taken up the calling that would possess her for life. But allowing for the time-lapse between the events of spring 1933 and their recollection – or perhaps we should say reconstruction – something about this account does not hang together. Perhaps the clue lies in the cable's ' . . . NAMELY SZILARDS WORK . . .'

25
Grant Pulls it Off

In seeking to understand the presence of Esther Simpson in our lives today, we need to return to her presence in Geneva in mid-1933, working in another charity, the World Alliance of YMCAs, in another personal assistant post that time and chance had offered, in a city without much opportunity to make music. It is difficult to pick up from Esther – her later recollections or contemporary correspondence – any sense of what Henry James called 'the hungry futurity of youth', though perhaps 'youth' is not quite right for a working woman of thirty in 1933.

Then comes the telegraphed offer of a job in London, which she takes up unhesitatingly, believing there would always be another job if that failed. 'I knew I could get a job abroad again if necessary. I was still young at the time.' Well, there always had been. We should note that the alternative job would be 'abroad again if necessary'.

Why was it that Esther evidently saw working abroad as a normal state of affairs for her, that taking this job in London would be a concession?

Working abroad could be seen as an adventure for a young single woman; it could also be seen as a back-turning, a necessary separation, an escape, a declaration of independence.

A similar question is when and why *The Green Leaf*'s, IFOR's or YMCA's Esther became the SPSL's Tess or with some friends Tessa. Her loving friend from Vienna days, Irene Grant, addressed her personal letters to Tessa. What seems likely is that something about the Esther working abroad in her twenties stirred the maternal instinct in the wives of her friends and employers, Irene Grant, Irene Soltau, Betty Macmurray. The diminutive usage 'Tess' might have been an expression of this feeling.[20]

Though Tess without an 'a' is an acknowledged diminutive of Esther, it seems more usually the diminutive of Theresa. [Hardy's Tess of the D'Urbervilles begins life as Theresa Durbeyfield.] Esther is habitually elided into Essy or Etti. Her mother's sister was Essy, perhaps the reason for Sora Liba's and Ilya's choice of Esther for their daughter.

Esther signed her letters to Engelbert Broda as Tess. Her round-robin letter to her friends announcing her second retirement in 1968 was signed Tess. And, of course, her autobiographical *Refugee Scholars* is subtitled *Conversations with Tess Simpson*. She remained Esther to her now Canadian brother Joseph.

We might suspect she saw her first name as a movable feast, distancing her or not from her Jewish heritage depending on the recipient's own standing.

We can hold back on (inevitably) speculation for a while.

In *Refugee Scholars* her account of joining the AAC is tied in to the Szilard narrative of the AAC's founding – but also contains inaccuracies of the kind that signal reconstruction.

For instance, she tells Cooper about the AAC's founding letter to *The Times* on 24 May 1933. Bear in mind that she did not come to London until July and does not describe herself as seeing the letter in Geneva or reading about the displacements in the press there.

The AAC was proposed to salvage the displaced academics, she says.

---

20 This is not how it seemed to the Grant's granddaughter Eleanor, who wrote to me, 'By the time I knew Tess they had been friends for decades and seemed quite equals. I was also a child and Tess a grown-up so I might not have been aware of such dimensions to their relationship early on. However, Tess seemed such a strong character herself that I find it hard to imagine she ever needed protection or support in that way. Of course she enjoyed the fellowship and nurture of close relationships with the likes of our grandparents but she was clearly an accomplished and determined person herself. Also, she was but seven years younger than Irene; I know that might not be the determining factor in how relationships develop but I was never aware of Tess being a sort of child/daughter figure to Irene and Donald.'

The letter itself made clear that this was not considered exclusively a
Jewish question, although at that moment it was those who were Jews
who were being sacked. Beveridge and the Vice-Chancellors saw that
this was a much wider movement and that a lot of other people would
be affected, because of the spread of Fascism.

The Times letter actually stated that

> the issue raised at the moment is not a Jewish one alone. Many of those
> who have suffered or are threatened have no Jewish connection . . .

[As we have seen, Hitler's Law for the Restoration of the Civil Service
excluded from state service 'non-Aryans' along with political opponents
– proof of political reliability was required. A personal oath of allegiance
to Hitler was demanded from members of the armed forces and the entire
civil service from 20 August 1934.]

And while she allocates to Beveridge and the other forty signatories
concern that a lot of other people would be affected because of the spread
of Fascism, *The Times* letter took care to delimit its coverage.

> Our letter implies no judgement on forms of government or on any
> political issue between countries. Our only aims are the relief of
> suffering and the defence of science and learning.

Next in her story, as narrated in *Refugee Scholars*, Esther is told – she does
not say by whom – that

> something had got started in London: there were two rooms in the
> Rooms of the Royal Society at the top of Burlington House where a
> man and a typist were established.

This is a strange mixture of the precise and the general: *something had
got started* but it involved the Rooms of the Royal Society in Burlington
House with *a man and a typist*. And, whatever it was that had started, that
something, Esther wanted Szilard – if he were going to London – to see if
there would be a job there for her, although she knew a typist was already
in situ, *because it was the kind of thing I wanted to do.*

Why was that *something* the kind of thing she wanted to do? Or to put it another way, how did she know she wanted to do that particular *something*?

> The people who were losing their jobs were the same sort as those I had played chamber music with in Vienna. I had the language and I had the interest.

In *Refugee Scholars*, Esther does instance two professors with whom she played in Vienna 'in a very fine string quartet': its leader Artur Schiff, professor of internal medicine, and Karl Popper's uncle, and the cellist, another medical professor, Professor Klar. Other professors and investigators there might well have been in her extensive musical acquaintance in Vienna. None would be at risk of forced retirement there until 1938 and unification with Germany, the *Anschluss*, though all Jewish academics were at risk from the rise in violent antisemitism in Austrian universities that led to Vienna University twice being closed during Esther's time in the Austrian capital. If the people with whom she played chamber music in Vienna had included the sort of top-flight scientists who applied to the AAC, then assuredly she would have said so.

The Quakers discussed and reported on the ugly scenes in the university. These find no place in Esther's account of her time in Vienna, although she had a student ticket and apparently attended four hours of lectures on philosophy: the course was in *Grundfragen der Philosophie* [Fundamental Questions of Philosophy]. From a letter to Broda in which she refers to Rudolf Carnap, perhaps they included logical positivism.

She might, of course, have worked with displaced German scholars and remained in Switzerland by offering her services to the *Notgemeinschaft* in Zurich, with, it was said, displaced professors on every corner.

If she had felt the need at that time in her life to do something for the unemployed, the poor and destitute, it would have been all too easy to find something. But London and displaced scholars? We might recall the resonance of her explanation to Cooper: 'This was something that I could do – well, you could say it was a call – and so I accepted.'

So it seems London and the something that had got started it had to be. A call to go to the aid of the displaced cream of German academics.

As well as Szilard, she also asked her former boss at IFOR and personal friend Donald Grant to put in a word for her with the AAC.

> As it happened, at the same time as Szilard went to London, Donald Grant went there too, and they both together called on the Honorary Secretary of this new organization, Professor C. S. Gibson. They told him about me. As a result I received a cable offering me a job . . .

Continuing with the narrative as told in *Refugee Scholars*, she was wanted at once and wanted to go, but needed to give the YMCA a month's notice and

> my boss was in America. My friend Frank Willis telephoned him to see if I could leave earlier. He agreed, not only that – he came back a day or two later and he and his wife insisted I should spend my last days in Geneva as their guest.

In this account the anxiety to take the post – whatever it involved – is palpable. Yet she can have had no clear idea of what she would be there to do. Another glance at this pivotal cable is worthwhile.

> SINOVITCH CHEZ BELMENT 5 RUE PIERRE FATIO GENEVA
>
> ACADEMIC COUNCIL HELPING GERMAN SCIENTISTS NAMELY SZILARDS WORK WANTS SECRETARY STOP IMPORTANT START MONDAY NEXT BUT TEN DAYS DELAY POSSIBLE STOP TERM AT LEAST ONE YEAR BEGINNING FIFTY SHILLINGS WEEKLY LATER RISE PROBABLE. I AM WIRING INFORMATION AND OFFER TO YOU

The cable remains a curious document. Although it is unsigned, the actual sender was Esther's former employer Donald Grant, who also sent the follow-up information. And neither he nor Szilard – 'namely Szilards work' – were officers of, or indeed anything to do with, the AAC. Perhaps this association with Szilard led Grant to write mistakenly of 'helping German scientists' as the purpose of the 'Academic Council'. And while 'namely' gives the phrase 'namely Szilards work' an unwarranted certainty, it was probably intended to provide Esther with a link between the AAC, this cable and Szilard rather than to make any direct connection between Szilard and the AAC.

While Esther tells Cooper that she had wanted Szilard if in London to see if there would be a job for her at this something that had got started, she does not directly mention also asking Donald Grant to do so. Grant, she tells Cooper, went to London at the same time as Szilard, and they both together went to see the honorary secretary of 'this new organization, Professor C. S. Gibson. They told him about me. As a result I received a cable offering me a job . . .'

Donald Grant, with whom she had worked at the FOR in Vienna, as secretary, and, it seems, henchwoman, and the Disarmament Conference in Geneva, came into the AAC story although Esther had ceased to work for him and he had not been working or living in Switzerland.

He and his wife Irene felt close to Esther. To them, she was Tess, and someone special. In a letter of 27 May 1933 from University College London, the moral philosopher John Macmurray, whom she had met in Vienna, tells Tess that Donald has been with them for quite a long time now and

he often talks about you in awe because of certain days in Vienna.

We know from the correspondence with Roger and Irene Soltau in 1932 that Tess had actively backed Donald in his problems of cooperation with a FOR senior colleague, to such an extent that Irene thought the two men would get on better if she, Tess, left Vienna. Gratitude for her actions might well have inspired Donald's interventions with the AAC. The problem had been solved, or put on ice, when Donald and Esther went or were sent to Geneva to cover the Peace Conference.

And what comes out of the archive is Grant's anxiety that she should have this job, to do with Szilard's work, in London. It seems she must have reached out to him for help in getting the job, and his personal involvement in the telegram and what negotiations followed testify to his sense of her urgent resolve to get to London.

We could assume that, having persuaded Gibson of Esther's high professional skills – only in January of that year Grant had given Esther a testimonial for the YMCA job in Geneva in which he wrote that no secretary he had had could be compared with Miss Sinovitch – and her desire to work for displaced academics, Grant offered to cable Esther on the Council's behalf, an offer the busy Gibson would have gladly accepted.

This version of events leaves much unexplained about both Grant's role and Esther's 'call' to work at the AAC.

A problem with the AAC end of the correspondence is that none of it is dated and much is unsigned, but the unsigned telegram offering the job came on Friday 9 June and appeared to have been followed up the same day by another from Grant 'on behalf Academic Council' telling her to wire her reply to the Academic Council at Burlington House.

Esther jotted down a note of her reply on this telegraph form: so soon was impossible, Gethman – her boss – was in London, she would write.

She omitted the phrase about Gethman when she telegraphed this, but wrote a blue aerogramme on the same day saying that she had received a telegram from Mr Donald Grant asking if she could make herself free within ten days to enter their service as secretary. She had wired at once that was impossible so soon. There was nothing, she wrote, she desired more than to work for them, but it was impossible at such short notice. Their general secretary was in London and did not return before the eighteenth of the month; she was his personal secretary. If it were possible for them to hold the position vacant for a longer period until she could see her chief (Mr W. Gethman) on his return from London and make arrangements for leaving, she would be more than grateful. Might it be possible to find a temporary secretary? If they could get personally in touch with Mr Gethman in London, a great deal of time and energy might be spared; if Dr Szilard was in London he might find time to do this and to explain to Mr Gethman that she was really willing to join them. Should they be able to effect anything in this way, she would be truly grateful, and would also then be glad to have further details.

She ended by writing she was with their work heart and soul.

A number of points catch the eye. One is how the reality differs from the recollection in *Refugee Scholars*. In the aerogramme her boss is named as Walter Gethman and he is in London, not the US, as recounted in *Refugee Scholars*, accessible to the AAC, not needing a call from an intermediary.

Another is the note of asperity inflecting her suggestions that a temporary secretary might be found (the AAC replied on 13 June 'we have already obtained junior clerical assistance'), and that a great deal of time and energy might be spared if the Council officers themselves got in touch with Gethman over her release. That asperity is far from unusual.

Then there is the revealing statement, that there was nothing she desired more than to work for the academic action – with which Dr Szilard (whom she had met in Geneva) was connected – and that he could be asked to intervene with Gethman on her behalf – not Donald Grant, who had already intervened on her behalf with the AAC and who would have been known to Gethman.

Is it the academic action's connection to Szilard that is bringing her to work in London at a sharply reduced salary? She desired nothing more. Is that an unconscious revelation of the 'call'?

So to how she was with their work, heart and soul. This last really brings the reader up short. A certain job-seeker's exaggeration might be sympathised with, though her work with the International YMCA was itself very worthwhile. But the newly founded AAC was just settling in, and she cannot have known much of it, such as it was so far. Not even its proper title, it seems.

The next turn in the story illuminates Donald Grant's role, his intervention with the AAC on her behalf, and offers some possible insights into Esther's position and state of mind.

On Tuesday 13 June, Donald Grant went to Burlington House and spoke to the assistant secretary Percy Gent (absent from *Refugee Scholars*) on Tess's behalf. He then wired her that the Council proposed some delay. He would write.

And write he did, showing his commitment to getting her to London. The next day, Wednesday 14th, he sent the first of two handwritten two-page letters, the central object of which appears to have been to reassure Tess that any delay in her coming to London was the responsibility of Mr Gent and Professor Gibson.

This reads all the more strangely when it is remembered that, delay or not, the AAC were actually offering Tess the job she wanted heart and soul.

He explains to her how the AAC's Mr Gent had qualms over her exchanging her secure job in Geneva for one in London with a developing organisation, its own future still uncertain. Gent could not have known Esther had heard a call. He, Grant, would go to see the professor mainly concerned with getting the Council up and running but she should not be perturbed by his wire about delaying her starting there. He went on oddly to explain that he had allowed the Council's Mr Gent to get away with that delay, believing a few weeks' delay would suit her. But after speaking to Szilard the previous evening he thought he should see Professor Gibson and bring matters to a decisive conclusion.

So the Reverend Grant felt he must justify his dealings with the AAC on her behalf by explaining how he had 'allowed' the assistant secretary, Percy Gent, 'to get away with' a legitimate concern on the part of the job-offering AAC. But after a conversation with Szilard he then revised his position. What could Szilard have said that made Grant determine to bring the matter so urgently to a conclusion?

This raises the question as to what pressure Grant felt under to get Tess to London as soon as possible, leaving a secure job with an established organisation for a less well-paid post with an uncertain future. It was a pressure that led him to write to her in terms that have nothing to do with any increased urgency in the German situation, pleading with her to hold on until she hears more, and asking her forgiveness for his not having pressed Gent finally to decide on her arrival. He felt she was coming to London, so she should exercise the calmness she could always command.

The second two-page letter is written the next day, Thursday, following Grant's further meeting with Gibson and Gent the day before. It opens with the assurance that they stood by the offer telegraphed to her and that they would like to interpose a delay before she took up her duties. This he explains as the timidity of a gentle professor in taking action.

Grant tells Tess he had pointed out to them how disturbing the prospect of delay must have been for her, and they were sorry and accepted the blame for suddenly notifying her of a delay in her taking up the post after they had originally pressed her to come at once. He added that they were really nice people, the work would be chiefly office work, and she would be much more than recently her own boss. He made two additions to the letter. In one he averred he was not responsible for the urgency in the original telegram. In the other he said he had spoken to her YMCA boss Gethman who was content if she could stay in Geneva for a week or two before leaving for London.

We have only Grant's version of his meeting with Gibson and Gent, but it seems curious if they considered a necessary delay a matter for blame, no matter how put out the recipient might be. The explanation of timidity (in an established professor whom he had just met) seems something of a rush to judgement. Honorary secretary of the AAC from its founding, Professor Gibson was head of the chemistry department at Guys Hospital Medical School. On his retirement, *Nature* wrote that

> he had maintained an impressive scientific output in spite of the fact that his students rarely specialized in chemistry. He secured considerable expansion of his department, found time to collaborate with his hospital colleagues on various professional problems and devoted considerable energy to studies of chemotherapeutic and dental materials.

But a key question is why Grant felt the need to shore up Tess so dramatically and when Gethman had been so cooperative on her leaving him.

In *Refugee Scholars*, the story is shorter, smoother, and without Gethman or Gent. Grant and Szilard tell Gibson about Esther and as a result she receives the cable offering her the job immediately. She has to give a month's notice and her boss is in the United States. But her friend Frank Willis telephones him there [not Esther herself] to see if she could leave earlier and he could not have been friendlier or more cooperative. So off she went.

This is far removed from facts that involved her great friend and former boss Donald Grant, who not only dealt with her getting the job but spoke to her Geneva boss Gethman. Yet it has the detail of Frank Willis's telephoning her [unnamed] boss in the US. Was this just the confusion and forgetfulness of old age? Or suppression of an ultimately painful episode? The urgency of Grant's reassurance to Esther that she will be coming to London reads as though she was hysterical at the possibility she might not get *to London,* but not, for instance, being thwarted over her 'call' to help academic refugees. She wanted to get to London. He ensured she did.

Grant's version of the AAC job as chiefly office work in which he thought she'd be interested and more than recently her own boss signals an assumption that she cannot know what the job involves – and singularly fails to live up to the drama of her wanting it heart and soul.

But her being 'more than recently your own boss', coming from her former boss, does reveal another possible reason for her wanting to leave the YMCA, that there she wasn't her own boss as presumably she had been at IFOR. Echoes of this are to be heard in her lack of enthusiasm for her much later job at the Wellcome Foundation, as well as briefly playing in an orchestra at Morley College.

And so it finally worked out; Esther settling the arrangements for her starting in Burlington House.

How well suited she will be to fight the refugee scholars' corner is already clear from the tone and directness of her letters:

to: ES
13 June 1933

Dear Madam,

I thank you for your letter of the 9th inst. and have today had a conversation with Mr. Donald Grant on the subject. I explained to him that, in all the circumstances it would be better to wait for a month or so until we have a clearer idea of the work of the Council and what is entailed. We have already obtained junior clerical assistance and I do not feel justified, at the present time, in encouraging you to leave a post in Geneva in order to take up duties with the Council. From what I have learnt about you I have no doubt your services would be very useful but I believe it would be more satisfactory, from every point of view if you take no steps to leave your present position until after you have heard from me again – probably in about a month's time.

Yours faithfully,
[unsigned]

On 17 June 1933 Esther wrote to Burlington House:

Dear Mr. Gent,

As a result of a note received from Mr. Donald Grant, I had expected to hear from you to-day. . . . Since it is important that I know as soon as possible when I am to leave Geneva, I am taking the risk of this letter crossing with one of yours . . . .

The organisation for which I am at present working is naturally anxious to know when it must dispense with my services. The Committee has been most accommodating in releasing me at such short notice, and I may not keep the whole office now in doubt as to when a substitute for me must be obtained. I suggest that I begin my work for you in London on Monday July 3rd. This would enable me to complete the month of June here and settle my outstanding matters at my office. It would also give you the required delay. . . . Mr Grant will have explained to you that I am really anxious to take part in the work you are doing. He may have mentioned as evidence the fact that I am at present earning rather more than twice the salary you are offering me!

from: [no author]

to: ES
22 June 1933
handwritten annotation: 'File Domestic S'

Dear Madam,

With reference to your letter of the 17th inst. and your telephonic conversation with Mr Gent to-day, I now have pleasure in confirming that the Academic Assistance Council is pleased to offer you a clerical post effective from the 17th July, at a salary of £2.10.0d. per week.

I shall be glad to receive your confirmation that this is acceptable to you.

Yours faithfully,
[unsigned]
from: ES

to: C. S. Gibson
26 June 1933

Dear Sir,

In reply to your letter of the 22nd inst. I am glad to inform you that I am able to take up my duties with the Academic Assistance Council on July 17th as required.

I propose to leave Geneva on July 4th; the address which will find me until I find permanent residence is:

BM/TVR2 [*sic*]

Monomark House,

High Holborn,

LONDON, W.C.1.

Looking forward to taking up service with you,

I am,

Yours sincerely,

Esther Sinovitch

from: [no author]
to: ES
8 July 1933

Dear Madam,

With reference to your letter of the 26th June, from Geneva, I should be glad to learn whether it would suit your convenience to commence work before the 17th of this month.

If so, I shall be glad if you will give me a call.

Yours very truly,

[unsigned]

from: ES
to: [no recipient]
11 July 1933
37, Simonside Terrace,
Heaton,
Newcastle-on-Tyne.

Dear Sir,

Your letter of July 8th has been forwarded to me here. I am afraid it would now be very difficult for me to alter my arrangements in order to be in London before July 17th. Had I known earlier I would perhaps have managed it. I have however only just joined my family and cannot get away from the end of the week – it is three years since I was last home.

I expect to arrive back in London on Saturday evening. My address in future will be:

6, Halliwick Road,

Muswell Hill,

London N.10

(Tel: Tudor 1175)

Looking forward to joining you on Monday morning next.

I am,

Yours very truly

Esther Sinovitch

And so the start – in a clerical post – of Esther's life's work was settled. We could also see it as an ending, a closing of the door on the future life opportunities this bright, adept, gifted, young woman had shown herself so capable of accepting in her voyage across Europe.

Two phrases in this last letter catch the eye – 'Joined my family' and 'home' – in the sentence: 'I have however only just joined my family and cannot get away from the end of the week – it is three years since I was last home.'

The address Esther gives is that of her school-teacher brother Israel. And while he and his wife are undoubtedly family, and home can mean England, we might ask why for Esther these two phrases appear not to mean her father Ellis and his home in Hayes Street Leeds. All the more as he was presumably living on his own after the death of Sarah only three years earlier, the occasion presumably for Esther's being 'last home'. The missing headstone comes to mind.

En passant we might note that this correspondence is at odds with Szilard's claim in his letter quoted in *Leo Szilard: His Version of the Facts*. The secretary Walter Adams had gone away for four weeks [to Germany] . . .

leaving the office in my care. Fortunately one of the lady secretaries is excellent and I hope we will manage to get useful things done in August. She is my invention in so far as I got her to come to London to this office from Geneva when I spent some days and did some work in which she helped me. I was impressed by her ability and devotion and got the London office to take her on their staff and now I get the benefit of my good deed as I would be buried by the work without her being in the office. The real problems have not been attacked at all and the office exhausted its energy in bureaucratic activity.

And Szilard's version becomes the historical version, such as in Shula Marks's introduction to the British Academy's *In Defence of Learning*,

As Lanouette shows in this volume, Leo Szilard . . . should be regarded as a co-founder of the AAC, his argument is further underscored by the correspondence between Esther Simpson and Engelbert Broda [ed: neither of whom had first-hand knowledge] . . . In Vienna in April 1933 it was Szilard, Lanouette maintains, who lent urgency to Beveridge's discussions and helped to elevate a scholarship scheme for displaced academics into the much wider project of creating an international network to settle Jewish and left-wing academics beyond the reach of the Nazis . . . [H]e was in an ideal position to link small bands of activists, collect the names of displaced scholars and publicise the formation and objectives of the AAC . . . All this was crucial to the early success of the AAC; perhaps as crucially, Szilard was also responsible for persuading Esther Simpson, then working in Geneva, to join the AAC as secretary.

Assistant secretary actually, together with Esther's needing no persuading to go to London, as her correspondence with Donald Grant shows. Szilard played no part in getting Esther to London – other than by having lunched and dined with her in Geneva when he was pursuing his phantom international university.

Why Esther should have gone along with, supported, a version of events of which she either had no direct knowledge or did know was not the case is open to speculation.

One thing becomes clear: her 'call' did not extend to helping or reaching out to other non-academic victims of Nazism, even when the appeal came from a personal contact.

In January 1935, Esther received letters from her friend Lily Schiff in Vienna, a relative of Karl Popper's, about the fate of Hans Litten at Nazi hands. The letters were probably part of an international campaign for his release from the concentration camps where he was held in so-called protective custody.

Litten was a German lawyer and steely opponent of the Nazis; his singular and lasting fame stems from his calling Adolf Hitler as a witness in the trial of some Brownshirts whom he was prosecuting for murder, and subjecting the future Chancellor to a fierce and revealing cross-examination on the violence practised by his party.

After Hitler came to power, Litten was arrested on the night of the Reichstag fire and sent to a series of concentration camps, endlessly brutalised and tortured, and finally to Dachau, where he committed suicide in 1938. Litten was Jewish by descent on his father's side; his father had converted to Lutheranism and was a devout nationalist.

Esther forwarded the Schiff letters to Bertha Bracey.

In mid-March, she received another letter from Lily Schiff in Vienna. This she sent to Mary Ormerod of the Germany Emergency Committee, with a note that, 'It is of course advisable that whatever publicity there is should be in the right-wing press.'

In mid-June, Esther, just back from a holiday in Vienna, wrote again to Mary Ormerod. Hans Litten's father had approached her – one tragic aspect was the father's being a Nazi supporter who'd broken off relations with his son.

Forwarding the letters apart, Esther seems not to have taken up the campaign on Litten's behalf. Was she simply too busy? It is easy to get the impression that once installed, Esther then worked non-stop, from morning until the Burlington House gates were closed late each night. In fact, she took holidays in England and Vienna and may possibly have contemplated another job.

On 23 November 1934 Roger Soltau wrote to ask if she anticipated starting a new job for next autumn, as a probable vacancy there might suit her.

The vacancy would be at the American University in Beirut, and the job would be mainly acting as editorial assistant for the Social Science department publications, where she would be given, Soltau wrote understandingly, 'a very free hand'.

Of course she did not take up Soltau's enquiry. But he and his wife Irene felt very close to Tess, and it seems unlikely that he would have written without their having some inkling of her wanting a move. Perhaps at this early stage, she had realised the futility of the hope that had brought her so urgently back to Britain, and was not enjoying a very free hand in the AAC in her clerical post as an assistant secretary.

26
Getting the Show on the Road

As Esther took up her 'calling' in July 1933, appeals from the displaced were surging into the two rooms at the top of Burlington House. In *Refugee Scholars* Esther describes how they worked till ten o'clock at night, stopping only because the gates of Burlington House were locked, and at weekends, 'whatever was necessary', responding to those appeals and putting in hand the paperwork required for compliance with government entry policy, establishing academic credentials and suitability for an academic or research post.

Contemporary documents give a somewhat modified view of that time.

Replying in May 1935 to a letter from Esther enthusing over her holiday in the countryside – they would have to bring some cows into the Burlington House quadrangle to make her feel at home, he wrote – Walter Adams bemoaned their not yet having moved from Burlington House, where they were turned out at 5 p.m. while the amount of correspondence from desperate Germans was steadily increasing.

The general line on which the hopes of applicants would be realised or not is set out in *Refugee Scholars* with a dismissive finality:

> ... it was obvious that while each country had to have a large contingent of its own mediocre people, in another country refugees had to be in a class ahead of the locals to get absorbed.

She also recorded her – professionally qualified – approval of the AAC's governing body:

I'm amazed to this day at the wisdom shown by our Executive
Committee as they were only academics. They showed great
understanding of the situation, which was not shown in some other
countries, particularly America.

It must be said this demonstrates an ignorance of a professor's managerial
duties and necessary political skills – perhaps C. P. Snow's novels had passed
her by – and a not widely shared view of the Americans' response to the
refugee crisis, operating under very different national circumstances.

With the former senior civil servant at the helm, the AAC was
conventionally structured, with officers, a governing council, an executive
committee, an allocation committee, a secretary – though never settled
office premises.

The allocation committee had been established to consider the
displaced scholar's suitability for assistance and the likelihood of their
finding a place. The prevailing economic depression, with its effect on
jobs, had to be taken into account: young British academics should not
have their jobs put at risk. The key lay in the phrase 'exceptional abilities
exceptionally trained'.

The committee was central to the placing of scholars and met as often
as business required. Its working was set out in the 1934 Annual Report:

> All applications are submitted to a panel of experts, and the scholars
> if possible are interviewed by a specialist in their own field. All cases
> are fully reviewed by the Allocation Committee, which decides, on
> grounds of the needs and the scientific qualifications of the applicants,
> which persons to recommend for research grants to the Executive
> Committee.

The scholars were expected to search for themselves. In the first Annual
Report it is stated that of the 1,200 displaced scholars, 178 were placed in
Britain and 211 placed abroad. The second Annual Report listed the areas
of scholarly interest for the AAC: art history, biology, chemistry, dentistry,
economics, education, engineering, history, law, mathematics, musicology,
philology, philosophy, physics, psychology, sociology and medicine.

Of course, the officers controlled the purse-strings, as this minute
displays:

The officers resolved themselves into an allocation committee to consider grants for the year 1937/8, and made the following authorizations on the basis of a memorandum of recommendations submitted by Professor Gibson. The memorandum showed that there was a free balance for the year 1 August 1937 – 31 July 1938 of £7155. The committee authorized payments from this balance not exceeding £1300 for the administrative expenses of the office in the year.

Every case had to be examined individually and to receive the exact treatment that was needed. It first met on 13 July 1933 with Beveridge in the chair, which he continued to occupy until the SPSL moved to Cambridge in 1939 and he discovered the impossibility of getting there from Oxford, where he was now Master of University College. Sir John Clapham took over. That first meeting dealt with twelve individual cases, Beveridge records, in one and a half hours. But later meetings could take up to five hours, as on 3 July 1934 when thirty-one new grants were made to individual refugee applicants and forty-one existing grants were renewed. Seven grants made by officers were approved and ten existing grants were terminated. It was, records Beveridge, 'an heroic occasion'.

In effect, the executive committee and the allocation committee were one and the same by membership, containing the stalwarts of the AAC/SPSL, meaning that the decisions on the running of the organisations and on addressing individual cases came before substantially the same people year upon year:

Executive committee:

KENYON, Sir Frederic George (1863–1952)

ADAMS, Sir Walter (1906–1975)

DEMUTH, Dr Fritz (1876–1965)

GIBSON, Professor Charles Stanley (1884–1950)

GREENWOOD, Professor Major (1880–1949)

HARTOG, Sir Philip Joseph (1864–1947)

HILL, Professor Archibald Vivian (1886–1977)

SALAMAN, Redcliffe Nathan (1874–1955)

TABOR, Professor R. J. (–1958)

'The General Secretary' [i.e. THOMSON, David Cleghorn
  (1900–1980)]

'The Assistant Secretary' [i.e. ES]

Allocation committee:

Sir William Beveridge – Chairman

Professor P.M.S. Blackett

Professor J. L. Brierly

Professor C. S. Gibson

Professor Major Greenwood

Professor A. V. Hill

Mr. A. J. Makower [Alfred Jacques Makower (d. 1941), electrical
  engineer and chair of the German-Jewish Aid Committee]

Dr. Redcliffe N. Salaman [physician and botanist, author of
  The History and Social Influence of the Potato (d. 1955)]

Of course, the allocation decisions could not be undertaken without the
relevant information on each applicant. The committee had to be serviced
with the necessary documentation for each of its decisions over a range
of academic subjects and careers. And that documentation in itself was,
in each case, the outcome of a fateful initial decision on qualification: the
applicant's meeting the AAC criteria, for assistance, or being advised that,
'We have registered the information you give us and will let you know
should we hear of any suitable opening.'

Beveridge lists thirty-two applicants with sixteen subjects from eleven
countries. Women were singled out: 'woman philosopher', 'woman
classicist', 'woman physicist', 'woman historian'. All the paperwork on
each individual case for the meetings, which would have been a heroic
amount, was assembled by the Burlington House office staff – and it was
here that Esther's outstanding administrative skills and tenacity made all
the difference to the lives of the displaced and their families.

The Allocation Committee continued its unsung work in war-time
Cambridge, meeting there initially on 1 October 1939 and holding forty-
nine recorded meetings up to 1943. Beveridge says,

... using as little money and as much thought as they could to give the maximum of help and secure the maximum of cooperation from other agencies.

The executive committee also dealt with individual cases. On 29 June 1939, Beveridge noted, German scholars who had succeeded in getting out were to a large extent already established in countries of refuge. Before the committee were nineteen from Austria; eleven from Czechoslovakia; six from Germany; three from Italy; two from Spain. A feature of all the meetings was the trouble taken, spending very little money. By January 1939 the executive committee had met thirty-five times.

Minus the names of applicants, the minutes typically showed the committee deciding their individual fates:

1.   Grantees in the year 1933–4 and 1934–5
'The Committee considered a list of scholars to whom the Council had made grants during the first two years of its existence, and noted that approximately 34 of these were re-established, and 3 deceased.'

2.   Grantees in the year 1935–6
'The Committee considered a list of scholars who had received grants in the past year and noted that 32 of these were not in immediate need of further financial help.'

Extension of grants

'The Committee considered individually the situations of the scholars in receipt of grants who were not yet re-established:–

In the following cases the Committee agreed that no extension of grants be made:–

12 individuals listed (name, subject)

'The Committee agreed to submit the following cases for consideration by the London School of Economics Academic Assistance Committee:–

2 individuals listed (name only)

'The Committee agreed to make a loan of £50 to ...'

'The Committee agreed to make the following grants if they should
be required:–'

5 individuals listed name, subject, grant amount, grant duration,
institution

3.   New Applications for Grants
'The Committee refused applications for grants from

8 individuals listed (name, subject)

'The Committee agreed to postpone, for consideration by the Society,
applications from

3 individuals listed (name, subject)

'The Committee agreed to make the following grants:

3 individuals listed (name, subject, grant amount, purpose). Of the
third individual listed, 'It was [also] agreed to recommend to
the Society further consideration of his position'

4.   Grant to Courtauld Institute
'The Committee agreed to postpone for consideration by the Society
an application for a block grant to the Courtauld Institute.'

5.   Emergency grants
'The Committee agreed that authority be given to the Honorary
treasurer, Professor Gibson and the General Secretary to make grants
in emergency cases in the Long Vacation, not exceeding £300 in total.'

And typically the attendance looked like this:

**Fifteenth Meeting of the Allocation Committee, at the Athenaeum
Club, on Thursday, 1st July 1937, from 6.45 to 7.30 p.m.: Minutes**

Attendees:

BEVERIDGE, William Henry, 1st Baron Beveridge of Tuggal;
GIBSON, Professor Charles Stanley; GREENWOOD, Professor Major;
HILL, Professor Archibald Vivian; KENYON, Sir Frederic George;
ADAMS, Walter [Secretary]; 'The Assistant Secretary' [i.e. ES]

Russian, Spanish, Portuguese scholars make an appearance, alongside German and Austrian.

An eye-catching minute for 1938 has twelve individuals listed. The first two listed are scholars who have not yet arrived in Britain, whose grants are to enable them to 'continue research' with a particular academic based in Britain. The grant for the sixth individual listed is 'conditional on suitable academic hospitality, on favourable judgment of his scientific qualifications from the Dean of St. Pauls, and on a statement from the Bishop of Chichester that he has reasonable prospects of re-establishment'. The grant for the seventh individual listed is 'towards expenses of lecture tour to United States'. And the grant for the tenth individual listed is accompanied by the 'request that Jewish Professional Committee share the grant'.

After the war the executive met for the first time on 17 October 1945, back in Burlington House 'where they had started twelve-and-a-half years before'.

Esther was now working for the Society for Visiting Scientists and J. B. Skemp was secretary until 1946, when he resumed an academic career, to be followed by Ilse Ursell [m.Eton] until 1951.

At the age of seventeen Ilse had come from Düsseldorf with her parents in 1939. She had taken the School Certificate in the summer of 1939 (and supplementary Latin in 1940) and had taken a degree in modern languages at Reading University. In July 1943 she worked for the BBC monitoring service and started work with the SPSL, where she took over as secretary from Joseph Skemp in April 1946, at a salary of £5.10. Esther mentions her, noting that her brother was a Fellow of the Royal Society. Ilse was later active in Düsseldorf and Cologne working with Holocaust remembrance groups.

Beveridge notes the subjects for the next twelve and a half years: Intolerance; return of refugees or not; fitting resources to a variety of human needs; ageing of membership; where to do work; policy for the future.

There were 2,541 displaced scholars on the SPSL register: 624 were in the US; 612 in Britain; 80 in Central and South America; 74 in the Dominions; 66 in Palestine; 62 in the rest of the Middle East; smaller numbers in smaller European countries.

Of the 612 displaced in Britain, 243 were in universities or parallel institutions; 170 in industry, commerce or private practice, 46 in government posts; 23 in the army; 17 in schools, etc.; 14 in the BBC; 38 unemployed; 61 not traced.

Post-war, the world was of course a different place. The era of displacement of mainly Jewish German-speaking world-class scholars, at which Esther would look back with a veteran's nostalgia, was over. Now scholars from Czechoslovakia, Poland, China, Portugal, Greece, Hungary and Romania would be knocking on the SPSL's door. Of forty-six applicants, only eleven were from Germany/Austria. A major preoccupation were claims for pensions owed by the defeated to the displaced.

Closing time advanced for the era of the founders. Beveridge succeeded Archbishop Temple as president in 1944. Professor C. S. Gibson resigned as honorary secretary in 1945. Professor R. S. Hutton took his place. Sir John Clapham died in 1946, succeeded as chairman of the executive committee by Professor A. V. Hill. Professor Major Greenwood died in 1949.

For all its elevated membership, the SPSL had always led a nomadic existence, signalling its hopes that the problem of displaced scholars would be temporary. It returned to London from Cambridge in 1951 to be housed with the Society for Visiting Scientists at 5 Burlington Street, recovering, as Beveridge puts it, the services of Miss Simpson 'who became our secretary as well. She had never really ceased to help us.'

In 1947 the SPSL's closure was envisaged to come in two years' time. But by 1948 the onset of the Cold War had changed the outlook and the executive committee decided that the Society still had a role in support of free learning, though quite how was unclear. Closure then returned to the agenda. But the Hungarian uprising in 1956 and applications from five Hungarian scholars made for a prima donna's farewell.

In 1959 Beveridge wrote,

> On the question of principle the answer is clear. With tyranny and intolerance established over so much of the world, can anyone who has known freedom doubt that the task which we set out to do twenty-five years ago, in defence of free learning, still has to be done? It needs to be done more than ever.

In the SPSL's reincarnation as CARA, the Beveridge principle is maintained.

Looking back, Beveridge had no illusions about the place of academic rescue in the greater refugee scheme of things.

> We were right, I am sure, to concentrate our own efforts on a special task of enabling university scholars to continue their services to learning. But we were reminded often that we covered a small fraction only of the refugee problem.

As to that fraction, in February 1940 a reminder had come from the Quaker Margery Fry. Just back from France, she told the executive committee how full that country was of refugees: 400,000 Spaniards, 42,000 Germans and Austrians, many Poles and Czechs.

As to that problem,

> The disadvantage at which all merely professional people – lawyers, doctors, administrators – were without SPSL to help them through the barricades of official delay. It took the Jewish organizations and the Home Office 6 months between them to issue a visa for a distinguished woman for whom a home was waiting in the USA – four months after I had written a special letter to the undersecretary at the Home Office urging expedition.

27

Across the Pond

From the pages of *Refugee Scholars* Esther's view of the SPSL's American counterpart emerges as disapproving if not disparaging, though after 1935 and the Nuremberg Race Laws, the displaced, equally well qualified as the initial wave, were redirected to America by means of funded lecture tours. British universities were already sated with the pre-Nuremberg displaced. 'We are a very small country,' Esther noted.

> We knew in America there were very many universities . . . We said to our refugees, 'It hasn't to be Yale or Harvard or Columbia. You have to concentrate on the Middle West, the smaller universities, just as any American has to do. You can go from there later to the other universities, but this is where there would be opportunities.' . . . It worked quite well, but we did have opposition from the American organization, which started at more or less the same time as ours. In our opinion, they did not show the wisdom shown by our own academics.

'Just as any American has to do.' Where did Esther get her ideas of 'any American'? She had not herself been to the US and never followed up the invitations from her transatlantic relatives to pay them a visit.

Curiously, Esther's (retrospective) account then turns into a critique of the American rescue organisation's attitude to Jewish participation.

> When we started the AAC, it was realized that this was not solely a Jewish problem. It was something much bigger. But that was not the

case in America. And we had representatives of the Jewish Professional Committee . . . However, the Americans regarded this primarily as a Jewish question, and so their committee was largely Jewish. We ourselves were extremely careful about our grants. The money for our grants was raised especially for that purpose. We were not interfering in any fellowships or grants available for British scholars . . . Unfortunately this was not the case in the United States, and the result of that was resentment in the universities. There was a great fear in the American committee then of anti-Semitism [sic] and in 1935 they sent an emissary over to us to say that there was no more room in America for refugee academics . . . To us their complaint was preposterous, for the reason that we had already absorbed more in this little country than they had in the whole of America.

The SPSL's officers had reservations about the American approach, as we see later, though this really expresses the cultural difference between the two countries over the funding of universities. But the official account of the American committee calls into question quite how well in fact Esther understood the American situation, then or all those years later:

The US Emergency Committee [in Aid of Displaced Foreign Scholars], located in New York City at 2 West 45th Street in the Institute of International Education, was organized in May, 1933, to serve the needs of the university professors who had been dismissed from German universities because of political opinions or anti-Semitic legislation, and to preserve their attainments for the benefit of scholarship in the United States. With the outbreak of Nazi aggression the Committee necessarily revised its mission so as to include refugee professors from all countries in Western Europe overrun by the Nazi armies . . .

The Committee[21] was in operation for twelve years and served to

---

21 Dr Livingston Farrand became chairman of the committee; Dr. Stephen Duggan [then director of the New York Institute for International Education] became its secretary, and after the death of Farrand, its chairman; and Fred M. Stein became its treasurer. Edward R. Murrow served as assistant secretary until 1935, followed by Professor John H. Whyte (1935–1937), Betty Drury (1937–1944) and, finally, by Dr Francis Fenton Park (1945). Professor Nelson P. Meade and Professor L. C. Dunn were added to Messers Farrand, Stein and Duggan to form an executive committee. The committee was disbanded in June 1945.

raise funds on behalf of refugee scholars. Relief was not made directly to the scholars, rather, funds were made available through a program of grants-in-aid to colleges, universities, and other institutions and later through fellowships that served mainly artists and writers. These funds were provided mainly through foundations, although many individuals did make significant contributions.

In 1938, as Nazi aggression spread throughout Europe, the Committee broadened the scope of its mission to include refugee scholars from all countries overrun by the Nazi armies. The Committee changed its name to the Emergency Committee in Aid of Displaced Foreign Scholars, in order to reflect this new mission.

Over the course of twelve years, the Committee provided grants for 335 scholars and assisted many others through references to other assistance organizations. The Committee disbanded in 1945.

As to how the Emergency Committee's modus operandi differed from the AAC, Isabella Löhr of the Institute for European Global Studies at the University of Basel has written:

> [T]he EC saw itself as a 'clearing house' operating as a go-between for universities, donors, émigré scholars, government institutions, and the public . . . To avoid criticism and public disapproval, and in light of the isolationist attitudes and financial distress of American universities in the wake of the Great Depression, the EC decided not to appeal for public donations. Instead, the EC approached philanthropic bodies to raise funds for fellowships, for which universities could then apply if they suggested the appointment of a particular refugee scholar and if they could guarantee the employment of the scholar on a permanent basis after the expiration of the fellowship. In this way, the EC helped many prominent scholars build a transatlantic career . . .

Of course, these relief organisations, the AAC, the EC and the NWA cooperated closely. When in December 1933 the University of Pennsylvania won the race to invite Rudolf Höber, the former professor of physiology at Kiel University and a pioneer in cellular biochemistry, to join its medical faculty, the letter was addressed to him care of A. V. Hill at University College School of Physiology. The Rockefeller Foundation contribution to his salary made the appointment possible.

With Whitehall's immigration policy discouraging stays of more than one year, displaced junior scholars in particular sought residence in the United States, where the Emergency Committee helped such scholars find positions and arranged temporary funding, very often from the Rockefeller Foundation. The SPSL's fifth report (1946) stated that:

> The great majority of the scholars registered with us who have found employment abroad are in the United States. We know of 624 placed there.

What stands out in the American reach to saving the Jewish victims of Nazism is the sheer number of bodies the effort spawned or called on:

The Hebrew Sheltering and Immigration Society of America

The National Co-ordinating Committee for Aid to Refugees and Emigrants coming from Germany (in cooperation with the High Commission for Refugees (Jewish and other) coming from Germany

Jewish Sheltering and Immigrant Aid Society

American Christian Committee for German Refugees

American Friends Service Committee

American Jewish Committee

American Jewish Congress

American Jewish Joint Distribution Committee

Emergency Committee in Aid of Displaced Foreign Physicians

Emergency Committee in Aid of Displaced Foreign Scholars

German-Jewish Children's Aid

We must add to those the War Refugee Board, set up in the US Treasury Department in 1944 by Roosevelt's authority, the story of which is grippingly told by Rebecca Erbelding in *Rescue Board: The Untold Story of America's Efforts to Save the Jews of Europe*. According to the jacket, it involved

... a team of D.C. pencil pushers, international relief workers, smugglers, diplomats, millionaires, and rabble rousers to run operations across four continents and a dozen countries. Together, they tricked the Nazis, forged identity papers, manoeuvred food and medicine into concentration camps, recruited spies, leaked news stories, laundered money, negotiated ransoms, and funnelled millions of dollars into Europe. They bought weapons for the French Resistance and sliced red tape to allow Jewish refugees to escape to Palestine ...

What the jacket copy does not say is that the WRB faced constant obstruction from the State Department and the opposition of the British government to some of its schemes. The British stance was that the best way to save the Jews of Europe was to win the war.

The Americans took in 1,919 refugees in 1933. The number went up by roughly a thousand a year until 1938 when it leaped from 12,012 to 44,848. And it then steadily climbed to a peak of 61,882 in 1939.

28
Calms and Storms

> Our committee met frequently and discussed each application very thoroughly. The members were all very helpful to refugees; panels of advisers for each discipline were formed quickly so that if, for example, a mathematician came I knew I could turn to Professor Hardy in Cambridge. The panel members consisted of the leading people in their profession and were all very helpful to their colleagues from abroad. (*Refugee Scholars*)

Esther's assistance went beyond the paperwork of the assistant secretary. In the 1930s she would also ask a friend of Irene Grant's from the Christian left to pick up arriving refugees and bring them to the accommodation she had arranged for them in London.

Later in life, Esther would describe with relish how she was being contacted by historical researchers wanting a picture of those desperate early days, with appeals for help and applications for assistance arriving by every post. Later still, she was to see herself as the last survivor of a celestial battle to save the scholars.

Many scholars would be taken care of through the deservedly high regard in which German universities and German scholarship were held; by their being part of the international fraternity of scholars, invitees to lecture, recipients of international prizes, attendees at international conferences, esteemed for their contributions to or reports of their work in learned journals, altogether seen as great catches.

As described in *Ark of Civilization*, the rule of 'who you know' assured the fortunate worthy (comparative) few a warm welcome and a continuing academic future.

For the deserving bur unconnected majority, Esther's gift of friendship, tenacity and administrative flair offered a lifeline when forced to relinquish and to leave behind the career, friends, society, home, wider family, language and culture that had been the substance of their lives.

The enforced emigration became a matter of international concern, leading to the establishment under the League of Nations in October 1933 of a 'High Commissioner for Refugees (Jewish and other) Coming from Germany'. An American diplomat, James McDonald, was appointed with the mandate to negotiate and direct the international collaboration necessary to resolve the economic, financial and social problem of refugees coming from Germany. He lasted two years in the post, resigning in December 1935 having concluded that:

> . . . conditions in Germany which create refugees have developed so catastrophically that a reconsideration by the League of Nations of the entire situation is essential.

His resignation letter included a coruscating summary of German policy,

> Tens of thousands are anxiously seeking ways to flee abroad . . . But except for those prepared to sacrifice the whole or greater part of their savings, the official restrictions on export of capital effectively bar the road to escape. Relentlessly, the Jews and non-Aryans are excluded from all public offices and any part in the cultural and intellectual life of Germany. They are subjected to every kind of humiliation. It is being made increasingly difficult for Jews and non-Aryans to sustain life. In many parts of the country, there is a systematic attempt at starvation. The number of suicides, the distortion of minds and the breaking down of bodies, the deaths of children through malnutrition are tragic witnesses.

The President of the United States, Franklin D. Roosevelt, called an international conference at the Hotel Royal in the French spa resort Evian-les-Bains on Lake Geneva between 6 and 18 July 1938. Thirty-two countries sent representatives – though Roosevelt sent a businessman friend Myron C. Taylor rather than any ranking official – and more than a hundred representatives of refugee organisations were also present. Poland, Hungary and Rumania were not invited. Germany, Italy and the Soviet Union chose not to attend. The United States put its immigration quota system off limits, as Palestine was for Britain.

The establishment of an Intergovernmental Committee on Refugees (ICR) to negotiate with Germany on an orderly exodus of refugees was one outcome of the conference – the agreement that it would continue to work on the refugee problem deferred any firmer conclusions. Notably, only Bolivia and the Dominican Republic agreed to take more refugees, something Hitler did not let pass without comment, Germany remarking how 'astounding' it was that the conference countries had criticised German policy towards Jews but none wanted to open their doors when the opportunity was offered.

Countries bordering Germany, France in particular, had taken the brunt[22] and the French delegate claimed his country had reached 'the extreme point of saturation as regards admission of refugees', while the British delegate averred that his country was, in effect, full while suffering from a high level of unemployment.

National established Jewish communities worked to succour their German-speaking co-religionists. Generally, though, they had to take account of the local constraints that also shaped government policy towards immigration beyond the general principle of limiting it. Commonly these included levels of unemployment consequent upon the Great Depression; the risk of exacerbating the strain of omnipresent antisemitism; competition for scarce employment opportunities; professional protectionism – as with the British Medical Association, though with this latter the situation was

---

22 As early as February 1935 the House of Lords had been told that of 35,000 unsettled German refugees in various countries, 'the vast bulk' were in France. HL Deb, 6 February 1935, vol 95 cc820–44.

far more nuanced than presented through the (in)famous adjuration from the then president of the Royal College of Physicians Lord Dawson of Penn. The number of refugee doctors that 'could usefully be absorbed could be counted on the fingers of one hand', he told the Home Secretary Sir Samuel Hoare.

In 'Medical Refugees and the Modernisation of British Medicine 1930–1960' Paul Weindling, Wellcome Trust Research Professor in the History of Medicine at Oxford Brookes University, writes:

> The medical refugees were less targets of a homogeneous and discriminatory establishment but caught in the divide on issues of the organisation, training, research, clinical outlook and public provision of health care. The situation was dynamic and rapidly changing, as dismissal and exclusion in 1939–1940 was followed in 1941–1944 by concessions and the recognition of the shortage of practitioners in a society at war.

A memorandum from Professor C. S. Gibson and Walter Adams of 24 June 1937 contemplated the future of the SPSL as well as offering a picture of the organisation at work:

> At the end of four years' work I feel that the officers of the Society for the Protection of Science and Learning should consider what policy the Society can usefully pursue in the future, and be ready to place suggestions before the Council at some opportune time in the near future. Mr. Adams and I have therefore drawn up this memorandum to facilitate an informal discussion of possible future policy.

The memorandum sets out the current position:

> Of the 1300 dismissed university teachers, 600 are still within Germany, 450 are permanently placed outside Germany, and 309 temporarily placed outside Germany. In Great Britain there are 100 permanently and 128 temporarily placed. Of the temporarily placed 64 are dependent financially on the Society; the others are dependent on the Jewish Professional Committee, local academic committees, special grants from universities or other academic institutions, or temporary posts, and very few of these are likely to need maintenance

grants from the Society in the future . . . Since the large numbers of dismissals in 1933 and after the Nuremberg legislation of 1935, there have not been many dismissals and few Germans have preferred the uncertainty of emigration to the discomfort of waiting inside Germany . . .

However, the position could change, for instance by the intensification of the persecution of Jews and 'non-Aryans'. The Society's help was called for beyond Germany:

> German scholars, Spanish scholars, Portuguese scholars, Russian scholars.
>   Political exiles from Italy and other countries Austrian, Roumanian and Polish scholars.

[*Refugee Scholars* does not mention non-German scholars and political exiles in these early years.]

Reservations are expressed over the workings of the American Emergency Committee in Aid of Displaced Foreign scholars, that while the AEC had made frequent use of the SPSL's office and information files,

> Its value as a cooperating agency in the USA is somewhat limited by the fact it can help only German scholars and only those who previously had official university positions (i.e. not younger scholars, scholars from non-university institutions etc), that it initiates no negotiations, and can make a grant only if a university initiates the suggestion, that it is not a place-finding or information service organisation, that it makes no public appeals for funds, and derives its money almost entirely from existing trusts and foundations.

A handsome tribute is paid to the *Notgemeinschaft*:

> The Notgemeinschaft Deutscher Wissenschaftler im Ausland, with its headquarters in London (for which the Society gives office accommodation) and branches in different countries, continues its activity as the most effective organisation working for the German scholars, technical experts, industrial specialists, etc. Its negotiations in S. America particularly are proving fruitful.

The memo notes positively the work of the Jewish Professional Committee, local academic committees, though their role depended on the future policy and initiative of the Society, which would also have to pick up the support of the particularly brilliant German students from the International Student Service.

The passage on the Home Office makes interesting reading:

> The Home Office and Ministry of Labour officials have come to depend for information about refugee scholars in Great Britain supplied by the office. The officials often unofficially ask the advice of the office both on individual cases and on general points. It appears the existence of the office and its information files is of value to them in their work.

The memo then gives a picture of the current activity of the SPSL, looking ahead to its possible futures:

Place finding and information service
The office, working in closest collaboration with the *Notgemeinschaft*, has steadily developed its employment and advisory service to a point where for the time being it has become far more important than the grant-making activity of the Society.

It has often proved possible to place a scholar directly from Germany without the intermediate process of a maintenance grant . . . It is this development, more than the reduction in the number of applicants, that accounts for the rapid decrease in the number of cases brought to the allocation committee.

In any policy adopted by the Society for the future it will be important to make provision for the maintenance of this service, though it must be recognised that it depends largely on the knowledge possessed personally by Mr. Adams and Miss Simpson.

Fellowships [By Nov 1937 the SPSL had set up four endowed research fellowships and was directly or indirectly maintaining eighty scholars. Numbers continued to rise. After the *Anschluss*, 200 applications were received from Austrian scholars.]

Finance . . .

Summary

The Society has sufficient funds, independently of any response there may be in July when the annual report is issued, to meet all its predictable obligations next year and to have a balance in hand of over £2,000 [£145,000 in 2022]. The period of great emergency has passed. The Society is no longer overwhelmed with legitimate applications for funds beyond its resources. Although there are still many eminent German scholars in need of re-establishment, the average quality of those outside Germany still unplaced is not high, and they include persons whose personality or whose speciality (e.g. law) make re-establishment almost impossible. Probably the continuation of the place-finding and information service and occasional grants for emigration will suffice to solve the existing problem of the displaced German scholars who have already left Germany.

Conclusions

(f) Provision must be made, both in personnel and in finance, for the continuation of the place-finding and information service not only for next year but for subsequent years.

Suggestions for consideration

I feel that the Council must now choose between a policy of contraction or expansion. If it adopts the former it should almost immediately reduce the office staff and accommodation to a skeleton service, able to continue the administration of funds in hand and to maintain a minimum of the information service work (e.g. a one room office, open three afternoons a week, with the part-time services of Miss Simpson and one typist).

If it decides to expand its activities it will be necessary to have the services, full time or part time, of Mr. Adams or another academic General Secretary, and to undertake new work:

It could take advantage of the present period of relative inactivity in its practical relief work to establish more effective organisation on an international basis to meet future emergencies, and to liquidate the existing problem.

The picture is of an agency that has passed peak activity and faces a fallow future – 'the average quality of those outside Germany still unplaced is not high', 'the present period of relative inactivity in its practical relief work'.

Four years after her 'call', Esther might have found herself making good on her belief that she could always find another post abroad.

Instead, two years of intense activity lay ahead. Less than a year after the memorandum, Hitler's annexation of Austria, the *Anschluss*, in March 1938, and the pogrom on 9 November – *Kristallnacht*, or *Pogromnacht* – that same year laid bare the brutal realities of the Third Reich's relationship with its Jews and started a mass exodus.

Four times as many enforced migrants were admitted, 40,000, as in the previous five years. The SPSL became in effect an arm's length government agency, an immigration gateway for refugee academics, particularly scientists, on behalf of the Ministry of Labour and the Home and Foreign Offices, handling entry requirements and work permits.

In Vienna, between March 1938 and August 1939, the Quaker Centre in Singerstrasse dealt with 11,000 applications for assistance in leaving, affecting 15,000 people. Detailed case papers were prepared for 8,000 families and single people; 4,500 were got away to different countries. Other figures say 6,000 cases representing 13,745 people were registered and 2,408 were able to leave – 1,588 men, 509 women, 311 dependents. Of these 1,264 went to England; 165 to the US; 107 to Australia.

Applications to the SPSL followed the pattern. 418 academics were displaced from Austrian universities, adding to the 1,400 displaced from Germany alone.

Public attention to the burgeoning refugee problem soared in 1938. In October the Lord Mayor of London, Sir Harry Twyford, opened a fund for Czechoslovak refugees. In December Lord Baldwin's fundraising broadcast-appeal for refugees raised £500,000 [nearly £40 million in today's money] by the following July. Pressure rose on the government to make refugees its concern. Beveridge noted the SPSL had to ensure its scholars were not forgotten in the rush.

The SPSL's officers formally recognised the burden this meant for Esther:

> The Council wishes to record its deep appreciation of the devoted work of the Assistant Secretary, Miss Esther Simpson, on whom a particularly heavy burden of work and responsibility has fallen during the past year.

The 9 November pogrom followed the death of a junior German diplomat in Paris, Ernst vom Rath, shot on 7 November by a young Polish Jew, Herschel Grynszpan. He was distraught at the treatment of his parents left on the border between Poland and Germany.

Following the *Anschluss*, the Polish government, fearing a mass return of Polish Jews from Germany/Austria (over half the foreign Jews living in Germany were Polish), had legislated to enable the withdrawal of citizenship from Poles who had lived abroad for more than five years. In response, on 28 October, in the so-called *Polenaktion*, the German government had ordered the round-up and deportation to the frontier with Poland of Jews with Polish passports. Grynszpan's parents in Hanover were among those chased to the border and dumped in no-man's-land at the Polish frontier.

In the House of Commons, the British Prime Minister Neville Chamberlain told MPs assembled for Question Time on 14 November that there was 'deep and widespread sympathy for those who have been made to suffer so severely' for the senseless crime committed in Paris. (He also told the House that the Government had protested to Germany about an accusation carried in Goebbels's propaganda sheet *Der Angriff* that Winston Churchill and Anthony Eden had more or less directly instigated vom Rath's murder.)

Much later, on the eve of war, Neville Chamberlain was moved to write to his sister Hilda with a much-quoted sentiment:

> No doubt Jews aren't a lovable people; I don't care about them myself; but that is not sufficient to explain the pogrom.

On 21 November 1938 the House of Commons held an emergency debate on the refugee question, opened by the Labour MP Philip Noel-Baker – 1920 Olympic silver medallist and recipient of the 1959 Nobel Peace Prize – with a horrific description of the pogrom:

What followed Grynspan's act in Germany? Every hon. Member knows the main outline of the facts. Dr. Goebbels has described it as the justifiable and comprehensible indignation of the German people. Let hon. Members think of that. Here is the 'Daily Telegraph's' first summary of what occurred: The entire Jewish population of Germany was subjected yesterday to a reign of terror. The pogroms started simultaneously all over Germany. No attempt was made by the police to restrain the savagery of the mob. Almost every synagogue in the country was burnt to the ground. Scarcely a Jewish shop escaped being wrecked. Looting occurred on a great scale. Parts of the fashionable district of Berlin were reduced to a shambles. Jews of all ages, of both sexes, were beaten in the streets and in their homes. Numbers were lynched. The caretaker of a synagogue is believed to have been burnt, with his family, to death. Let me give the House some details, which I can guarantee as facts. As part of the general destruction of Jewish institutions, a boarding school at Caputh, near Potsdam, was invaded and utterly demolished at 2 a.m. The young children were driven, without adult guidance or protection, into the night. At Bad Soden, the only Jewish home for consumptives in Germany was destroyed and sacked. The patients were driven away, wearing nothing but the shirts in which they slept. At Nuremberg the inmates of the Jewish hospital were forced to line up on parade. Some had just had serious operations, and one of them, my informant says, dropped down dead. At Ems, an asylum for aged Jews was raided, and the old people were driven out. A paralysed old man was driven from his bed, and his wife refused to leave his side. She was assaulted with an axe and her crippled husband was dragged away; at Bernsdorf, in Silesia, the boys in a Jewish camp were summoned to parade, and some 1430 were missing. A storm trooper, so says my informant, at the point of the pistol, asked a young Jew if he knew the whereabouts of the others. The young Jew was either afraid to answer or really did not know anything about it, and he was shot dead immediately. As he was lying on the ground the storm trooper kicked him with his heels.

In a concentration camp at Buchenwald, near Weimar, 70 Jews were killed during the night of 8th–9th November. That is to say, before it was known that Vom Rath was dead. Dr. Goebbels tells us that these acts were the spontaneous outbursts of national anger. In our view there would be no justification if that were true, but there is too much evidence not to think that the attacks were organised, and that they were organised in advance. In all the raids on Jewish institutions a common plan was followed, such as the cutting of the telephones, the disconnecting of the electric current, and the smashing of the central heating system before the actual assaults on the buildings were begun. British journalists are unanimous in their testimony that the attacks were not spontaneous, but, as the 'Times' said, all the indications point to centralised direction. Everywhere the police allowed them to go on. In the Fredrichstrasse district of Berlin traffic was diverted half an hour before the looting actually began.

At Questions in the Commons on Monday 21 November 1938 the Prime Minister Neville Chamberlain, fresh from Munich, had demonstrated the limitations on admitting enforced emigrants felt by his government:

In conformity with the recommendations of the Evian meeting in July last, His Majesty's Government have had under constant examination the contribution which they could make, in respect of the United Kingdom and of the Colonial Empire, to the international effort to facilitate the admission and settlement of involuntary emigrants from Germany. They have also had in mind the view expressed by the Evian countries that the country of origin should make its contribution to this problem of migration by enabling intending emigrants to take with them their property and possessions. The extent to which countries can be expected to receive emigrants must depend very largely upon the conditions in which they are able to leave their country of origin. His Majesty's Government have been greatly impressed by the urgency of the problem created by the anxiety to migrate overseas of sections of the population in Germany and of individuals who, in consequence of recent events in that country, have found temporary asylum in countries of first refuge. In the light of these circumstances and of the recommendations of the Evian meeting, His Majesty's Government have again reviewed the situation.

With regard to the United Kingdom, the number of refugees which Great Britain can agree to admit, either for a temporary stay or for permanent settlement, is limited by the capacity of the voluntary organisations dealing with the refugee problem to undertake the responsibility for selecting, receiving and maintaining a further number of refugees. His Majesty's Government are keeping in close touch with the Committee which has been set up to co-ordinate the activities of the voluntary organisations engaged upon this task. The United Kingdom has, since 1933, permitted about 11,000 men, women and children to land in this country, in addition to some 4,000 or 5,000 others who have since emigrated overseas.

As regards the Colonial Empire, it must be remembered that, although covering a great extent of territory, it is not necessarily capable of the immediate absorption of large numbers of refugees. Many of our Colonies and Protectorates and our Mandated Territories in East and West Africa contain native populations of many millions, for whom we are the trustees, and whose interests must not be prejudiced. Many large areas, which at present are sparsely populated, are unsuitable either climatically or economically for European settlement.

[As for the League of Nations mandated Palestine]:

Finally, I must mention Palestine. It is generally recognised that that small country could not in any case provide a solution of the Jewish refugee problem; but Palestine has been making its contribution. No less than 40 per cent of the Jewish immigrants entering the country during the last 12 months have come from Germany

In practice, worried by Arab unrest, the government announced a new policy on immigration to Palestine in a White Paper of 1939 on the trust territory's future status. It drastically limited Jewish immigration that had seen nearly 33,000 Jews admitted to Palestine between 1933 and 1936.

His Majesty's Government hope that the other countries represented on the Intergovernmental Committee to continue and develop the work of the Evian meeting, will also endeavour to make what contribution they can to the urgent need of facilitating emigration from Germany and from the countries of first refuge.

In conclusion, I must emphasise that, however great may be our desire and that of other countries to assist in dealing with this grave situation, the possibilities of settlement are strictly limited.

However, as mentioned earlier, the United Kingdom admitted 10,000 unaccompanied Jewish children on an emergency basis in a truly humanitarian programme initiated by the Quakers during 1938–1939. The immortal *Kindertransport*.

An American attempt in February 1939 to admit 20,000 children under the age of fourteen by the Wagner-Rodgers Bill failed twice in the Senate, the opposition citing the risk to aid for American children.

In Britain, the crucial point appeared to be that as children they did not pose any sort of challenge to employment, as the Independent Conservative MP Daniel Lipson, a former headmaster, made plain in a question to the Prime Minister on 21 November 1938:

> While thanking the right hon. Gentleman for his statement, may I ask whether the Government will be willing to consider favourably the admission into this country of young children from Germany, who will not be competing in the labour market?
>
> The Prime Minister [in his response did not say no]:
>
> We shall be having a Debate on this subject later in the day, and perhaps the matter could be discussed then.

The *London Remembers* website records the 2006 placing of a *Kinderstransport* memorial in London at Liverpool Street station.

Alongside a sculpture of children with suitcases on a railway track, the text reads:

> [On a plaque on a nearby wall:]
> Hope Square, dedicated to the Children of the Kindertransport, who

found hope and safety in Britain through the gateway of Liverpool Street Station.
Association of Jewish Refugees, Central British Fund for World Jewish Relief, 2006.

[On a plaque behind the statues:]
Children of the Kindertransport
In gratitude to the people of Britain for saving the lives of 10,000 unaccompanied mainly Jewish children who fled from Nazi persecution in 1938 and 1939.
'Whosoever rescues a single soul is credited as though they had saved the whole world.' Talmud

[To the sides of the statues are sixteen bronze blocks carrying place-names:]
Cologne, Hanover, Nuremberg, Stuttgart, Dusseldorf, Frankfurt, Bremen, Munich, Danzig, Breslau, Prague, Hamburg, Mannheim, Leipzig, Berlin, Vienna

[On a plaque attached to the railway track behind the statues:]
Frank Meisler, Arie Ovadia, 2006

And the rescue of so many children, bringing them into a safe haven, but alone and uprooted from family, society, language, remains a powerful memory.
On Thursday 1 September 2022 a memorial sculpture, *Safe Haven*, was unveiled at the east coast port of Harwich. On the webpage marking the unveiling, Kindertransport.memorial.org wrote:

The port of Harwich was the main point of entry for most of the 10,000 children who came to Britain on the Kindertransport, from December 1938 to the outbreak of war in September 1939. Nearly 2,000 children spent their first weeks at the Dovercourt holiday camp just two miles from the Harwich docks.

Safe Haven. © Ian Wolter (www.ianwolter.com)

29
Dots of Light

With the *Kindertransport*, a wave of voluntary aid committees spread across the country. In his 'The Dudley Refugee Committee and the Kindertransport, 1938–1945' (2020), in which he tracks the futures of the *Kinder* children taken on in Dudley, Richard A. Hawkins says:

> Little is known about most of the local refugee committees formed in response to the government's announcement of the Kindertransport scheme and the subsequent creation of the Lord Baldwin Fund – there were at least 170 – apart from a few in places such as Manchester, Cambridge, Gloucester, Worthing and York where records have survived.

Dudley, in the West Midlands industrial area known as the 'Black Country', was among the first such committees, formed initially at a meeting called in December 1938 by the then mayor of Dudley, Alderman A. Elliott Young. It had a link to the AAC, as Richard Hawkins explains:

> One of the reasons why the Dudley Refugee Committee was among the first wave may have been because one of the founders, [Dr Hans] Honigmann, was a refugee himself. He had studied zoology and medicine at Heidelberg University and then at Breslau University where he was awarded a doctorate in zoology and an M.D. His son Ernest later recalled that his father had worked tirelessly to help other persecuted Jews find refuge in Britain. Honigmann was the former

Reichsgesetzblatt

Teil I

1933   Ausgegeben zu Berlin, den 7. April 1933   Nr. 34

Gesetz zur Wiederherstellung des Berufsbeamtentums.
Vom 7. April 1933.

Die Reichsregierung hat das folgende Gesetz beschlossen, das hiermit verkündet wird:

§ 1

(1) Zur Wiederherstellung eines nationalen Berufsbeamtentums und zur Vereinfachung der Verwaltung können Beamte nach Maßgabe der folgenden Bestimmungen aus dem Amt entlassen werden, auch wenn die nach dem geltenden Recht hierfür erforderlichen Voraussetzungen nicht vorliegen.

(2) Als Beamte im Sinne dieses Gesetzes gelten unmittelbare und mittelbare Beamte des Reichs, unmittelbare und mittelbare Beamte der Länder und Beamte der Gemeinden und Gemeindeverbände, Beamte von Körperschaften des öffentlichen Rechts sowie diesen gleichgestellten Einrichtungen und Unternehmungen (Dritte Verordnung des Reichspräsidenten zur Sicherung der Wirtschaft und Finanzen vom 6. Oktober 1931 — Reichsgesetzbl. I S. 537 —; Dritter Teil Kapitel V Abschnitt I § 15 Abs. 1). Die Vorschriften finden auch Anwendung auf Bedienstete der Träger der Sozialversicherung, welche die Rechte und Pflichten der Beamten haben.

(3) Beamte im Sinne dieses Gesetzes sind auch Beamte im einstweiligen Ruhestand.

(4) Die Reichsbank und die Deutsche Reichsbahn-Gesellschaft werden ermächtigt, entsprechende Anordnungen zu treffen.

§ 2

(1) Beamte, die seit dem 9. November 1918 in das Beamtenverhältnis eingetreten sind, ohne die für ihre Laufbahn vorgeschriebene oder übliche Vorbildung oder sonstige Eignung zu besitzen, sind aus dem Dienste zu entlassen. Auf die Dauer von drei Monaten nach der Entlassung werden ihnen ihre bisherigen Bezüge belassen.

(2) Ein Anspruch auf Wartegeld, Ruhegeld oder Hinterbliebenenversorgung und auf Weiterführung der Amtsbezeichnung, des Titels, der Dienstkleidung und der Dienstabzeichen steht ihnen nicht zu.

(3) Im Falle der Bedürftigkeit kann ihnen, besonders wenn sie für mittellose Angehörige sorgen, eine jederzeit widerrufliche Rente bis zu einem Drittel des jeweiligen Grundgehalts der von ihnen zuletzt bekleideten Stelle bewilligt werden; eine Nachversicherung nach Maßgabe der reichsgesetzlichen Sozialversicherung findet nicht statt.

(4) Die Vorschriften der Abs. 2 und 3 finden auf Personen der im Abs. 1 bezeichneten Art, die bereits vor dem Inkrafttreten dieses Gesetzes in den Ruhestand getreten sind, entsprechende Anwendung.

§ 3

(1) Beamte, die nicht arischer Abstammung sind, sind in den Ruhestand (§§ 8ff.) zu versetzen; soweit es sich um Ehrenbeamte handelt, sind sie aus dem Amtsverhältnis zu entlassen.

(2) Abs. 1 gilt nicht für Beamte, die bereits seit dem 1. August 1914 Beamte gewesen sind oder die im Weltkrieg an der Front für das Deutsche Reich oder für seine Verbündeten gekämpft haben oder deren Väter oder Söhne im Weltkrieg gefallen sind. Weitere Ausnahmen können der Reichsminister des Innern im Einvernehmen mit dem zuständigen Fachminister oder die obersten Landesbehörden für Beamte im Ausland zulassen.

§ 4

Beamte, die nach ihrer bisherigen politischen Betätigung nicht die Gewähr dafür bieten, daß sie jederzeit rückhaltlos für den nationalen Staat eintreten, können aus dem Dienst entlassen werden. Auf die Dauer von drei Monaten nach der Entlassung werden ihnen ihre bisherigen Bezüge belassen. Von dieser Zeit an erhalten sie drei Viertel des Ruhegeldes (§ 8) und entsprechende Hinterbliebenenversorgung.

§ 5

(1) Jeder Beamte muß sich die Versetzung in ein anderes Amt derselben oder einer gleichwertigen Laufbahn, auch in ein solches von geringerem Rang und planmäßigem Diensteinkommen — unter Vergütung der vorschriftsmäßigen Umzugskosten — gefallen lassen, wenn es das dienstliche Bedürfnis erfordert. Bei Versetzung in ein Amt von geringerem Rang und planmäßigem Diensteinkommen behält der Beamte seine bisherige Amtsbezeichnung und das Diensteinkommen der bisherigen Stelle.

(Vierzehnter Tag nach Ablauf des Ausgabetags: 21. April 1933)

Reichsgesetzbl. 1933 I

The Civil Service Law in action: a school teacher is dismissed for political unreliability (Clause 4).
(© United States Holocaust Memorial Museum, courtesy of Peter Englemann)

Memorial plaque listing the names of more than fifty professors and lecturers of the University of Göttingen dismisse and forced to leave between 1933 and 1945 as a result of t racist purges carrie out by the Nazi regime. Among th included outstandi scientists Max Born, James Franc Richard Courant a Emmy Noether.
(© Simon Hornblower)

(ab*ove*) From left to right:
~~rah,~~ Ellis, Esther and
~~ael~~ Sinovitch.
Courtesy of Julia Simpson)

ght) Esther Simpson:
~~ob~~ Kramer's portrait.
*iversity of Leeds Art
'ection/Estate of John David
erts. By permission of the
sury Solicitor)*

To Esther from Jacob
August 1929

Jacob Kramer

Dr Esther Simpson O.B.E. *(© Courtesy of the* Yorkshire Evening Post*)*

In 1911, 22 Crawford Street, in Leeds' so-called Little London area, north of the city centre, was home to the whole Sinovitch family – Ellis and Sarah, Joseph, Isaac, Israel and Esther – as well as boarders Phillip Samuel, Jack Miller and Israel Vurl. *(© West Yorkshire Archives)*

Sarah and Ellis Sinovitch lived at 5 Patti Street, also in Little London, from 1918 until 1927. *(© West Yorkshire Archives)*

Professor A. V. Hill from *Refugee Scholars*.

William Beveridge in his study at University College Oxford, 1943. *(© Piemags/Alamy)*

J. G. Crowther. *(© Courtesy of Smithsonian Institution Archives)*

Director of Breslau Zoo. He had been dismissed on 31 March 1934 because of the new antisemitic laws in Germany. His friend Julian Huxley (the brother of the writer Aldous) had worked with the Academic Assistance Council, the predecessor of the Society for the Protection of Science and Learning, to secure Honigmann a research position at London Zoo in 1935, funded by private donations including £200 from Honigmann's friend the City financier Walter H. Laband, and £50 a year from the Academic Assistance Council. Honigmann was joined by his wife and three sons. In early 1937 he secured the position of Scientific Adviser at the new Dudley Zoo which opened on 18 May of that year.

Hans Honigmann continued to help other victims of Nazi persecution. In December 1938 he applied to the Home Office for permission for his cousin Antonie (Toni) Milch (née Honigmann) and her husband Dr. Werner Milch to join him in Dudley. Werner Milch was a fellow 'non-Aryan Christian' incarcerated in a German concentration camp. His only hope of release was to secure a foreign visa to allow him and his wife to emigrate. Honigmann undertook to support and maintain his cousin and Milch. Honigmann's application was supported by another, more distant, relative, the émigré nuclear scientist Professor Rudolf Peierls. It was eventually successful and the Milchs took up residence with the Honigmanns in late summer 1939.

Professor Sir Rudolf Peierls CBE, FRS, Wykeham Professor of Physics at Oxford, who was among those working to create the atomic bomb, was also an alumnus of the AAC. He was among Esther's guests, with his wife Genia, when she received her London University honorary doctorate in 1984.

It is noteworthy, Hawkins records, that of the six *Kinder* assisted by the Dudley Refugee Committee, at least five went on to study at university, among them the mathematical genius Georg Kreisel, who went from Dudley Grammar School to Trinity College, Cambridge, on an Open Major Scholarship in Mathematics. However, Hawkins remarks that, 'The experience of the Dudley Kinder was unrepresentative of the Kindertransport children as a whole.' This was possibly due to the cosmopolitan outlook of the teachers at the Dudley schools.

The common accounts of *Kristallnacht* are of antisemitic violence in public spaces and buildings, but in her autobiographical *The Ninth of November*, Hannele Zürndorfer gives a terrifying account of the pogroms reaching into her liberal-Jewish childhood home in a suburb of Düsseldorf, a city on the Rhine in western Germany, initiating a process that led inexorably to her and her sister's boarding a *Kindertransport* train away from parents, home, country, to start a new life in England.

She had already experienced a frightening change of atmosphere on the streets, with local non-Jewish children no longer her playmates; being forced to go to a Jewish school in nearby Düsseldorf; and in her home with their non-Jewish maids leaving. Now at about three or four o'clock in the morning the sound of smashing glass woke her. She and her sister went to their parents' room . . .

> Seconds later there burst into the room a horde of violent monsters, their faces contorted into raving masks of hatred . . . wild hands flailing, jackboots kicking. They were wielding sledgehammers, axes, hammers, stones and knives. They rushed about the room, smashing, throwing, trampling . . . A chair hurtled into the wardrobe mirror, glass flying everywhere.' [Her mother still in bed narrowly escaped having her legs cut off by a Brownshirt wielding an axe. Then they were gone . . .] Other images succeed each other; the piano on its side its guts ripped out and scattered on the floor like the bones and sinews of some huge animal; every single oil painting hanging in strips out of its frame or lying impaled on the spikes of upturned furniture . . . My mother's cherished collection of old china cups – not one left unbroken . . . old oak and walnut tables and chairs were legless; the carpets hacked, curtains torn down, floorboards splintered, and many windows smashed with the cold dark night crowding in.

The assault had been organised by a neighbour, a leader of the local Brownshirts who wanted to be the first to have cleared the Jews from his district, their suburb of Düsseldorf, Gerresheim. The synagogue and the adjacent Jewish school had been burned down. Hannele's father had his little bag packed – 'the bare necessities' – in case 'they' came for him.

Indeed, the question of emigration now confronted the Zürndorfer family. Hannele's father Adolf, she recounts, found it hard to contemplate. He was – or at this point had been – managing director of a publishing firm which he combined with a calling as a well-known drama critic. He had been asked to resign, and his pension was shortly to be cut. But Hannele recalled how, at that moment,

> He floundered. It meant recognizing the utter hopelessness of life in Germany. Everything he had spent his life building – a comfortable home, prospects for his family, a full and civilized life, full of friendships and the enjoyment of beautiful things and ideas – had been destroyed . . . Perhaps at sixty-four he lacked the resilience of younger men who were able to plunge impulsively into the uncertainties of a new life abroad. He could see only too clearly what it would mean to start afresh in another country at his age, without means of support, without language, and the thought that he might be dependent on the charity of others appalled him beyond anything.

He and his wife Elisabeth had the advantage of relatives in America and London. But, from Hannele's account, Adolf lingered; displacement took the form of helping others before himself. The children would be sent on ahead, though, through the *Kindertransport*.

They took the one suitcase each they were allowed on to the last but one children's train that stopped at Düsseldorf on 3 May 1939. All that Hannele retained of her English lessons in the Jewish school, she remembered, were 'good morning', 'thank you very much', 'strawberry jam' and 'porridge'.

Though they could not know it, time to follow their girls was shortening for Adolf and Elisabeth. From her father's letters Hannele reconstructs his attempts to work with the demands of German, British and American migration policy. By August 1939 success is in sight when,

> Tomorrow I will have to start from scratch all over again. The office in Cologne drew up our forms in the name of Zwidorf instead of Zürndorf and so I had to go to Cologne to the passport office and start again.

He was now spending two to three hours a day with the authorities, he wrote on 17 August, and they were having their passport photographs taken so as to be ready. He hoped peace would last, in which case they might be with the children in five or six weeks. But then he wrote to the children – now evacuated from London – that the British Consulate in Cologne had stopped working – meaning no visas, meaning their German passports were unusable.

The war was little more than a week away.

Emigration to America remained open, though it required some twenty documents from Adolf's American relatives and dollars for the passage out. They could attend the American consulate in Stuttgart only when the twenty papers were all in order, and letters from the US could take three months to arrive.

Learning to make their way as evacuees in provincial war-time England, encouraged by their hosts to become as English as possible, Hannele and Lotte were forced to keep in touch with their parents by letters sent through their American relatives; only occasional and very brief International Red Cross notes came the other way. Via America the children heard of

> complicated negotiations and repeated setbacks. They must be patient;
> the visas would be issued, the sponsors would yet be found, there was
> a possible route through Lisbon . . . or Cuba.

Up to the end of 1941, third- or fourth-hand tidings that their parents were well came from America. Then, silence . . . until 1943.

The children were informed by the Red Cross that their father, the sixty-four-year-old former publishing director, had died in 1942 of a heart attack after being deported with their mother to the ghetto of Lodz in 1941. No trace of their mother was ever to be found. It seems they had managed to take berths on a ship to Cuba, but the Nazi official in charge of their suburb had deliberately delayed their departure and had put them into the first batch of deportees from Düsseldorf.

30
And Now Visas

The initial entry framework had a certain built-in looseness allowing a more flexible approach to immigration from Germany. But that was sharply reduced in 1938 when a new requirement for entry visas was introduced. For desperate applicants this brought inevitable problems of access to consulates and dealing with the paperwork. Previously, travel from Germany had been visa-free and the Foreign Office had opposed the introduction of visas as threatening good relations with that country.

By October 1938 the Home Office system was at breaking point, representatives of voluntary organisations were told; 15,000 files were awaiting action, possibly as many as 20,000. Otto Schiff suggested calling a halt: 'Visas had created an administrative catastrophe.'

The requirement for visas, for entry or transit, also produced some truly heroic action on the ground in Germany or occupied countries.

A leading example is that of Frank Foley, the MI6 officer in Berlin, who doubled as Director of the Passport Control Office. He is said to have saved 10,000 lives by giving visas for Palestine or Britain.

Michael Smith writes in *Six: A History of Britain's Secret Intelligence Service*:

> Most wanted to go to Palestine, but the very strict quotas imposed by the British meant that few were eligible. Foley realised the danger they were in and tore up the rulebook, giving out visas that should never have been issued, hiding Jews in his home, helping them to obtain

false papers and passports and even going into the concentration camps to obtain their release.

The Spartacus Educational website[23] has an entry by John Simkin on Margaret Reid who worked for Frank Foley in Berlin. In the entry he describes the impact of *Kristallnacht* on the British Embassy:

> A journalist, James Holburn, who worked for The Glasgow Herald, reported large numbers of people outside the British Embassy: 'Desperate Jews continue to flock to the British passport control offices in Berlin and elsewhere in Germany in the hope of gaining admission to Great Britain, Palestine or one of the Crown Colonies . . . A visit to the Passport Control Office here this morning showed that families were often represented only by their womenfolk, many of them in tears, while the men of the family waited in a concentration camp until some evidence of likelihood of emigration could be shown to the Secret Police. While harassed officials dealt firmly but as kindly as possible with such fortunate applicants as had come early enough to reach the inner offices – about 85 persons were seen this morning – a far larger crowd waited on the stairs outside or in the courtyard beneath in the hope of admittance. The doors were closed and guarded much to the annoyance of Germans seeking visas, some of whom complained angrily of being forced to wait among Jews and demanded preferential treatment, though without success.

A further entry by John Simkin is on Frank Foley's role,[24] as described by his wife Kay:

> Jews trying to find a way out of Germany queued in their hundreds outside the British consulate, clinging to the hope that they would get a passport or a visa. Day after day we saw them standing along the corridors, down the steps and across the large courtyard, waiting their turn to fill in the forms that might lead to freedom. In the end, that queue grew to be a mile long. Some were hysterical. Many wept.

---

23 https://spartacus-educational.com/Margaret_Reid.htm
24 https://spartacus-educational.com/Frank_Foley.htm

All were desperate. With them came a flood of cables and letters from other parts of the country, all pleading for visas and begging for help. For them, Frank's yes or no really meant the difference between a new life and the concentration camps. But there were many difficulties. How could so many people be interviewed before their turn came for that dreaded knock on the door . . . He (Frank Foley) worked from 7am to 10pm without a break. He would handle as many applications himself as he could manage and he would walk among his staff of examiners to see where he could assist them, or give advice and words of comfort to those who waited.

As well as demanding visas, the enforced migrants' most favoured destination, the United States, was determinedly sticking to its country-based quota system established by the Congress in 1924. For Germans this was 27,370; in practice from 1933 to 1945 a third of that number were allowed in.

In late 1938, American consulates were flooded with 125,000 applicants for visas, many coming from Germany and the annexed territory of Austria. But national quotas for German and Austrian immigrants had been set and there was no budging. By July 1939, 309,000 German, Austrian and Czech Jews had applied for the 27,000 places available under the quota.

Visas came under the State Department. There the effective head of the Visa Division, Breckinridge Long, was an uncompromising antisemite and xenophobe, seeing his responsibility as to keep immigration as restricted as legally possible. Along with maintenance of the 1924 quotas, the later (1930) prohibition of entry for immigrants under the mantra 'likely to become a public charge' was used to the full.

Widespread hostility to the idea of foreigners coming to take Americans' jobs in the wake of the Great Depression also had to be taken into account.

A counter to this was the work of the New York-based Emergency Rescue Committee, set up by New York's intellectual, social and philanthropic elite and funded by donations made at a series of starry lunches and dinners. The principal concern was the fate of refugees caught in occupied France.

Article XIX of the armistice agreement in June 1940 between Germany and the Vichy government of France obliged France to 'surrender upon demand all Germans named by the German Government'. Among these were the refugees who had been waiting in France for Hitler's government to fall, Jews, political oppositionists, leading figures in the arts and literature, academics.

In Vichy France some 20,000 foreign refugees were imprisoned in the Gurs and Rivesaltes internment camps in the south-west. The Germans also deported 14,000 Jews to Gurs from Baden in Germany and from Belgium. Between 1940 and 1942, while the camps were administered by Vichy, some 2,000 Jewish inmates were released and permitted to emigrate. (Hannah Arendt, who had been briefly imprisoned by the Gestapo in 1933, was interned in Gurs in 1940 but managed to get liberation papers and leave.) These decamped to Marseilles in search of the US visa that would secure their future or a path over the Pyrenees into Spain and on to Portugal.

The fate of the remainder was death in the camps or deportation by the Germans, though an unknown number escaped. From Rivesaltes in 1942 2,313 foreign Jews were transported via Drancy to their deaths in Auschwitz and Sobibor.

To help the escape of refugees trapped in the south of France, the Emergency Rescue Committee sent a young Harvard graduate to Marseilles. Varian Fry's role was to assist the refugees to get visas and entry permits into Spain and on to Lisbon.[25]

While Walter Adams credits Esther with saving civilisation, a list of the refugees Fry rescued reads like a directory of twentieth-century culture: in his words 'the novelists, poets, painters, historians, philosophers, scientists, doctors' – as long as they were not communists.

The saved include artists Marc Chagall, André Breton, André Masson, Max Ernst, Marcel Duchamp, Jacques Lipchitz, and writers Lion Feuchtwanger and Heinrich Mann. With Fry's help Alma Mahler crossed the Pyrenees with her third husband the writer Franz Werfel (his bestselling *The Song of Bernadette* was written in gratitude to nuns who had helped him escape). Their flight symbolised the entire emptying out

---

25 The critical part played by Hiram Bingham Jr, a vice-consul in the visa section of the American consulate in Marseille, must also be acknowledged, cf. *Americans and the Holocaust*, United States Holocaust Memorial Museum – https://exhibitions. ushmm.org/americans-and-the-holocaust/personal-story/hiram-bingham-jr

of Viennese culture. Alma Mahler was carrying the score of Bruckner's Third Symphony. Fry arranged the transportation of her first husband Gustav Mahler's scores. The harpsichordist Wanda Landowska crossed, as did Hannah Arendt (who carried the text of Walter Benjamin's last work *Theses on the Philosophy of History* over the Pyrenees, after Benjamin committed suicide on being turned back from Spain; a day later he would probably have been admitted).

And nearly 2,000 others.

As this book was being written, the *New York Times* published the obituary [18 November 2021] of Justus Rosenberg who had died at 100. A Jewish boy from Danzig [Gdansk] who had been studying in Paris, he acted as Fry's runner in Marseille, delivering messages and fake documents, buying passports on the black market, accompanying Fry's escapees across the Pyrenees. He then fought with the French resistance, emigrated to the US at the end of the war, and became a languages professor at Bard College.

The émigré Russian writer Victor Serge was also in Marseilles, on his beam ends and desperate to escape France, though as a communist he could not get an American visa.

His experiences are retold in his 1946 novel *Last Times*. In his introduction (2022), Richard Greeman notes that Serge lived briefly in the Villa Air Bel, a Second Empire house just outside Marseilles, together with Fry and the surrealist writer and poet André Breton, who invited friends including Jean Arp, Marcel Duchamp and Max Ernst to play surrealist games every Sunday.

Serge named the house '*Chateau Espère-Visa*/Chateau Hope for Visa', and *Last Times* contains a powerful account of the labyrinthine processes for escape from Marseilles.

The hope was for an Ecuadorian immigration visa that might arrive in about a month, cable expenses paid.

> On what passport should he take it? The préfecture might grant a
> stateless travel paper, the American Aid Committee would support
> the application, which would have to be filed at the same time as the
> application for an exit visa, with a certificate of unfitness for military

service (cost, three hundred francs), a certificate of residence, a letter (promised) from the Abbé N. Would the Spanish transit visa be granted to a Lithuanian? . . . The Portuguese visa was contingent upon the Spanish visa and on a certificate from a steamship agency in Lisbon attesting that the price of a tourist-class passage from Lisbon to New York or Havana had been paid. The United States would probably not grant a transit visa. Cuba would demand a deposit of $500, this would be reimbursed on his departure from Cuba – but meanwhile where was he to get the money? . . . The danger is that in view of three thousand seven hundred applications, the Ecuadorian visa might expire while I'm waiting for a place on the boat. Or if it doesn't, one of the transit visas might expire, or the Spanish border might be temporarily closed.

As for Serge himself, with the help of his American publisher he managed to leave Marseilles in March 1941, sailing with other Fry refugees to Martinique, his final destination Mexico.

Consuls with humanitarian impulses could and did use their visa-issuing powers to save lives. In Lithuania, the Japanese consul Chiune Sigihara issued transit visas to over 2,000 Jewish refugees enabling them to find safety in the Far East.

Stories of other similar saviours still emerge. On 11 August 2022 the Guardian carried a 'long read' headlined 'How Bolivia's ruthless tin baron saved thousands of Jewish refugees'. The story by journalist Dan Collyns was subtitled:

He has been described as 'the worst kind of businessman', but we now know that industrialist Moritz Hochschild also rescued as many as 20,000 Jews from the Nazis.

The story told us that according to recently discovered documents from Hochschild's Bolivian companies,

Moritz Hochschild had helped to rescue as many as 22,000 Jews from Nazi Germany and occupied Europe by bringing them to Bolivia between 1938 and 1940, at a time when much of the continent had shut its doors to fleeing Jews. The documents, which included work permits and visas for European Jews, tracked Hochschild's efforts not only to ensure Jews escaped Europe but also to resettle them in Bolivia, investing his own fortune and using his influence with the country's elite to secure protection and employment for as many refugees as possible.

Many organisations emerged in Britain and the United States to assist the émigrés.

Set up in 1927 to help European Jews emigrate, HICEM[26] was formed from the merger of three Jewish migration associations and had offices in Europe, South and Central America and the Far East. In 1940 it moved its headquarters from Paris to Lisbon. The Shoah Resource Centre says,

> All in all, some 90,000 Jews managed to escape Europe during the Holocaust with HICEM's assistance.

Then there were the American-Jewish Joint Distribution Society, Jewish Aid Committee, Christians' Council for Refugees, British Committee for Refugees from Czechoslovakia, Central British Fund for the Relief of German Jewry, Central Council for Jewish Refugees, Council for German Jewry, Germany Emergency Committee (Society of Friends), German-Jewish Aid Committee, Jewish Refugees Committee, Jews Temporary Shelter, National Committee for Rescue from Nazi Terror, World Jewish Congress, German Refugee Hospitality Committee, Jewish Refugees Committee, the International Hebrew Christian Alliance, Free German League of Culture, Austrian Centre, Czech Club for the Sudeten Germans, German Lutheran Congregations.

---

26 The name HICEM is an acronym of HIAS, ICA and Emigdirect: HIAS (Hebrew Immigrant Aid Society), which was based in New York; ICA (Jewish Colonization Association), which was based in Paris but registered as a British charitable society, and Emigdirect, a migration organisation based in Berlin. See https://www.yadvashem.org/odot_pdf/Microsoft%20Word%20-%206368.pdf

And among the social and political groupings, the Communist *KPD, Union Deutscher Sozialistischer Organisationen, Sozialdemokratische Gruppe Neubeginnen, Internationaler Sozialistischer Kampfbund, Deutsche Freiheitspartei, Reichsbanner Schwarz-Rot-Gold.* (German and Austrian refugee politicians hoping to have some post-war influence on the British government were destined to be disappointed.)

Of course, the AAC/SPSL was the first port of call for up to half the 2,208 scholars who had emigrated from Germany by 1938. But only those who might be classified as the elite, of the first order, exceptional were seen to merit the AAC's full assistance, while rank-and-file academics would be helped with job-hunting funds and advice, and teachers entering on short visits would be advised to re-emigrate. By mid-1935, 148 refugee academics had temporary positions and sixty permanent. And, as we've seen, by 1940 the US had emerged as the prime host country.

It should not be forgotten that a third of all refugees who came to Britain in the 1930s came as domestic servants; more than half women. They took posts as housekeepers, companions, nannies, governesses if they were fortunate, menial domestics if not. In 1936 the number of foreign domestics increased to 8,449, twice that of the previous year; in 1937, 14,000 permits were issued. But in terms of escape from Nazi Germany, as well as persecution in Roumania [sic], Hungary and Poland, the domestic route offered a benign outcome: the middle-class was happy, costs were low, the refugee organisations – the coordination committee had a domestic bureau – enthusiastic.

So, in Germany and former Austria and the German-speaking Czech lands, Jewish managing directors retrained as butlers and gardeners, and pharmacists acquired new skills as cooks in the hope of finding a place in domestic service. Young men and women learned agricultural skills that they could take to Palestine. Kitchener Camp in Kent was a training and transit camp for this purpose, the inhabitants having undertaken to move on.

And all over the country, local relief committees were set up, such as that in Dudley.

Esther's alma mater, Leeds University, had its own Academic Assistance Committee set up in 1933 at the instance of an economics professor John Harry Jones to collect funds for academic refugees from Germany.

Later it became an outpost of the SPSL. (Esther doesn't mention it in *Refugee Scholars*.) In the Brotherton Library at Leeds University it is recorded as having

> sponsored three scholars – Dr. Robert Bloch, a Jewish botanist from Rostock who was enabled to emigrate to the United States; Dr Boris Kaufmann, a Jewish mathematician from Heidelberg who soon went to Cambridge, and Dr Lothar Richter, a Lutheran and civil servant from Berlin who subsequently had a distinguished academic career in Canada as an expert on unemployment.

And then there were the children who were consigned by desperate parents to a new life with new guardians in England by the *Kindertransport*. Among the most tragic documents of this period are the English newspaper small ads seeking an English family to take a child.

On 6 May 2021 the *Guardian* included an article by Julian Borger on the 1938 surge of classified advertisements as parents, including his own grandparents, scrambled to get their children out of the Third Reich:

> Scores of children were 'advertised' in the pages of the Manchester Guardian, their virtues and skills extolled in brief, to fit the space.

But what of women academics? The story of how The British Federation of University Women [now the British Federation of Women Graduates] 'embarked upon a unique humanitarian mission to aid their counterparts in Europe' is told in Susan Cohen's 'The British Federation of University Women helping academic women refugees in the 1930s and 1940s'.

Crucially, the BFUW set up an emergency sub-committee for refugees in 1938, after the *Anschluss*, to secure grants, jobs, research and teaching posts for women. It had its own secretary, Dr Erna Hollitscher, Holly, from Vienna, originally hired for thirteen weeks, but still with the BFUW in 1950. She called the refugees her 'little lambs'. The needy included dentists, psychologists, a physicist, a neurologist, political economists, lawyers, laboratory assistants, biologists, teachers. By 1945 the sub-committee had assisted some 400 women academic refugees.

Not changing its exclusive basic approach, the SPSL offered to assist with women applicants who were of special merit and whose academic

work should be continued. No suggestion could be made that Esther saw
any need for special measures for women graduates, or the management
for extra funding, though the American Relief Fund of the American
Association of University Women donated £3,000 [£168,328 in 2022]
between September 1940 and May 1941.

31

At the Coal Face

Nothing Esther, or Ray Cooper, tells us pictures what work on the front line of refugee assistance was like. But for something of that we can turn to Yvonne Kapp.

Born in England of German-Jewish lineage in the same year as Esther, Yvonne Kapp (1903–1999) was a writer, novelist, co-author with Margaret Mynatt of the first study of internment, *British Policy and the Refugees, 1933–1941*, and acclaimed biographer of Karl Marx's daughter Eleanor.

While waiting for her fourth and last novel, *The Houses in Between* (1938), to come out she took a job with the main Jewish refugee organisation, the Jewish Refugee Committee. In her autobiography *Time Will Tell* she has left us a vivid picture of the scenes there and of what working to secure the refugees' future meant in non-elite daily practice. Reading it, we might remember how Esther recalls the early days at Burlington House when she joined the AAC. She found that

> very many letters were reaching the Council from or about scholars
> who were being displaced in Germany and that we were also receiving
> visits from many scholars who were already in this country. We
> worked until 10 o'clock at night . . . We worked over weekends . . .

Esther herself was an experienced secretary and plainly had a gift for administration. 'Determined' is a common description by those who knew her. And while the 'work escalated quickly', we have a hint that it never went beyond the manageable when she mentions how a volunteer, Charles Milne Skepper, came to help.

> . . . [a] rich young man who was bilingual in English and French . . . It was he who put me on to having coloured cards for the different discipline: green for instance was economics, red was physics and so on, helpful things like that, because he had been trained that way.

The AAC office was also well staffed, which we will come to later.

It is five years after the above and at the Jewish Refugee Committee Yvonne Kapp has been assigned to deal with doctors and dentists in . . .

> . . . what was misleadingly called the Medical Department. This consisted of one quite small, rather dark room whose walls were lined neck-high with piles of letters from and correspondence about individual doctors and dentists desperate to come to Britain. There was no indication that they had ever been answered. However terrible their plight, all those seeking refuge here had to have a guarantor in this country . . . to ensure they did not become a charge upon the state. Doctors and dentists were not allowed to practice as such in this country. That was the problem and, as I looked more closely into these heartrending letters, I realized that, in some cases and however urgent their appeal, they were many months old.

Yvonne used small gangs of young male refugees working there to sort and classify the letters so that she could take up the cause of those not beyond help. The organisation was in urgent need of a professional administrator:

> The day-to-day running of this charitable organization had, until then, relied largely upon the services of voluntary workers: for the most part benevolent Jewish ladies of a certain age who had generously abandoned their tea parties and bridge tables to devote themselves to this cause, but who had no more idea than day-old kittens on the management of the administrative problems presented by an ever-increasing flood of German Jews, now swollen by their Austrian and Czech co-religionists, who had escaped from Nazi persecution . . . The gloomy pool of the great vestibule of the building was daily thronged with unhappy men and women who had nothing better to do and

nowhere else to go, sitting on benches and hopelessly waiting for something or other, like out-patients in a hospital for incurables.

Or perhaps waiting literally just up the road, as pictured in Louis MacNeice's 1939 poem, 'The British Museum Reading Room', where the refugee situation is caught precisely in one plangent line:

The guttural sorrow of the refugees.

A professional administrator was brought in, a retired senior civil servant Sir Henry Bunbury.

As a non-Jew he was looked upon with some disfavour by many of the good-hearted ladies who swarmed about the place and whom he started easing out.

Meanwhile, Yvonne was concentrating on her prime duty, preparing

with the utmost care, week by week, at least six cases of doctors and dentists in dire need. At the end of every Friday afternoon I would make my way to the Home Office department dealing with these matters and submit my applications. Since I had made absolutely sure that they fulfilled all the conditions laid down for the immigration of such individual, they were never refused.

Personal contact with her applicants was not part of Yvonne's scheme of things:

It took time to build up the cast-iron cases on which I worked with the help of an efficient secretary so that, unlike my predecessors – the kindest of scatterbrained ladies – I refused to receive visits from those who had safely reached England, beyond a formal meeting of welcome. It was far more important to work on trying to rescue those still in danger.

However, I did not wish to give offence and, now that the organization had moved to larger premises – a former hotel in Bloomsbury Street (and therefore known as Bloomsbury House) where the Medical Department occupied several rooms and a corridor – I arranged for one or two of the older and more mature refugees who worked in the place to intercept the callers, explain how the land lay, and give them friendly and helpful advice.

While early on in the refugee crisis, Yvonne recounts, doctors had been allowed to requalify in Edinburgh, that facility was speedily withdrawn and the medical profession set its face totally against foreign doctors practising, no matter how well qualified.

In the summer of 1939 a small chink was opened in this blockade, with the Royal Colleges agreeing that a committee of the most eminent medical practitioners could admit fifty refugee doctors to practice.

Yvonne had some 3,000 refugee doctors on her books, but with the assistance of her own allocation committee of two highly qualified medical men, both Jewish, two selections of fifty doctors each were made for consideration by a practice committee. One 'whose impartiality', Yvonne remarks,

> had been badly shaken at the outset when its members were bombarded by those who, at one time or another, had treated in some foreign spa or in their private sanitaria a minor royalty or other persons of social influence and now expected to be singled out for recognition and reward.

The outbreak of war brought the necessary recognition that all refugee doctors should be allowed to practice. Yvonne's Medical Department was wound up. But she had already been seconded to the government-funded Czech Trust (The British Committee for Refugees from Czechoslovakia, later the Czech Refugee Trust Fund), from which she was abruptly ejected in 1940, on MI5's advice, as a communist. With invasion feared, the 1939 Nazi-Soviet pact made all communists objects of suspicion.

Reds under the dossiers would also play a part in Esther's future. Meanwhile, the AAC had prepared to take on a political role.

32
Advancing to the Future

From its first days, the AAC stands out as a tightly focused relief organisation, hewing to its core purpose of saving excellence while still devising means to help the less eminent of its applicants.

In 1936 it changed its name, and widened its public purpose, from the Academic Assistance Council to The Society for the Protection of Science and Learning, thus allowing it to play its part in promoting the cause of academic freedom.

The 2021 CARA website, relating its history, quotes Lord Rutherford in its account of the name change:

> By 1936, it was clear that a new, more formal, structure was needed to take over the AAC's work. Rutherford explained the rationale in an open letter in 'Science' (Vol 83, No 2155, 17 April 1936):*The council hoped that its work might be required for only a temporary period, but is now convinced that there is need for a permanent body to assist scholars who are victims of political and religious persecutions. The devastation of the German universities still continues; not only university teachers of Jewish descent, but many others who are regarded as 'politically unreliable' are being prevented from making their contribution to the common cause of scholarship.*
>
> As a result, he announced the creation of a permanent successor, the Society for the Protection of Science and Learning (SPSL). In a joint letter on the same page, Albert Einstein, Erwin Schrödinger and Vladimir Tchernavin paid tribute to the work of the AAC in its three

short years: *The warm sympathy extended to all who approached the Academic Assistance Council has helped in hundreds of cases . . . The Academic Assistance Council is coming to an end in its emergency form, but we and our friends will endeavour to make it remain unforgotten. May we hope that the continuation of our scientific work – helped in no small measure by its activities – will be an expression of our gratitude?*

The phrase 'warm sympathy' might have been written as a direct description of and tribute to Esther.

The change in name and vision came very much at the urging of the Nobel laureate scientist who had become a central figure in the management of the SPSL and in Esther's future.

A full biography of Archibald Vivian Hill is sadly lacking, though his eighty-page obituary for the Royal Society by his former student Sir Bernard Katz gives a full and engrossing account of his life, character and many achievements. A highly informative overview is also to be found, and has been drawn on in what follows, in 'Nobel Laureate A. V. Hill and the refugee scholars, 1933–1945' by Jack A. Rall in the American Physiological Society's *Advances in Physiology Education* 2017. A. V. Hill was a physiologist with a background in mathematics who was awarded the Nobel Prize for physiology or medicine in 1922 jointly with German scientist Otto Meyerhof, who himself became a displaced academic. Hill, who was married to John Maynard Keynes's sister Margaret, was biology secretary of the Royal Society and a founding officer of the AAC.

His own research career spanned sixty years and three future Nobel laureates trained with him. He believed passionately in the freedom of science and learning and that the purpose of the AAC went beyond assisting displaced academics into new posts to maintaining the freedom of academics to work as they could.

As early as November 1933, in a lecture given in Birmingham, A. V. Hill made clear his understanding that the displacing of German academics was a matter of far-reaching political substance:

Germany, however, has lately rendered such intellectual co-operation impossible by offending the first and most fundamental rule, that providing freedom of thought and research . . . It seemed impossible in a great and highly civilized country, that reasons of race, creed, or opinion . . . could lead to the drastic elimination of a large number of the most eminent scientists and scholars, many of them men of the highest standing, good citizens, good human beings. This, nevertheless, has happened: the rest of the world of learning is gasping and wondering what to do about it. Freedom itself is again at stake.

And in 1935, at a time when British tourists were flooding into Germany to see (and often vocally admire) the new regime's works, he refused an invitation to participate in an international sports medicine congress in Berlin, linked to the forthcoming 1936 Olympics. He insisted it would be too distasteful for him to go 'when Jewish and other colleagues were being persecuted'.

In the same year he was invited to join a committee that would make a vital contribution to Britain's technical ability to fight in the Second World War: the Tizard Committee for the Scientific Survey of Air Defence. The chairman was Sir Henry Tizard (1885–1959), the scientific adviser to the Air Ministry. The committee was concerned with the development of radar.

Hill was not new to government service: already in the First World War he had directed an Anti-aircraft Experimental Section of mathematicians and scientists within the Munitions Inventions Department of the Ministry of Munitions (1915), bringing science to bear on the problem of shooting down moving aircraft.

Crucially for the refugee cause, Hill became a member of parliament – at that time the only MP to have been a Nobel Prize winner.

He stood for one of the Cambridge University parliamentary seats as an independent Conservative in a by-election on 23 February 1940. He took 64.6 per cent of the popular vote (if that is the right phrase for an electorate exclusively of Cambridge graduates) against his opponent the Regius Professor of Physic John Ryle, standing as an Independent Progressive. Professor Ryle had also been active in helping displaced German academics. The university had hoped that Keynes would stand. He declined and the opportunity was passed to his brother-in-law.

While in no sense a professional politician, Hill's urbanity, penetrating intelligence and wit were a gift to the war-time House of Commons. They were on full display in the debate on the refugee problem of 19 May

1943 [Hansard Vol 389], centring on what should be done to answer the situation caused by the Nazi massacre of the Jews – immediate help to those in immediate danger, as Hill put it. He chided the Home Secretary for the government's delay – and in words that have a sadly perennial feel to them:

> If the Home Secretary were to see a drowning child in a pond he would jump in at once to save it regardless of his clothes. He would not argue that he had saved other children already, or that the shipping position made it necessary for him to be careful of his trousers, or that it was essential first to call a conference of all those others who might equally well jump in, or even say that some people do not like children anyway. He would forget his dignity and past virtues, he would forget his trousers, he would forget other people's obligations, he would forget his rich uncle who does not like children, and would go straight into the pond . . . To count the probable cost too closely or too long is to deny the common humanity which no community, great or small, can afford to give up if it is to hold together.

He dealt with the government's position that the best/only way to help the Jews was to win the war, and ended by looking ahead to the challenge common humanity would set the victors:

> The task of rescue from Nazi massacres is only the beginning or the end of the beginning. The much greater task lying before us is restoring shall we say 50,000,000 refugees to their homes all over the world and of bringing back order and civilization to a distracted world.

When war came, Tizard had asked Hill to go to the United States and Canada to promote the possibility of exchange of ideas and technology in the war effort. In March 1940, before taking his parliamentary seat, Hill sailed to America. Upon his return to London in June, he produced two key reports that advocated free exchange of information with the United States and Canada regarding the development of technology for the war effort.

A. V. Hill was a man of warmth, wisdom and wit, who made time to become a governor of Highgate School in north London, a short walk from where he lived in leafy Highgate Village. His wife was active in setting up philanthropic housing in the same area. A Jewish refugee found a home with them in the years before the war.

One of his future Nobel-winning students, Sir Bernard Katz, wrote in his obituary for the Royal Society in 1977:

> . . . committed though he was throughout his life to work in the laboratory, it was his concern for others, the encouragement he gave to young colleagues, his upright defence not only of the cause of science, but of scientific men who had been driven from their places of work and needed help, in short it was his devotion to such wider issues, outside the boundaries of his own research, through which he exerted his most important influence on other people's lives and on the course of events.

Sir Bernard also called him, 'The most naturally upright man I have known.'

After the war, A. V. Hill returned to his laboratory at University College and to active research at the age of fifty-nine, producing a stream of research papers that ended only in 1970 with the publication of a monograph entitled *First and Last Experiments in Muscle Mechanics* at the age of eighty-four. His generosity in supporting and bringing on younger colleagues is clearly on show in any account of Tess Simpson's life. As she wrote to him on 26 September 1976 in anticipation of his ninetieth birthday,

> Looking forward to your ninetieth birthday I look back, with so much gratitude, on our long friendship. I think of the immeasurable help you have given to innumerable people at times of anguish and stress, and not only to 'our' scholars and their families. With wonder I think of your great kindness to me over the years, of your unobtrusive thoughtfulness and consideration – and of your humour, which enlivened so many sessions of our various committees . . . I have no really adequate way of expressing my appreciation, and that of countless others, for all you have meant in our lives, so I just thank you, and hope we shall celebrate many more of your birthdays.

If there is a moral to this as a story of refugees, it must be left to A. V. Hill, as quoted in Norman Bentwich:

> Tolerance and intellectual freedom cannot be established once for all
> in human society, but demand continual watchfulness and effort.

That watchfulness and effort were to be called for from the SPSL in its next
major challenge – and triumph – internment.

33

Don't Collar the Lot

With the outbreak of war, the SPSL office was evacuated to Cambridge, first to rooms in King's College, then the Scott Polar Research Institute, then in the Appointments Board, this itinerant life nothing new.

Esther found yet another room; this one, according to the 1939 Register, with the Baster Household, St Andrew's, 99 Chesterton Lane. Eight people were recorded as living there, including three private secretaries.

The outbreak of war meant the effective end of the influx of refugees from Germany, Austria, Czechoslovakia. Work continued on finding posts or creating opportunities for those already in Britain. The allocation committee continued to meet, though without Beveridge, now in Oxford as Master of University College. A. V. Hill's laboratory closed and he was occupied with war work.

But the British debacle in Norway and the German lightning invasion of the Low Countries and France in May 1940 brought in their trail a new challenge for the SPSL and for Esther in particular, one that she met magnificently: Britain's internment of 'enemy aliens'.

Internment was not a novel expedient, though historically seen as a distasteful one. In the First World War, some 30,000 German and Austrian enemy aliens had been interned, starting almost immediately after war was declared, many were not released until 1919.

In 1940, fear of a German invasion prompted the government into mass internment of 'enemy aliens', among whom, of course, were the

SPSL's newly placed displaced academics. The German refugees were not stateless but had travelled to the UK on German passports and retained their German nationality, if not naturalised.

They retained that nationality until 25 November 1941 and the 'Eleventh Decree to the Law on the Citizenship of the Reich' of that date. This laid down that Jews living outside Germany could not be German citizens.

In 1933 2,274 refugees had come from Germany. By 1939, at least 50,000 had come, though in 1943 the War Office declared that there had been 78,000 émigrés in Britain in 1939.

Initially, sentiment was against a First World War-style mass internment. But with the coming of war, the new coalition government instituted an aliens' control policy under the Emergency Powers (Defence) Act of 1939, passed in the last month of peace. This instituted 112 dedicated Tribunals to assess the risk posed by enemy aliens over the age of sixteen (including Italians after 10 June 1940, when Mussolini declared war) whom they allocated to three categories:

> Class A: those whose loyalty and reliability were doubted and who might constitute a present security risk. They were to be arrested and interned immediately.

> Class B: Aliens whose loyalty was not absolutely certain. They should be exempt from internment but subject to personal restrictions and kept under supervision. They were not allowed to move further than five miles from their homes without police permission nor to be in possession of cameras, maps, field glasses, arms, etc.

> Class C: All those whose loyalty was not doubted. They were free from restrictions.

The government stated that only between 1,000 and 1,500 enemy aliens, a little over 1 per cent of the 70,000 aliens, would be interned.

The Security Service, whose principal concern was communist spying after the Molotov-Ribbentrop Non-Aggression Pact of 23 August 1939, grumbled that the system was too lax.

The Tribunals, much criticised historically for their variable quality, began their work in October during the so-called 'phony war'. By the end of 1939, they had reviewed 73,000 cases, allocating 64,200 to Class C and only 1 per cent, 569, to Class A.[27]

Then, from early May 1940, with the *Blitzkrieg* bringing German forces up to the Channel coast, threatening invasion as Hitler's next move, this tempered approach went into a sudden reverse. Broad-based internment of enemy aliens became policy.

First, on 15 May the arrest was ordered of all male refugees in Class B between the ages of sixteen and sixty, followed by women in Class B at the end of the month.

Then, following the Dunkirk evacuation between 26 May and 4 June 1940, the declaration of war by Mussolini on 10 June, and the French surrender on 22 June, the mass round-up was ordered of 25,000 men and 4,000 women in Class B; and, finally, all remaining Class C German and Austrian enemy aliens between the ages of sixteen and seventy.

Some 4,500 Italians were taken on Churchill's order, many of whom had been resident and working in Britain for years.

Excluded were those with important functions in the war economy and/ or under the special protection of a ministry. Several thousand would be shipped to Canada and Australia.

As to the decision to go for mass internment, the story is one of pressure from the military, the chiefs of staff and the Joint Intelligence Committee on an unwilling Home Secretary that ended in his defeat and the ceding of authority by the Home Office to the War Office.

---

27 This is still a live issue for families of the interned. As this book was being written, a moving discussion on the fairness of Class A classifications and internment took place on Tony Hausner's 'interned-on-iom' Google group. Rachel Pistol, historical adviser to World Jewish Relief, wrote: 'There certainly was a postcode lottery with the tribunals, with certain areas giving more A or B classifications than others. Overall, the average percentage of Category A given within all tribunals in the UK was 0.8%. Out of the 91 different tribunals in the UK, only 11 of them classified more than 2% of those who came before them as category A. There is no way to separate those who were Jewish from those who weren't as part of the data. There were many reasons an individual could be classified as A. It is important to remember that the British were most concerned about who was pro-British, rather than who was anti-Nazi.'

On 4 June Churchill spoke to the House of Commons, describing in detail how a German 'scythe-stroke' had culminated in the Dunkirk evacuation.

> Nevertheless, our thankfulness at the escape of our Army and so many men, whose loved ones have passed through an agonising week, must not blind us to the fact that what has happened in France and Belgium is a colossal military disaster.

The Prime Minister moved on to discuss the question of home defence against invasion, including putting

> ... our defences in this island into such a high state of organisation that the fewest possible numbers will be required to give effective security ...

And this meant internment.

> We have found it necessary to take measures of increasing stringency, not only against enemy aliens and suspicious characters of other nationalities, but also against British subjects who may become a danger or a nuisance should the war be transported to the United Kingdom. I know there are a great many people affected by the orders which we have made who are the passionate enemies of Nazi Germany. I am very sorry for them, but we cannot, at the present time and under the present stress, draw all the distinctions which we should like to do. If parachute landings were attempted and fierce fighting attendant upon them followed, these unfortunate people would be far better out of the way, for their own sakes as well as for ours.[28]

The undifferentiated mass of enemy aliens – refugees, victims of Nazi violence, business people, lawyers, artists, shopkeepers, waiters, journalists, factory workers, intellectuals, scholars – found themselves, Jews and non-Jewish political opponents alike, living cheek by jowl with avowed Nazi supporters, sharing the holiday camps, unfinished council housing estates, race-tracks, derelict factories, a circus's winter quarters, schools, barracks,

28 HC Deb, 4 June 1940, vol 361 cc787–98.

prisons, any accommodation that the authorities could rustle up at such short notice to serve as immediate transit camps on the way to internment proper.

Beveridge reflected,

> Practically all our 500-odd academic refugees from Germany, Austria, Italy disappeared overnight. Our academics were about one in fifty of all the internees on this occasion.

On the other side of the channel, the SS was drawing up its list of refugees to be arrested post-invasion, known as the *Black Book* of over 2,000 names.

After Dunkirk, the nation's impoverished defences had been put on an anti-invasion footing. The German planning under the rubric 'Operation Sea Lion' was known to British Intelligence from Czech intelligence sources. That the German navy, the *Kriegsmarine*, had severe doubts over attempting an opposed channel crossing without German control of the air – a superiority never achieved – was not.

Churchill's famous speech on 4 June 1940 predicting resistance beyond *the beaches, the landing grounds* . . . actually anticipated the invasion forces landing successfully and progressing inland, meaning: *we shall fight in the fields and in the streets, we shall fight in the hills* . . .

Fearful memories of how French refugees had clogged roads prompted the immortal 'Keep calm and carry on' invasion poster, happily never officially issued for use.

Later that year, the chiefs of staff decided evidence of an immediate threat of invasion warranted sending out the code word for 'Invasion Imminent' – *Cromwell* – putting defensive forces on full alert. At seven minutes past eight in the evening of 7 September, General Headquarters transmitted *Cromwell*, bringing all home defence forces to 'immediate action'. It was cancelled the following morning.

But the authorities, and the public, were anticipating a threat at home as well as from across the channel.

Drawn from Franco's successes in the Spanish Civil War, particularly the capture of Madrid, the idea of a 'Fifth Column' of civilian Nazi sympathisers assisting the invasion forces was a potent one. Rumours were rife of active spy networks preparing the way for the landing forces.

A thousand-word report by London's freshly escaped Envoy Extraordinary and Minister Plenipotentiary to The Netherlands, Sir Nevile Maltby Bland, described in horrific detail how German paratroopers abetted by Dutch fifth columnists had overwhelmed Dutch defences. It called for the immediate internment of German refugees as potential fifth columnists:

> We cannot afford to take this risk. ALL Germans and Austrians, at least, ought to be interned at once.

The popular press demanded the safeguarding of the realm from the Germans living in its midst. Internment now!

The Home Secretary Sir John Anderson was not much in favour of mass internment, but the military chiefs were, together with the Security Service MI5. Challenged on the unlikelihood of Jewish refugees assisting the *Wehrmacht* and the SS (with the threat of its *Black Book*) they would have replied that however unlikely that assistance might seem, the threat of pressure on any family and friends remaining in Germany could work unfortunate wonders on the most grateful of refugees.

President Roosevelt made the point at a news conference held after France, with its army of 117 divisions, had fallen in six weeks; a defeat blamed by apprehensive Americans on fifth columnists and spies. And, said Roosevelt, as quoted in Rebecca Erbelding's *Rescue Board*, among refugees were some spies, as other countries had found:

> And not all of them are voluntary spies – it is rather a horrible story, but in some of the other countries that refugees out of Germany have gone to, especially Jewish refugees, they have found a number of definitely proven spies . . . The refugee has left Germany and then has been told by the German government, 'You have got to conduct this particular spy work and if you don't make your reports regularly back to some agent in the country you are going to – we are frightfully sorry but your old father and mother will be taken out and shot.

No cases are recorded in Britain of refugees spying for Germany – for the Soviet Union is another matter – though an MI5 agent posing as a Nazi successfully entrapped the Austrian-born naturalised Briton Hans

Kohout, who was attempting to pass air defence secrets to the Gestapo. But after Dunkirk, with the *Wehrmacht* seemingly poised to bring its *Blitzkrieg* strategy to British beaches, fields and streets, anxieties ran high across the country.

In 'Fifth Column Fears in Richmond 1939–1940: A Brief Survey', an article in the *Richmond History Journal*, historian Steven Woodbridge notes:

> Even refugees who had escaped from Nazi persecution and taken jobs in Britain came under deep suspicion as there were fears that some of them might be Nazi spies or potential collaborators in the event of invasion . . . As the news from the Continent became more and more gloomy, the local press tended to stoke such fears as to who could be trusted and who could not . . . On the 18th May 1940 the Richmond Herald in a weekly column penned by the mysterious 'Mr X' asserted, 'By this time everyone has heard of Hitler's Fifth Column. It consists of German spies and English traitors . . . Make no mistake. It is right here in your midst.

The atmosphere of suspicion reached into the Rickmansworth home to which the *Kindertransport* refugees Hannele Zürndorfer and her younger sister Lotte were evacuated from Hampstead. A postcard written in German had arrived:

> Mr H confiscated the card without letting us see it. He wasn't going to have anything of this sort in his house! How did he know we weren't spies? I suppose he thought that if German paratroopers could disguise themselves as nuns – as they were then rumoured to do – a team of dwarf spies might be disguised as children. At any rate, he continued quizzing us whenever we were in his presence, taking great care not to discuss anything to do with the war in front of us.

And when Hannele and Lotte joined a crowd in their local high street waving and cheering lorry loads of newly uniformed soldiers on their way to the coast:

> Suddenly I heard a woman say to another, 'Look at those two little Germans. What are they doing here? The cheek of it, cheering our soldiers. It oughtn't to be allowed. It ought to be stopped.

'Collar the lot', in the phrase attributed to Churchill, would have seemed reasonable. Though Peter and Leni Gillman, who popularised the attribution in their 1980 study of internment by the same name,[29] amplified their use of the phrase in a letter to the *Guardian* on 29 August 2019:

> The internment of 27,000 'enemy aliens', principally German, Austrian and Italian, occurred mostly at the height of the fifth column scare that followed the fall of France. Most were refugees, around two-thirds of them Jewish, but they also included German, Austrian and Italian nationals who were resident in Britain. When reviewing government papers while researching our book on the subject, we found no evidence that the policy was driven by antisemitism. The predominant fear was that this group might contain spies or saboteurs; and when one internment camp officer discovered that most of his charges were Jewish, he exclaimed: 'Dammit – I knew we'd got the wrong lot.' The British government soon began vetting the internees and releases started within three months; 10,000 had been freed by the end of 1940, although a further 6,000 had been deported to Canada and Australia, where many of them decided to stay. Your report cites Churchill as giving the order 'Collar the lot!' to start the arrests. It is not clear whether he said this or whether it was attributed to him as a paraphrase. However, we did adopt the phrase as the title of our book, first published in 1980.
> **Peter and Leni Gillman**
> *London*

If 'Collar the lot!' is to join 'Panic, what panic?' in the lexicon of prime ministerial-quotes-they-never-uttered, it is to be hoped the story will survive of Churchill's shock at the disappearance of familiar Italian waiters in his favourite restaurant, Quaglino's.

In fact, the lot were not collared. While an elderly German professor of ancient Greek philology was taken from his bed to a transit camp, a refugee weaver of webbing belts for the army in a clothing factory in Wales remained at work.

---

29 *'Collar the Lot!' How Britain Interned and Expelled its Wartime Refugees*, Quartet Books, 1980.

The press described the SWOOP ON GERMANS IN BRITAIN as an anti-fifth column measure – reporting that on 16 May Scotland Yard had brought in 2,000 internees within an hour of starting the round-up – and quoted the Home Office announcement:

> The Home Secretary has as a further measure of precaution directed the temporary internment throughout Great Britain of all male Germans and Austrians over the age of 16, and under the age of 60, whose present classification as a result of examination by a local tribunal or regional advisory committee is 'B'; that is to say who though exempted hitherto from internment have been required to comply with special restrictions.

The immediate destinations for the internees were transit camps, cobbled together at the last moment. Some, such as closed holiday camps, were tolerable. Others, like the notorious derelict cotton mill Warth Mills at Bury and closed racecourses (Kempton Park and Lingfield), were downright inhumane. The final destination was the Crown Dependency of the Isle of Man, usually described as windswept and in the Irish Sea, with its many hotels and boarding houses, and its heritage of First World War internment camps from 1915 to 1919.

The island accommodated so-called camps – areas of hotels and boarding houses that were surrounded with double rings of barbed wire. The names that have gone down in history include Hutchinson, Onchan, Sefton; 10,000 men in nine camps. Four thousand women and children were in Rushen across the island from the men's camps.

For Churchill, the Isle of Man was not far enough. He came to an agreement with Canada and Australia that they would take 7,000 and 6,000 internees respectively, in the event all male.

In one respect, the transported internees could have been fortunate: were Germany to have mounted a successful invasion, they at least would have been beyond the reach of the SS and the Gestapo.

In other respects, the transportation was a blot on British government: the internees' status was confused with their being prisoners of war. They were transported in company with Nazis, Nazi sympathisers and actual POWs. And, tragically, those on the *Arandora Star*, en route to Canada,

were torpedoed by a German U-boat on 2 July with the loss of 800 lives –
700 internees and 100 crew. The dead internees included eighty of the 254
former passengers from the ill-fated German cruise ship *St Louis* who had
finally been allowed to enter Britain (many then interned) after the ship
had been turned away from the Americas.

2,542 internees were shipped to Australia on what became known as the
'Hell ship', the *Dunera*, with both inhumane living conditions and savage
treatment on board, the internees being robbed of personal possessions by
their British Army guards, some of whom were later charged, including
their commanding officer. Churchill later described the *Dunera* ordeal as
'a deplorable and regrettable mistake'.

One of the *Dunera* internees, Heinz Lippmann (1921–2004), an electrical
engineering student who escaped from Berlin at the last moment, leaving
his family behind, commented to the Australian Sea Museum:

> There is tremendous pressure from not knowing, when actually you
> are alone and homesick. You left your place, you left your country, you
> left your people and you're uncertain what happened to them. All that
> I had was my friends. And we [Dunera] boys, we stuck together, till
> now. That created a bond of very strong friendship, cause I've been
> together with these boys from Berlin till today. And we still stick
> together . . . if you keep on looking at the sad side, if you look only at
> documents, it's very miserable. But if you look at what you can really
> do and how you can pull yourself out of misery, even at the worst
> possible moments, that is really something you can learn from.
> Something good can come out of it.

In a 1985 article in the *New Yorker* magazine recalling his internment
experiences, the Nobel laureate Max Perutz spoke for them all,

> Having first been rejected as a Jew by my native Austria, which I loved,
> I now found myself rejected as a German by my adopted country.

Having been uprooted from their native land, the internees were now
uprooted a second time from their safe haven; 4,000 to Canada and 2,000
to Australia.

A Quaker observer from the Friends Relief Service, William Hughes, who had been expelled from Germany for helping Jewish families, noted the troubles of the ordinary internee in West Huyton: close confinement behind barbed wire was combined with insufficient privacy; complete separation from family and family life; and lack of work and occupation. The camps were, he noted, all overcrowded and understaffed. Leaders, Hughes observed, lived strenuous and busy lives, but the rank and file were suffering from lack of occupation.

Not so the academic, professional and artistic occupants, who had the blessing of cultural interchange with similar fellow internees – while well-placed British colleagues agitated for their release.

They set up a now famed 'university', with courses on maths, physics, law, economics and languages. The brilliance of the internees who participated and their memorable activities in the 'university' across so wide a range of cultural and academic callings, the subject of many a contemporary lecture or exhibition, risks blanking out the horrors of internment for the rest.

At the time, Hughes was impressed by the internees' educational activities in Hutchinson Camp ('The most elite university in the world in terms of the pool of scholars it contained', according to the introduction to *Ark of Civilization: Refugee scholars and Oxford University 1930–1945*). Also impressive were the physical training at the Metropole, the production of *Julius Caesar* in English and in modern dress at the Sefton, and the home farm at the Sefton. A great demand existed for lecturers on the English way of life.

As for the women's camps, the Quaker observer Margaret Collyer noted that the beautiful weather and the sense of novelty helped to balance the difficulties of the early days. But the gay images of the front at Port Erin hardly suggested what lay behind: personal anxiety about relatives, the sense of injury at being interned, the renewed sense of insecurity, the incompatibility of various people, the lack of money, possessions and work; for those with relatives in the cities, anxieties at their fate in the Blitz.

The internees' sense of indignity is caught exactly in a widely quoted poem by one of the '*Dunera* Boys', internee no. 35271 Oswald Volkmann at Tatura Camp, Victoria, who was said to have been a First World War fighter pilot alongside the Red Baron. Caustically the author notes the internees have long been Hitler's enemies. Now they are the King's

Most loyal internees.[30]

On the other side of England, in a Cambridge denuded of most loyal interned scholars, internment and the campaign for the release in the national interest of the (selected) interned meant Esther's hour had truly struck.

---

30 Copyright the Estate of Oswald Volkmann.

34

Esther's Hour

The internment crisis lasted from June 1940 to mid-1943 when releases came to an end. The round-up caught refugees and refugee organisations by surprise. Esther records in *Refugee Scholars* how she was staying with friends for the weekend when she heard the news. She returned immediately to Cambridge and took part in the meetings of the Refugees Association to discuss what steps to take. She was distressed to find that some participants were on the side of the government, one feeling that the round-up had not included enough women, for instance, and another that sixteen-year-olds could be Nazis.

She wrote an immediate letter of protest to the Home Office, pointing out how the SPSL's refugees were well-known public figures, but received no answer.

It took the return of A. V. Hill from his Tizard Committee visit to the United States for the SPSL's voice to be heard in the campaign for the release of the non-Nazi internees. It would be difficult to imagine anyone not actually in the Cabinet better placed to bring pressure on the government over internment. [Though Bentwich records that Maynard Keynes personally achieved the release of four economists: P. Sraffa, E. Rothbart, H. W. Singer, E. Rosenbaum. Rothbart died at Arnhem.]

Hill's standing as a leading member of the Royal Society and Nobel laureate, as well as adviser on air defence, underpinned his opportunities as a backbench MP to make a case direct to government for the release of those internees who, in the broadest sense, could contribute to the war effort.

He was not alone. A. V. Hill was one of a small number of MPs who regularly harassed the Home Secretary over the continuation of internment and the conditions experienced by the internees. Among them was Eleanor Rathbone (1872–1946), who sat as an Independent for the Combined English Universities seat from 1929 to her death in 1946. She became known as the angel of refugees.

In a Commons debate on the deadly situation of the Jews in German-controlled Europe on 19 May 1943, Hill named her the 'patron saint of refugees'. In 1943 she formed the National Committee for Rescue from Nazi Terror, of which A. V. Hill became a member, and published *Rescue the perishing: a summary of the position regarding the Nazi massacres of Jewish and other victims and of proposals for their rescue: an appeal, a programme and a challenge*; five editions were published in 1943 in English and German. Also *Continuing terror; how to rescue Hitler's victims, a survey and a programme*.

Immigrant organisations and refugee committees of all persuasions had gone into action immediately on behalf of the interned, supporting them with donations of money and goods. Between 10 July 1940 and 2 February 1941 a perturbed House of Commons held full debates on internment on 10 July, 23 July, 22 August and 3 December. Beveridge noted,

> Fourteen hours of parliamentary time devoted to the interests of enemy aliens in the year of greatest danger that Britain has ever known.

Regular questions were also put to the Home Secretary, Sir John Anderson, who made it plain in August that the policy was at the instigation of the military leadership, and to his successor from October 1940, Herbert Morrison. The Home Office would take over administration of the camps with the War Office responsible for security.

Concern was cross-party. Eleanor Rathbone and A. V. Hill were Independents; Graham White Liberal; Victor Cazalet and Viscount Wolmer Conservative; Josiah Wedgwood Labour. Colonel Cazalet, Colonel Wedgwood and Graham White were members of the Commons committee on refugees, visiting the internment camps and harrying the government on conditions and on release in the five debates on internment in 1940–1941.[31] In the House of Lords, Bishop Bell added the weight of the established Church.

Those calling for an immediate review of the internment policy were kicking at an open door. On the question of release, the issue for the administration was not if but how, who and how soon. By the end of July 1940, the Home Office issued a White Paper proposing eighteen categories of internees to be released, focusing on those who could contribute to the war effort. The following month, Churchill called for a less rigid attitude in regard to the internment of aliens. At the end of August, a second White Paper proposed the release of those who had distinguished themselves by political or journalistic work in the struggle against fascism. Then, in October, a third White Paper added artists, scientists and writers, together with students and long-term residents unfit for service with the Auxiliary Pioneer Corps, for which enemy aliens were eligible: digging latrines rather than trenches.

By the beginning of 1941, 8,700 internees would be released. Only some 5 per cent of the internees were refugee scholars, including scientists, but the scholars' principal advocate gave them a voice out of all proportion to their numbers.

Just as in the 1930s, the Home Office had sub-contracted academic refugee admission procedures to the AAC/SPSL, so now, in the summer of 1940, the administration gave the learned societies a key role in the process of internees' release in the national interest. The echo of corridor conversations is to be heard here. Hill had paved the way with the Home Office in June, writing to ask if the SPSL could submit a list of internees for whose integrity and academic worth it could vouch. The Home Office replied such a list would be welcome.

---

31 'I am sure that public opinion is being profoundly shocked by individual cases which have come to the attention of all of us. I know several cases in which I am perfectly certain that the men interned are innocent of any pro-Nazi feeling – as certain as I am about all the occupants of the Front Bench opposite or of this bench.' – Viscount Wolmer, House of Commons, 10 July 1940 (HC Deb, 10 July 1940, c1208)

In a Commons debate on 18 July, as the Home Office was actively considering the principles and mechanisms for a release programme, A. V. Hill (Cambridge University MP, Nobel laureate, biological secretary of the Royal Society, Tizard Committee member, vice-president of the Society for the Protection of Science and Learning) rose to ask the Home Secretary, Sir John Anderson, a leading question:

> ... in considering the categories of aliens who, in the absence of any suspicion on personal grounds, may be exempt or released from internment, will he interpret work of national importance as including contributions of significance to science and learning?

Anderson's reply came as interestingly pat and positive:

> Yes, Sir. I shall be ready to give sympathetic consideration to any case where I am advised by bodies of recognised standing in the sphere of science and learning that an alien's work is of importance for the promotion of science and learning.

Sphere of Science and Learning ... Promotion of science and learning ... Protection of Science and Learning?

'Outstanding contributions to art, science, learning or letters' became one of the categories for release.

A. V. Hill's idea was that the learned societies, the 'bodies of recognized standing' – the Royal Society, the British Association, the British Academy – should set up panels to advise on the professional standing of interned scholars and the propriety of their release, vouching for their integrity and the value of their work for its quality and significance.

In the scheme of national governance, the learned societies would take this responsibility and the administration accept their doing so. Other professions, architects, dentists, followed suit. The British Academy and the Royal Society panels procured the release of some 500 interned scholars, many by spring 1941, almost all by the middle of 1942.

However, the panels could not act from expressions of opinion, as Hill pointed out to Esther. Dossiers for the applicants had to be founded in fact as to both the applicants and their work.

So Esther's devotion to refugee scholars, her administrative skills and her capacity for unremitting work were at the heart of the SPSL's internment-release effort and her contribution to the release process became her finest hour.

The crucial moment for the SPSL – and its refugee scholars – was the meeting of its officers on 28 June 1940 in Burlington House.

> ... the meeting was called in order to discuss the special problems raised by the Government's policy of a general internment of male aliens.
>
> The Secretary had written to the British professors with whom a limited number of outstanding refugee scholars and scientists had been working, for a statement on the interned refugees' academic or scientific capacities, their personal integrity and loyalty to this country, and after consultation with the two Honorary Secretaries and the Honorary Treasurer, had appealed for the release of these scholars from internment.

The meeting decided that the SPSL would process their scholars' applications for release, making Esther – but not Esther alone, it must be said – the scholars' immediate contact and the repository of their hopes.

In *Refugee Scholars*, Esther says she drew up about 500 applications for release:

> As far as procedure was concerned I had to obtain the curriculum vitae of the internees for whom I was to prepare an application for release. In addition references from British citizens were required, about three if possible; I obtained the names and addresses of such referees and wrote to them myself. Once I had the information, I put it together as succinctly as I could and sent the applications to the tribunals of [the Royal Society, the British Association, and the Royal Society of Medicine]. They met several times a week, and forwarded these applications to the Home Office with or without their recommendation. It was nearly always with. The Home Office considered them and eventually the internees were released. It took nearly three months for this process, from my writing to the individual internee and processing the result.

A typical letter in pursuit of a reference for a not-so-prominent SPSL/AAC scientist was sent by Esther from the SPSL at the Scott Polar Research Institute in Lensfield Road Cambridge on 5 November 1940 [identities withheld]:

> I have been approached to appeal for the release of Dr XXX, who gives your name as a reference. I have been completely unsuccessful in getting any statement from some British scientists on Dr XXX's scientific work, and the only comment I have on his character comes from a Mr YYYY.
>
> For our application, which has to be submitted in the first place to a special tribunal of the Royal Society, I need a brief description of Dr XXX's scientific work by some authoritative British scientists, and assurances of his personal integrity and loyalty to this country. If you can help me I shall be grateful.
>
>   Yours sincerely,
>   Esther Simpson
>   Secretary

In 1946 the first Annual Report since 1939 looked back at the Society's internment role:

> In 1940 the invasion of the Low Countries was followed by a series of general internments, and the work of the Society in the summer and autumn of 1940 was chiefly concentrated on preparing cases to be submitted to the special Tribunals set up by the Royal Society, the British Academy and the Royal Society of Medicine. Refugees whose cases were approved by these Tribunals were then the subject of applications by our Society for release from internment. 518 applications were prepared by the Society in this way, of which only 20 were refused. This work of securing the release of scholars and scientists able and willing to assist in the war effort in their various ways was of benefit to the nation as well as to the refugees. Its success was largely due to the untiring labours of the Secretary, Miss Esther Simpson, who had most valuable help from the late Miss Eleanor Rathbone and from Professor A. V. Hill, both in their personal capacity and as Members of Parliament.

That meeting also reflected on the working of the Cambridge office:

> Since the office moved to Cambridge on the outbreak of war in 1939 the main work of administration has fallen to Miss Esther Simpson and her assistants. Among these, long and valued service was rendered by Miss Nancy Searle, Mrs. Gisela Perutz. Mr. Adams, when available, had the valuable advice that would be expected and Professor C. S. Gibson was very helpful. *The Committee at Cambridge cannot overpraise Miss Simpson's devoted service over a period of eleven years from the first days of the Academic Assistance Council. They had the greatest difficulty in inducing her to take any holiday or rest. Her knowledge of individual cases, of the Society's policy and of the records is unparalleled. She was, and remains, the friend of all expatriated scholars* [author's italics].

Esther accepted the need for internment in the circumstances of 1940 but was angered by the process:

> It was quite appalling for all of us, and particularly for the refugees themselves, for them to be interned in such a peremptory way. We all understood that we were facing the threat of invasion and that the Government had to take some action, and this was recognized by most of the refugees I know and by me. What I protested about was the way it was done, the lack of preparation. The camps weren't ready to receive the numbers involved . . . The authorities performed most unprofessionally as I saw it. After all, this was done by officials in our Home Office who should have known better, who should have been better prepared and had more understanding.

To which the hard-pressed civil servant might have replied, 'Don't you know there's a war on?'

But for Esther, a silver lining was also to be found.

> However, some of the scholars interned quite enjoyed that period of internment. The first thing some of them did was to establish a 'university'. Several of them told me how much they learned from being with other people of a different calling. My academics learned

a lot from the internees who were not academic. The non-academics were very grateful to hear lectures on subjects they found of interest.

And with a reservation, she noted:

> It was really like flaunting the old school tie: 'My camp had the best university'; 'We had the best musicians'; 'We had the best actors' and so on . . . That was incidental. They were not interned in order to have these experiences.

But 'these experiences' were central to the internees' life of internment, the confinement, and the forced separation from their new-found world of exile. Together with 'old school tie', these phrases must call in question Esther's comprehension of her scholars' outlook and the culture of their *Heimat* [homeland], hinting at the solipsistic nature of her sympathies.

Bentwich notes the categories eligible for release as 'scientists, research workers and persons of academic distinction for whom work of importance in their special fields is available; persons of eminent distinction who have made outstanding contributions to art, science, and letters.' He says that SPSL staff put testimony together for over 550 applicants. The recruitment of all available scientific skill was central to the war effort.

> In the end it could be said that one of the great English contributions to the Allied cause was the direct and systematic utilisation of all available scientific skill for war operations.

We could liken it to the role of Polish and Czech fighter pilots in the Battle of Britain.

Norman Bentwich listed the subjects, as seen in 1953.

First, during the war: nuclear physics/fission; physical chemistry; mathematics; astronomy; thermodynamics; radio-therapeutics; Pluto [Pipeline Under The Ocean]; Fido [Fog Investigation and Dispersal Operation]; ice-carriers; medical science (penicillin, surgery, Guttmann's pioneering work); machine tools; aluminium.

The mobility of science at the highest level could not have been better demonstrated, particularly in nuclear physics, by the work of Otto Frisch, and the development of the first atomic bomb. But Bentwich instances the involvement of refugee scientists leading to the Trondheim Raid to destroy the Norwegian stock of heavy water; FIDO – Fog Investigation Dispersal Operation; PLUTO – Pipeline Under the Ocean, vital for D-Day; the present author's favourite Operation Habakkuk, a proposal for a floating aircraft carrier constructed from ice and wood pulp. Besides these, there were contributions to medical treatment, liquefying helium, dry batteries and machine tools.

They combined, says Bentwich, 'German thoroughness with the English practical approach'. And he quotes the head of the German navy, Grand Admiral Dönitz, as saying to the Head of Scientific Staff at the German Admiralty in 1943, 'The enemy has rendered the U-boat war ineffective through superiority in the field of science.'

Including the war influx, the total number of academic refugees registered with the SPSL was 2,541 – double the number registered in 1935. Rather more than half came from Germany. Bentwich shows how 600 academic scholars and scientists worked in universities and science institutes, research outside universities, hospitals and industry, government, the forces, schools, broadcasting.

Of Esther he remarks that her contribution to the war effort was to help make possible

> defence of civilization against the common enemy of the human race who had marked down their own race as the first victims.

Then, moving on to peacetime: physiology, biochemistry, psychiatry, neurology, vitamins; fertilisers; law; social sciences; art history; Latin; biblical archaeology; Egyptology; antique music; classical archaeology; fine arts; philology; theology; jurisprudence; comparative law; private international law; Roman law; conflict of laws; moral philosophy; oriental scholarship; archaeology; semitic epigraphy; classical scholarship; sociology; modern and ancient history; fine arts; music, academic and production.

A reflection on refugees' contribution to Britain at war comes from Paul Weindling in 'Medical Refugees and the Modernisation of British Medicine 1930–1960', referring to:

... the significant wartime medical contribution made by refugees, who were rightly proud of their service, whether it was as auxiliary fire-service personnel, as officers in the RAMC or in ensuring the medical and dental fitness of allied troops or auxiliaries such as the Merchant Navy. The refugee physicians looked after civilians at a time of upheaval, including a range of fellow refugees, while supporting the medical services of a country at war ...

35

Behind the Wire

In the crowded exclusion of the internment camp, the *Kultur, Bildung* and *Muttersprache* [culture, education/cultivation, mother-tongue] from which as exiles these German-speakers had been so decisively and painfully uprooted were theirs again; the internees were, without choice or warning, re-rooted behind barbed wire.

The release of their rooted creative and cultural energies followed. Survival skills recalled from service in the German army at the front during the First World War were also called into play.

Both are evident In *Refugee Scholars* Chapter Eight, entitled 'The Long Vac 1940' by Paul Jacobsthal (1880–1957), Professor of Classical Archaeology at Marburg until 1935 and then Student of Christ Church and Reader in Celtic Archaeology at Oxford. He was recognised as a world expert in Celtic Art.

Professor Jacobsthal's unpublished narrative of his internment was sent to Esther by her friend Lady Simon, and Ray Cooper decided to include it in *Refugee Scholars* though it has no references to the SPSL or to Esther.

As a narrative of an internee's lived experience, it brings the realities of internment behind barbed wire for one exiled German professor to vivid and insightful life.

Professor Jacobsthal was arrested:

> On Friday July 5 1940 in the morning when I was peacefully writing
> on Celtic Geometric Ornament a knock came at my door in Christ

Church and a plain clothes officer entered producing a warrant of arrest.

Although other scholars had already been interned, Professor Jacobsthal had felt safe as the judge at his Aliens Tribunal hearing in 1939 had said it was an honour for the country to have him there.

He returned to Oxford on Monday 30 September, having experienced the staggeringly inhumane transit camp at Warth Mills, Bury, and then one of the forty spartan (House 24: nine small rooms, one bathroom, one WC) seaside boarding houses ('built of yellow brick in a style of timeless undatable ugliness') of Hutchinson Camp, Douglas, Isle of Man ('We often thought it would have been much worse to have a voluntary holiday in this place'), keeping enforced company with a mix of fellow Oxford scholars, chemists, engineers, pastors, trade unionists, lawyers, factory owners.

A former civil servant in Hamburg had taken a course in cookery before emigrating, when he became a butler to 'a decent family in Oxford'. He became House 24's cook.

Professor Jacobsthal and his wife had left Germany early:

> Now I was living with men who had terribly suffered; they spoke rarely, but the more impressively, of their ordeals in concentration camps; once far better off than I, they had lost everything and now with dignity led a life of privation in exile, eager to emigrate to America and to build up, if they could, a new existence.

The camp contained some 1,200 internees, of whom 80 per cent were Jewish.

> Of these approximately 150 were Orthodox and lodged in Kosher houses . . . Many of them did not speak German, but Yiddish or English with a funny accent; it was not always easy to find out what they were really speaking.

Inevitably, on arrival tensions arose between the different groups over sleeping arrangements. Professor Jacobsthal gives himself a pat on the back for using his First World War experience with Greek officers or soldiers in 1917 to bridge the divisions.

Many ordinary household fixtures and fittings were missing in their house,

> ... but we had Richard Cohn, a man with an inventive mind and a sound training in occupied countries 1914–1918 who searched for scrap in basements, stole wood, nails and screws and made shelves, commodes or lampshades out of nothing.

The camp was run by the internees' self-administration ('they had all the virtues of the German race, efficiency and the gift of organisation') under the control of military authorities, who generally won the professor's approval, even admiration, for their attitude and, in some cases, command of German.

What he does complain about is the 'cruel, scandalous treatment of our mail', its delays, its limitations, its censorship, the increasing strictness of control when, say over release, extra correspondence was necessary.

> The internees were very much embittered and hardly any other aspect of internment has done so much harm to the sincere and profound admiration for everything English they had felt before.

Yet,

> It goes without saying that there was much Kultur. There was a Kulturabteilung [Cultural department] and each house had a Kulturwart [Culture representative].

An extraordinary range of lectures apart, a 'highly respectable musical life' won his approval.

> It was moving when fifty unhappy men gathered in one of the narrow shabby rooms and listened to Professor Glass playing Bach, Mozart or Schubert on a worn-out piano or to Rawicz' masterly melancholy jazz improvisations ... I never went to any of the very popular performances of the Cabaret Stacheldraht [Cabaret Barbed Wire] which had, as I was told, the character of Jewish Varieties in certain quarters of Vienna. Some of the English officers went.

This was *Kultur* for the *polloi*, he remarks. [Post-war, Marjan Rawicz and Walter Landauer became an immensely popular piano duo, performing their duets regularly on BBC Home Service variety programmes.]

Always, the cultural ground bass, as it were, was the return to the German language and culture. While Liverpool and London were bombed, he reflects, a German holiday,

> . . . a complete relapse – after a short and imperfect acclimatization – into former language and habitats, bowing and introduction . . . and people addressing each other 'Herr Geheimrat, Herr Hofrat'. The German past which during the last years had sunk to the bottom of consciousness came to the surface again . . .

For Max Eschelbacher, a religious scholar and rabbi who had been one of the last two rabbis in Düsseldorf, his stay in Hutchinson proved a spiritual release. In the camp he took up again his calling as rabbi, religious and pastoral, for the camp's Jews – a microcosm of central European Jewry. It was a blissful time for which he was deeply grateful.[32]

In a January 1993 letter to Cooper, Esther makes a singular call on her German with reference to a page from 'a German list' Ray has been sent. The page included a notice on Paul Jacobsthal:

> I suggest that 'get.' stands for getauft, i.e. baptised (taufen means to dip, getauft meaning 'dipped' becomes the technical word for baptised. In philology 'dip' and 'tauf' would come from the same root word.

Of Jewish parentage, Jacobsthal had been baptised a Protestant – an irrelevance in the application of the Nazi race laws. His wife was the daughter of a Protestant pastor.

The use in the document of the abbreviation 'get.' to indicate 'Christian convert' is interesting. Denomination – Protestant, Catholic – might have been expected if religious affiliation was to be shown, or 'dissident' for a non-religious political exile.

Of course, socially, whether a Jew had been baptised had long been something to be discussed out of the side of the mouth, as it were, particularly what was termed *liegend getauft* – baptised as a baby, lying

32 Max Eschelbacher: *Meine Internierung*. S. 58, courtesy of Barbara Suchy.

down. However, Esther did not stray beyond philology into the historical significance of 'get.'.

The inevitable focus on the intellectual and artistic life of the Isle of Man internment camps, the so-called university, tends rather to mask the realities for the families of the interned and indeed for the non-artistic, non-scholarly inmates who had been scooped up in the internment panic.

In early 2022 an article by Nick Pryer in the *Mail on Sunday* (29 January 2022) was circulated on interned-on-iom@googlegroups.com, an internment group curated by Tony Hausner:

> British WW2 prison camp where every inmate was a genius: A painter despised by Hitler. A pianist adored by the royals. A Prussian prince and a London elephant keeper . . . all among perhaps the most extraordinary set of captives ever assembled.

The topic was the Hutchinson Internment Camp. Among the internment group subscribers who were prompted to write in about their parents' or grandparents' internment experience was Judith Elam:

> Thank you for this article. I was particularly interested by the fact that the 'elite' were the ones who successfully obtained early release. My grandfather, Peisech Mendzigursky, was at Hutchinson. He was a mere 'commercial traveler' back in Leipzig, very religious and certainly not an intellectual. He had already been deported to Buchenwald during Kristallnacht, and interned at Kitchener [ed: a disused army camp in Kent used by the Central British Fund for German Jewry to receive some 4,000 adult male German Jews after Kristallnacht, many of whom had been in concentration camps]. After Kitchener he had returned to Manchester and was employed as a machinist by a British-born Jew called Benno Kessler, along with about 5 other Jews who were also Polish-born refugees like my grandfather. Benno Kessler wrote to various governmental departments to try and get all 6 of his employees released, as he was unable to fulfill his government contract. I have copies of all the letters. He was simply bounced around between departments. But to no avail. My grandfather remained at Hutchinson for 14 long months.

It was definitely a question of your education and background
and whom you knew, which determined your early release . . .
or not.

Later, Judith Elam wrote to me with additional details of her grandfather,
deeply moving:

My maternal grandfather Peisech Mendzigursky was not a scholar in
the traditional sense. But he was an acting rabbi and very learned in
Torah. A deeply religious man, whose religion gave him the ability to
survive and continue with his life post war in England, despite having
lost his six-year-old and only son to pneumonia in June 1933, and then
his father, wife and six-year-old daughter, who were all murdered. He
would say 'if that is God's will, who am I to question it'.

36

The Cave and the Spider

In terms of contribution to the war effort, this is not the place for a debate on the comparative worth of weaving webbing belts for infantrymen or producing equations for nuclear fission. What counted was access to the internment decision-makers, and what mattered there was being part of the same social and educational group – avoiding the term elite.

As Jeremy Seabrook puts it in *The Refuge and the Fortress: Britain and the Flight from Tyranny*,

> Those who lent their support to the AAC all knew each other. Many had attended the same schools and universities. A word in the right place, the lifting of a telephone, a friendly note could galvanize like-minded others into action. Their friendships, family relationships and common experience ensured they would be heard. It was no doubt patrician and elitist; but it was effective. One can admire their energy and commitment, without necessarily approving of the hierarchies of privilege, to which, in part, they owed their capacity to get things done.

To which should be added hierarchies of scholarly attainment and recognition.

If the interned scientist or scholar had no direct access to a word in the right ear, a friendly and committed go-between would, and frequently had to, serve.

Esther Simpson in the AAC/SPSL's engine-room was also that, though 'go-between' is not extensive enough.

As well as collecting and copying all the relevant papers for the consideration of the learned societies' panels, she made time to offer personal support to the Society's internees, soothing anxieties over the release process, keeping contacts with their families, addressing personal needs.

It was in that context that in July 1940 she had the noted exchange of letters with Dr H. Schlossmann, who was writing from the Central Promenade Camp on the Isle of Man, quoted in *Refugee Scholars*. Esther wrote on 9 July:

> I am glad you have written to A V Hill. Lots of other people are writing to him too and my impression is that the more letters are sent the merrier. A V has of course at once taken steps on our behalf and the next fortnight or so may see our first releases. You know the story of Bruce and the Spider? I am that spider. About myself there is of course nothing to write in these days. I haven't had much of a private life these last seven years and just now there is no question of one.

On 10 July Schlossmann wrote [given the dates, possibly referring to another letter]:

> Your children were very glad and grateful when I read the official part of your letter to them. We appreciate every token of friendship these days more than you might realize, and therefore your letter was a treat for all concerned.

Also on 10 July Esther wrote:

> . . . I faced one or two anxious moments last week worrying about my 'children'. One naturally always has someone to worry about when one has a family of six hundred in this country . . .

It is not to detract from the objective value of her contacts with the internees to note some of the idiosyncrasies in Esther's letters that will tell us a little more about her.

Curiously, she writes of A. V.'s steps on *our* behalf and *our* first releases, presumably meaning the SPSL's and indicating the primacy she felt over the refugees, implicit in her use of 'children'. But of course A. V. was taking steps in his role as an officer of the SPSL of which Esther was an employee, and those steps were on behalf of the internees – *your* behalf, *your* first releases.

Then as to the curious reference to the legend in which the fourteenth-century fugitive King of the Scots Robert the Bruce is given a lesson in tenacity by a spider in his cave hideout – apart from the question of a German-educated scientist's knowing 'try, try, and try again', what the recipient is being invited to see is Esther's personal primacy, leading the way.

Her having no time for a private life is assumed to be of interest to the inhabitant of a crowded internment camp; and, of course, the assumption of maternal standing over the refugee scholars is implicit in the phrases 'my 'children' and the 'family of six hundred', implying that the uprooting of the refugee results in her or his re-infantilisation requiring a mother-figure.

Altogether, in this correspondence we might see the whole run of her language as also demonstrating her ownership of the release process, the ownership that backgrounds the contribution of others, and underpins her future idealisation.

37

Hush! Establishment at Work

Cooper saw release from internment as a great story, virtually written by Esther and A. V. Hill in their constant correspondence between June and December 1940.

Cooper's research on the role of the SPSL and its officers in creating and setting up the release process for scholars with the Home Office and its Permanent Under-Secretary Sir Alexander Maxwell became a detailed Chapter 7 of *Refugee Scholars*, titled *Bruce and the Spider*. He took as its epigraph:

> 'Do you know the story of Bruce and the Spider? I am that spider' – Esther Simpson in Cambridge 9th July 1940 to Dr. H. Schlossmann Central Promenade Camp Douglas Isle of Man

Cooper's chapter develops the centrality of the SPSL in securing the release of some 500 scholars, beginning with a letter as early as 4 June 1940 from its joint honorary secretaries Walter Adams and Professor C. S. Gibson to Sir Alexander Maxwell raising the possibility of the release of scholars for whose integrity the Society would vouch and whose work was in the national interest.

Nothing came of this, but the principles of SPSL agency and recognition of work in the national interest as a gateway to release were carried through by force of an establishment that could transform the position: the sheer closeness of the SPSL to the Royal Society and in particular the situation of

A. V. Hill as vice chairman of the executive committee of one and biological secretary of the other, as well as MP for Cambridge University. For non-scientist scholars, the British Academy lined up alongside the Royal Society; its chairman Sir Frederic Kenyon was also a joint-vice chairman of the SPSL executive committee.

The point was, in terms of their influence on and access to government, these people and their organisations mattered where it mattered. Their willingness to commit themselves is beyond impressive. (In the age of email, we should also not forget their dependence on letters sent and received through the Royal Mail during the Blitz.)

Cooper gives figures:

> From June to December 1940 Esther Simpson in Cambridge wrote sixty-one letters to AV Hill dealing with the release of refugee scholars and he sent forty-nine to her, all signed personally. In many cases the letters consisted of two or more closely typed pages, dealing with queries about individuals, all of which required further research and prompt action. Most were dealt with by return of post. Esther Simpson was, of course, also frequently in touch with Sir Frederic Kenyon at the British Academy. The SPSL archive contains seventeen letters from Kenyon, all in longhand, written to Esther Simpson between July 1940 and April 1941, dealing with the release of humanist scholars.
>
> In all 532 recommendations for release or exemption from internment were made by the two tribunals [the Royal Society and the British Academy]. This figure includes recommendations for 56 doctors which AV Hill had referred to the Royal Society of Medicine . . . No less than nine copies of each application and supporting documents seem to have been required.

The Home Office rejected only twenty of the 532 recommendations made by the tribunals. On its willingness to follow them, the Home Office was also accepting the agencies' grasp of a criterion reaching beyond the applicants' qualifications and work: their integrity.

Here Esther's personal connection with her 'children' now took on an unforeseeable significance, a vital role in the release process: it was in many cases the sole source of judgement. Conscious of the responsibility this thrust on her, she questioned, what of applications from scientists not registered with the SPSL, not 'her' children?

By October 1940, the SPSL was preparing applications for scientists who, she wrote to Hill,

> were not refugees in any sense: they held comfortable positions here chiefly in industry and if they did not return to Germany on the outbreak of war, the reason was not necessarily their attachment to this country and its institutions.

Hill took the point. The Royal Society had neither the time nor the staff to do anything except examine scientific credentials. She must take extra precautions.

> I am afraid that this more careful scrutiny of the new type of applicants may mean enlargement of your responsibilities and efforts . . . It is most important, however, for you to maintain the high standard which has been set so far and not to be tripped up by one or two bad eggs getting into your list of applications.

But in one case, cited by Cooper, with an applicant who had an elderly mother still in Germany, and whose referee worried that he could easily be taken in by a competent spy, Hill told Esther simply to put all the facts to the authorities.

With the panel system set up, notices were placed in internment camps publicising the various panels that provided gateways to release for the qualified. (The internee-in-the-street, as it were, had to apply direct to the Aliens Department.) Applications via the SPSL for scientists and technologists were dealt with by Royal Society panels, confusing a Home Office official into addressing 'The Royal Society for the Protection of Science and Learning', an understandable slip. An Oxford panel under the vice-chancellor existed for Oxford scientists and humanists. Cambridge had a separate panel. The British Academy panel under Kenyon for all humanists at universities other than Oxford took applications via the SPSL. A joint vice-chancellors' panel was for other people teaching or administering at universities.

But the panels had to have the information on which to make their recommendations. And from that requirement came what was possibly Esther's finest hour, as she assiduously compiled the dossiers containing the applicants' academic and employment history, qualifications, family circumstances, and all-important references, all the while keeping in touch with the internee and his family, advising and reassuring. What also comes across is the manifest trust A. V. Hill and the other SPSL officers placed in her capacity to carry through this work to a standard on which they could rely in the national interest.

Cooper quotes extracts from Esther's correspondence with Dr Hermann Lehmann between 10 June and 11 October 1940. Dr Lehmann, a specialist in sickle cell anaemia, later Professor of Biochemistry at Cambridge, interned in Huyton and Central Promenade Camps on the Isle of Man, sent particulars of interned scholars to Esther.

On 21 August he groused to her about the national usefulness criterion of the White Paper's Section 8. Esther's reply by return showed she was feeling the pressure:

> Please tell [our scholars whom you see] not to be upset by the shortness of our letters and any bad temper in them or in letters from other official bodies. It is most extraordinarily difficult to keep equable in view of the continuous delays and disappointments and it is sometimes irritating beyond bearing to have unreasonable requests from internees, though this should not be so.

Lehmann struck a mollifying note in his last letter on the 7 October:

> . . . Naturally the para 8 people here are somewhat sad that the term starts without their being back at work. The White Paper came in July and here they still are, with a few exceptions, where a special pressure was brought to bear on the Home Office. But everyone sees that the aged and infirm ones have to be released first and the feeling of impatience and the loss of sense of proportion which cannot be averted in internment *do not diminish* a bit the confidence and gratitude we all have, knowing that our affairs are in your hands . . . Everyone coming into contact with you expresses his admiration in general, and especially for you personally for the work done by the Society.

Cooper noted to Esther his disbelief at how she managed to get through so much work, particularly between July and September 1940. It meant four or five letters a week exchanged with A. V. Hill at the height of the process, over 200 pages altogether. Each letter dealt with the positions of an individual and included papers for the Royal Society Committee of three or four, including one or other of the two secretaries, meaning Esther had to prepare copies. Then papers recommending release would be sent to the Aliens Department of the Home Office. Pause here to recollect we are talking of office typewriters, ink ribbons, carbon paper and erasers.

Having explored the SPSL archive, Cooper wrote,

> The archive shows that Esther Simpson was indefatigable in her efforts to alleviate the plight of refugee scholars, whether it was by highlighting the many inexplicable restrictions under which they had to live or by exerting every pressure she could on the government departments responsible for handling their applications for release.

Following up on the applications for release and the incessant delays in the system, even when release had been agreed, was part of the load she carried. It is understandable that nearly forty years later in a letter to Engelbert Broda, referring to a scientist who had been a refugee she remarked: 'I got him out of internment along with some 560 others in 1940.'

She might well have said that this was the moment for which life had been preparing her. If so, patience was a prime lesson, given the delays in communication between the internee, the aid agency and the Home Office.

A. V. Hill took this up in the Commons in the 3 December debate, when he ingeniously told the House that a letter from an internee on the Isle of Man took forty days to reach the Royal Society. This 'works out at a quarter of a mile per hour or less than the speed of a tortoise'.

On 6 December the *Daily Telegraph* disagreed, averring that the Home Secretary's department 'moves three and a half times faster than the speed of a tortoise' as evidenced by the tortoises in the US Oklahoma City Tortoise Derby.

No, no, Hill responded on 11 December. He had been referring to Greek tortoises. Because of the higher temperatures in Greece, they moved faster.

He wrote to a friend serving in Greece, asking him to send some tortoises for an experiment.

If you were an internee pressing your own case for release on the Aliens Department, talk of a Tortoise Derby would be cold comfort. But some 10,000 were released by the beginning of 1941, and the Isle of Man held fewer than 5,000 by the beginning of autumn 1942.

38

A N Other

The commonly accepted version of Esther at work in these turbulent days of the AAC/SPSL, in the 1930s and 1940s, is essentially that of the solitary warrior, carrying all before her, an impression she did nothing to dispel.

But a glance at the organisation's correspondence as well as its salary rolls confirms that, with the success of its financial appeals, the AAC/SPSL was well staffed. Walter Adams, the first secretary, and his voluntary assistant Charles Milne Skepper (who died in 1944, serving in France with the SOE) had letters typed by 'PF' and 'MW' between 1933 and 1935. Esther's salary was increased in 1935 to £5 [£365 in today's money], with the promise that if Walter Adams left the AAC in that year, she would be asked to run the office and a further £5 added.

The office had other secretaries who dealt with the refugee scientists and their families. Esther's account in *Refugee Scholars* has a passing reference to David Cleghorn Thomson, who followed Walter Adams as the AAC secretary, making his first appearance at an allocation committee meeting on 21 July 1938. Nancy Searle, who may have been his personal secretary, is recorded as working for the Society between 1938 and 1940; she also dealt with refugees and their families.

The Society's General Secretary's Progress Report for March 1939 gives an idea of a busily crowded office:

> In addition to the Appeal Secretary (Miss Avril Wood) , who is incidentally handling all the secretarial work for public relations

activities in the office, committees and outside bodies, press contacts etc., it was found necessary to take on one temporary junior typist. Now that the appeal work is slackening, she will undertake certain pieces of important copying, the Home Office 'crisis' register, the publications questionnaire for the Medical Committee, the lists of subscribers and members (by areas) and case lists for India, before her appointment ends. We have been fortunate in securing the services of two regular voluntary workers, skilled editing assistance has been several times made available to our great profit. The regular staff has continued as in the earlier quarter to work long hours (and frequently over-time) to overtake arrears piled up with the increase of applications consequent on the appeal publicity.

The Society used Miss Kerr-Sanders London Secretarial Agency. Miss Kerr-Sanders Secretarial Training College was intended for 'well-educated girls wishing to qualify for the higher branches of the secretarial profession' and with 120 words a minute shorthand and sixty words a minute typing.

The 1946 Annual Report (the sole report produced after 1938) covers the period 1939–1945. It thanks Esther Simpson 'and her assistants' for undertaking 'the main work of administration' since the move to Cambridge. Nancy Searle is named as one such assistant, as is Gisela Perutz (1915–2005). And the meetings of the SPSL's Executive and Allocations Committees, the members of which all had full-time posts, in the case of A. V. Hill several, impress by their sheer number and frequency.

It is easy to get the idea that she, Esther, was working non-stop from the July day she took her seat in Burlington House, overrun with applications and with looking after the applicants and their families. But she was still able to take summer holidays travelling to Vienna with her violin and viola to visit friends each year up to 1937. As recalled earlier, in 1946 the officers recorded that, 'They had the greatest difficulty in inducing her to take any holiday or rest.' Presumably they had succeeded.

The solitary warrior is the impression given by *Refugee Scholars* and in heroic accounts of her life.

I certainly approached Esther assuming this was the case. Focusing on her, it is easy to forget, for instance, that the Society had a full-time general secretary, her boss, in this period – though now plausible to think that if

Esther had been male, she might have been appointed general secretary earlier. As it was, in an age when broadly the boss classes were not open to women, the AAC meant an opportunity for Esther to be her own boss, the importance of which Donald Grant had recognised when he was fixing it for her.

Then, in the course of research, Father Costello directed me to Esther Saraga and her memoir *Berlin to London: An Emotional History of Two Refugees*. It is a compelling and deeply moving account of her German-Jewish parents', Lotte and Wolja Saraga's, enforced migration to England, a story of exile, separation and internment. She kindly sent me copies of her parents' correspondence with the SPSL.

It includes a letter (8 August 1940) from Albert Einstein in Princeton in support of Wolja's application for release from internment. He is vouching for Wolja on the basis of assurances from Einstein's absolutely reliable assistant Dr V. Bargmann who had known Dr Saraga since the days of early youth.

> On the basis of my information I am able to take any responsibility for the personal and political reliability of Dr Saraga.

Dr Saraga, a physicist, had been in touch, initially from Berlin, with the Society and Esther Simpson since July 1935, with Esther assisting him to find a post in his special field, oscillation research. But, to my surprise, the SPSL's letters between November 1939 and May 1940 were signed – the work was being done – not by Esther alone but by Nancy Searle, in sequences of letters that included some from Esther.

Nancy Searle does not appear in *Refugee Scholars* but her SPSL employment seems to have been from September 1938 to May 1940. She is mentioned by Beveridge in *A Defence of Free Learning*:

> As soon as the Executive Committee of S.P.S.L. discussed the Government's offer, at our meeting of February 8 [sic], 1940, we realized that we might find difficulty in getting as much money as we should like to have. So, after a preliminary talk between Sir Herbert [i.e. Herbert Emerson – Chair of Central Committee for Refugees (also League of Nations High Commissioner for Refugees)] and myself, we

sent Miss Nancy Searle to put our case to the Central Committee as a
whole on March 13th, 1940.

That is, Nancy Searle was seen as capable of putting 'the SPSL's case to
the Central Committee as a whole' – i.e. of the League of Nations High
Commission for Refugees, the Emerson Commission, in March 1940.

The name Gisela Perutz is also missing from *Refugee Scholars*, the
omission the more surprising as she was married to the Nobel laureate
Max Perutz, who is, of course, mentioned and who spoke at the launch of
Refugee Scholars.

> Perutz's Cambridge friends . . . included his future wife, the beautiful,
> Berlin-born Gisela Peiser, who worked in the Cambridge-based Society
> for the Protection of Science and Learning (Obituary Max Perutz,
> The Times, 7 February 2002)

Yet the Royal Society of Medicine's web-page[33] recording the part played by
the RSM's panel in the internment release process for enemy alien doctors
pays a tribute to both Esther Simpson and Gisela Perutz.

As mentioned earlier, there are four 'assistants' described in the 1946
annual report as having undertaken 'the main work of administration'
after the move to Cambridge, including Nancy Searle and Gisela Perutz.

In *Berlin to London*, Esther Simpson and the SPSL play an active and
significant part in securing residence and work for Wolja and Lotte Saraga.
He was released from internment on 3 September 1940, writing to express
his and his wife's deep gratitude to Esther and the Society. He also wrote
separately to Nancy Searle to say how glad he was and grateful for her
never-ceasing efforts to obtain his release. He wanted to thank her, he
wrote, for her great kindness to his wife and to him during the whole time
of his internment. He also thanks her for her last letter to him at Onchan
Camp, just before his release. Esther acknowledged the letter on behalf of
Nancy Searle 'who happens to be away just now'.

Esther Saraga also illuminates beautifully the life-long reach of Esther
Simpson's commitment to 'her' refugees. She quotes Jeremy Seabrook's

---

33 https://www.cara.ngo/wp-content/uploads/2017/07/Royal-Society-of-Medicine-
Committee-for-the-Release-of-Aliens-from-Internment-Poster-exhibition.pdf

view in *The Refuge and the Fortress: Britain and the Flight from Tyranny* that
Esther Simpson

> became an 'idealized figure' who embodied many of the values of the
> time – altruism and duty and a devotion to welfare, associated in
> particular with women shaped by the events of the First World War . . .
> She showed a personal interest in and friendship to every single
> refugee with whom she had contact, networking on their behalf.

Evidence of all her activities on behalf of the internees appears in Wolja
Saraga's internment file, 'as does evidence of her expectations of gratitude
from refugees', and 'to imagine this multiplied by the number of refugees
seeking her help is truly amazing. I can see how easy it would be for me
to idealize her.'

(Idealisation continues, with the invitation to the grand opening of the
Esther Simpson Building at Leeds University, quoted earlier, celebrating the
'[twenty-first century] values that she stood for, which included inclusivity,
community and support for marginalised groups . . .')

After Wolja Saraga's death in 1980, Esther Simpson wrote to Lotte in
response to a notice in *The Times*:

> I have such warm recollections of him and was always proud of his
> achievements and the contribution he made to the intellectual life of
> this country.

A reply from Lotte giving news of the children then drew this response:

> My work for academic refugees gave meaning to my life and I have
> been particularly interested in the next generation and their
> contribution to the cultural life of our society.

Later, after Lotte Saraga's death in 1984, Esther Simpson wrote:

> I remember your father very well; he was once a grantee of my Society
> and we were very proud of the career he made for himself. I esteemed
> him also as a person, so friendly, so appreciative. I felt so deeply for
> you all when he died, and was grateful that your mother had you and
> Peter. You will miss her, but will be grateful that her suffering came
> to an end.

Esther Saraga remarks,

> In her letters to Lotte and to me she emphasizes again Wolja's achievements and contributions and how 'appreciative' he was. At the same time I have direct experience of Esther Simpson's warmth and personal interest in every individual.

However, the lines ' . . . he was once a grantee of my Society and we were very proud of the career he made for himself. I esteemed him also as a person, so friendly, so appreciative', written so long after the event, raises the question of the possible underlying motive for these words and this approach.

They can be read as casting the once unassimilated, uprooted refugee, now assimilated and re-rooted, back to those days of living with apprehension and loss, of becoming uprooted, of 'guttural sorrows', of dependence on the AAC/SPSL and on Tess, who was always there for them. We might call it refugeeisation. (The later cherishing by their family and admirers of a refugee's cultural achievements is wholly distinct from refugeeisation.)

With that return, the writer, looking back as the sole survivor of the rescuers' glory days, can revisit her (long distant) role as the saviour of the elite of the elite, in so doing recalling the dependence of the displaced.

In another question mark over her self-awareness, she seems to have had no sense that in thus continuing her presence in the lives of her 'children', by her deliberate reminders of the desperate circumstances of their arrival in exile, she might also be recalling that breakdown in their lives and their refugee origins for her own gratification.

However, to contemplate this continuing attachment to her 'children' from another angle, that her work for academic refugees 'gave meaning to my life', should we rather see it as simply a continuation of life's meaning for her? In the absence of anything quite like the glory days as her life went on, a necessary continuation.

39

Cambridge Over and Out

With the cessation of internment and the dwindling of new academic refugees, the *raison d'être* of the SPSL looked increasingly doubtful. The question of its future came on to the management agenda.

Esther records fire-watching and music-making (of which more later) and friendship with Greta Burkill who ran a charity for refugee children. But what else occupied her in the protection of science and learning is unclear. The allocation committee met very infrequently but had to be serviced; the torrent of the pre-war heroic days had eased to a trickle, presumably for good.

We might question why Esther didn't take her undoubted skills, secretarial and administrative, into the war effort as the number of new refugee scholars diminished to vanishing point. Her scholars contributing to the war effort had just been a major reason for claiming their release from internment.

Her command of German and French; her having lived and worked in Breslau, Paris and Vienna; the insights into Hitler's Germany and its academic society from her SPSL work – the combination of these could have made Esther an invaluable resource for the British war effort. Walter Adams had joined the Political Intelligence Department of the Foreign Office at the beginning of the war and would surely have been pleased to find her a suitable post.

No doubt Cambridge with fire-watching and chamber music recitals was a good place to see out the war. But was the reason for not seeking an opportunity to serve her country a simple unwillingness to relinquish management of the SPSL to someone else? A rejection of having to work as part of a team, of not being her own boss?

When, in 1944, she does take another post, she is still constantly on the telephone to her successor Ilse Ursell. And when, finally and very much later, she hands over the secretary's post to Liz Fraser, she is constantly remarking in her letters how Liz needs her continuing help; as the text of *Refugee Scholars* emerges, she resists Cooper's suggestions that Liz be consulted and asked to read it – a revelation to Liz Fraser when shared with her as this book was being prepared.

In 1944 A. V. Hill instigated a change for Miss Simpson, perhaps anticipating the need for her to move on; with the war and the era coming to an end, the SPSL's activities would inevitably diminish in size and scope. Moving on rather than moving up: with all her experience and gifts, a post as an assistant secretary, this time the hostess of a newly established club for foreign scientists.

That anticipation of the SPSL's future is clear through the formal language of the minutes of the sole executive committee meeting of 1944 – its forty-second meeting and the first since 1942, held at 3 p.m. on Tuesday 19 September in the Royal Society's rooms at Burlington House. The committee fielded a full house of AAC/SPSL officer stalwarts:

Sir Frederic Kenyon – in the chair, Sir John H. Clapham, Dr F. Demuth [of the *Notgemeinschaft*], Professor C. S. Gibson, Professor M. Greenwood, Professor A. V. Hill, Professor R. S. Hutton, Dr Redcliffe N. Salaman. And the secretary (Miss Esther Simpson).

The secretary, Esther, reported on the difficulty of managing even routine work because of the shortage of staff – a part-time bookkeeper and no typist until July – while the two rooms currently occupied at the Cambridge Appointments Board looked to become one room in the autumn, though they could manage with one room.

The Committee looked at the changes that lay ahead for the Society when peace came:

> The Committee were of the opinion that the maintenance of the Society's work was essential for some time to come. The probable

situation of emergency at the end of the war was stressed, when many
of the scholars would be temporarily without employment. However,
the Committee looked forward to the time when the refugee scholars
in this country would cease to be 'refugees', as they would either be
absorbed into the community as British citizens or would be reinstated
in posts in their country of origin. The activities of the Society would
gradually be reduced to the maintenance of a number of elderly
scholars and in due course the need for a separate organisation for this
purpose would cease. The Committee were agreed that it would take
some considerable time before this end was reached. It was agreed
that it was undesirable to prolong the life of the organisation beyond
that time.

At that point the secretary made formal what had already been set up: her
taking a new post in London:

> The Secretary informed the Executive Committee that it had been
> suggested that she might be appointed to the full-time office of
> Assistant Secretary to the newly-formed Society for Visiting Scientists
> in the near future (about the end of October).
>
> While contemplating with very great regret the possibility of
> Miss Simpson's terminating her official connexion with the work
> of the Society the Committee hoped and desired, if it were in her
> own interest, that Miss Simpson should regard herself as free to
> accept the position if and when it were offered to her. At the same
> time, the Committee wished to place on record its high appreciation
> of the manner in which Miss Simpson had carried out her duties for
> the Society since 1933. This unique and difficult work could not have
> been better performed and the Executive Committee and the Officers
> of the Society desired to record their gratitude to Miss Simpson for
> the work she had so ably done. Many scholar refugees from Nazi-
> Fascist oppression would have reason to be grateful to Miss Simpson
> for the efficient and tactful way in which she had carried out her
> work on their behalf as Secretary of the Society for the Protection
> of Science and Learning and for its predecessor, the Academic
> Assistance Council.

And this elaborate dance included Esther's replacement, on an if-and-if-so-when basis:

> Dr JB Skemp, Assistant Secretary of the Cambridge Refugee Committee and Secretary of the Regional Council for Refugees, Civil Defence Region IV, and Fellow of Gonville and Caius College, should be appointed to maintain and carry out the work of the Office if and when Miss Simpson vacated her post.

But vacating was precisely not what Esther had in mind:

> The Committee gratefully accepted Miss Simpson's offer to give Dr. Skemp advice and help and to serve in a consultative capacity without prejudice to her future work. The settlement of the details of the change-over were left to the Allocation Committee.

Joseph Bright Skemp, thirty-four, was a Greek scholar and unofficial Drosier Fellow of Gonville and Caius College between 1936 and 1947. He was secretary of the SPSL from 1944 to 1946, when he went to Manchester University as Lecturer in Greek and Latin. He is not mentioned in *Refugee Scholars*.

40
Keeping Going Keeping Going

As assistant secretary, then secretary, Esther would stay with the Society for Visiting Scientists for the next twenty-two years, twice as long as she had so far spent with the AAC/SPSL.

Working for the SVS might have been a step away from the SPSL, but it was far from a separation, which plainly she would not have allowed to happen. Not that she ever really lost touch with the SPSL at any stage. In 1944, when she left for the SVS,

> In London, as a member of the SPSL Council and of the Allocation Committee, I was in daily correspondence with my successor in Cambridge, and by telephone also. I never lost sight of what was happening. This successor [Ilse Ursell] . . . continued the work and was always in touch with me.

Or as Ilse Ursell remembered it – Esther constantly on the phone to her. (Other members of the SPSL's Council and Allocation Committee did not feel the need to be in unremitting touch with the new secretary.)

Esther also became a member of the Society of Friends' refugee committee, though an agenda mainly concerned with the practical needs of refugees – food, clothing – seems not to have been her cup of tea. She remarked to Broda about a forthcoming meeting that 'as usual' she would be the one who disagreed on the proposed measures.

From 1951 to 1966, when the SVS was wound up, she also worked as the

SPSL's secretary in a voluntary capacity from her SVS office in its 5 Old Burlington Street premises.

> I took over the SPSL again as its Secretary, dealing with what remained . . . From 1951 until 1966 I ran both the Society for Visiting Scientists and the Society for the Protection of Science and Learning from the SVS office in London. The SPSL paid the SVS a nominal sum for my services and those of my staff.

The SPSL had closed its Cambridge office in 1951 for lack of refugees. She recorded in a 1951 letter to Broda,

> On August 2nd the furniture and files of SPSL came from Cambridge, and I am once again Secretary of SPSL. There is rather a lot to get hold of, after seven years' absence. I have kept in intimate touch, but the bulk of the work is accounts and I never used to do those anyway.

On the SVS's closing in 1966, the SPSL moved into Esther's flat until she retired in 1978. The honorary officers, the Council, and the Allocation Committee continued their work, but to the veteran and longest-serving employee, she and the organisation had become one.

She had told Broda in December 1969 that the last holiday she had taken was in 1937. Heaven knew when she would get another; she was so tied now by her SPSL work.

On finally retiring as secretary in 1978 at the age of seventy-five, she noted,

> I realized I would still remain closely involved because there was nobody left who knew what had happened before the war.'

Though it is not immediately obvious why knowledge of aiding displaced scholars between 1933 and 1945 should be so significant to aiding scholars from, say, Bangladesh in 1972.

She remained on the Council of Management and the Allocations Committee.

> I like to feel I can still contribute in this way.

Whether it was in the interests of the SPSL in a fast-changing world that Esther should have remained at the helm for so long, cherishing those pre-war memories, needs consideration. Where Miss Simpson's whole life was tied into the Society, we might understand if her managers found it difficult to, as it were, drop the pilot.

Though a foreign scientist's home from home, the Society for Visiting Scientists, the SVS, was altogether a different beast from the SPSL.

Originally it was seen as a necessary provision for scientists coming to Britain from newly liberated and war-torn countries in the final year of the war and early years of peace and reconstruction. It offered a residential club and professional centre for the increasing numbers of foreign scientists seeking a fresh start, coming to Britain to research, study, work, catch up, make contacts. The initial idea was to provide a meeting place, a limited amount of accommodation, a restaurant for lunches. In the years of peace, it also became prominent for its lecture programmes, in which leading scientists spoke about their current work.

Unlike the AAC, Esther was in at the creation of the SVS, and she was still there at its demise when its political and financial support ran out in 1966.

In her letters to Broda of this period, two constant refrains, threnodies really, are to be heard. One is her working a seven-day week, often till 11 p.m., and having no time for private correspondence:

> I always work all day Saturday as well as late every evening and this is the first time for months I've taken time off for writing a personal letter. [1949]

> I've had no respite for so long. Not that I'm likely to have any for some time to come; it looks as though again I shall have no holiday.

She did manage to get to a Royal Society Conversazione, where a 'sweet sight was A. V. Hill plunged in the deepest and most earnest conversation with a Bishop'. But later,

> I have no news of myself as I haven't time to live. It's so long since I had any time to myself that I've forgotten what it's like – which is probably just as well.

However, she spent the August 1949 bank holiday reading Chaim Weizmann's autobiography *Trial and Error* – 'a book which has a lot of meaning for me'.

Caveats need to be entered here. Once again it is easy to have the impression that she was the sole employee. In fact, the staff included a full-time secretary and a housekeeper, whose husband also played a part, and domestic staff.

A second caveat relates to her extensive music-making in this period, as recorded in *Refugee Scholars*, which we will come to. And a third to her yearly excursion to the British Association's annual meeting, mentioned below.

The second refrain is the SVS's constant financial fragility, dependent as it was on continuing British Council largesse.

In November 1956 she also had to cope with a large volume of extra work for the SPSL caused by the Hungarian exodus after Soviet troops suppressed the popular uprising led by the Chairman of the Council of Ministers Imre Nagy. Interviews during the day meant that she could only start her SVS routine work at night. She was dealing with some fifty displaced Hungarian scholars and the problem was very different from pre-war. (Who greeted SVS visitors or dealt with their queries while she was occupied with SPSL business is not explained. The housekeeper, Mrs Robinson, presumably.)

For all this, her account of her twenty-two SVS management years takes only part of a chapter of six pages of *Refugees Scholars*, which also includes an account of the Overseas Science Students Association and work she did at the annual meeting of the British Association for the Advancement of Science, assisting with the reception of overseas guests 'who enjoyed special privileges'. She had a room specially for their use:

> They came to me for their documents, not to the reception centre where the other participants went, and for their invitations, and with any queries or problems they had. Although it was a strenuous assignment, it was most enjoyable and I made friends with many of my overseas guests.

She did this for the British Association for eighteen years, until 1970, 'making many friends on the way'.

OSSA, the Overseas Science Students Association was founded

> to bring graduate science students from overseas into contact with the scientific life of Great Britain and to bring such students into contact with one another. It is affiliated to the Society for Visiting Scientists, Ltd., where its meetings will be held. The Association proposes to fulfil its objects by arranging scientific meetings and visits to places of scientific interest and by other means.

It is curious that Esther should say so little about the SVS in *Refugee Scholars*, even if her SVS clients were not in that category, or open to becoming 'her children', or Fellows of the Royal Society.

For its lifespan from 1944 to 1966, the SVS was significant for British science, its development and reputation, and always successful in meeting its founding aim of providing a useful London base for visiting scientists. And unlike with the AAC, Esther really was in at the very beginning. At its bitter end, she was still there.

41
J. G. Crowther is Missing

In *Refugee Scholars* Esther gives her account of the founding of the Society for Visiting Scientists: a group of concerned scientists getting together with the Foreign Office, the British Council 'and, of course, the Royal Society', and deciding to set it up. They acquire the lease of 'a lovely old house in Old Burlington Street, which was immediately behind Burlington House'. The French scientist Louis Rapkine (1904–1948) was appointed secretary of this new organisation, she says, but he was not able to take up the secretaryship in time,

> . . . and he himself suggested to AV Hill that I be asked to take this post.
> AV Hill, who had known me since 1933, thought it would be a good idea.

Esther describes how initially she resisted leaving the SPSL but was persuaded when it was pointed out that eventually the refugee work would come to an end, 'a prophecy that unfortunately was not fulfilled', and that, as a member of the SPSL Council and Allocation Committee, she would not actually be leaving it – a prophecy that was more than fulfilled. A distinct impression remains that with a falling away in new refugee scholars, the SPSL's officers, A. V. Hill in particular, thought she should move on. She required some persuading, and her retaining a connection with the Society was part of the deal.

So the decision to move was taken, though the SPSL long outlived the SVS.

'It was run by a committee with an honorary secretary and honorary treasurer and some of the committee were connected with the SPSL. AV Hill himself became President. Naturally I did most of the work.

As with the SPSL, in her telling the SVS and Esther Simpson became synonymous.

Although in at the creation of the SVS and spending twenty-two years doing 'most of the work', Esther's recall in *Refugee Scholars* of her time with it is limited in scope compared with her account of the SPSL. But one omission remains startling.

In fact the SVS had been the 1942 brainchild of the pioneer science-journalist J. G. Crowther (1899–1983), at that time working as director of the science division of the British Council. From his initiative the SVS was established by the British Council with the support of the Royal Society.

James Gerald Crowther became the SVS's first honorary secretary and Esther worked for him as assistant secretary when she joined the enterprise in 1944, sharing the excitements and pains of getting the club up and running successfully until Crowther resigned in 1948 – a forced resignation in which Esther played a part.

Though it must have required another major feat of forgetfulness, in her reminiscence of the SVS in *Refugee Scholars*, Esther makes no reference to J. G. Crowther.

Not even a passing mention. Nothing on his contribution to the SVS, nothing on how they worked together to get the Society up and running, nothing on his leaving.

In fact, the post strangely offered to Louis Rapkine had been assistant secretary. J. G. Crowther was the honorary secretary. (Rapkine's place in this history is discussed below; his priority was always the post-war reconstruction of French science and his own return to a laboratory in Paris.) On Rapkine's and A. V. Hill's advice, Crowther then offered Esther the post as assistant secretary at a salary of £300 a year (or £13,600 in today's money), an amount close to the average wage in Britain.

It may be significant that in *Retrospective Sympathetic Affection*, his self-published 1996 follow-up book to *Refugee Scholars*, Ray Cooper devotes a detailed chapter to the SVS and the part played by J. G. Crowther in its early history, including a photograph of Crowther.

At no point in his assiduously researched account does he refer to Esther's omission in *Refugee Scholars*, but in his Preface notes that:

Esther Simpson mentioned only in passing her work with the Society for Visiting Scientists (SVS) where she was assistant secretary throughout the Society's existence from 1944 to 1966.

But he goes on to summarise that:

The Society for Visiting Scientists was founded in 1944, shortly after D-Day, by a group of scientists in cooperation with the scientific representatives in London of the Allied Nations and sponsored by the British Council, with the encouragement and support of Fellows of the Royal Society . . . Between 1944 and 1966 some four thousand foreign scientists used the Society's building as a pied-à-terre and its staff as a source of information when visiting London during the difficult post-war years.

Again, in the light of this summary, we might wonder why Esther, assistant secretary throughout, felt that only a passing mention would suffice for the SVS. (No 'children', no friends, no FRSs?)

In his detailed chapter on the SVS, Cooper makes clear the fundamental part played by Crowther in its birth and also the political beliefs on science and society that underlay its importance for him.

Born in 1899 in Halifax, his parents both teachers, James Gerald 'Jimmy' Crowther was educated at Bradford Grammar School and won an exhibition to Trinity College Cambridge to read mathematics and physics. The First World War then took him into a scientific job in the Ministry of Munitions Inventions Department, mentioned earlier, working with a dozen scientists and mathematicians in the Anti-Aircraft Experimental Section on anti-aircraft gunnery using an invention of A. V. Hill's.

Going up to Trinity after the war, he left at the end of his first term in a crisis over his choice of subject. He then taught science for a short period, married, and with two step-children to support became a travelling salesman for Oxford University Press science books. He began to publish articles on science and, in 1926, persuaded the legendary editor of *The Manchester Guardian*, C. P. Scott, that he should become the paper's first science correspondent, a position he held until after the Second World War.

Prolific work in science journalism, with contributions to *Nature*, *Scientific American* and *New Scientist*, as well as the *Sunday Worker* and *Plebs*, together with a stream of popularising books under such titles as *An Outline of the Universe* (1931) and *The ABC of Chemistry* (1932) published by Penguin and Pelican, earned the respect of scientists for the speed and accuracy with which he brought developments in science to the public. The London Library catalogue lists twenty-four works under his name. On a political footing *The Social Relations of Science* (1941) won praise as occupying a genuine niche position in the 'science and society' literature of the 1930s and '40s.

A note on the book in *Nature* 148, 5 July 1941, by the physiologist R. A. Gregory FRS said that:

> He has long been esteemed as a clear interpreter of scientific development to general readers, through his articles in the newspaper press and other literary works; and he realizes fully the relations between these advances and the structure of society.

Crowther's work took him to Weimar Germany, to France and the US, and on several visits to the Soviet Union, where he was particularly impressed by the role of the state in the organisation of science. He met his second wife there, a German filmmaker named Franziska Zarniko.[34]

Crowther saw himself as a writer with a social purpose. He had absorbed left-wing views from a boyhood friend, Ralph Winston Fox, later a devout communist and supporter of the Soviet Union who died fighting for the International Brigade in Spain.

Crowther became an active member of the Society for Cultural Relations with the USSR, along with such prominent scientists as J. D. Bernal, P. M. S. Blackett, J. B. S. Haldane, Joseph Needham and Solly Zuckerman. But his cultural connections ranged beyond science, notably reaching out to the founder of the Bauhaus movement, the German architect Walter Gropius, and the painter László Moholy-Nagy.

---

34 Through Franziska, Crowther became the brother-in-law of Kurt Mendelssohn FRS, married to Franziska's sister Jutte.

Cooper quotes from Crowther's autobiography *Fifty Years with Science*, where he sets out how his views on the politics of science had taken shape:

> The rise of Nazism and the Second World War made these connections more important, for they had provided knowledge of the forthcoming scientific and technological power of the USSR, and enabled me to help in welcoming scientists and others who had to leave Germany, and after the outbreak of war, the occupied countries of Europe.
>
> These events, and the personalities and knowledge with which they acquainted me, sharpened my perceptions of the importance of the social and political relations of science, both in national and international affairs. I began to write on science from that point of view.

He also developed a relationship with the BBC, broadcasting and advising on science programmes. Among those he advised was an Overseas Service producer, Eric Blair.

With Britain at war, in 1941 Crowther was invited to become part-time secretary of the British Council's new Science Committee and Director of its Science Department. There he played a significant part in the setting up of the international body that became UNESCO, ensuring that its mandate included science. He also saw through the setting up of a Cultural Scientific Office in Chungking headed by Joseph Needham.

And in 1942, following a conversation with a colleague on the problems of helping visiting scientists find accommodation in London, he had the idea that led to the creation of the Society for Visiting Scientists.

> Many of the scientists in London in 1942 had serious personal problems. They had difficulties in finding accommodation and jobs, and were worried about relatives in occupied countries.

The idea was for a club 'not unlike those of the *Fondation Universitaire* in Brussels and the Harnack House in Berlin' [where Leo Szilard had lived]. The initial move was an approach by the Chairman of the British Council, Sir Malcolm Robertson, to the President of the Royal Society, Sir Henry Dale, to suggest that the Royal Society might form a society where visiting scientists could meet. The society would be regulated by a joint committee with the British Council. But in a bureaucratically skilful manoeuvre, while declining the proposal that it should form the society, the Royal Society established its future control by offering help in the form of cooperation by its Professor F. G. Donnan.

In consultation with A. V. Hill, the professor drew up proposals from which a skeleton plan emerged for what became the Society for Visiting Scientists. Professor Donnan would be president, Lord Rothschild treasurer, Crowther secretary, and Dr Louis Rapkine assistant secretary.

Crowther wrote:

> I suggested that [Louis] Rapkine, who was then in New York, might be brought in to run the new Society because, in spite of his unique efforts in saving French scientists, he had no adequate means of support.

In this account Rapkine agrees to take the post, and in his brief time with the SVS it is he who finds a home for the SVS at 5 Old Burlington Street – going there and returning in twenty minutes having taken the property, according to Rapkine's Royal Society memorial meeting in 1949.

However, this account is not without problems. The major difficulty is taking account of Rapkine's total commitment in his then post with the French Scientific Mission to the UK to the re-establishment of French science, and also his determination to return to the laboratory, which he finally did in 1946. How could his acceptance of a full-time job as an assistant secretary for a London club fit with his commitment to the Mission? He was also in London from the liberation in 1944, working to re-establish French science.

The French historian Diane Dosso records that:

> The [French Scientific] Mission in the UK originated in Rapkine's trip to England in 1943, where he observed the 'systematic and direct use of the scientific method for anything associated with war phenomena' – in other words, operational research, which was the British contribution to the Allied victory. Considering 'all that France would have to gain', he decided to establish 'close collaboration between French scientists and British scholars', who had opened their laboratories to the French.

Dosso also notes that the Anglo-French Society of Sciences resumed its meetings in September 1944:

> Two plenary sessions (French group and English group) were held in London on 16 and 23 September. French participants: P. Auger, B. Ephrussi, F. Perrin, L. Rapkine and R. Wurmser; British participants: J.D. Bernal, P.M.S. Blackett, J.G. Crowther, C.F. Darlington, P.A.M. Dirac (on 16th), Waddington (on 23rd) and Zuckerman. (Fontainebleau, CAC, 80 0284 – 60, Folder Anglo-French Society of Sciences.)

It was in September that Esther told the SPSL executive committee that she had been invited to be the SVS's assistant secretary; it remains unclear quite when Rapkine would have accepted and then rejected the post while working with and urging on the French Scientific Mission.

A brilliant young biologist, French by naturalisation, Louis Rapkine is described by Esther as 'one of the heroes of my life'.

A fuller account of his war-time significance comes later, but he can be credited with keeping the flame of independent French science burning during the war. He was involved in setting up a Free French scientific mission in the United States under de Gaulle and organised the escape of scientists from France. Midway through the war he came to London to organise a scientific mission there, the importance of the missions being to have a French scientific stake in the western alliance and to keep French scientists up to date. After a break of seven years in laboratory work, he joined the Pasteur Institute in late January 1946 to lead a cellular chemistry department, but he died from lung cancer on 13 December 1948. He was forty-four years old and among other attributions was saluted for his war work enabling France immediately to enter the nuclear age.

The British Council took the lease on 5 Old Burlington Street in October 1943 on behalf of the SVS. A housekeeper and domestic staff were hired, and the restaurant opened in June 1944. Delayed by the threat of flying bombs, the official opening took place on 17 October 1944, though it was up and running well before that.

In Crowther's words,

> The Society had a restaurant in the basement, and a lounge on the first floor. A stream of scientists from all quarters of the world visited the

Society, where they could meet and eat with their friends and colleagues, and continue their conversations in the lounge. There were also some bedrooms, where visitors could be accommodated for a few days.

Cooper tells us that on 4 October the BBC recorded a lunchtime broadcast from the house, introduced by Professor Donnan:

> Here we are in the refectory of 5 Old Burlington Street, London. This is the club house of the Society for Visiting Scientists. Here the scientific men of our Allies meet their British colleagues from Great Britain and the British Commonwealth. We are a jolly company of friends. We eat and we talk and we smoke. This centre of friendly and mutual intercourse has been established by the wise and far-seeing policy of the British Council.

Perhaps a programme suggestion of Crowther's, it must have made quite a contrast with the lunchtime variety programme *Workers' Playtime*, broadcast three times a week from war-working factory canteens across the nation, particularly given the international range of speakers – from France, Australia, Norway and Poland.

At the official opening, where again the BBC recorded the proceedings, membership was reported to be over 200, including Madame Irene Curie and Professor Frédéric Joliot-Curie, noted both for nuclear research, notes on which he had sent to London from Paris just ahead of the German invaders, and for his role in the French resistance.

The SVS's first officers were all British scientists, and the executive committee was a mix of eminent scientists from Britain and from Belgium, France, Czechoslovakia, Greece, Holland, Poland, South Africa and the US.

In his tribute that 'This centre of friendly and mutual intercourse has been established by the wise and far-seeing policy of the British Council', was Professor Donnan gracefully giving all the credit to the British Council? Or was there a wider political purpose?

The SVS had taken the form it did because the Royal Society had held back from taking on the British Council's original proposal, offering limited cooperation instead. When the design of the SVS emerged from the British Council's exploratory committee, with its own premises and offering accommodation, the Royal Society still envisaged it 'should function in a modest way on a temporary basis and that its future should be discussed at a later stage near the end of the War'.

As it was, Crowther's brainchild grew into a popular, lively, bustling resource for scientists visiting London, both in the capital's dilapidated post-war state and later.

In an offprint from the *Report of the Proceedings of the 21st Conference of Aslib [Association of Special Libraries and Information Bureaux], 14–15 September 1946,* Esther noted,

> At the present time there are nearly 1,000 members of the Society for Visiting Scientists, from 42 different countries, all of whom have visited the Society at some time during the past two years. The personal contact facilitated by the Society should prove most valuable for international scientific cooperation and for the advancement of knowledge and mutual understanding essential for a lasting peace.

She also notes the availability of advice as one of the Society's strengths:

> During this past summer the Society has been able to deal with very many questions concerning the numerous international scientific conferences which have taken place for the first time since the war, and to provide particulars for and about the delegates from other countries.

It seems surprising that the part played by the SVS in helping to establish post-war London as an international science centre was not better recognised by the government and science establishment.

Cooper gives figures for the usage of 5 Old Burlington Street, which provided a lounge, a library, a refectory that provided up to forty lunches on weekdays, a dormitory with four single beds, and two single rooms.

> 309 members from 25 countries spend 1400 nights there during 1954 and 247 members from 35 countries spent 1200 nights in 1960, an occupancy rate of about 60 per cent.

Amid the returning prosperity of the post-war years, demand did not falter. In 1961 some 3,200 scientists were registered members of the Society, and at least fifteen new members used the Society's facilities for the first time every month. The membership was spread across eighteen countries from Africa, the Americas, Asia, Australasia and Europe.

To have provided visiting scientists with a welcoming pied-à-terre would have been enough. But what has come down to us as a hallmark achievement is the SVS programme of discussion meetings, each chaired by an eminent authority in the subject under discussion. The central feature was the specialist topic's being opened up to questions, comment and discussion by scientific minds from other disciplines.

Crowther arranged for 'trained scientific stenographers' to record the meetings, leaving an archive of twenty-two years of contemporary scientific history – the early meetings include three on 'Growing Points in Science'. Glancing down the list of discussions between 1945 and 1966, the eye is caught by the second meeting, on 29 September 1945, on 'The Social Implications of the Atom Bomb' (Hiroshima and Nagasaki were on 6 and 9 August) and by the last speaker listed for the 1950 meetings, on 'Computing Machines and Brains': A. M. Turing.

Crowther himself took part in five meetings between 1945 and 1948, either as speaker or chair. Broadly, the topics related to the place of science in society, an area where he held strong views on the desirability of the central organisation and direction of science by government in the national interest, and on the recognition of the social relations of science as implicit in scientific work.

Cooper also narrates the circumstances in which Crowther left the SVS in 1948 – and the part Esther played in them. The heading he chooses for this part of the SVS story is

That Communist cell round the corner.

According to Crowther's autobiography, that was how the SVS under his management was seen 'in certain quarters'. Those quarters included the Special Branch, who had Crowther and his wife under observation as communists or communist sympathisers. Yes, in his younger days Crowther had flirted with communism, and his political beliefs were firmly of the left, but they had evolved into a looser and more pragmatic leftism. The Security Service accepted he was not a communist, but had his wife Franziska marked down as a member of the Holborn Communist Party in 1951.

(In her autobiography Yvonne Kapp tells a salutary tale of her exclusion from her post at the Czech Trust in 1940 on the advice of MI5 for her Communist Party membership – and how the MI5 dossier, based on a misapprehension as to the identity of her brother, followed her from one refused job application to another.)

Nonetheless, the SVS under Crowther acquired the reputation among the science and civil service establishment of being a red cell, a reputation that haunted it into the 1950s and probably made its fundraising more problematical. The developing Cold War in Europe has to be taken into account here, with the uncovering of Soviet spies and the Attlee government's adoption of more stringent security procedures in Britain.

Crowther's position as a bulwark of the British Council's standing and influence in the promotion of science, together with the use of the SVS for promulgation of his left-wing view of the social relations of science (or 'that communist cell round the corner'), had brought him hard up against the science establishment represented by the Royal Society. He suspected that Esther's mentor A. V. Hill, a secretary of the Royal Society, was involved in its policy of clipping the wings of the British Council's Science Committee. In fact, A. V. Hill became the Royal Society's representative on the British Council Science Committee and President and Chairman of the SVS, working hard to keep the Society financially afloat.

Some background to Crowther's ejection from the SVS can be found in the diaries of the Royal Society's then assistant secretary and future executive secretary, Sir David Martin.[35] Sir David was with the Royal Society from 1947 to his death in 1976.

When executive secretary, he put Esther on his personal list of invitees to Royal Society events.

Sir David's role at the Royal Society is a fascinating subject in itself, as the introduction in 'Doing Diaries' makes clear:

---

35 See the Royal Society's 2012 publication 'Doing Diaries: David Martin, the Royal Society and Scientific London, 1947–1950'.

During his long tenure he oversaw the modernization and expansion of the Society's administration, finances, publications and premises, and worked closely with the Officers, Council and the Society's many subcommittees. He was closely involved with the national and international aspects of the Society's work, and with the Fellows, visitors and external relations at all levels. The key link between the Royal Society and Whitehall, he developed strong informal contacts with civil servants in the Treasury, other government departments and the research councils, which greatly facilitated the Society's work.

We learn from his diary that he went to an SVS meeting in October 1947 and found it:

> . . . very poorly attended, the number not being more than about ten in all. Sir W. Wavell Wakefield, M.P. and Captain A. R. Blackburn, M.P., spoke about the Parliamentary and Scientific Committee, somewhat laboriously and without bringing matters to a point.

He also met Crowther over lunch in November 1947 and listened to him giving 'a glowing account' of a visit to Poland.

Quoting the diaries for 1948–1949, the paper continues:

> If the talks were eye-openers in different ways, there were significantly larger management problems at the SVS, in which Martin became involved. He attended a meeting of its Executive Committee, which 'had been informed in a very roundabout and unbusinesslike manner that its liquidation was imminent. A considerable discussion on the management of the S.V.S. and its possible future took place. I advocated a go-slow movement and an interview with the Chairman of the British Council and it was agreed that Sir Harold Spencer Jones should do this.' Martin was becoming a shrewd tactician, which was a valuable asset in his work for the troubled SVS. In mid-1948 the organization was thrown into crisis 'when the British Council withdrew £2,000 of its £4,000 annual grant'; there were also 'political difficulties . . . some of the key offices being held by a communist'— presumably J. G. Crowther—and 'the British Council threatened to withdraw all support.' A change of officers was made and a 'great deal

of effort has since gone into re-organizing the affairs of the Society. The first step was to regain the goodwill of organized science in this country and secondly, to increase the membership. Steps towards this end are being taken.' These 'steps' seemed to work, because within a couple of weeks the British Council was 'taking a more favourable view of the Society's activities', and a meeting with its representatives on 19 January was 'useful'—to the extent that the Council found £500 a week or two later 'to help in the redecoration of the premises'.

As to Crowther's defenestration, Cooper describes how, working on the SVS papers, he was astonished to find the following minutes of the sixteenth meeting of the Society's Executive Committee held on 27 May 1948:

> ... 186 THE PRESIDENT [Sir Harold Spencer Jones (1890–1960) Astronomer Royal] explained the reasons that had led him to submit his resignation. Letters containing submission of resignation from the Treasurer (Lord Victor Rothschild) and the Assistant Secretary (Esther Simpson) were read and discussed.
>
> 187 IT WAS AGREED that every effort should be made to persuade the President, Treasurer and Assistant Secretary to withdraw their resignations.

Crowther, whose autobiography records only Spencer Jones's resignation, immediately offered his resignation. On his resigning, Spencer Jones and Simpson thereupon withdrew their letters. Lord Rothschild did not but, says Cooper, 'made a very generous donation towards the Society's funds'.

What are we to make of Esther's participation – not mentioned in her letters or in *Refugee Scholars* – in this ambush?

The assistant secretary's resignation could not have been necessary to force Crowther's; it is not easy to imagine the president and treasurer asking the assistant secretary to join with them behind her manager's back, to strengthen their hand. How could they be sure she was not a supporter as well as a colleague of Crowther's?

At this point, we might ask if here we have the answer to why Esther omitted Crowther totally from her account of the SVS in *Refugee Scholars*. (Why she did give Louis Rapkine such prominence is another matter.) We might surmise that she did not want to touch on Crowther's departure. But why not at least acknowledge his role in the SVS's setting up and early success?

Then, how did she come to join the 27 May ambush? Did she see the resignation offers when putting the papers together for the meeting? And decide to join in? But if so, why?

Contemplating her role in Crowther's leaving, we might look back to her letters from Vienna to Roger and Irene Soltau in Beirut, with the accusations against the FOR's managers that so disquieted them, her friends. Did she play a similarly active part in Crowther's going? Did she simply want to demonstrate that she was not a Crowther person or hope to be asked to take Crowther's place? If the latter, she was to be disappointed. Professor F. J. M. Stratton DSO OBE FRS took Crowther's place. Esther remained as assistant secretary until the Society foundered financially in 1966.

Was the move politically inspired by her opposition to Crowther's left-wing, science in society, 'communist cell' views? Or her wanting to signal that? She described herself as a 'life-long socialist', and theoretically should have been a supporter of his social relations approach to science; she joined the Quaker peace initiative towards the Soviet Union led by Kathleen Lonsdale. (Or at least so she claimed, again in letters to the communist Broda, though in a letter to Broda she mis-stated the name of the Quaker committee and there is no reference to her membership in the Quaker records.)

Writing to Broda in October 1949 with 'news of the crisis in the SVS coming to a head', she told him,

> Big guns have been got out – organised science (which includes the President of the RS) versus the self-satisfied pen-pushers in the administrative jobs – the folk the French so aptly call ronds de cuire, folk who shudder if confronted with even the ghost of an idea.

In the end, the most likely explanation for Esther's joining in the resignations was that she wanted to side – be seen to side – with the Royal Society.

This receives some support from another of Cooper's discoveries. He does not discuss her taking part in the ambush. But what he does of significance is to record the problem that initially arose over Esther's drafting of the tribute to Crowther to appear in the SVS's Annual Report for 1949.

The draft went to Dr Dorothy Needham, a member of the SVS executive committee. 'Quite inadequate' was Dr Needham's reaction.

Cooper describes Esther's response as written with 'consummate tact':

> The report which I had drafted, and which was very brief, was subsequently added to by others. However I should like it to be more representative of the Council as a whole, and I should be grateful indeed to you if you yourself would rewrite the paragraphs concerning Mr Crowther . . .

'Consummate', maybe, but it is not clear that 'tact' is quite the appropriate term.

This reply admits that her draft acknowledgement of Crowther's work for the SVS was not what the SVS Council would consider sufficient. But rather than attempt something more representative of the Council as a whole – in other words more appreciative of Crowther – she would hand it over for redrafting.

In other words, it seems that even with Crowther disposed of, Esther could not bring herself to give him (her fellow grammar school pupil from Yorkshire) his public due. Offered a second chance, she still could not. Nor even on a third chance forty years later in *Refugee Scholars*.

What was her Crowther problem? The 'red cell'? Or that he had never lost his flat-capped northern character? In later life she wrote to Engelbert Broda's son Paul about the difference between people from Yorkshire and Lancashire, adding,

> Even in Yorkshire we discriminate; the people of Leeds have little use for the citizens of Bradford and vice versa; they are ten miles away from one another and that's all built up.

Or was it simply the idea of giving someone else public credit for the SVS? Cooper has the 1949 Annual Report's redrafted text:

> We would record here our special gratitude to Mr Crowther who, Secretary of the Society from its beginning early in 1944, resigned last October. The idea of the Society and the translation of this idea into reality were due to his vision and tireless work. During four difficult years he guided the activities of the Society with enthusiasm and

initiative, carrying out also such extra onerous tasks as the preparation
for UNESCO of the report of the Society.

Was that, or something like it, so difficult? But also in 1949, and after
the British Council had cut its grant to the SVS from £4,000 to £2,000,
the Society's Annual Meeting, Cooper records, saw Esther saluted:

> The Council cannot speak too highly of Miss Simpson's services and
> wish to assure you that but for her great spirit and devotion to the
> Society's interest, they might not be in a position to come before you
> with a report with the few gleams of hope for the future it contains.

The work of the housekeeper Mrs Robinson and her husband was also
saluted,

> for the splendid way they have stood by the Society in this time of
> difficulty.

In Esther's account – her 'naturally doing most of the work' – Mrs Robinson
and her husband join J. G. Crowther in nameless obscurity even though
for twenty years they had looked after the guests and held the fort while
Esther was fulfilling SPSL duties, out playing chamber music, or away with
the British Association. When complaining to Broda of how late she works
or working at weekends, she neglects to mention the amount of time she
spends away from the SVS enjoying her other activities.

Writing to Broda in December 1964, Esther had yet another version of
the SVS's origins. With the Society's future far from clear, she sent Broda
a copy of the Annual Report, '(my nineteenth)', which would give him an
idea of the Society's background, and added:

> (what it doesn't reveal is that the original initiative was mine alone).

Perhaps that was how she recalled it after twenty years, just as she saw
herself as an originator of the AAC.

She was also very critical of the honorary officers for being too busy to
take action to press the government for support.

Whatever its financial straits, Esther remained with the SVS until its
demise in 1966. Her work running the club through its constant financial
uncertainty, welcoming and befriending its foreign visitors, keeping records

of the Society's distinguished lectures, and documenting guests' careers won her the warmest of tributes and two decorations. Her French *Ordre des Palmes Académiques* first grade in 1949 was for her work with the SVS, as was her OBE in 1956, coupled in A. V. Hill's 1955 letter of recommendation with her assisting academic refugees.

She wrote to Broda about the shock of finding her name in the British New Year Honours list – had she not been informed in advance?

> I can't find out how or why but I have good reason to think it was largely due to the work with academic refugees. It caused quite a flutter as the SVS is not a government organisation that automatically has a quota of such things and nobody thought of me in such a connection. It was an awful shock to me.

The SVS work could not have offered a greater contrast to the running of the SPSL, particularly in its pre-war heyday. Esther moved from engaging with a small and highly selective group of refugees, helping them and their families to put down roots in a strange land and new culture and find new posts there or abroad, to operating a club with a constant turnover of new guests. A. V. Hill described her as the Society's hostess.

Esther's letters to Broda provide a running commentary on the affairs of the SVS as it teetered on the brink of financial demise.

Ray Cooper did not have the advantage of reading these letters, but his research produces a picture of the SVS as popular with its visiting scientists and the scientific community and honoured for its lecture programme, but unloved by its sponsors and financial backers, the Royal Society, which had a seat on the British Council's Science Advisory Committee, the government of the day, which had other financial priorities, and the British Council itself.

The Royal Society's approach was that it should be the sole official arbiter and channel to government on science policy. Thus the British Council should keep out of science. The British Council was under attack by the popular press for its claimed waste of public money – for instance, sending 'Morris Dancers to Kazakhstan'. And although the sums were very small comparatively, governments were unwilling to find the money. The reflexive 'red cell' reputation did not help during the Cold War.

The Society's own fundraising initiatives, membership fees and club charges could never end dependence on the British Council's grants. After the British Council's subsidy was cut by half in 1949, subsequent years saw a temporary increase. But £4,000 [£140,000 in today's money] remained out of reach. The Society could not fulfil its objectives unless the annual grant of £2,000 was increased to £4,000.

Esther wrote to Broda describing with increasing exasperation the failure to raise the necessary funds. But her letters also constantly depict her as overwhelmed by the day-to-day work of keeping the Society running. If she hasn't written to him, it's because she has no time to write any personal letters so busy is she with the SVS.

(But not only the SVS. She had also taken on organising the reception of foreign guests for the British Association's annual conference. From 1951 she took on voluntary SPSL duties. And all the while she enjoyed an extensive musical life playing chamber music with a variety of groups.)

Esther had no role in the Society's financial affairs. But until his frustrated resignation from the Council's Science Committee in 1956, A. V. Hill fought for that increase in subsidy with her future in mind. Cooper quotes a letter Hill wrote in February 1956 to the Society's secretary Alan Lang Brown when the Society's future was in the balance:

> It will be no good lingering on in hope, to die of starvation (and let Miss Simpson kill herself) during 1957/58. Perhaps someone will have better ideas than I have where we might look for additional support of this magnitude . . . Whether we should risk breaking Miss Simpson's heart at this stage before the formal decision of the British Council reaches us you must decide.

The Society did linger on for another ten years, with Esther and her staff doing all they could to keep its ideals alive in the face of the British Council's inability to increase its grant – another refusal came in 1957 – and fundraising efforts bringing in paltry sums.

The death blow came in 1962 with the end of the lease on 5 Old Burlington Street. Esther noted with disgust in a letter to Broda that it was to be pulled down to make way for a multi-storey car park.

The Society limped on. The discussion groups were hosted by the

English Speaking Union and office space found on a temporary basis. The final two discussion meetings were held in 1966, on 'The Shape of Ships to Come' and on 'Teaching Methods in Biology and Medicine'. But, as Esther told the Society's friends, 'without being able to put up members or offer them a restaurant', they lacked the two 'club' functions at the heart of the Society. She still found grounds for hope in the Society's joining with another organisation, perhaps the British Association.

Would the Labour government, with its aim of forging the new Britain 'in the white heat' of the technological revolution, prove financially sympathetic, as the Society's managers hoped? The Annual Report to the Eighteenth General Meeting in December 1965 noted that:

> Although Government help has not in so many words been refused, continued deferment of the consideration of the possibility of helping us amounts in practice to much the same thing.

Close readers will see in the phrase 'the consideration of the possibility' an expression of futility.

The Society's winding up was approved on the 24 October 1966.

Esther was sixty-three and taken to have retired on the SVS's closure.

42

Esther SPR

Though she had left the SPSL for the SVS all those years ago, and was currently acting as SPSL secretary with no hint of relinquishing the post, her 'children' and others who had worked with her in the cause of academic refugees now held a retirement celebration for her. A collection was made, of which the biologist Wilhem Feldberg was the main organiser, culminating in a cheque to be presented to her towards the purchase of a flat.

Six of her refugee scholars: David Daube, Wilhelm Feldberg, Hans Krebs, Max Perutz, Nikolaus Pevsner and Otto Skutsch sent out an appeal to her children:

> Some University teachers and scholars got to know her because they were given grants by the Academic Assistance Council, others received encouragement and advice from her, but what we all probably remember best is that she was always there, that her life centred round one problem only, how to help all of us. Whenever a colleague needed help we could send him to Esther Simpson, knowing he would be befriended, and effectively assisted towards obtaining the maximum help available in those days.

Money came in from Australia, the US and Canada, Germany, Austria, Switzerland and Israel. In a typical response, Eugene Wigner wrote on 5 November 1965,

I hardly know of any other cause as worth and deserving as this one!

Three hundred and twenty of her refugee scholars, her 'children', contributed to the cheque for £3,500 [£71,000 in today's money] that was presented to her at her retirement celebration on 9 June 1966. She was also given a book with their names. Its message read:

> To Tess with thanks from all her friends and to remind her of the occasion on 9th June 1966.

Other messages all stressed her always being there to help, the sweetness of her personality, her courage when demanded, her friendship.

Sir Walter Adams's remains the most full and striking, also touching on the theme of her family of refugees:

> I do not know what your present score of Barons, Knights, Fellows of the Royal Society is, but your family – of which you are mother and sister – is without doubt the most talented and distinguished in the world.

He also refers to her as a colleague:

> My personal debt to you is something I cannot put into words. Never could anyone have had a more loyal colleague, tireless, non-irritable, full of insight into personal problems, unswerving in devotion to the principles for which the AAC/SPSL stood . . .

When she wrote to Broda describing the event, she was marking out her future and retirement was not what she had in mind:

> I am quite overcome by the kindness and generosity that has been shown me by our refugee scholars . . . The reception was like a dream. I was quite overwhelmed by the volume of affection shown by the scholars, who some of them came quite long distances; about 150 accepted the invitation. [Ninety-five-year-old Professor Stefan Jellinek came from Oxford.] I intend to carry on the Secretaryship of the Society for the Protection of Science and Learning indefinitely; our help is still needed and will be, I fear, for many years to come. Our latest refugee scholars are from South Africa. My concern just now is

to find a new home for the SPSL; when this is achieved, all our scholars will be notified. Then I shall look for some paid employment, because I am not really ready to retire.

For our understanding of Esther's view of herself and the SPSL, all we have to do is remember the phrasing of that letter:

I intend to carry on the Secretaryship of the Society for the Protection of Science and Learning indefinitely; our help is still needed and will be, I fear, for many years to come.

The semi-colon says it all. Thirty-three years earlier she had started as assistant secretary at the AAC. Now she and its SPSL successor were in her eyes inseparable.

Ten years earlier, in 1956, when she was at the SVS, it was on the basis of her professionalism in dealing with the refugees that A. V. Hill recommended her for the OBE:

... Her knowledge, critical judgement and experience were invaluable; by what she did then not only did she build up a fund of goodwill towards this country when it was most needed but she made a substantial contribution to the national cause.

At the 1966 celebration, he added the initials SPR – Supreme Protagonist of Refugees – to her OBE.

Many would have questioned whether so comprehensive a title should properly have gone to his late fellow member of the House of Commons Eleanor Rathbone, with whom he worked to secure the release of the mainly Jewish German-speaking refugees interned in May 1940.

The SPSL 1946 annual report notes that the success of the 'work of securing the release of scholars and scientists able and willing to assist in the war effort' was 'largely due' to Esther, assisted in particular by A. V. Hill and Eleanor Rathbone.

Born in Liverpool in May 1872 into a Quaker family, Eleanor Rathbone was an indomitable campaigner for women's rights. Elected Independent MP for the Combined English Universities from 1929, she was an early vocal critic of Hitler's and became known as 'the honourable member for refugees'. It was said she died from exhaustion in January 1946 from her tireless work for them.

Eleanor Rathbone had already participated in the rescue of 4,000 Basque children from the Spanish Civil War when, in 1938, she responded with a frenzy of action to the waves of refugees generated by the *Anschluss*, the *Kristallnacht* pogrom and the Munich Agreement handing over the Sudetenland to Hitler.

She set up the voluntary Parliamentary Committee on Refugees, gathering 200 Parliamentary supporters. Its remit was

> to influence the Government and public opinion in favour of a generous yet carefully safeguarded refugee policy, including large-scale schemes of permanent settlement inside or outside of Empire; also, since 1,000s of refugees would perish while awaiting such schemes – temporary reception homes in this country where refugees can be maintained, sorted out and eventually migrated, except in cases where there abilities can be profitably utilised here without injustice to our own workers.

In a post for Refugee Week 2016, celebrating Eleanor Rathbone's humanity and determination, Dr Susan Cohen, author of 'Rescue the Perishing: Eleanor Rathbone and the Refugees' and co-founder of the website Remembering Eleanor Rathbone[36] wrote:

> Deputations, questions, letters, phone calls, liaising with every refugee committee and activist, and enlisting the support of other MPs were all part of her armoury. The mass internment of around 27,600 enemy aliens in May 1940 served only to exacerbate an already challenging situation and to plunge Eleanor and her committee into a maelstrom of activity as they sought the release of 1,000's [sic] of refugees. She put over 80 parliamentary questions on internment alone, the issues pursued including the importance of separating Nazi internees from non-Nazis, the shocking living conditions in many of the camps, the food shortages and lack of medical care . . .

36 https://rememberingeleanorrathbone.wordpress.com

The response to Rathbone's urgent requests for a more generous immigration policy followed a pattern, including claims that it would fuel domestic anti-semitism, and in a desperate effort at countering this assertion, she established, in late 1942, the National Committee for Rescue from Nazi Terror.[37]

In her study of British Women Humanitarians 1900–1950, *Doers of the Word*, Sybil Oldfield quotes Rathbone's fellow MP Harold Nicolson,

... recalcitrant ministers would quail before the fire of her magnificent eyes.

And says herself,

Eleanor Rathbone was, unquestionably, the most tireless and wide-ranging of all the British women humanitarians of the twentieth century ... A monument to [her] should be set up in the Home Office. Every politician in future who holds that place would work with her watching eye upon him.

Of course, as a man of supreme intelligence, A. V. Hill might have argued that 'supreme' as a qualifier does not necessarily denote a singular. After all, he was a joint Nobel laureate. 'Protagonists [pl] for Refugees' could include Eleanor Rathbone, yes, and equally certainly Bertha Bracey.

Born into Quaker stock in 1893, Bracey had been in charge of Quaker relief operations in Germany and the Netherlands, and became secretary of the Quakers' Germany Emergency Committee set up by the Meeting for Sufferings on 7 April 1933 (coinciding with the passing of the Law for the Restoration of the Civil Service) to help victims of Nazi persecution to find refuge outside Germany, working with Jewish organisations in Britain and Germany. Its first meeting was on 12 April. Her name became synonymous with the rescue and care of thousands of Jewish children from Germany, Austria, and Czechoslovakia both before the war, through the *Kindertransport*, and after the defeat of Germany.

Awarded an OBE in 1952, she was recognised as a British Hero of

37 https://refugeeweek.org.uk/remembering-eleanor-rathbone-the-mp-for-refugees/

the Holocaust in 2010 by the then Prime Minister Gordon Brown. The inscription on her statue at Friends House in London reads:

> To honour Bertha Bracey (1893–1989)
>   Who gave practical leadership to Quakers in quietly rescuing and resettling thousands of Nazi victims and lone children between 1933–1948

The SVS years over, her 'retirement' generously marked by her SPSL family, Esther continued to work as secretary of the SPSL, taking it with her to her newly acquired Buckland Crescent. But she also looked for paid work to carry her through to sixty-five. She found a post, or one was found for her, with the Wellcome Foundation, set up in 1936 to support scientific research and the study of medicine.

43

What Retirement?

Esther wrote to Broda that when she was offered the position at Wellcome, as an Information Manager, she assumed it was for the records she had compiled at the SVS on scientists and scientific activity. She continued to compile them as far as she could long after she ceased work, going from her Buckland Crescent flat to Finchley Road – so much the haunt of German-speaking refugees it had been known as *Finchleystrasse* – at nine o'clock each morning to buy *The Times* and the *Guardian* newspapers to be scoured for snippets on the lives of 'her children' and their children.

She shopped for her economical groceries at Sainsbury's and the local department store John Barnes, complaining about rising prices – butter, milk, bread, rolls – though music helped her to cope with the world situation, price rises and inflation, as did *The Times* crossword that she did every day 'to keep my brain ticking over'. She also did the *Observer* version every week, as well as the music crossword in the local Hampstead paper, the *Ham & High*. She had been introduced to *The Times* crossword, she told Broda, by her friend, the economist Karl Polanyi in her 1932 Vienna days.

She clipped records of student turmoil at Berkeley and other universities, so she wrote to a friend, and noted the state of the world. In August 1983 she wrote to Broda,

> I must say I do not miss holidays. Typhoid in Greece, shoot-out in Avignon, hotels unbuilt in Spain, strikes at airports etc. etc.

These records, the cuttings from the press and science journals, were not a hobby or pastime. She started the SVS information system on scientists, their activities and whereabouts, on her own initiative, though a possible source of inspiration is noted later. She remarked to Ray Cooper how pleasantly surprised the visiting scientists were to find their particulars were already in the Society's records. (If they came from authoritarian regimes, perhaps they were not so pleasantly surprised.) The records also provided an information service for those wanting to get in touch with scientists working in specific fields.

Ray Cooper lists the formidable weight of pre-internet hard information deposited at the University of Sussex:

> 66 stiff-backed files containing alphabetically biographical career details of scientists; 1 card index of international scientific societies; 2.5 card indexes of titles of scientific conferences and names of participants; 140 card indexes of individual scientists with name, address, and relevant contributions to scientific societies and periodicals; 1 card index of participants in SVS discussion meetings and chronological list of SVS members; 1 card index of scientific societies, British and international; 1 card index of donors and scientific journals; 27 card indexes of individual SVS members, master cards with all particulars.
>
> In addition, at least twelve cardboard boxes of assorted press cuttings covering, between 1944 and 1966, every conceivable scientific topic likely to be of interest to scientists.

Bear in mind Esther was not a scientist.

Her keeping records of scientists was an activity of great significance to her. Individually she followed the careers of her 'children' – grantees – and their children. She also compiled records of scientists generally:

> . . . my job was a day and night job, and even weekends, because I found it necessary to compile an information service, although nobody asked me to do so. I kept track of people who contributed to scientific journals. I collected names and addresses of the contributors so that if I was asked by a visiting scientist about getting in touch with British

> equivalents whom he may not have known, I would be able to turn
> up what was necessary. That was quite a big job but I did it because I
> thought it was a contribution to the Society.

Why a visiting scientist should have asked the SVS hostess rather than
use his own scientific contacts about getting in touch with 'British
equivalents he may not have known' is unclear. Equally, keeping records
of her 'children's' lives bespeaks an unusual sense of closeness or of that
refugeeisation discussed earlier.

A comparison is irresistible with Mrs Heeny, the masseuse in Edith
Wharton's *The Custom of the Country*. Mrs Heeny's black bag is stuffed with
the 'piles and piles' of newspaper clippings, the strips of newspaper she
keeps recording the public lives of her clients and their contacts, clippings
she will bring out to satisfy another client's curiosity. She also brings them
out to satisfy the remarrying heroine's son, Paul.

> He had the feeling that Mrs Heeny's clippings, aside from their great
> intrinsic interest, might furnish him the clue to many things he didn't
> understand, and that nobody had ever had time to explain to him. His
> mother's marriages, for instance: he was sure there was a great deal
> to find out about them.

But Mrs Heeny's newspaper clippings will not satisfy Paul's curiosity about
his mother and her latest husband; nothing personal is recorded there, only
the public facts about a limited class of the highly privileged.

44

Unwelcome

Esther's time with the Wellcome Foundation is not mentioned in either of Ray Cooper's works. Possibly she simply did not want to remember it.

In December 1966 she told Broda that with the SPSL parked at the British Association, she had put off taking a job while her flat was put in order, but she now needed to bolster her income and had taken this post, which she later described to him as Information Manager.

> I did not replace anyone; the post was created with me in mind, inspired by the information service I had built up with the SVS. No one was clear as to what I was expected to do, and after six weeks I am still feeling my way. The job is radically different from any previous ones in two important ways. I am not responsible for running the whole show and if I want any equipment, I ask for it and get it. The weak spot is secretarial assistance, which is inadequate and almost not existent. I can manage for the moment, but if I get ambitious, I shall ask for a proper secretary.

This is all interestingly remote from the facts. The scanty Wellcome record of her being employed shows only she was taken on as Administrative Assistant in charge of Records at their Queen Anne Street office, starting on 1 November 1966.

We might assume she did not enjoy her time at Wellcome, whatever her title; not her own boss, no longer running the whole show or honoured as a veteran of 1933. To Broda she described it as 'a job. Not entirely uncongenial.' And that

> I'm not yet sacked but doubt whether I'll go on for long. It does good work by giving money away for constructive purposes but I'm not keen on its office aspect. At present I need the money.

Two of 'my' children had won medals, she added. As for her 'rogues' gallery' – her massive collection of cuttings on her children's progress – 'At the Wellcome Trust I am trying something on a smaller scale.'

To move from the status of founding member and pivotal figure in the SVS and SPSL to a quotidian employee of the well-established Wellcome Foundation cannot have been easy. On 28 October 1967 she wrote to Broda she was not 'overenthusiastic about my job at the WT'.

She left Wellcome without any recorded ceremonial.

In a letter of 30 March 1968 to a musical acquaintance she says she is giving up her job at the end of July: she found it too much to have a full-time job and a strenuous voluntary one [for the SPSL] as well. But she strikes a different tone when she adds that she will look for a part-time occupation where her qualifications will be of use and welcome, and remuneration won't be the first consideration. She had wanted the salary to cover the expenses in acquiring the flat; had she really enjoyed the job she might have gone on with it in spite of having really no leisure, but she did not care for it.

In a round-robin Christmas letter dated only December 1968, she tells her recipients she has left her post as what she names Information Assistant at the Wellcome. She found that in the long run she could not manage to hold down a full-time paid position and cope with her voluntary job as secretary of the Society for the Protection of Science and Learning, which came first with her.

Of course, that was not her only voluntary job. She was, she went on, looking after overseas guests as usual at the British Association annual meeting when the Soviet occupation of Czechoslovakia took place.

> As a result my voluntary job is more like full time; I am translated back into the nineteen-thirties, in touch with many of the same

organizations and many of the same people as then. It is rather grisly! The difference is that I have no office personnel, so there is not much leisure for me. In addition to Czechoslovakia and South Africa, we have to be prepared for an influx from Greece and Poland if the scholars who have been displaced will be allowed to leave. In spite of everything I do manage to continue with my chamber music.

Esther as the self-conscious veteran of the 1930s is on display here, though the spur comes from conflating three very different if approximately simultaneous European political events in the light of their bringing refugee scholars in the same period. The April 1967 extreme right-wing putsch by the Greek colonels; the Moscow-required Warsaw Pact invasion of Czechoslovakia in August 1968, to repress an attempt to liberalise the communist regime; and the wave of virulent antisemitism, with thousands of its Jewish population forced to leave the country, that formed part of the repression of liberal tendencies by Poland's ruling Communist Party also between 1968 and 1972.

In September 1968, fresh from her stint with the British Association in Dundee, Esther wrote to her brother Joe, who was on a visit to England, that she had time for nothing but work, with news of displaced Czechoslovaks coming thick and fast, and the size of the problem meaning that some official action would have to be taken. She had given up looking for a part-time job now her voluntary work was more than full time.

Not quite a year later, in July 1969, she is telling Joe and Florrie that her work has escalated to such an extent that she has almost no leisure: the Polish crisis had taken her back into the 1930s, the persecution being entirely and unashamedly antisemitic. All Jews were 'Zionists' and 'Zionists' were the enemies of the Poles. In a step further than the Nazis, she wrote that one Jewish great-grandparent made a person Jewish. Poles were allowed to go only to Israel having paid over all they had. She had to deal with the Czechs and also now Brazilians. There was no end. She supposed she should be grateful for having too much work to allow herself to brood.

Although we learn next to nothing of these academic refugees from *Refugee Scholars*, at this period Esther really was coming to their aid on her own, a retired sixty-five-year-old volunteer secretary of the SPSL.

However, this was not the 1930s. She remarked to Broda at the same time that it was obvious there were not likely to be future FRSs or FBAs among any Polish scholars who got there. In 1970 it became,

I was now, alas, dealing with displaced Polish scholars.

Alas?

45

Academic Possibilities

Back full time to the SPSL did not mean back to the glory days of succouring existing and future Nobel Prize winners or other academics of pre-eminence, days on which she would look back as might the sole survivor of Dunkirk, the last and only one to remember what it was like on the beaches.

'Academic possibilities' replaced 'exceptional abilities, exceptionally trained' or 'elite of the first order' as the bar for help. No new 'children' were added to her family after the fall of Nazi Germany.

In *In Defence of Learning*, Shula Marks notes the concern aroused

> . . . among some members of the SPSL's allocation committee that recent refugee academics no longer met the high standards set by their predecessors. A far greater stretch of the Council's imagination and generosity was now required. The Society would have to redefine its role. Council members were by no means unanimous in approving the Society's change of direction, harking back – as many did – to the great days of Nobel Prizewinners, Knights of the Realm, and Fellows of the Learned Societies. Arguably this signalled perhaps a degree of amnesia about the very many less celebrated academic refugees the Society had assisted in the 30s and 40s. Nor was the existing Council with its roots in the European world of learning ideally placed to support them as Esther Simpson was only too aware when she

discovered that South Africa's apartheid government was dismissing academics on political and racial grounds from the University of Fort Hare.

The common cultural ground between saviours and saved that existed in the world of 1930s, 1940s and 1950s science and learning had existed in a world of colonialisation. Post-war Britain had still ruled some seventy overseas territories. Now that world was in its death throes, though the colonialists' historic attitudes were not always keeping pace with the facts on the ground.

Shula Marks quotes from a letter Esther wrote to a South African correspondent in the 1960s:

> When this [flight of academic refugees] happened on the Continent in the 1930s it had an effect on the universities there from which they have hardly recovered, yet they had sufficient reserves to carry on their university teaching. What is to happen to the South African universities? I hope that wisdom will prevail before there is an academic catastrophe.

And in 1981 when Esther was standing in for (her eventual successor as secretary) Liz Fraser on holiday,

> The applications we have now are very different from the earlier ones and are quite difficult to decide as the standard is so different.

The reach of scholastic assistance moved still further afield with the introduction of the apartheid regime in South Africa, and the political upheavals in Greece, Biafra, Bangladesh, Rhodesia, Argentina, Chile. The challenge for the SPSL – and Esther – was over its continuing adherence to the original academic criteria, the highest, for assistance or recognising that time and circumstance now dictated helping academic victims of political oppression who were less recognisably eminent.

In 1970 she wrote:

> Did I tell you [Engelbert] our latest grantee is a Biafran?

She was so taken with this, she asked him twice.

Engelbert Broda's son Paul, to whom Esther had stood in as a surrogate godmother, wrote:

> I think she would have been less at ease with subsequent waves of refugees from the Africa and Middle Eastern worlds, though she certainly engaged with Chileans and South Africans. She was definitely elitist.

Certainly, readers of *Refugee Scholars* looking for a detailed accounting of post-war, post-colonial assistance similar to the pre-war will not find it; her 'children' and 'friends' seem to have been confined to those she helped from the Continental influx of the pre-war glory days.

At the end of August 1971 she wrote to her brother Joe that she had been busy chiefly with South African displaced scholars, as well as having to prepare for the SPSL's yearly Council meeting and its Annual General Meeting. There was a lot of work, she wrote, and she had not succeeded in finding someone locally to help her and eventually take over from her. As for holidays, she was never dependent on holidays, she says, but if she could find the right clerical assistant she would go abroad the next year – but not if it meant flying, as the condition of her ears would not allow that.

On 11 January 1972, Esther wrote to a Canadian friend:

> Alas! I am kept as busy as ever. Since 1968 there have been waves from Czechoslovakia, Greece, Poland, Brazil, some South Africans, the occasional Hungarian, Rumanian, ex-Biafran, Bangladeshi – there is no end.

She could not absent herself as she couldn't find a stand-in and could not leave the job unattended even for a short time. Grants had to be paid each month, and one never knew what emergencies might arise.

They even had a Bangladeshi grantee, she writes to Joe in January 1972. Florrie, Joe's wife of fifty-seven years, had died, and in this same letter Esther demonstrates her capacity and willingness to go where angels fear to tread in the giving of advice on matters of personal difficulty or distress.

Taking what might be seen as authoritative command in a troubled situation, rather than offering an empathetic reaching out, she tells her bereaved brother it was good to know his family were there for him; he should not feel so alone, though he would always miss Florrie. Perhaps by now he has established a routine that keeps him busy, and he must have friends he can see. It was good to know he might come over. She expected there was still some business outstanding with Florrie's family, so she looked forward to seeing him.

In a letter of May 1972, the tone is just as brisk as she tells him she realises how he misses Florrie and always will. But he is lucky in having his family with whom he can always stay, on the doorstep almost. She has friends who have no such consolation. Life for them is very hard, she says consolingly.

The first sentences of the letter are an apology for not writing earlier, but she had been so busy that she had had little leisure to give her anything to write about. There were constantly new applications for grants. They already had two Bangladeshi scholars, and there were always new applications from Czechs and Poles and South Africans, and so on. There was correspondence of all kinds connected with the job, and she had very little clerical help. She was doing a great deal more herself than a few years ago. Her evenings were taken up with music and meetings, which was a great safety valve. But in the day she had almost no time to herself, which was rather tiring. Visits to the dentist and that sort of thing were the only breaks.

She complained to Joe at length about the price inflation brought by both decimalisation and the introduction of packaging for food like rolls, which meant having to purchase five where one or two would do. She had complained to the local consumer group about the change, as the ordinary old-age pensioner was not sufficiently articulate to fight his own battle. (No ordinary old-age pensioner, Esther.)

A January 1973 letter from Joe comments on the ending of the war in Vietnam and the UK's entry into the Common Market. Later letters discuss Watergate and British sex scandals, inflation and Canadian opposition to Chilean refugees. They point up the narrow compass of Esther's letters: how hard she is working, new academic refugees and the price of rolls.

But in a letter of 18 March 1982 she speaks about the discouragement of encountering the same thorny problems as when they began nearly fifty years earlier. Having learned to accept facts rather than dreams, they could give a little help, saving a few lives, and bringing hope of a better future for a few families.

She could look back to July 1933 and know she had certainly done that.

46

Times are a-Changing

For Esther, the overthrow of the democratically elected government of Chile in 1973 was a personal turning point, just as Hitler's taking power had been forty years earlier.

The violent ousting of Salvador Allende's *Unidad Popular* government on 11 September 1973 by a right-wing military junta, led by the commander-in-chief General Augusto Pinochet, was also a generational turning point for the SPSL, now under Esther's roof.

In the repression that followed the coup, with Pinochet declared President, tens of thousands of the junta's political opponents disappeared, were imprisoned or interned, tortured, murdered. Those who could fled abroad. Those already abroad looked for means to extend their stay.

The response in Britain saw the founding of 'Academics for Chile', one of a number of popular groups that erupted spontaneously to support the people of Chile. Echoes of the 1930s can be heard in the summary of how Academics for Chile came into existence written by one of its moving spirits, Alan Angell, in 2010:

> Academics for Chile developed from a series of conversations between academics in various universities in the UK deeply concerned with the plight of academics and students in Chile following the coup of 1973. A group of us – a dozen or so – met in London and decided that we would organise a campaign to try to help those academics and students

already in detention or in danger and bring them to continue their studies or research in the UK. We were also concerned with the plight of those Chileans studying in the UK who lost their grants following the coup and in many cases were denounced by the military government and hence were unable to return to their country.[38]

Academics for Chile was one of three separate organisations that were set up to organise different aspects of the resistance to General Pinochet's regime: the 'Chile Solidary Campaign', 'Chile Committee for Human Rights' and 'Academics for Chile'.

Again, echoes of the 1930s are distinct:

> We secured a list of sponsors who, deliberately, were mostly establishment figures – Lord Kahn a prominent Cambridge economist, the Archbishop of Canterbury, Richard Keynes an eminent scientist and others – to show that we were appealing on the grounds of academic freedom in general and not because we as an organisation sympathised with the aims of the Allende government (even if of course many did). We also had support from the highly respected and long-established Society for the Protection of Science and Learning – a source of much useful advice and help from its then secretary Esther Simpson.[39]

Lord Kahn was the SPSL's treasurer, but the SPSL and its 'supreme protagonist of refugees' were seen as a source of advice rather than as central to the Chilean crisis.

In 1974, Esther wrote to Broda, presaging the SPSL's future, and her own:

> The Chile emergency is too big for our little Society. There are some 600 academics affected, who are either in other Latin American countries, in prison or concentration camps. 'Academics for Chile' together with the WUS [World University Service] has set up a special

---

38 https://warwick.ac.uk/fac/arts/history/research/projects/chileanexileinuk/ testimonies/documents/alan_angell.pdf

39 https://warwick.ac.uk/fac/arts/history/research/projects/chileanexileinuk/ testimonies/documents/alan_angell.pdf

office for Chile. Meetings of both bodies take such time. Our Society
was concerned with those who happened to be in this country at the
time of the coup d'état.

At the same time, she reported that Lord Kahn was very concerned and
thought the Society would have to pack up in a couple of years.

At the height of the German academic refugee crisis, the question of the
AAC's being too small to participate had never arisen. The Chile crisis was
exactly in the SPSL's *raison d'être*.

If its officers had been firm on making Esther's retirement a reality, even
if she was the only one who could remember how it was forty years earlier,
would a younger secretary have been able to take the SPSL into the heart
of the Chilean battle where it belonged? As it was, this became a watershed
moment for the SPSL and for its secretary.

Alan Angell and his academic colleagues had a tiger by the tail; the
amount of work and financial administration was too much for them to
manage along with their personal academic responsibilities. In October
1973 they wisely proposed to Alan Phillips, general secretary of the World
University Service 1973–1981, that it should take over the scholarship
programme for Chilean refugee students; though small – no more than
five full-time staff – it already had some experience of such programmes
for Hungarian and Czech refugee students.

At this point in the narrative, I had originally written that popular
funding had poured into Academics for Chile. Kindly correcting this, Alan
Phillips recalled for me how the AFC/WUS situation had actually evolved:

> When Alan Angell and I met in October 1973, popular funding had not
> poured in. There had not been any fundraising, although some
> Oxbridge colleges were offering to waive fees or to provide free
> accommodation to existing stranded scholars for a term. Popular
> fundraising began in November with a joint appeal led by WUS as an
> education charity and publicised by Academics for Chile ACF as ACF
> had no legal status nor a bank account as far as I am aware. ACF was
> an informal grouping of academics that met in London on a few
> occasions and liaised often on the phone. Their support was crucial
> to the success of the WUS programme.

Once the fundraising took off in November offers of funding did indeed pour in and by March 1974, 50 academics and post-graduate students were found fully funded places in universities through our joint efforts. Additionally, the fundraising campaign raised over £39,000 from public donations and grants from charitable trusts and foundations [£298,000 today]. This sum included the one-off grant of £7,000 to WUS from the Ford Foundation for WUS's work for Chilean refugee academics and students with Academics for Chile. Alan Angell and I had lunch with a Vice President of the Ford Foundation in London late in 1973, which was a good example of how we worked together.

In discussions with government ministers and officials, I was able to use the breadth of public support as a powerful argument to persuade them to fund the WUS Chilean Refugee scholarship programme. Eventually, the programme grew from being a tiger that mewed to a tiger that roared, providing over 900 scholarships and spending over £11 million pounds from 1974–1985. At today's prices that may be worth 10 times that figure [£84 million today].

The generous grant from the Ford Foundation made possible the appointment of a part-time – three days a week – administrator, Liz Fraser, a former lecturer in French at Southampton University. The election of a Labour government in October 1974 produced further funding at the instance of the Minister for Overseas Development Judith Hart. The programme saw 900 Chileans achieve their studies in the UK.

The University of Warwick WUS history programme recalled:

The WUS programme was very complex. On the one hand, many of the people assisted were or had been in danger, some had been tortured, were in hiding or in prison; and there were many challenging issues of adaptation and settlement, of understanding British culture, the English language, the social and educational system while coping with the pain of exile and the hopes for the future. On the other hand, WUS had to organise long, sometimes secretive, lines of communication, extending from those in secret addresses in Chile to FLACSO and CLACSO in Chile and Argentina, to WUS in London, to University Departments and to individual academics, who offered crucial advice matching individuals to courses.[40]

The Society for the Protection of Science and Learning was naturally among the refugee organisations to which WUS reached out for assistance, though with its lack of resources and the paucity of academic posts appropriate for the Chilean refugees, the amount of direct help the Society could give was limited. But in the chapter he contributed to *In Defence of Learning*, 'Refugee Academics from Chile', Alan Phillips noted:

> Nevertheless, the SPSL did what it could, working closely and diligently with ACF to assist academics and with WUS to assist postgraduate students. Much of SPSL assistance was indirect – contacting influential academics, writing to universities and colleges and approaching trusts that it knew, using its high reputation and the contacts of its distinguished Council members, including Lord Ashby and Lord Kahn.
>
> In the small number of cases where the SPSL was itself able to give grants, the recipients received them gratefully. Limited as they were, the grants went some way to convincing them that they were welcome in the UK, and provided them with an opportunity to continue their work for a short time and allowed them a breathing space to plan for their future.

As for Esther's part, an unmistakably elegiac note is to be heard:

> The SPSL frequently pooled resources with both AFC and WUS in their respective fields. Advice and information was readily shared and, on a few occasions[,] money was pooled to overcome financial limitations. Esther Simpson, who was still then the Secretary of SPSL, was a regular, albeit unofficial presence at WUS and AFC meetings in 1973 [she was seventy] and 1974, and both organizations viewed her as an invaluable source of advice and contacts. WUS had substantial

---

40   https://warwick.ac.uk/fac/arts/history/research/projects/chileanexileinuk/ wusprogramme/https://warwick.ac.uk/fac/arts/history/research/projects/ chileanexileinuk/wusprogramme/

funds to support postgraduate and undergraduate students from Chile, while the AFC had a strong network of scholars who worked on Latin American and Chilean issues. Nonetheless the expertise, reputation, and historic contacts of SPSL were valuable. Esther Simpson played a coordinating role within SPSL, showing her customary deep commitment to those scholars in need and their families. She deployed her rich experience to each and every inquiry, and it is clear that she took and maintained a personal interest in the outcome of it all.

Esther had always worked by the SPSL book in her response to applicants – but Chile put an end to that.

Valuable as 'the expertise, reputation, and historic contacts of SPSL' may have been to WUS and AFC in the crisis, contemporary history had bypassed Esther's attachment to the pre-war refugee world of German academic brilliance, of *Bildung* and *Kultur*.

Besides the Chilean scholars – and those who were already there were, she told Broda, placed with Cambridge colleges by Lord Kahn – she also had a South African and a Hungarian to deal with, and was wondering about Portugal.

Without any clerical help, in the whole of 1974 she was away from London for one day – for a few hours in Cambridge for a memorial service and in 1975 for a Twelfth Night Feast at Trinity. '"We" have four Fellows of Trinity.'

As for the future, in *In Defence of Learning* Alan Phillips summarised the train of events:

> The relationship that had begun between WUS and SPSL through the links with Esther Simpson and Lord Ashby, then Chairman of SPSL, and also Vice-President of WUS, was strengthened through the collaborative work undertaken by the two organizations. Mutual trust and community of purpose led in due course to a compact between the SPSL and WUS, which assured the continuation of the SPSL as an independent body. WUS was able to provide a room in its offices and put forward Liz Fraser as a possible successor to Esther Simpson; she was initially seconded from WUS to the SPSL as its Secretary for one day a week, in 1978. Close collaboration was also assured when a

number of members of Academics for Chile network, including Alan
Angell, became member of WUS Executive Committee and its awards
committees. In due course a number were also invited to become
members of the Council of the SPSL.

The fact that WUS was able to house the SPSL in its offices from
1978 and the formal compact between them meant that not only was
its organizational and administrative structure secure, but it
was embedded in the organization most clearly linked to its own aims.
The flow of information on refugee issues, and its access to first-hand
knowledge of the needs of refugees from countries all over the world,
as well as of individual scholars, established the SPSL at the heart of
refugee work in the UK. According to Liz Fraser, without this lifeline
it could not have survived.

Not only survived, of course, but lived on to fight the cause of academic
freedom, in 1999 changing its name to the Council for Assisting Refugee
Academics, and again in 2014 to The Council for At-Risk Academics.

In June 1974 Esther described WUS's involvement with the SPSL to Broda:
WUS would carry out the clerical work under Esther's supervision.
She would also continue to see displaced scholars, telephoning on their
behalf and advising as best she could. Alan Phillips notes that Esther's being
on the board of a Rothschild charity for Jewish intellectuals made possible
grants to two Chilean authors.

Writing to Broda in July 1974, she remarked that she was attending
meetings on Chile. WUS had applied to the government for help. Ministers
were sympathetic but not the civil service and the Treasury so negotiations
were dragging on.

> I took the General Secretary of WUS [Alan Phillips] to the Royal Society
> conversazione, and he was duly impressed by seeing in the flesh so
> many living legends . . . I enjoy the Conversazione because it is an
> annual opportunity to see so many of 'my' children in all their glory.

But Esther also recorded how she was shattered when she told Phillips she
was attending a meeting of the JD Bernal Peace Library – and the name
meant nothing to him.

It had meant the 'red cell' in Crowther's SVS. The eminent scientist J. D. Bernal (1901–1971) was a passionate socialist and peace campaigner. The library was opened in 1968 as a centre for peace research and was donated to the Marx Memorial Library, of which he had been president, in 1979. It is not clear when or how Esther became a supporter of his life and works.

Recalling that conversazione, Alan Phillips remarked to me:

> I was delighted to be taken to the Royal Society by Esther, I knew little about its events and I was undoubtedly impressed by its ambience and the participants.
>
> Esther was greeted kindly, if somewhat patronisingly, by some of those who knew her at the Royal Society. I am saddened that Esther was 'shattered by my lack of knowledge of the JD Bernal Peace Library' but I was in my twenties with many things for me to learn as there still are today! My good fortune was that Esther did not hold this against me as I was invited back to a Conversazione on two other occasions.

She was only seventy-three, but by June 1976, Esther's correspondence with Broda is starting to describe the setting sun of her SPSL life.

> I am overwhelmed with new refugees and so conscious of our lack of funds. We have practically no income, and the value of our investments has slumped to a frightening degree. We have been saved by the existence of a special fund [a Rothschild trust] for Jewish intellectuals, which has so far reimbursed our grants to Jewish refugee scholars (nearly all the Poles were Jewish and some Czechs). But I fear that fund is at a low ebb.

A list of countries displacing academics since 1968 included Czechoslovakia, Brazil, Poland, Biafra, Bangladesh, Uganda, South Africa, Chile, Zambia, Rhodesia, Argentina 'and even the USSR'. The three Argentinians were all Jewish, so was at least one Rhodesian and one from Zambia. That a grantee was an Orthodox Jew (from Russia) prompted a surprising reaction: 'I had not realized it was still possible to find younger orthodox Jews – he is in his 40s.'

> To prevent a catastrophic hiatus should anything drastic happen to me, I have been briefing a member of WUS staff on our procedure,

she comes every three weeks or so and I tell her what has happened since the last time. She is the secretary of their Chilean section, and was a lecturer in French at Southampton University – Liz Fraser.

And in December 1976, reflecting on events in Chile and Argentina

> . . . the latter place they are lucky to escape with their lives. Uruguay also is a very ugly place. I still have no clerical help, but the time has come to think of when I can no longer cope. I have had ideas on this for some time, but delicate negotiations are required.

In February 1977, she wanted 'to hang on to the job for a while yet, if they will let me'. But a year later,

> In theory I 'retire' at the end of July, on my 75th birthday, but in actual fact I shall be going on with a great deal of the work as 'Honorary Consultant'. The takeover period is bound to be a very long one indeed.

She also had to read *The Times* and the *Guardian*, she told Broda, to keep her work of reference and cuttings up to date.

But the road taken in July 1933 from the two rooms on the top floor of Burlington House had reached a crossroads for its last traveller. A meeting at King's College Cambridge between the WUS UK chair Iain Wright, the SPSL's two senior officers, the chair Lord Ashby and the treasurer Lord Kahn agreed that the WUS should find office space in its north London headquarters in Highbury Fields for the SPSL, in effect removing it from Esther's grasp, and that the WUS's Liz Fraser should take over as secretary.

Alan Phillips was at the King's College meeting:

> It was my first visit to King's College and recall walking up the staircase to Lord Kahn's room with Iain Wright to be greeted by a formidably large oak door on which the name 'Professor, The Lord, Kahn' painted in gold leaf. I was duly impressed, although I had already been told that he was probably one of the most esteemed economists never to have received a Nobel Prize. Apparently, his short 36-page essay on the multiplier theory had been crucial to Keynesian economics. Inside the room, the Lords Ashby and Kahn had already gathered. It quickly became clear that Lord Kahn was very hard of

hearing and the conversation would effectively be limited to Eric Ashby (then described as Chairman of SPSL), Iain Wright (Chairman of WUS UK) and myself (General Secretary of WUS UK). Lord Ashby, who was also a Vice President of WUS, had already broadcast a description of WUS's work on Radio 3 and valued highly the work of both SPSL and WUS.

WUS was already well funded through large grants from the Overseas Development Ministry for several major scholarship programmes and had recently moved into 19/20 Compton Terrace. These were two delightful, early 19th-century four-storey houses in Highbury that WUS had bought for a song (£110,000) from the BP pension Fund and had refurbished. WUS offered to provide free accommodation and office facilities to SPSL while putting forward Liz Fraser as a possible successor to Esther Simpson.

I suspected that Lord Ashby thought that we would want SPSL's work to be subsumed by WUS and for its work to become supervised by a sub-committee of WUS. Lord Ashby was delighted at the offer we made which he commended for its generosity and for the independence that SPSL would retain. It only took a minute or two for Lord Ashby to summarise the proposal for Lord Kahn and receive his acceptance in principle. They agreed they would present the proposal to the SPSL (Council?) for its approval. It did not take long for the compact to be approved formally by SPSL and WUS.

So Esther 'retired' again, making her last appearance as secretary of the SPSL at the Council meeting on 23 May 1978. She said she had been coaching Liz for some time. Liz Fraser told me she had found Esther 'extraordinary but not unique'.

Esther was not at all happy with the transfer to Highbury Fields. She complained to Broda how difficult it was to get there, and that the room allocated to the SPSL was far too small. She would not be able to find any papers she wanted, and she had an accumulation of documents and papers that needed filing – but she wanted to visit Highbury as little as possible. The transfer was a watershed for Esther, and she plainly found navigating it difficult. Liz Fraser recalls:

Esther considered the office which I was allocated within the World
University Service building at Highbury Corner was HER office and
that she could come into it at any time. I had to insist that she had to
respect the admission rules for the entire building.

Esther remained on the Society's allocation committee and council of
management. She had also become a trustee of a Rothschild charity for
Jewish intellectuals. Her continuing involvement with Jewish refugees
is plain. September 1981 saw her invited to a Refugee Council dinner for
services to the Jewish Refugee Committee. The dinner was at the Mansion
House for the Central British Fund for World Jewish Relief.

However, as honorary consultant, she would become a regular member
of the SPSL Council. It was, she thought, or hoped, clear that her activities
would continue indefinitely, as it would take a very long time for her
successor to become independent.

A former academic and experienced administrator, Liz Fraser had all
the relevant and up-to-date experience and insights from her work with
WUS and on Chile. But Esther imbued her own role at the AAC/SPSL since
1933 with something like the divine power of a priest of the ancient Greek
Eleusinian Mysteries, commanding secret rituals that would give initiates
a god-like afterlife.

Letting go is not easy, as innumerable tea towels assure us, particularly
of what has been one's whole *raison d'être*. In a letter to Engelbert Broda
dated 20 March 1978 Esther's intention is clear:

> At the end of July I retire officially, on my 75th birthday, but it is quite
> clear that I will remain involved indefinitely.' [Retirement party at the
> CIBA Foundation on 13 July] which seems to me a redundant idea as I
> had one 12 years ago, though that was the result of a misunderstanding,
> when it was assumed I was retiring because the SVS was packing up
> – they didn't ask me.

And in two letters to Paul Broda at the opening of 1979 and another to
Engelbert Broda in the spring of that year the tenor is the same:

> My successor has still a lot to learn. [23 January 1979]

> While work has eased off somewhat since my 'retirement' I am still

much involved, as my successor will need my help for quite a long time yet. [6 March 1979]

The Society keeps me busy still. There are so many matters my successor Liz Fraser can't deal with. We have had a spate of inquiries concerning pre-war and war times. I will be spending tomorrow afternoon with Liz on the account books – this is something she finds difficult to learn, but I go over each monthly statement from the bank with her, and the entries in the account books. [10 April 1979]

In June 1980 she was still helping her successor with the accounts and with problems that arose where, as she explained to Engelbert, more experience was required than Liz Fraser yet had.

In fact, as Liz Fraser recalls, accounts were far from Esther's own forte; she had constant help from the SPSL's accountants and auditors, who also assisted her with her personal accounts. As for enquiries about the pre-war and wartime periods, Liz Fraser arranged for the relevant records to be accepted by the Bodleian Library in Oxford. Again, we might suspect that it was not the objective historical record that mattered to Esther so much as its ownership.

Anyone hoping that *Refugee Scholars* will offer Esther's view or memories of the Chilean crisis will be disappointed. She makes no reference to the agonies of the Chilean academics and students under Pinochet, to the energy and generosity of the British response, or even to her successor from WUS, Liz Fraser, who had worked closely with her on taking over the post.

Perhaps if a Chilean refugee Fellow of the Royal Society had emerged, her narrative might have stretched to the Chilean crisis and Academics for Chile. In describing her friendship with Greta Burkill of the Cambridge Refugees Committee, a member of the SPSL council, Esther recalled,

We had fun boasting of 'our' F.R.S.s. My supply was drying up, as my scientists were ageing; hers were just coming on!

But in 1983,

Greta has her refugee children all over the world, including a Vice-Chancellor!

Greta Burkill had what we might call a head start: her husband was an eminent mathematician and an FRS.

Esther's constant criticisms as shared with Broda came as a shock to Liz Fraser when I shared them with her. The younger woman, a former academic, was a veteran of the refugee organisation WUS, and experienced from 1973 in a culture of refugee work where:

> There was no such thing as clocking off at the end of the day. Everyone worked flat out to bring in and settle people who were fleeing from persecution.

But Esther's comments on Liz Fraser's needing her help were essentially not about Liz but demonstrating her own indispensability, albeit at Liz Fraser's expense.

As we have seen, it is evidently difficult to speak of Esther Simpson and retirement (as commonly understood) in the same breath. October 1990 saw her writing to Ray Cooper complaining of lack of time to attend to her personal correspondence. Liz Fraser kept her busy, she told him, as they had a spate of new applications for grants. Applications had come in the last few days from Afghanistan, Colombia and Iran. More were in the pipeline.

Her devotion to the AAC/SPSL since she began work there in July 1933 had not been rewarded with any pension provision organised by the governing Council, themselves all in pensionable occupations. (Though Beveridge had noted that Walter Adams had given up his LSE pension on joining the AAC.) In state pension terms, even post-Beveridge report, women were not seen as requiring the same provision as men. Esther herself, so she told Ray Cooper, had never been interested in money – but thought that lack of interest had saved her a lot of agony in her life.

Now the Council asked Esther to withdraw while they considered the question of a pension. On her being recalled, she was told that she would receive a pension from the SPSL of £2,000 a year (£10,000 in today's money). But that was not all. From a source that had to remain anonymous, so Esther was informed, she would also receive £500 a year (£2,500 today). Members of the Council had to remain in ignorance of the source of this generosity. But the retiring Chairman Lord Ashby confided the name to Tess after the meeting.

We might suspect she already knew the source, an Anonymous Rothschild Trust: she was on its board. She wrote next day to Dorothy de Rothschild, widow of James de Rothschild, to express her immense gratitude. The extra payment would make a great deal of difference to her situation. She also stated her undiminished concern for the SPSL.

She lived a simple life in her Buckland Crescent flat, as a former neighbour recalled to me, emphasising what he described as her modesty; she never cared for money and the suggestion she might take a lodger offended her. She had nothing new unless it came as a present. She liked giving her neighbour's daughter little presents, but always modest.

Occupying a single floor of the Buckland Crescent house, the flat included a bedroom, a small office and a huge library. She passed her time reading and writing and playing the violin, and was always ready to talk about the prominent people she had known, becoming close to them, helping them settle down after fleeing the Nazis. She was a walking encyclopaedia for the shape of Europe in the 1930s and '40s – and had no time for modern politicians. She had no washing machine – her neighbour offered the use of his – but did have a television set. She was always first to pick up the mail in the mornings and would go for a walk to nearby Finchley Road to collect her newspapers. She didn't cook, but lived off ready-made sandwiches and supermarket chicken. She was, naturally, the secretary of the House committee. Her one priority remained the Society. A giver not a taker. [She did not die in penury. Under her will she left pecuniary legacies totalling £32,000 – or some £64,000 in 2022's money.]

47
Roll Call

If her commitment to succouring academic refugees, broadly stated, absorbed her working life, two further interests, passions we might say, absorbed Esther Simpson's own life: friendship and music, the two not being separable.

In her accounts of the 1930s academic refugees whom she worked to rescue, the word 'friend' is curiously frequent, a stress on the personal relationship, founded on her having been there professionally for the displaced, uprooted exile.

It is also striking how many of her letters to Engelbert Broda are recitations of the (well-known) people with whom she has had contact. A typical passage is in a letter of February 1968:

> Many years ago I read the book by GH Hardy whom you mention. I was particularly interested as I knew Hardy – he helped us very constructively with advice about our mathematician refugees and financially too . . . I am glad you have been reading Bertrand Russell too; only recently I was with one of his students who is now Professor at Smith College Mass. Dorothy Winnick. I wonder if you ever came across her? . . . I first met her when I was living in Vienna. She was a great friend of the Singers (History of Medicine).

In 1970, on a weekend in Cambridge, she had been completely intoxicated by all she crammed into two and a half days:

Bondi, Pevsner, Burkhill, Hutton memorial service, Hill, Perutz, Lehmann, Frisch. Szilard whom I knew so well.' [Written without first names]

And in 1971, at a memorial service in Oxford:

I met so many of ''my' FRSs there – Katz, Neuberger, Feldberg, Edith Bülbring, Marthe Voigt, Blaschko . . .

And the deceased?

I wonder if you ever knew Sir Lindon [sic] Brown, the physiologist [George Lindor Brown] who died a few months ago.

Bernard Katz, she informed Engelbert, was what 'Sir Lindo' was before him:

Professor of Physiology* at University College and biology secretary of the Royal Society. *Sorry no. Professor of Biophysics following AV Hill.

The Ciba Foundation held a symposium

in connection with the Hering-Breuer centenary and I was proud to tell the Director that the Breuer family were friends of mine.

This – perhaps coining a term is required: *philonominalism*? – is at full stretch in the most distinctive feature of *Refugee Scholars*, Esther's list of scholars with honours – members of 'her family', as already quoted.

In other autobiographies they might be reserved to an appendix. Here they come – as she proposed to Ray Cooper they should – as the main narrative, the *ipsissima vox*, a narrative that goes beyond giving assistance to familiarity and inevitable friendship.

Her memory sometimes lets her down, as in an anecdote about Sir Nikolaus Pevsner as a 'Bevin Boy' clearing blitzed London streets in 1940 and being awarded a CBE, much to his amusement, as a labourer. But Bevin Boys were conscripted into the mines and his CBE came in 1953. (This 'recollection' might also be an example of her desiring her friends and 'children' to be generally exceptional.)

Anyway, to return to Chapter 5 and the eminent who were such a source of pride to her,

> ... They include not only those displaced university teachers with
> whom the S.P.S.L. has been concerned but also scholars of the next
> generation. Now I follow with keen interest the achievements of their
> children. Their contribution to the intellectual life of this country has
> been immeasurable. Of course it is not possible for me to describe all
> of the scholars who are now numbered in their thousands. I shall
> mention some in special categories, starting with the Nobel laureates.
> There are sixteen of them but I shall mention only a few. Details of
> their careers can be found in Who's Who, Who Was Who and the
> International Who's Who ...

As for the next category,

> Now for those refugee scholars who received knighthoods. Some of
> them are second generation and the Society was not in touch with
> them personally. No doubt many more are to come.

The selection of knights, including some household names, extends over
four pages and ends with the four who became Masters of Oxbridge
Colleges.
Next,

> I come to the refugee scholars who were Fellows of the Royal Society
> followed by those who became Fellows of the British Academy.

In 1954 she had written to Engelbert Broda: '"I" now have 29 FRSs ...' Here,
seven pages and twelve Fellows later, we come to six refugee scholars who
were Foreign Members of the Royal Society, and then to Fellows of the
British Academy who were originally refugee scholars registered with
the SPSL.

> Now for those Fellows of the British Academy who were originally
> refugee scholars registered with our Society ...

She had thirty-three refugee Fellows of the British Academy on her list and
eighteen Corresponding Members who lived abroad.
This section of the chapter concludes with three CBEs and an OBE,
before turning to individuals of particular significance for her: Sir Francis
Simon and Lady Simon; Sir Karl Popper; the Gombrichs ...

After the war I continued to see the Gombrichs quite often, sometimes with Nikolaus Pevsner at little dinner parties Pevsner held in the Isokon Club in Hampstead; I really don't know him [Sir Geoffrey Elton] very well but his parents were good friends of mine [Professor Victor Ehrenberg]; Sir Ludwig Guttmann, who has become world famous for his work with paraplegics. I knew him personally . . . Peierls speaks many languages, including excellent Russian; Sir Nikolaus Pevsner, who is very famous . . . I have known him since he came, which was about 1935 . . . He liked to know people, and used to invite his friends to occasional dinner parties . . . I was invited as a personal friend and also by virtue of my job because the occasional refugee scholar joined us . . . I wasn't in any way involved in Pevsner's architectural survey of British buildings but, of course, I knew about it. I now come to the refugee scholars who were Fellows of the Royal Society followed by those who became Fellows of the British Academy. Professor Franz Bergel I knew quite well . . .; Dr Hermann Blaschko is a very good friend of mine . . . With Blaschko, a man of culture and widely read, I have been able to talk about books and other objects of interest to me.

The late Professor Edith Bülbring, whom I also wish to mention, has the distinction of being one of the early women Fellows of the Royal Society. A very fine pianist . . . I myself played sonatas with her in Professor Feldberg's house in 1933 . . . and continued to see her from time to time until her death; Professor Wilhelm Feldberg CBE I have known well since 1933 when he came to London. During the war I saw a great deal of the Feldbergs as I was myself living in Cambridge. One of my jobs when I visited them was weeding their garden. I watched the children grow up and I remained in touch with Feldberg. Feldberg was, along with Sir Hans Krebs, responsible for organizing my first 'retirement' party in 1965; Professor Otto Robert Frisch OBE I knew very well indeed from when he first arrived and worked with Professor Blackett. [Though he did not mention her in his short autobiography *What Little I Remember.*] His aunt was the famous Lisa [sic] Meitner. He was a very good musician . . . we played together sometimes. He had another aunt who was a well-known photographer Lotte Meitner-Graf. She photographed almost all the eminent people you can think of whatever their field . . . One of our most recent Fellows Professor George Kalmus is a second generation refugee . . . His father Professor Hans Kalmus was Professor of Genetics at University College London. He discovered that UC had been connected with more than one hundred refugee scholars. A few years ago he delivered a most interesting lecture on the subject which I attended. The late Professor Hermann Lehmann CBE was also a very good friend of mine; Lehmann's wife, Benigna, whom I see, is a pianist and teaches the piano; Professor Albert Neuberger I have known since the 1930s . . . one of his sons is a Fellow of Trinity College Cambridge and one is married to Rabbi Julia Neuberger who has become well known on television.

A characteristic of her friends is generally to excel and to excel generally: Peierls's autobiography *Bird of Passage* is in excellent English.

A British scholar of considerable eminence, who read another autobiography by a British scientist which appeared about the same time, told me how superior Peierls's English was to that of the native British writer.

Albert Neuberger got in touch with the head of the phonetics department. The result was his English became far better than that of many other refugees because he learned to speak it correctly.

In December 1971 she pays a Christmas visit to elderly retired refugees and their families. The letter to her brother Joe describing the visit is a roll-call of professors, classical scholars . . . the distinguished . . . making a name for himself. But she also wishes she had no new grantees.

The reciprocal warmth of 'her' children is unmistakable. A visit to Oxford or Cambridge for, say, a refugee scholar's funeral will always include her meeting some of her 'children' over tea or dinner, brought together by one of her refugee friends.

And in an example of her children's continuing sense of closeness, a former South African grantee, now on the staff of an Australian university, brings his Australian-born wife (the daughter of refugees) and baby daughter to meet her.

48
Friends

Esther's diction in *Refugee Scholars* tends to the formal. A rare colloquialism taking the reader back to Esther's Leeds origins is also a moment of sudden warmth. Here, although 'peeky' is put in the mouths of two German refugees, we can assume Esther's usage. 'Peeky' means sickly looking, pallid, ill. (For the opposite she might have said 'gradely'.)

> It was about 1935 when Professor Saxl and Dr Bing [of the Warburg Library] told me I looked peeky. They thought I needed looking after and they invited me to stay with them for several weeks . . . During the war I even spent some days with them in Elstree, where they had moved.

Although Gertrud Bing was not a Fellow of the British Academy, Esther said, she wanted to add this tribute:

> When Hitler came, though she was not Jewish, she left with the Warburg Institute and renounced her own research in order to do all the administrative work of the Institute as well as the personal side because, like a mother, she looked after all the individuals connected with the Institute. I should like to mention something about her that the great conductor Otto Klemperer wrote when she died. 'I could talk to her about everything.' And everybody thought that was so very characteristic. Gertrud was a very great, very fine woman.

In writing this tribute, did Esther see something of herself in Gertrud? It was a pity she omitted Gertrud Bing's having driven an ambulance for the London Auxiliary Ambulance Service until she was dismissed for being an enemy alien.

The insistence on the personal relationship that follows or arises from her handling the refugee's case is striking: plainly, having managed the refugee's escape from Germany and resettlement in Britain or abroad, supporting them every step of the way, with all the work and determination that required, was in the end not meaningful enough. Something more, something involving her as a person, had to be part of the outcome.

> Lise Meitner: a very fine human being who took a great interest in what was happening in the world. I was in touch with her after she came to this country from Stockholm where she lived and worked during the war. After the war she lived and worked in Cambridge; I saw quite a lot of her because she often came to see me in London.
>
> Dr Walter Pagel was outstanding as a polymath. I saw a good deal of Walter Pagel and his wife Magda.
>
> I now come to the longest story about any Fellow of the British Academy, my friend, and he was a close friend, Professor Walter Simon CBE, who had been Professor of Chinese at the University of Berlin. I made friends with the Simons early on . . . Occasionally I would spend the night in Twickenham and read stories to their two little boys in bed.
>
> I now come to the Corresponding Fellows of the British Academy, of whom there are eighteen, but I will mention only one whom I knew well, Ernst Kitzinger.
>
> There are three CBEs . . . I would like now to mention Hermann Brueck. Again, he is one of the very few of my pre-war refugees who was not Jewish. He was a devout Catholic . . . He had a wife and two children and I used to have tea with them occasionally at the [Cambridge] Observatory.
>
> Again, a very close friend was Dr Paul Rothschild, who arrived here early in 1933. I knew him very well indeed, and I remained in touch with his widow, who died a couple of years ago.
>
> A well-known international lawyer, Professor Georg Schwarzenberger. What I remember about him particularly, because I

knew him and his wife and son very well, is that he never stopped working. I used to see them quite often and regularly on Christmas Day.

There are two other refugee scholars about whom I would now like to say something. The first is [the neurologist/psychiatrist] Dr Karl Stern. He and his wife became close friends . . . I found that Karl was an accomplished pianist, a fine musician. We played violin sonatas very often. The only time I have been in the Albany[41] was in Graham Greene's chambers there, because he had offered Karl the use of them while Karl was in London, he himself being away, I think in Vienna filming *The Third Man*.

On Karl's last visit, I said to him that he should try to come back to England as often as possible, *as there was very little chance of my going to Canada* [author's italics], and I wanted to see him in this world, since it was very unlikely we could meet in the next as I was not a Catholic. [She had evidently not mentioned her extensive family in Canada.] Karl replied: 'That is very bad theology.'

Esther also picks out three people whom she says (inaccurately in the case of Szilard): 'I first met through our work for refugee scholars.' Leo Szilard, Louis Rapkine, and Ludwig Wittgenstein.

I have already spoken about how I first met Leo Szilard and how this resulted in my joining the Academic Assistance Council in 1933. He was such a remarkable man that I must add something more. His name will be familiar to anyone who has anything to do with the development of atomic energy, because he was one of the people who wrote papers on it at the very beginning. He was one of the first to envisage the possibility of an atomic bomb: I know that because he told me about it.

Esther also tells us how Szilard had called, with Einstein, on President Roosevelt to tell him that the Germans were working on the development

---

41 Secreted just off Piccadilly and dating from 1803, the Albany was one of London's most exclusive sets of apartments. As well as Graham Greene, tenants included Byron, Gladstone, Macaulay, J.B. Priestley, Isaiah Berlin and Edward Heath.

of an atomic bomb . . . 'Appropriate measures should be taken in the USA . . .' (Conventional accounts have Szilard drafting a warning letter that Einstein signed and Alexander Sachs, a banker friend of Roosevelt's, read to the President. Szilard also drafted a technical memorandum to go with the letter.)

Hopes of a reminiscence of their dinner and lunch in Geneva are in vain. Perhaps he talked then only about his work.

> He used to talk to me about his work, which I couldn't understand as it was all concerned with physics. He said to me on one occasion: 'What would you think of being able to get a fresh peach out of a tin?' I said that sounded very nice.

Next comes Louis Rapkine, who 'was quite intimately connected with us. He is one of the heroes of my life', though in *Refugee Scholars* the heroics seem to have supplanted the facts.

Rapkine was born in Russia, raised in Canada and studied biochemistry in Paris. Esther's account of his connection to London is refracted through her need to privilege the SPSL. What follows is taken from Diane Dosso's account: [42]

After being granted French nationality on 28 September 1939, Rapkine strove to make himself useful to his country under threat while waiting to be called up (with the class of 1940). On 11 May 1940, a director of the CNRS [*Centre national de la recherche scientifique*] entrusted him with an information assignment to develop the Franco-British scientific collaboration in biological chemistry and experimental biology. It was the start of a major role in the preservation of independent French science after the fall of France.

Esther's extraordinary account of Rapkine's rescue of French scientists from German-occupied France reads like a spy thriller.

Louis, she says, was with a French scientific mission in London when war broke out and stayed there:

---

42 Diane Dosso, 'Rapkine Louis', pp. 704–705 in *Dictionnaire des étrangers qui ont fait la France*, under the supervision of Pascal Ory, Paris, Robert Laffont, [collect. Bouquins], 2013.

When France was overrun by the Germans he realized how many academics were in grave danger, and wanted to do something about rescuing them. He didn't know where his wife and child were, because he had left them in Paris; they were in danger too, being of Jewish origin. After consulting AV Hill, Louis went to Washington, America not yet being in the war, to discuss means of rescuing these scholars who were in danger. We don't know exactly how it worked because of course it was dead secret at the time, but Louis got word to upwards of eighty scholars in France to be at certain French ports on a certain date with their families, when there would be American ships to pick them up to take them to America. Fortunately Louis's wife and little daughter were included. Louis once told me: 'You know you have no idea here what red tape is like. You have got to go to Washington for that.' At any rate, he managed it and that was just on his own initiative.

The 'red tape' remark at least rings true, as the rescue of French scientists was in fact organised in Washington through the regular American visa system, backed by the financial clout of the Rockefeller Foundation. And not by Rapkine alone.

The facts are set out in Diane Dosso's detailed account in *France and Nuclear Deterrence – A Spirit of Resistance*, 'Louis Rapkine and the Free France scientists at the dawn of the Atomic Age'. Rapkine had gone to the United States with, and at the invitation of, one of the two directors of the CNRS, Henri Laugier. Laugier, fifty-two, spoke little English; Rapkine, thirty-six, was bilingual. Laugier had already written to 'his dear friends' at the Rockefeller Foundation about saving 'French intellectualism'. The Foundation's invitation came at his request and the recommendation of A. V. Hill and W. H. Bragg.

Diane Dosso writes:

The aim of the Rockefeller Foundation was to lastingly enrich the United States through the European elite fleeing the Nazi threat. They were not looking to save lives, but to safeguard outstanding intellects. This was also Laugier and Rapkine's aim, at a time when unprecedented world conflict had just begun.

In 1940 the United States still had diplomatic relations with Vichy France, and this allowed the possibility of legal travel between the two countries, subject to differing academic visa requirements being met on both sides. Laugier and Rapkine worked with the Rockefeller Foundation to enable visits by French academics on a perfectly legal basis, though this meant gaming the system on both sides of the Atlantic, as Diane Dosso describes:

> In the end, the following subterfuge was developed: the Americans spoke of a one-year invitation in its correspondence with the French Embassy in Washington or with French ministries. The invitations sent to the American consulates in France, however, specified the true duration (two years) so that the scientists could obtain an American visa.

Who would come?

> Finally, Laugier and Rapkine accepted the crippling responsibility that the Rockefeller Foundation had refused to shoulder, drawing up a list of French scientists to welcome to America . . . The main criterion in the selection of an individual was clearly his or her scientific value. They then considered whether or not the person was Jewish, in any particular political danger, and his or her age. Finally, they determined whether or not the individual wanted to leave France. Some, like Frédéric Joliot, Henri Cartan, André Lwoff and Edgar Lederer refused the exile they had been offered . . . Throughout the procedure of receiving an invitation and leaving France, Rapkine worked in liaison with staff at the Rockefeller Foundation. For each scientist selected, he wrote a detailed record of biographical information, explaining the interest of his/her research and drawing up a list of publications. Finally, he took legal responsibility as guarantor before the immigration authorities . . .

In June 1941 Rapkine's wife Sarah and his nine-year-old daughter finally joined him in New York. In December General de Gaulle authorised the creation of a *Bureau Scientifique* [Scientific Bureau] with Rapkine as director. 'This was the first official recognition of Rapkine's work in support of French scientists.' For de Gaulle, the setting up of an official organisation for the deployment of French scientists was a politically significant step. For Rapkine it was the gateway to the participation of French scientists in American defence work, contributing to victory, for which he worked tirelessly in frustrating conditions.

Dosso quotes a letter from him:

> I continue to focus my efforts in this direction, but the going is tough because our American friends consider the fighting French to be 'enemy aliens' with regard to secret war research . . .

and their contribution remained marginal.

> This is why French scientists, still led by Rapkine, formed the French Scientific Mission in the United Kingdom.[43] They left America for London, arriving shortly after the Allied landings in Normandy (6 June 1944). Rapkine was now in the forefront of moves for cooperation between Free French and British scientists. On 28 April 1945, two decrees from the French Ministry of War created a 'Service Scientifique et des recherches intéressant l'Armée et les operations militaires' (Department of Science and Research for the Army and Military Operations). Pierre Auger and Louis Rapkine were the lead scientific advisors.

Diane Dosso wrote to me:

> Louis Rapkine's work concerning refugee scholars was built from the outset in collaboration with the English committee.
>
> It seems to me that Walter Adams and then Esther Simpson were, for Rapkine, correspondents and advisers essential to the success of the action of the French committee.
>
> People entirely devoted to the cause they defended on a daily basis.[44]

---

43 Mission Scientifique Française en Grande Bretagne.

44 'Le travail de Louis Rapkine concernant les savants réfugiés s'est construit dès l'origine en collaboration avec le comité anglais. Il me semble que Walter Adams puis Esther Simpson ont été, pour Rapkine, des correspondants et conseillers indispensables à la réussite de l'action du comité français. Des personnes entièrement dévouées à la cause qu'ils défendaient au quotidien.'

Esther's acquaintance in Cambridge with Ludwig Wittgenstein (1889–1951) has become one of the labels commonly attached to her, along with saving sixteen future Nobel Prize winners from Hitler. And, after all, she does mention him 'because he was so famous'.

When they met, Wittgenstein, born in Vienna but then a naturalised British subject, was a Fellow of Trinity College and had held the Chair of Philosophy since 1939.

In *Refugee Scholars* Esther says:

> The third person I am going to mention at this stage is somebody who was not himself a refugee but who did his best to help a refugee. I mention him because he is so famous. He is the philosopher Ludwig Wittgenstein. I am talking about him because I can, perhaps, illustrate one side of his character that does not often appear in all that has been written about him.

The refugee was a Polish-Jewish philosopher, Rose Rand (1903–1980), who was a direct link to the logical positivist Vienna Circle, on whose approach to philosophy Wittgenstein's *Tractatus* had been so influential. Her special interest was logic. As a doctoral student she had kept minutes of the Circle's meetings; she had also shown considerable aptitude for working with psychiatric patients. A Jew, she was barred from starting a university career in Vienna after completing her doctorate in 1938. And while on the SPSL's books from 1939, her lack of any previous university post meant she had no chance of the Society's assistance in finding one, though she was admitted to the Cambridge Moral Science faculty as a 'distinguished foreigner'. The full story is told in David Edmonds' *The Murder of Professor Schlick: The Rise and Fall of the Vienna Circle*, where he quotes Esther's response to Rose's plea for help in finding an academic post:

> There is no chance whatever of an academic position . . . I am afraid I can only advise you to register with the Labour Exchange.

Nonetheless Rose Rand did receive small grants and loans from the SPSL to help her survive. However, the money came from Wittgenstein and was put through the SPSL's books with Esther's cooperation to preserve his anonymity. The payments continued for several years.

As Edmonds shows, Esther did not echo his sympathetic generosity to this admittedly very difficult personality. But in 1943 she secured Rose Rand's release from a psychiatric hospital to which she had been committed after threatening to kill herself. Esther wrote to Wittgenstein, then working as a laboratory assistant at the Royal Victoria Infirmary in Newcastle, again quoted by David Edmonds,

> There's a good distance between being queer, which Miss Rand certainly is, and insane, which I felt sure she was not.

In *Refugee Scholars*, the emphasis is somewhat different. Esther does not name the refugee Wittgenstein wanted to help:

> ... an Austrian woman who had been a good philosopher, but then became mentally affected. She had been a grantee of ours, but she could no longer continue research. She had the illusion that she would one day become Professor of Philosophy at Cambridge. Wittgenstein had given us money for a grant, because he was sorry for her ... He wanted to help, but the day came when I had to tell him that we could not accept his money any longer, because there was no future in philosophy for this lady; we should not encourage her to think there was.

A suitably professional approach, most would think.

This was not the only time Esther put personal charitable support through the SPSL books. A close friend from Vienna came to Britain with her husband as refugees. He fell seriously ill and life became very hard for them. Esther, in war-time Cambridge with the SPSL, used her contacts to find them support, particularly over somewhere for the husband to live and be looked after. She made regular contributions towards his living costs, disguising them as coming from the SPSL so that her friend would not know.

A common story is that when Wittgenstein told Esther he was going to Newcastle upon Tyne to do war work in a hospital, she suggested he stay with her brother Israel who had a spare room in his house there. She thought the room simply furnished enough for Wittgenstein's spartan preference, but he declared it much too grand for him.

It is not quite clear when she could have suggested that. Wittgenstein had been working in Guy's Hospital London since September 1941. He left on 17 March 1943 and spent some time in Swansea before going to work at the Newcastle Royal Infirmary on 29 April 1943, remaining there until February 1944. In Newcastle he lodged initially in Jesmond in the same house as the two doctors, Reeve and Grant, with whom he had worked at Guy's and who had invited him to follow them to Newcastle.

Nonetheless, that anecdote is widely quoted, together with Esther's memory of Wittgenstein's queuing at the bread shop 'Fitzbillies' to buy her buns for tea:

> . . . he prepared tea and produced a huge mound of buns, but didn't touch any himself.

She does not say how many, if any, of the buns she consumed.

An anecdote confirming Wittgenstein's musicality (and hers) begins with her apologising to him for playing the Brahms clarinet quintet the previous evening 'with another Fellow of Trinity, William Rushton, whose rooms were immediately over Wittgenstein's [in Whewell's Court, Trinity]'. She made some comment about one of the variations in the last movement.

> He disagreed with me and I said: 'I wonder if we are talking about the same variation?' He said: 'Oh yes we are,' and promptly whistled it. I then found that he could whistle the second theme of the third subject of any symphony you could mention. Of course, he had grown up in a musical atmosphere . . . On music he was immensely knowledgeable. I remember on one of our walks in the Fellows' Garden at Trinity I mentioned something about our knowing too little about the music of Bruckner, which was hardly ever performed here. He said: 'Oh, the English are not capable of understanding Bruckner.' I am mentioning this because this was a side of Wittgenstein that a lot of people didn't know.

(This is also one of the few occasions in *Refugee Scholars* when she names a piece of music she played.)

49

A Musical Gift

As you know, music has been one of my greatest interests so I shall now say something of the musicologists I know. *Refugee Scholars*

The agency of music in Esther Simpson's life deserves a closer look. That she was an accomplished violinist, devoted to playing chamber music at every opportunity, stands out in her life story.

We should pause for a moment to consider the role of her parents in prompting and supporting her first steps into music, finding the money for an instrument and for lessons at the Leeds College of Music, taking her to organ recitals in the local parish church, and to free concerts organised by Quaker philanthropists, with an early introduction to string quartets by players from the Leeds Symphony Orchestra.

As we saw earlier, she performed publicly as well as at events such as prize-givings and plays in the Girls Modern School, as she recalls in *Refugee Scholars*, playing in the Music College orchestra, which she continued while at university, and for the Leeds Welsh community. Her talent took her across Yorkshire to play in Selby and Wakefield. In Leeds she played for the YMCA's amateur theatricals, and with an actors' group in the Civic Theatre.

Refugee Scholars offers a portrait of Leeds in the early twentieth century as a culturally lively and vibrant city for the daughter of Russian-Jewish refugees to grow up in and assimilate.

While still at school, Esther attended celebrity lectures at the city's Albert Hall – she instances Stephen Leacock and Walter de la Mare – and performances by the touring Carl Rosa Opera Company. Concerts were held in the Albion Hall, the Masonic Hall and the YMCA. She went to recitals at the university. When there, she joined the university orchestra and a small group, the Twenty-Five Orchestra:

> We went in for competitions and won them all, so I enjoyed myself.

Curiously, we learn nothing of Esther's own musical preferences, but in her account of these youthful days she recalls hearing Schumann's fantasy piece for piano *Aufschwung* (Op.12 No.2) for the first time and her introduction to the songs of Hugo Wolf, and how as a student in Caen she bought the César Franck violin sonata 'together with a lot of French music'.

Then, after university and teacher training, her account of the ten miserable weeks as the Weiss family's governess in Breslau includes her musical activities – joining the city's orchestra, playing sonatas with Martha Steinitz's brother Georg – though without detail or recollected enthusiasm.

Musically, Paris is then apparently unrewarding:

> It was so difficult to get to know French people, although I lived with
> a French family, along with three or four research students from
> Leeds.

But her twin gifts for the violin and for friendship conspired together at the end of her time in Paris to change the direction of her life.

As we have seen, an invitation came from Roger Soltau, who had been one of her French lecturers in Leeds, to act as an interpreter at the annual international conference of the International Fellowship of Reconciliation held that year at Vaumarcus in Switzerland, with wonderful views of Lake Neuchâtel. Soltau had left the university to work for IFOR.

There she made an English acquaintance. Marjorie Davis was a lecturer in music at Goldsmith's College London and a pianist with whom Esther could play sonatas 'for fun'. Back in London, working as Roger Soltau's secretary, she joined in Marjorie's regular musical evenings.

Through Marjorie she met the Viennese law student Lisl Kallberg, also a pianist and longing to find someone with whom she could play violin

sonatas. Esther played with her once a week. And in 1928 when she told
Lisl her job was moving to Vienna but she didn't want to go, Lisl persuaded
her to accept Soltau's invitation to work with him in Vienna. Through her,
Lisl promised, Esther would know everybody she needed to know.

This proved true. For Esther, Vienna was a musical paradise.

> I could have played three quartets a night, because almost everybody
> played. Playing chamber music was just taken for granted. It was like
> cleaning your teeth. Everybody learned to play a musical instrument.
> It was part of the social climate. I had a wonderful few years in Vienna.

In recollecting her time in Vienna in *Refugee Scholars*, Esther said,

> I should like to make the point that music enriched my life by providing
> me with wonderful friends and experiences I would not otherwise
> have had. So often meeting a single musician was like a pebble cast in
> a pool whose resulting ripples go on to eternity.

Esther's account of her musical life in Vienna presents a picture of non-stop
activity, her talent propelling her on from one group to another.

> . . . In Vienna I played second fiddle in a very fine string quartet led by
> Professor Artur Schiff who was a professor of internal medicine and
> the uncle of Sir Karl Popper. The cellist was another medical professor,
> Professor Klar, and the viola was Professor Schiff's niece, Gertrud
> Schiff, a professional viola player and cousin of Karl Popper. Mrs Schiff
> was a sister of Dr Robert Breuer, which is how I came to play with
> them.

She had come to know the Breuer family through the Kallbergs.

The chain continued, and not only in making music. In the IFOR office,
she was working for Donald Grant as his secretary (though she records
that she herself had a secretary). In 1932, with Donald Grant she went to
Geneva, where he was to report on the Disarmament Conference. They
were there for five months of the Conference, and once again 'music was
a tremendous passport'. She made friends with Helen Willis who played
the cello and they played chamber music. Helen Willis's husband Frank
worked for the YMCA. And when IFOR decided to move to France, and

Donald Grant left, Esther was offered a position as personal assistant to the
Director of the World Alliance of YMCAs at their headquarters in Geneva.
There she continued to play with Helen Willis and her friends, though she
records the native Swiss as unforthcoming.

In London from July 1933, it was a tale of continued musical activity with
old musical friends and new performers from the community of refugee
scholars, for whom the musical contact must have been a morale-boosting
boon.

She lists sixteen or more refugee academics with whom she played in
this pre-war period, noting: '(Ultimately I had a few purely English string
quartets as well.)' She even managed some orchestral playing, but 'At this
time, before the war, I was playing very often, sometimes several times a
week, as I had in Vienna.'

Her musical life was not only her own playing. She records going to
the premier London concert venues, the Queen's Hall, the Albert Hall,
the Wigmore Hall, hearing Arturo Toscanini, Pablo Casals, Bronislaw
Huberman, the Busch and Lerner Quartets, Yehudi Menuhin and his sister
Hephzibah, and Sergei Prokoviev conducting his own work.

> . . . Looking back, I wonder how I managed to get so much music in,
> as I was working very hard, often into the late hours and through the
> weekend.

Given her own account of playing 'very often, sometimes several times a
week', we might join her in wondering that, particularly as her attachment
to Vienna and its music did not come to an end in January 1933. She records
that she returned for a holiday every summer until 1937, 'taking my fiddle
with me'. In 1937 she was also carrying a viola along with her violin in a
bulky case as she holidayed in Yugoslavia first, playing chamber music,
before going on to Vienna.

In 1982 she recalled Ljubljana

> . . . when it was Bled. We drove from Paris to Zagreb (the Hermanns
> and me) stopping off at various places over ten days. We were not
> allowed to drive through Bled, because the young king was staying
> there at the time . . .

Quite how she managed these travels on her meagre AAC salary and while apparently working from dawn till dusk in Burlington House on desperate applications from displaced academics is also not clear.

Music did not come to a halt with the onset of war and the removal of the SPSL to the sanctuary of Cambridge. Far from it. Her musical life seems to have become even more extensive – and, she says, to have contributed to the war effort.

Refugee scholars in residence proffered opportunities to play and introductions to other musicians, to the Cambridge University Music Society and its orchestra, and to another local orchestra. She records how she formed a regular quartet with Elfriede Allen (violin), Jean Robson (viola) and Betty Leach (cello) that was invited to give a lunch-hour recital in the Guildhall for charity. 'For this we had ourselves coached in Haydn Op. 76 No. 5 by Sam Kutscher [sic], a violinist living in Cambridge at the time.' (A rare note of what music she played.)

This performance led to an invitation from the YMCA to play at aerodromes and soldiers' camps round Cambridge, at first as an experiment:

> . . . [t]his was such a change from the entertainment usually provided in these places.

Conscious of the cultural challenge posed by their classical string quartets, they took it cautiously.

> The YMCA representative sang songs, and Elfrieda [sic] and Betty played solos, between the more difficult quartet fare. The first time we went, we played not a whole quartet, but one movement of a couple of quartets, but the next time they got a whole quartet, of course carefully chosen. Jean always gave a little talk about what we were going to play before we started.

Performing within a thirty-mile radius of Cambridge, they had a petrol allowance as being part of the war effort.

Esther recalls one occasion about which the quartet were 'particularly dubious'. This involved playing at the YMCA headquarters in Cambridge itself to an audience of US servicemen, whose 'reputation was not high'.

Perhaps to their relief they found many officers in the audience. Further reassurance was to come:

> As Jean talked I looked at the audience and it seemed to me as though they understood and recognised what she was saying.

After the performance all was revealed, to Esther's particular pleasure.

> [M]any came over to speak to us; they were mostly refugees from Europe now serving in the American army, and were chamber music players themselves. We certainly hadn't expected that.

Perhaps the servicemen refugees included some so-called 'Ritchie Boys', German-speaking Jewish refugees trained at Camp Ritchie in the United States for special operations.

Across Britain, civilians found relief from the stresses of the war with American servicemen putting on shows, bringing a taste of Hollywood, Broadway, Chicago and Nashville to theatres, town halls and schools in provincial towns and cities.

Another of Esther's contributions to the war effort in the SPSL's Cambridge days came with her fire-watching duties; these too involved making music, but also affording security for a particularly fine grand piano, a Blüthner.

The owner of the Blüthner was the mother of one of Esher's refugee scholars, the biochemist and pharmacologist Hermann Blaschko. Her lodging had no room for the grand piano. Esther offered it a home in the SPSL's office in Lensfield Road. There it could also be played once a week at least, on Thursdays, the regular fire-watching night.

> As I had to stay on the premises overnight, I arranged chamber music for that evening . . . Although we got all the sirens that London got, fortunately we didn't get all the bombs. The sirens didn't go off until after 11 p.m., so we had a clear evening's music.

Cambridge did get some bombs. The city was targeted in the early part of the war; no basis can be found for the common story of an understanding between Britain and Germany not to target each other's ancient university towns. In Cambridge itself, according to the *Cambridge Historian* website, between 1940 and 1942 German raids killed thirty and injured up to seventy more. High explosive and incendiary bombs damaged some 1,300 properties in the city, while other attacks missed the city and scattered their bombs across neighbouring beet fields. The *Luftwaffe*'s targets seem to have been factories, railway lines and the local airport.

The Blüthner seems to have survived. Esther and her fellow musicians played on, performances that stayed in her memory. 'My war-interlude was full of music', she recollects. War-working women might have thought she had quite a cushy number.

> Once we played a Haydn quartet in the Cambridge Music Club, and I tend to think of that performance every time I have played it since. That also applies to the Haydn op 76 No 5 we played in the Cambridge Guildhall. Occasions in Vienna still come back to me when I play certain quartets. Outstanding in my memory is playing the Mozart Requiem in the chapel of King's College, with Kathleen Ferrier and Isobel Baillie as soloists.

She learned to ride a bicycle and would cycle in the dark to rehearsals, her fiddle slung over the basket. Her engagements were not just for quartets; she played sonatas with a number of pianists, some of them refugees.

Again, it was a matter of making new academic friends, she records.

> You see how music brought me the acquaintance and friendship of fine people I might otherwise not have met.

And just as she had revisited Vienna to play, so, once back in London, she would go back to Cambridge to make music.

When Esther came back to London in 1944 to work for the Society for Visiting Scientists, the music flowed on.

> The first decade after my return to London was to prove exceptionally rich for me in chamber music . . . I had so many regular quartets, quintets, trios, the occasional sextet, some all strings, some with piano, that I played several times a week, three or four times with different ensembles. Sometimes on Sundays I played with one quartet in the

afternoon and another in the evening. We played either at weekends or during the evenings.

In the absence of her diaries, there is no answer to how this fits with her 1949 complaints to Broda:

I always work all day Saturday as well as late every evening and this is the first time for months I've taken time off for writing a personal letter.

I've had no respite for so long. Not that I'm likely to have any for some time to come; it looks as though again I shall have no holiday.

The names of her musical partners flow over the pages of *Refugee Scholars*. But perhaps what is indicative of Esther's own superior quality as a chamber musician is the number of professionals with whom she played in that most exposed and demanding of musical genres.

First must come the virtuoso violinist and violin teacher Max Rostal, who had been a professor at the State Academy of Music in Berlin until 1933.

He had taken on Esther as a pupil in Cambridge and now introduced her to an industrialist, Martin Cahn, an amateur chamber music player who could afford to pay professionals to play with him. One instanced by Esther was Norbert Brainin, not yet leader of the Amadeus String Quartet. Esther became part of Martin Cahn's ensemble playing with his professionals for two years or so.

I was privileged to play string quartets with them and have been able to boast about it ever since.

Esther's partners as those post-Cambridge years go on also seem predominately former refugees.

She records having regular quartets, 'by which I mean those that lasted some years', one of which included Max Rostal's first wife, Sela Trau, a professional cellist, and was the jewel in the crown of Esther's chamber music.

The standard of this ensemble was superb.

But inevitably her fellow players moved on. She records a non-refugee quartet in the early 1950s and joining an eminent medical practitioner Dr John Horder and his wife to play chamber music in an ensemble of shifting membership, with musically eminent friends available to coach or give hints on particular pieces, such as Kathleen Long on Mozart's E flat Piano Quartet.

As with 'her' children, few participants, if any, seem not to have been eminent in their professional fields and/or musically, even with a bit of a stretch:

> The second violin of that ensemble was a professional singer, Roger Gage, who had at that time recently divorced. His former wife was Joan Plowright, the actress who married Lawrence [sic] Olivier, later Lord Olivier.

But by the early 1960s 'my quartets had disintegrated'. Esther found herself suddenly in a musical vacuum. 'I felt I was suffering from withdrawal symptoms.' To keep her hand in, 'in sheer desperation' she joined the Morley College Orchestra, in Lambeth, but did not enjoy the experience of playing with young college students.

Coincidence – and perhaps what she would not have called *chutzpah* – came to her rescue.

She records how she was at a 'gathering' where she happened to meet Guy Barnett, Labour MP for South Dorset from 1962 to 1964 and Greenwich from 1971 to 1986, with an interest in overseas aid and development. (He'd been to Highgate School, of which A. V. Hill was a governor.)

At that moment, the SVS was in a dire financial position and Esther determined to approach the MP to see, she says, if he could help. As she approached him, she heard that he was going that evening to hear Yehudi Menuhin play at the Royal Festival Hall. Was he interested in music? she asked. He'd been brought up in it; his mother played and taught the violin.

And she played chamber music. And she lived a stone's throw from Esther. And the MP left with Esther's phone number and instructions to tell his mother that if she needed a second violin for her chamber music to think of Esther Simpson.

Esther does not record if she also asked for his help for the SVS, but a phone call from his mother Elaine Minchin followed with an invitation to come and play that Esther recognised as a test – music for two violins and piano. Then, when Elaine heard that Esther already knew her pianist, Ada Goldschmidt, whom she had met often with Sela Trau, the invitation was changed to include supper.

The approach to Guy Barnett had proved a musical watershed.

> [Elaine Minchin's invitation] was the beginning of chamber music which, in one form or another, with some people dropping out and others coming in, has persisted to this day [1988], from 1963.

What Esther called 'many years of intense music activity' followed through the musicians to whom Elaine Minchin introduced her – more than sixty, she calculated, in regular quartets, meeting in different houses sometimes as often as four times a week, often the same musicians in more than twenty different venues.

The Hampstead Music Club in north London became part of her musical beat. The club met in Burgh House, a fine Queen Anne house in the heart of Hampstead and a short walk from the Friends Meeting House of which Esther was an active member. (Sadly, at the time of writing, the Club was unable to discover any record or reminiscence of Esther's participation.)

In a 1972 letter to Broda she described her life in chamber music. She had not much time for concerts, but:

> Regular string quartets on Wednesdays, when I play the viola, an almost regular Tuesday one, where I lead, and one at about six weekly intervals where I play second violin. In addition there is a regular monthly Saturday evening music session in which I take part. This is at the house of the new member for Greenwich Guy Barnett's mother whom I met through Guy, when he tried to get help for the SVS [sic]. So I am able to lose myself into a better and truly international world for a time.

In an autumn 1972 letter, she returned to that theme:

> It gets me into another world for a little while, a world not without argument, but this is confined to discussion of how a certain phrase is to be interpreted, and we don't come to blows about it.

At this time she was also dealing with 'a new Bangladeshi, a Czech, and latest of all a Bulgarian'. And awaited 'with apprehension what Uganda will bring'.

The Minchins, Elaine and her husband Leslie, known for his translations of German Lieder – 'Several recitals of his translations have been given by eminent singers' – also organised with a friend of theirs, Jerry Shields, thematic programmes by period or country, with the players in costume. Musical partners from the past – Leeds, Vienna, Cambridge – reappeared in her musical life.

A visit to Cambridge in August 1972 brought a reunion of her war-time string quartet:

> . . . we played together again three nights running after 28 years.

New partners came out of the blue, such as a professional string player Pauline Jackson who occupied the flat below Esther's.

Inevitably, time took its toll. Esther developed hearing difficulties, her musical contemporaries departed. But she could look back and know that music had had a decisive influence on her life as well as deeply enriching it.

We should recognise how it enabled her also to reach out to her refugees with a rapport that touched their inevitable sense of uprootedness and offered them a sense of belonging in a strange land. As Ray Cooper put it:

> Who else has played with Sir Ernst Gombrich, Karl Stern, Friedrich Buxbaum, Robert Frisch, Norbert Brainin and Hans Keller, to name but a few, and once even led a quartet in which Max Rostal played the cello?

Who indeed? And in coming to an understanding of Esther Simpson, we must note what little we get of the music in her account of her musical life – for all Cooper's attempt to get her to talk about her musical taste and development – and how much of her partners' success and standing. The undoubted richness of her musical experience exists in the background of her story, its unheard context.

50

Getting to Know Esther Simpson

It is my privilege to have known and had as friends people of
outstanding quality . . .

Esther's rehearsing the qualities of those whom she placed within that
category also tells us something about her outlook and priorities, invaluable
for understanding someone for whom personal reticence seemed a way
of life.

In *Refugee Scholars* Chapter 5, 'Refugee Scholars And Others', after
discussing the Nobel laureates, FRSs and FBAs, the OMs, CHs, knights,
Oxbridge heads of houses, musicologists . . . Esther arrives at 'the people I
worked with in the SPSL and the SVS'.

I have of course to start with Lord Beveridge as he was the founder of
the organization, *after he met Leo Szilard in Vienna in April 1933* [Author's
italics].

She goes on to mention his being the third SPSL president, director of the
LSE and Master of University College Oxford, author of *A Defence of Free
Learning*, and initiator of the proposal to deposit the SPSL records in the
Bodleian Library. She makes no reference to his part in the operations of the
AAC and SPSL. For that matter, she makes not even a passing reference to
the historic Beveridge Report, his 1942 blueprint for post-war social policy.

Perhaps his five giants – Want, Disease, Ignorance, Squalor and Idleness – were of no great interest to her.

However, she pays a strikingly modified tribute to Nicholas Baldwin who catalogued the SPSL records in the Bodleian in 1987–1988.

> I was gratified that he was able simply to build on the way I had catalogued the records originally.

Reading this, we might ask how self-aware she was.

Sir Walter Adams, who praised Esther at her 1966 retirement for saving civilisation, is elegantly honoured:

> Walter gave up what would obviously have been a fine academic career in history in order to enable displaced scholars to continue theirs.

Her remarks on his later post as the first principal of the University College of Rhodesia are in terms that will catch the contemporary eye:

> The political situation in Rhodesia was such that Walter had to struggle to preserve this institution while trying to develop its potential. He really had to walk a tight-rope to keep the College as a multi-racial one and at the same time maintain its standards.

The last sentence of her tribute to Sir Walter has the ring of genuine feeling:

> He was a very great human being and a brilliant administrator, whom I shall always revere.

Adams's successor as general secretary was David Cleghorn Thomson (1900–1980), his appointment announced in *Nature* on 30 July 1938, with a summary of the Society's work to date:

> ... So far, of the 1350 displaced scholars registered with this Society, 520 have been permanently placed in 38 countries, apart from more than 300 who have temporarily found work. Within the last three months, the Society has received 340 applications from scholars who have had to discontinue academic activity in Austria. The offices of the Society are at 6 Gordon Square, London, W.C.1.

Although Esther dismisses him as appointed as a fundraiser, and he had been secretary of the Oxford University Appeal Committee, he had also been the BBC's chief official in Scotland for seven years. He'd also been a Liberal Party candidate.

The word 'friend' crops up again here, though not for DCT:

> He brought with him, as his secretary, Avril Wood, daughter of the conductor Sir Henry Wood who founded the Promenade Concerts. Avril and I became friends and remained so until her death.

Avril was the second of Wood's two daughters with his second wife Muriel Greatrex, and had a much wider role than appeal secretary.

At least Cleghorn Thomson receives a mention, unlike Esther's successor as secretary for two years when she moved to the SVS in 1944, Joseph Bright Skemp (1910–1992), a distinguished Cambridge Greek scholar mentioned earlier.

It has to be said, and indeed Esther says it, she was not a scientist, nor for that matter an art historian; she left no record of a personal interest in science or art. Yet she measured the fulfilment of her life by her proximity to measurably successful, often recognised as great, scientists and art historians. Not her service to them, essential in their happily transient hour of need, but the proximity that service brought her, extending into friendship.

An exception to the tendency – leading scholar as friend – appears initially to be A. V. Hill. Mentor perhaps. But no sense of personal closeness is to be felt – unlike with Donald Grant – although A. V. worked so closely with her from 1933, particularly over internment. It was not until 1941 or '42, as Ray Cooper noted with surprise, that Hill had any idea of Esther's musical interests. Esther explained to Cooper that there had never been any need to mention music and she didn't know whether he had musical interests. If he did, they weren't to the fore.

However, her account of A. V. stands out for its feeling, as she speaks of his rare humility, his immeasurable kindness to her, and the value she placed on his friendship, more than she could say.

In the same letter, in a passage on Professor Major Greenwood, who was in at the creation and served as honorary treasurer to 1949, she sets out the standards by which she judged others also not categorised as her friends. She had the highest respect for him. Not a glamorous person but most conscientious and intelligent, not himself taken in by fame or glamour. In withholding admiration for Beveridge, he was not alone, she said. What remained in her mind was his comment when Chamberlain returned from Munich: something like his feeling was one of relief and intense shame.

Moving into the 1980s, her letters to Broda become necessarily records of disappearances – 'we have lost a few more of "our" scholars' – but the names still hold her. She reads *Britain and Atomic Energy 1939–1945* by Margaret Gowing:

> . . . photos of so many old friends. Just looking through the index revives so many memories.

She records going to the memorial service in Oxford for Hans Krebs – she stayed with Lady Simon, the widow of her 'first knight', Francis Simon – but says nothing on the memorial service itself, eulogies, music. Lady Simon held a little party for Esther's Oxford friends. Seventeen sat down to tea – among them she numbers four FRSs with their wives, one single FRS, three FRS widows.

Reading Esther's life as a commitment to refugees – in practice the limited class of refugee scholars – should not be allowed to displace her from her historical context, the gifted woman whose life began in an east European immigrant ghetto in industrial Leeds in 1903, at the beginning of an era of struggle but developing opportunity for educated women such as she. That needs an extra word of qualification for Esther's particular position. A woman and Jewish. A Jewish woman who appears to have cut herself off from her inherited east European Jewish culture and traditions. Perhaps that explains her compulsion to find 'friendship' and a family among her, principally, assimilated German-Jewish scholar refugees. And perhaps that also explains the severely constricted career she, with all her abilities, imposed on herself in mid-life.

Eighty-seven years after she first saw the light of a Leeds day, she wrote to Ray Cooper, with whom she had just had some political disagreement, of the disillusionment of her generation that was to have had a land fit for heroes to live in.

It was not to be, and she listed: the depression of the late 1920s, the fiasco of the 1932 Disarmament Conference, the rise of Fascism and Nazism, the Spanish Civil War, the Second World War. (Curiously, she omits one epochal event.) But then the Labour victory in 1945 brought a different orientation, with the welfare state, not perfect but on the right lines. Then, at the time of writing [April 1990], when she contemplated the deliberate running down, with a view to elimination (sometimes called privatisation) of nearly all that was worthwhile: health, education, housing, the arts, she could not keep her cool.

She saw this as brought about by a government that she characterised as dilettante, arrogant, lacking in intelligence, obsessed by a catastrophic ideology, wholly anti not pro. She couldn't remain calm in the face of the damage done to the people of her country. Education policy was destroying the seed corn. Materialism was triumphant.

She added a postscript. She was not a member of any political party. To use a Quaker phrase, she spoke to her condition. (This seems her only direct Quaker reference in the correspondence.)[45] She thought she belonged to an extinct species, one flourishing briefly at the end of the last century – a few painters, writers, artists. They had a vision diametrically opposite the one now ruling.

We have no further references to that species in her letters to take that further. But in a letter to Broda in 1958, she had written,

> As a life-long socialist myself, I realise more and more that privilege entails obligations; that where there are rights there are duties also, and this alas! has largely been lost sight of. Equality of opportunity must entail equality of service, if the whole thing is not to end in chaos . . . Unless there is reverence for each individual as a human personality, there can be no ethical system.

And in a further letter,

> I don't believe in privileges for one group and lack of them for another . . .

---

45 ' . . . for I saw there was none among them all that could speak to my condition' George Fox, *Journal*, 1647.

She also thought,

> The world is in a ghastly muddle and I suppose we are merely a reflection.

And in 1959 she added:

> Growing up a socialist among pioneer socialists in England. Expect simplicity, perhaps slightly puritanical among those who have suffered for their principles.

'Growing up a socialist among pioneer socialists in England' is a resonant phrase. More's the pity that, though Leeds had its share of early socialists and was even the site of a Labour and Socialist Convention held to follow Russia in 1917, no recorded fact in Esther's life in Leeds fits it. Put that alongside the sentiment quoted earlier that 'She thought she belonged to an extinct species that flourished briefly at the end of the last century – a few painters, writers, artists' and we might wonder about her self-image as an early socialist modernist, as well as a Quaker chamber music devotee and saviour of displaced scholars.

But in practice, away from expressions of moral principle, her approach to philanthropy, as practised by her fellow Quakers towards starving children in Vienna after the First World War, had its limits.

She wrote to Broda in May 1947 commenting on a plea for food parcels to the Royal Society by the Vienna Meteorological Society, who were too poor to buy food on the black market and pointed out there had been similar action at the end of the 1914 war on behalf of university people. The letter, she wrote, gave her quite a jolt. No doubt the people were hungry and poor, but the letter took for granted that it was their job to succour these people and showed no sense of responsibility of any kind.

> Reading that letter, I got a vision of this going on for ever and ever . . . I recalled the creatures I met myself at the Friends Centre in the [Vienna] Singerstrasse; as children they had been taken for years into English homes; the Quakers had started a club for them to keep up their English and help them as they grew up – and they grew up into Nazis. I felt I wanted to write to the staff at the Meteorological Office

and say: will you kindly tell me just how much help you gave to any
of the groups persecuted by the Nazis – Jews, political prisoners, slave
labourers? Which is very bad for my morale and not at all the way a
Quaker should feel. Only a letter like that depressed me, like the talks
I had with German scientists who were brought over here. No sense
of personal responsibility whatsoever, not even a tiny part of collective
responsibility.

The reference to 'talks I had with German scientists *who were brought over
here* [author's italics]. No sense of personal responsibility whatsoever, not
even a tiny part of collective responsibility' is intriguing.

It raises the question, was Esther somehow involved in the top-secret
programme for the Allies' occupation of Germany of 'enforced evacuation'
of German scientists to Britain by the so-called T-Force for questioning?
Perhaps using the SPSL or SVS as cover.

An article in the *Guardian* by Ian Cobain (29 August 2007), 'How T-Force
abducted Germany's best brains for Britain' tells how:

While it has long been known that German scientists and technicians
worked in the US and Britain after the war, it has generally been
assumed they were all volunteers, lured by the promise of good pay
and accommodation. However, the declassified papers make clear
that for more than two years after the cessation of hostilities the British
authorities were subjecting them to a programme of 'enforced
evacuation'.

That these were scientists who had worked in Germany during the war is
indicated by her reference to 'collective responsibility'. And if so, was that
experience the spur to her starting her own information system?

The reference in the letter to 'groups persecuted by the Nazis – Jews,
political prisoners, slave labourers . . .' is also noteworthy as a rare, perhaps
the only such, reference.

In her earlier letter to Ray Cooper listing the causes for disillusion of her
generation, she includes the rise of Fascism and Nazism and the Second
World War. We might expect an explicit reference to the Holocaust from
a Jewish person whose life had been devoted to mainly Jewish refugees
from Nazism, but, as noted earlier, she makes none.

Two years earlier, the ill-fated Suez intervention had roused her moral ire, according to reflections in a 1957 letter to Broda:

> Suez was an appalling shock, whatever consolation there is in the immediate reaction of the sensible element of the population. These 'incidents' terrify me, because they show so clearly how ready people are to plunge into senseless wars – how doped and hypnotized they become willingly and delightedly. The 'civilized' European is still thoroughly savage only a little way down . . . Mankind is very, very sick but thinks it is fine because it has technology – as if that is the answer to the sickness of men's minds and souls. I am horrified at the prevailing frivolousness in face of the dangers from mad children with their lethal toys. I feel I would like to plunge the whole earth into a delousing bath . . . I have never had the illusion that my race, tradition, government, political party had the answer to mankind's problems, but the irresponsible excursion of my own country last October found me still with an illusion to lose.

The contemporaneous crushing of the Hungarian uprising by Soviet tanks is not referred to, perhaps in deference to Broda's communist affiliation.

Again, she appears to feel no incongruity between her condemnation of 'mad children with their lethal toys' and her hero worship of her 'children' who had worked to produce the first nuclear weapons. Nor did her view of mankind as very, very sick but thinking it was fine because it had technology hold her back from lunching at the Royal Society. Still, we must remember that she was writing both to and for Broda.

She returned to then current politics, and Mrs Thatcher's Cabinet, in a letter of April 1990. It was obvious, she wrote, that most of them had not been selected on account of outstanding moral qualities or exceptional intelligence. The quality they had to have was obedience to their master's dictates. At the beginning [Mrs Thatcher] had slipped up by having a few who were not only intelligent but had a fatal flaw of cultural attainments. Ray Cooper had mentioned the notion of 'evil'. Evil results had been produced by certain measures, but their perpetrators were not necessarily evil, only misguided in their arrogance, which was a deadly sin as RC knew.

And although she didn't call people evil, she did call some 'saintly', so she did not wholly avoid the theological.

She did not avoid it in explaining her reaction to the then prime minister, Mrs Thatcher; it arose from an awareness of the qualities that were missing, those that gave meaning to life and made life worth living, that recognised the worth of people, that guided us as something to live by. You might call it, she said, religion.

Much earlier, in July 1954, she had written a thoughtful analysis of the human condition:

> There is misery in every party and much is avoidable – would be if we paid anything like the same attention to learning about ourselves, our humanity, as we do to economic factors or the laws governing inorganic matter. We reach middle-age hopelessly ignorant of ourselves, of our fellow men and of what makes them and us tick. And we then take refuge in 'systems', trusting to formulae to bring about what only God can – and by 'God' I mean the sum of those qualities, attitudes, philosophy, spiritual development – without which human life is barren indeed, however logically watertight the formulae. We all of us make ghastly mistakes about one another, very often because we are mistaken about ourselves. The important thing is to recognise them as mistakes, to be humble before our own inadequacy and profit from them to glimpse where human happiness or spiritual content is really to be found, or rather profitably sought, because it's never found, only experienced during the search.

This plea for self-awareness of our humanity demanding the same attention as the laws governing inorganic matter and humility before our own inadequacy sit somewhat uneasily with her own comprehensive dedication to the intellectual elite and her hero worship of the Royal Society and her FRS 'children'. 'Humble' is not a characteristic one would normally associate with Esther. And just as well for her refugees; humility would not have got her far dealing with the Home Office.

She had reflections, too, on Protestants (blame ourselves) and Catholics (blame the Church). What the letters do not directly discuss are her Quaker beliefs or Jewish inheritance.

For all the accolades on saving civilisation, Esther Simpson comes across as curiously remote from the historic issue that underlay her work for academic refugees, the existential threat to European Jewry. We are left with no idea of how she received the news of the Holocaust and what impact it had on her.

Her exact contemporary Yvonne Kapp writes in *Time Will Tell*:

> He, my father, had acquired British nationality long before my birth but, with my thoroughbred German-Jewish ancestry on both sides, I shall, for as long as I live, suspect every German national over the age of eight in 1933 and neither in exile or a concentration camp in the course of the following twelve years, of complicity in mass murder. How often have I reflected that there, but for the merest chance, go I among the millions for whom the lamentations will echo through the world for as long as humanity survives.

Esther Sinovitch had Russian-Jewish not German-Jewish roots. And while there is no evidence that she took any interest in her family's antecedents or ancestral home, her condemnation of her parents' failure to assimilate as she had assimilated means she had grown up with the sound of Dvinsk echoing in her ears.

The cruel fate of the Jews of Dvinsk at the hands of the SS and local Latvian nationalists is described in dreadful detail by *Generalleutnant* Heinrich Kittel in one of MI6's secretly recorded conversations at Trent Park between high-ranking German prisoners of war in late 1944:

> For instance, in Latvia, near Dvinsk, there were mass executions of Jews carried out by the SS or Security Service. There were about fifteen Security Service men and perhaps sixty Latvians, who are known to be the most brutal people in the world . . . there was a terrific bitterness against the Jews at DVINSK, and the people simply gave vent to their rage.

Did Esther ever reflect that 'but for the merest chance', she would have gone 'among the millions for whom the lamentations will echo through the world for as long as humanity survives'?

Nothing says so directly, for instance in the Broda correspondence. But perhaps her devotion to displaced scholars also bespeaks that reflection.

51
The Gift of Friendship

It would be enough if Esther were remembered only for her gift of friendship to the enforced migrants with whom she dealt. Those uprooted from the society of which they had believed themselves rootedly a part, nationally, professionally, socially, linguistically . . . to eat what Dante called 'the bitter taste of others' bread'.

In *Survivors in Mexico* (2003) Rebecca West outlines what the editor Bernard Schweizer calls '[t]he exile's trauma of deracination':

> Many people can, of course, tear up the roots and go to live in a strange country without a pang, but the very fact that a man has been exiled shows that when the blow fell he was happy where he was and hoped to continue to be there. Now he is in a place he never chose as his home: he will almost certainly have lost some of his family and his friends, and perhaps all of them; he may have made a fortune in his new country, but he has nevertheless not got the tables and chairs and beds his grandfather left him; he cannot open the shutters of his bedroom in the morning and look out on the field where the old white horse used to graze. He perhaps endures the most frustrating experience of all. As he gets into his seventies and eighties, he may long to go back to his own country, on any terms, making any submissions that are demanded, only that he may die in a particular house . . .

In a single short phrase Louis MacNeice caught their situation in his poem 'At the British Museum', when he wrote of 'the guttural sorrows of the refugee'.

If, that is, fortunate enough to be allowed entry. W. H. Auden in his 1939 poem 'Refugee Blues' pictures a public meeting where the speaker warns that if the refugees are let in 'they will steal our daily bread'.

In 1935 Auden had married the German exile and critic of the Nazi regime Erika Mann to give her a British passport.

And Bertolt Brecht, who fled Germany for Scandinavia on 28 February 1933, the day after the Reichstag fire, finally leaving Finland for America in 1941, complained in his poem 'On the Label Emigrant' that 'emigrants' was the wrong term: they had fled, they were 'the persecuted, the banished' – those who should not bother with a strange grammar, he advised in 'Thoughts Concerning the Duration of Exile', as the news that called them home was 'written in a familiar language'.

Brecht dramatised the experience of the ordinary refugee in a series of dialogues, *Refugee Conversations*, *Flüchtlingsgespräche*, between two German exiles, a bourgeois Jewish scientist and a left-wing worker, who meet in the Helsinki railway station café. The worker, Kalle, had been held in Dachau concentration camp and recollects how an SS man there was the most orderly person he, Kalle, had ever met:

> When he beat us with his leather whip, he did it in such a conscientious manner that the weals on our skin formed a pattern you could have measured with a protractor. His sense of order was so deeply ingrained that he would have preferred not to beat us at all rather than beat us untidily.

Esther's great friend Irene Grant, Donald's wife, is rightly hailed as a heroine for risking the concentration camp in her daring rescue of Bertolt Brecht's two-year-old daughter Barbara from the Gestapo.

Barbara [Brecht-Schall] wrote about Irene's mission in her Foreword to Brecht's *Love Poems*:

> Just as the Reichstag [February 1933] burned down, Papa lay in the hospital in Berlin, recovering from appendicitis. My mother went to his room and asked what they should do, and he told her they

must leave immediately. Perhaps just as serious as his condition was the fact that I was not in Berlin, but with my grandfather in Augsburg. The situation appeared so dire that they could not even wait for me. Even though he was hardly recovered, they left the hospital and took the next train to Vienna, still five years away from the Anschluss. The problem remained how to squire me, a little girl, out of a country whose borders were now patrolled and sealed. Arriving in the Austrian capital, they met up with Irene Grant, an English woman and a Quaker, who had a passport not only for herself but for her young son. It could not have been more perfect. She agreed to help, so I, a three-year-old girl, [Ed: two-year-old: born in October 1930] left Germany as a four-year-old boy, and was reunited immediately with my hugely relieved parents, who then promptly left Austria.

Irene's own account, broadcast in 1976 as an interval talk on BBC Radio 3 under the title *Conspirators*, makes clear the risk she ran. The Gestapo planned to hold Barbara hostage for Bertolt's return to Germany. Hence she had to be spirited out of the country by train as soon as possible. Irene also describes the unsolicited help she had from two women in traditional Bavarian dress in her compartment. Their sharp looks at Irene and Barbara had made Irene very anxious: would they say something to the border guards? But as the two got out at the last stop before the Austrian frontier, the point where passports were checked, they pushed between the border guard and Irene, saying how like the baby was to her mother. They had never seen such a likeness . . .

Loss of language, the immediacy of socially nuanced understandings, is central to the emigrant experience. The refugee Austrian actor Fritz Kortner coined the phrase *Sprachheimat*, one's language home. Thomas Mann in California considered that the exiled German writer had a duty to continue writing in the German language.

An interchange in the 1942 film *Casablanca*,[46] which is *par excellence* a refugee film, literally so in terms of its casting – the language on the set is

---

46 Curtiz, Michael, 1942, *Casablanca*. United States: Warner Bros. Producer Hal Wallis. Screenplay Julius J. Epstein, Philip G. Epstein and Howard Koch.

said to have been German, with so many German-Jewish refugee actors playing Nazi and other German roles – as well as its story, catches the misfortune of lost language.

In Rick's café an elderly couple are celebrating the arrival of their US visas with his head waiter Carl:

Mrs Leuchtag:	At last the day's came!
Mr Leuchtag:	Frau Leuchtag and I are speaking nothing but English now.
Mrs Leuchtag:	So we should feel at home when we get to America.
Carl:	A very nice idea.
Mr Leuchtag:	To America.
Carl:	To America.
Mr Leuchtag:	Come sit down. Have a brandy with us.
Carl:	To America!
Mr Leuchtag:	Liebchen – sweetness heart, what watch?
Mrs Leuchtag:	Ten watch.
Mr Leuchtag:	Such much?
Carl:	Hm. You will get along beautiful in America, mm-hmm.

Perhaps one of the scriptwriters – Julius and Philip Epstein and Howard Koch – had overheard such an interchange on a Los Angeles streetcorner.

Carl is played by a Jewish Hungarian stage and film actor, S. Z. Sakall, many of whose relatives died in concentration camps; Mr Leuchtag by an Austrian actor Ludwig Stössel and Mrs Leuchtag by a German actress Ilka Grüning. All three were stage and film stars before their enforced emigration, working now in essentially bit parts.

Language acquisition might well have been easier for the emigrant children, though the mother tongue still carried a high emotional charge, as Hannele Zürndorfer describes in her *Kindertransport* memory of her English school:

Somehow my English must have improved quite quickly. I don't know
at what point it became my first language. I continued to write poems,
diaries and letters to relatives in German. For some time Lotte [her
younger sister] and I continued to speak in German when alone
together, for I felt that German was the link between my parents and
us. It was the language of our lives together and I felt in some
indefinable way disloyal at abandoning its use altogether. But we heard
only English spoken and it became a necessity for survival. Gradually
Lotte and I started conversing in a hotchpotch of English and German,
but quite soon English became our spoken language, and I remember
waking one night and realizing that I had been dreaming in English.

Bernard Schweizer describes the exile's changing world:

[T]he flight from one's home may lead to initial elation about being
safe, followed by homesickness, gloom, and economic hardship,
which, in turn, are often succeeded by a slow acculturation to the new
environment, an evolving, hybrid cultural identity and, sometimes,
artistic and social success.

No aspect of life was untouched by the experience of exile, and the higher
up the academic tree, the more challenging the experience, whether
it was shared laboratory facilities, reduced salaries, unusually familiar
relationships with local staff, perceived lack of respect due to a professor,
or reduced living conditions.

In *Refugee Scholars* Esther's view of the professional and personal
acculturation of the exiled German professor is optimistic and somewhat
at odds with the received view over, say, scholars *welcoming* the change into
the British academic culture.

Clearly the educational pattern in this country was very different from
that in Germany and Austria and this could create a problem for some
refugee scholars. But it was really only true in certain individual cases
because many of the scholars welcomed the change. They thought
the British system of university education was, in some respects,
superior to their own. Originally some of those who had been
professors had a little difficulty in adjusting to the situation because

as I found when I was at the University of Caen, and also when I went to lectures at the University of Vienna, there was little or no contact in those countries between students and staff. The Professor was on a pedestal and he always wore a dark suit; whereas in Cambridge the professors could be slightly scruffy, in flannels, and that was something which it was difficult to come to terms with. But as the refugee scholars were going to live here and their children went to school here and grew up with our habits, generally they assimilated pretty quickly.

We cannot ignore that the AAC/SPSL's applicants were privileged in having a dedicated gateway to pass through to safety.

Not for them the fearful position so tautly described by Erich Maria Remarque in his 1962 migrant novel *The Night in Lisbon*:

> [T]he coast of Portugal had become the last hope of the fugitives to whom justice, freedom, and tolerance meant more than home and livelihood. This was the gate to America. If you couldn't reach it, you were lost, condemned to bleed away in a jungle of consulates, police stations, and government offices, where visas were refused and work and residence permits unobtainable, a jungle of internment camps, bureaucratic red tape, loneliness, homesickness, and withering universal indifference. As usual in times of war, fear, and affliction, the individual human being had a ceased to exist; only one thing counted: a valid passport.

To confine the experience of loss to migrants would be wrong: the fate of those Jews who remained was increasingly to become exiles in their own land, experiencing homelessness, loss of status, defamiliarisation, exclusion, even a loss of language as Victor Klemperer demonstrated.

It is also important to recall that not all the AAC/SPSL's applicants were big enough names to be celebrated in the pages of *Refugee Scholars*.

Historians, musicologists, sociologists, bearers of names without instant recognition, also passed through its registers, some to receive this:

> 28 Jan 1939: We have had your name on our lists for some time, and we regret that until now we have been unsuccessful in finding an

opening for you. History is one of the most difficult subjects to place . . . We shall continue to look out for possibilities for you, though world conditions are now against us.

Esther wrote that to Karl Süssheim, a sixty-one-year-old associate history professor at Munich University, Jewish, married with two children, with oriental languages noted as his special field. Dismissed from his university post in 1933, he remained in Germany until 1941, when Turkish friends helped him to emigrate with his wife and daughters to Istanbul, where he found work at the university.

But Charlotte/Lotte Schlesinger had success with Esther's support. Born in Berlin in 1909, unmarried, a teacher of music, a pianist and composer, her file extends from 1934 to 1947, showing her working in Kiev and then Prague, and finding a position in the US, at the famous liberal arts Black Mountain College in North Carolina.

Another less known in 1933 was the sociologist Svend Riemer. Born in Berlin in 1905, he became Professor of Sociology at University of California, Los Angeles from 1952 until his retirement in 1975. Not Jewish, he was married to a Jew and had been active in the SPD. While an assistant at Kiel University, in 1932, on the eve of Hitler's coming to power, he had written on the sociology of national socialism, a work said to have irritated the Party. In 1933 he and his wife fled to Sweden, where he lectured at Stockholm. The AAC/SPSL then helped him to find positions in the United States, with the aid of a Rockefeller grant. Beside Esther, the volunteer Charles Skepper managed his case.

52

Why?

We have no idea of Esther's prior knowledge, if any, of the extent of German academics displaced in those first months of Hitler's April Civil Service Law – what newspapers she read while in Geneva, or whether the displacement of German scholars was a topic of conversation at the World Alliance of YMCAs. She was certainly wrong about their all being Jewish. But that 'the people who were losing their jobs were the same sort as those I had played chamber music with in Vienna' is simply insufficient as an explanation for such an urgent resolve to return to England; to leave the well-paid security of the YMCA to work in London at a comparative pittance for the nascent AAC, as reflected in Donald Grant's letters to her.

On taking the secretarial post in the AAC office in July 1933, she cannot have known or conjectured that she would thereby be committing herself for life to the succour of academic refugees. Was the motive the simple desire to get to London – Grant's promise was she would get to London – to join Szilard there?

An alternative explanation, or speculation, might lie in her being prompted by a rediscovery of the Jewishness she had supressed.

In *Refugee Scholars* Esther recounted how, early on in her post as personal assistant to the Director of the World Alliance of YMCAs in Geneva, she was faced by the antisemitic incident remarked on earlier.

At the end of Thursday mornings, as she told Cooper, the staff would hold little religious services, and I remember being very shocked when, on an occasion soon after I joined, the French parson said that while rather awkward happenings were taking place in Germany, we had to ask ourselves what was the will of God. Quoting from Isaiah, he proved to his own satisfaction that it was the will of God that the Jews should be persecuted until they all became Christian. That was a little much for me.

She mentioned the incident to her friend Frank Willis, who ran the institution for training YMCA leaders.

When I told him about it he was quite furious.

This shocking incident seems to have coincided with Szilard's contacting Esther. She says, significantly,

It was while all this was happening – I hadn't thought then of leaving the job because, after all, I was fairly new to it and my colleagues were extremely nice and so was my boss – that I got a letter from somebody I didn't know . . .

That somebody was Szilard, who

had a great concern about the University staffs and students who had been displaced in Germany.

Plausibly we might see some sort of epiphany for Esther at this point, with the parson's attack on Jews in her workplace and Szilard's account of the actual attack on German Jews in their workplaces. It is clear that she saw the displacements as affecting only Jews. But when she says 'the same sort as those I had played chamber music with in Vienna', what did she mean by 'sort'?

Again plausibly, this could be a reference not to their academic standing – if they had been Nobel laureates we can safely assume she would have said so – but to their degree of acculturation. Their academic lives in Vienna may well have been disrupted by Nazi students. Accounts of Esther's life tend, unsurprisingly, to focus on her engagement with the musical life of Vienna – the Vienna where playing an instrument was as natural as cleaning your teeth.

Vienna had meant something to her from the first days with IFOR. Even when, as she says, pleas from displaced German academics were swamping the AAC, she took time off each summer up to 1937 to visit Vienna.

Was it just the music? A reasonable guess might be that the society of assimilated, cultivated German-speaking Jews was a magnet for her. More than 10 per cent of the city's population was Jewish or of Jewish background, and were to be found in significant numbers among its professional classes, artists and musicians.

The late nineteenth-century flight west to Austria and Germany of Jews of Eastern European/Russian Jewish culture, away from pogroms such as in the Bessarabian capital Kishinev in 1903 and 1905, was a problem for assimilated German-speaking Jews. They feared their hard-won status in society would be compromised by their exotic *Luftmenschen* co-religionists, conventionally pictured as a people of caftans, sidelocks, the shtetl[47] and loud bickering in Yiddish. (At this time, more than half of world Jewry lived in Imperial Russia, and the vast majority of Russian Jewish emigrants were simply in search of a better life or avoiding service in the tsars' armies.)

In a letter to Broda, Esther remarks that her parents never assimilated. We might coin the phrase for them that, 'The Jew may leave Dvinsk, but Dvinsk may not leave the Jew.'

For Esther in Leeds that would have meant growing up with at least some elements of that total way of east European and Russian Jewish life summed up in the phrase *Yiddishkeit*, hearing Yiddish itself, the language of everyday life that also carried the traditional spirit, rhythm and vitality of the shtetl, and living life with echoes at least of the charismatic Chasidism of which, together with tailoring, Dvinsk was a historic centre.

The Esther Sinovitch who was a bright star at Leeds Modern Girls School, was awarded a City scholarship to Leeds University, and took a first-class degree in French and German, appears to have stepped aside from her unassimilated parents' east European *Yiddishkeit*. (Her elder brother Israel also.) Of that, more later.

Besides non-stop chamber music, Vienna brought a close acquaintance with the Quakers, and she took steps to become a Quaker, though first at

---

47 A small Eastern European town peopled by observant Jews.

arm's length. But like the early-nineteenth century Berlin *salonnière* Rahel
Varnhagen von Ense, in Hannah Arendt's account, did Esther have to leave
her native Judaism in order to reconnect with a new, different, and now
personally acceptable version of it?

The shock of the parson's attack on the Jews coupled with the Nazi
assault on Germany's highly educated and assimilated Jews perhaps
prompted a new acceptance of her Jewishness – these were the Jews with
whom she could associate, a new family. Nonetheless, it comes uneasily
to read her description in *Refugee Scholars* of the makeup of the AAC's
management:

> On our Council we did not have a single Jew. We had them on the
> Executive Committee . . .

Them? But, for instance, Ray Cooper makes no reference to her immigrant
Jewish antecedents in his opening chapter of *Refugee Scholars*, and it is
plausible that he and his family did not know of them.

So she would straddle two worlds: that of being an active Quaker by
choice and that of her inescapable Jewishness through her 'family' and her
interest in Israel, with membership of the Anglo-Israel Association.

Sir Walter Adams's words in tribute to Esther might seem extravagant,
but they catch that association.

> I do not know what your present score of Barons, Knights, Fellows of
> the Royal Society is, but your family – of which you are mother and
> sister – is without doubt the most talented and distinguished in
> the world.

(Bearing in mind that Sir Walter was Esther's boss at the time and
responsible for everything she did in the AAC/SPSL, should we regard
him as father and brother of this distinguished family?)

Of course, non-Jewish academics displaced under the 7 April law for
political reasons may have been members of the 'family', but Esther does
not specify this.

That the displaced refugee academics became Tess's own extended
family – even metaphorically – must be unique among the refugee aid
workers of this period – excepting the refugee children from Germany,

Austria and Czechoslovakia that many actual families took in. And they are not just members of her family – though it was a term she used in 1940 over internment, 'I faced one or two anxious moments last week. One naturally has something to worry about when one has a family of six hundred' – but her 'children'. In her letters to Broda that word, or sometimes 'my', is always in inverted commas.

Even given the tragic circumstances that brought them together, something irresistibly comic infuses the notion of the displaced German professor as the 'child' of the Council/Society's unmarried English assistant secretary. Nonetheless, a word of caution is appropriate in how we approach her use of 'child' or 'children'.

Such usage in relation to an adult – child, childlike – is usually dismissive or pejorative where that person's abilities are concerned, as well as an assertion of morally-charged superiority in the user. Even more so in Esther's day in relation to indigenous colonial subjects.

Uprooted, bewildered, at a loss linguistically and culturally, feeling the novel effects of being hard up, the enforced academic migrant (and possible future Nobel Prize winner) and family were not infantilised by their experience. The AAC/SPSL ethos was also that applicants should take responsibility for themselves. Why did she diminish them by characterising them as children?

An answer may be that Esther's usage was for herself: she saw (or needed to see) herself not as an AAC secretary doing her job, no matter how efficiently and sensitively, but as having a significant relationship beyond that role, as *in loco parentis*: the refugees' stand-in parent, a relationship that required continuation in its nature long after the exile had left his or her refugee station and entered into quotidian life.

For an account of how this was the distinguishing characteristic of Esther Simpson's dedicated work we need look no further than the foreword to *Refugee Scholars*.

The distinguished botanist Lord Ashby, President of the SPSL, a former vice-chancellor of Cambridge University and chancellor of Queen's University Belfast, asked in his foreword to *Refugee Scholars*,

> How does it happen that an assistant-secretary should turn out to have had the star-role in the Society's history?

He responded,

> [The Society's] enviable reputation is due to the personality of a
> woman who was recruited at the age of thirty, in 1933, as assistant
> secretary . . .

He added,

> [s]he was a superb secretary, managing the massive pile of paper-work
> without fuss . . . Undismayed by frequent crises and with a dogged
> determination to resolve them; dismissive about overwork . . . Well,
> there are other secretaries like that. Tess's rare gift was an immediate
> and evident empathy towards each individual refugee. In their
> desperate plight she was often their first contact with British
> officialdom. To those that were qualified the Society was able to offer
> reassurance and financial help; but Tess offered them more than this.
> It was, so to speak, an invitation into an extended family, for she has
> been able, with total sincerity, to extend her gift of friendship to
> include hundreds of those who came to her for help. She became so
> dedicated to the work that she became possessed by it.

Lord Ashby's scientifically objective, if somewhat dismissive, 'Well, there
are other secretaries like that' points up the singular characteristic of
Esther's gift of friendship, extended with total sincerity to hundreds of the
lost and vulnerable seeking support. But it also recalls Gombrich's reference
at *Refugee Scholars*' launch to Esther as embodying 'the ethos of secretaries,
that unsung array of heroines who prevent our world from going to pieces'.
Esther, even to her warmest supporters forever the secretary.

Reading the draft text of the book before writing his foreword, Lord
Ashby was struck by how the transcribed interview tapes carried the sound
of Esther's voice. And it is her account in *Refugee Scholars* that produces the
impression it was the refugee scholars' becoming her friends, her successful
friends, and thereby members of her extended family, that was significant
for Esther. Though the recorded acknowledgement extends only to cover
German-speaking assimilated Jewish people before 1944.

As for Esther's becoming possessed by the work, perhaps 'possessive of
the work' would fit better.

Eric Ashby is not alone in focusing on the significance of the attachment between Esther and the enforced migrant. Ray Cooper noted:

> What stood out from our conversations was Esther's total commitment to the refugee cause and her instinctive ability to involve herself in each and every one of the hundreds of refugee scholars who appealed to the Society for help.

This raises a further question. How can anyone involve themselves in each and every one of hundreds? Not over a life career, but in this case focused on the pre-war Hitler period.

A different analysis might conclude that distinction or success was the further qualification for 'friendship'.

Her lifelong attachment to the SPSL, determination really that no one take her place, perhaps displace her at the Royal Society, requires that we look at its origins, what was it that drew her to the world of enforced and mainly Jewish German-speaking migrants?

The key may be in her remark to Engelbert Broda that she had assimilated while her parents never did. Unlike them, she was born, brought up and educated to degree level in Leeds, including a musical education. But she could still use the word 'assimilated' about herself, perhaps a reference to her memory of Crawford Street as a little Dvinsk from which she needed to become British as though she herself had immigrated.

In 1959 she had written to Engelbert's scientist son Paul that there were worse things than being a cultivated English scientist with that 'plus' that foreign ancestry and travel give.

> Of course I am not objective in this, but I have experience growing up in England, of British birth, but of Russian Jewish parents in a community cosmopolitan at home, English at school.

Of course, her first school, Lovell Road, the ghetto school, was far from wholly English in classroom and playground, but does this comment signal that the key to knowing Esther is understanding her sense of lacking authenticity as an Englishwoman? Did she see herself as detached from her 'cosmopolitan' family by acculturation but still inauthentic: remaining a stranger as a Russian Jew and a woman in what was her own land? Was this an impulse behind the long period working abroad after university? Then, behind the attachment to these uprooted, cultivated, mainly Jewish migrants, a sense of sharing their assimilation, a process in which she had a head start, making them members of the same family?

In March 1951 she writes about the Society for Visiting Scientists,

> It's been quite gratifying to see how high our little SVS stands in scientific esteem, and whereas some time ago I might have been inclined to add und damit kann man Schabbas [*sic*] machen [and you can make Shabbos with it] – I don't think so now.

But in March 1949, a religious reference on Louis Rapkine's death was Christian:

> I think particularly of one saying of Jesus, where one or two are gathered together in his name, he would be there . . . I have always held that immortality consists on the continuation of a person's influence in the soul of others . . . If the Jesus handed down to us in legend ever existed he must have been like Louis. New Testament in modern terms.

While accepting the exceptional personal involvement – not easily undertaken when hundreds are involved – claims of her 'total commitment to the refugee cause' might give us pause. The individual refugee and family, yes. The cause or causes that brought that individual scholar or scientist to her door? Lobbying, marching, banner-waving, boycott-organising, letter-writing? No mention of any is to be found. From that angle, Esther was no Ethel de Keyser, a point made in a conversation about her.[48]

However, it would be wrong to see Esther as personally without a child. In her correspondence she refers to her 'ward', a woman only thirty-four when she died.

The ward and her twin brother were the children of a great friend of Esther's from Vienna. The friend and Esther were the same age and had shared so much, she told Broda.

Her sense of bereavement on her ward's death was plainly as if her

---

48 (1926–2004), South African-born anti-apartheid activist, secretary of the Anti-Apartheid Movement.

own child had died. Indeed, in a letter to Roger Soltau's wife Irene, Esther described her ward as 'almost a daughter to me'.

But in an article in *The Times* for 1 July 1992 when *Refugee Scholars* had been published, she is quoted as saying she has no regrets about never being married.

> I don't like doing things badly and I would not have made a good wife
> or mother.

From her willingness to advise friends on their relationships and her own sense of maternal relationship to her ward, we might surmise that what Esther rejected was the partnership and its obligations involved in marriage. Being her own person was all.

53
Berti

No account of Esther's life can be complete without including her relationship with the leading Austrian scientist Engelbert Broda – Berti – and his son Professor Paul Broda, born in England in 1939, to whom she stood close as his unofficial godmother. Paul Broda was involved with the SPSL and its successor CARA for an uninterrupted thirty-five years, including serving on the SPSL's and then CARA's councils and as chair of the Allocation Committee and as honorary secretary.

Engelbert (1910–1983) and his German wife Hildegard, Hilde (1911–2004), a medical doctor, were married in 1935 and fled to Britain in April 1938, Engelbert coming from Zurich, having left Austria in March, and Hilde coming from Cologne with a visa to join her husband. Both were half-Jewish; both were left wing. More, as Paul narrates in *Scientist Spies*, Engelbert had been a devoted communist since his days in Vienna. He had been imprisoned as a communist in both Germany and Austria and had paid an extended working visit to Russia from the end of 1935 into most of 1936.

In Vienna, he had probably met Edith Suschitzky, born in 1908 and a communist from the age of fifteen; a photographer who had trained at the Bauhaus. She came to London as Edith Tudor-Hart, having married a British doctor, Alexander Tudor-Hart, and became an intermediary between the British Communist Party, of which she had become a member under the name of Betty Grey, and an Austrian communist group set up in 1938 by Engelbert Broda at the Austrian Centre in London.

She was an agent for Soviet intelligence and is said to have been a key figure, a talent-spotter whose stars included Kim Philby and Anthony Blunt. Blunt is said to have described her as 'the grandmother of us all', though it is highly unlikely that she described them as her grandchildren.

It was through Edith Tudor-Hart that Engelbert later himself made contact with Soviet intelligence in London. Esther does not mention her, but may well have met her at the famous modernist Lawn Road Flats dining club, the Isokon club, in Hampstead, to which Esther was so pleased to be invited. Esther lived in Lawn Road for a period.

Engelbert met Esther at the SPSL in May 1938. She helped him to find work in a new field – visual purple, a key component of the retina – though this seminal research was interrupted on the outbreak of war by his internment as a communist enemy alien. Initially he was interned only briefly. Sir William Bragg and Sir Edward Mellanby, secretary of the Medical Research Council that had funded his research, and Esther all contacted the Home Office to argue for his release. But then he was interned again six months later in the general round-up. Esther had 600 internment cases to deal with, but she again helped to achieve his freedom after thirteen weeks.

In 1950 he wrote from Vienna to seek her help over the release of two friends of his second wife's held by the Yugoslav authorities:

> You know that it is not for nothing that one's mind turns to you when somebody among one's friends is in trouble. I often think back to your words in a letter during my first internment 'that you will leave no stone unturned'. You did not.

She told him that she was

> . . . plotting to get [Norman] Bentwich to write the history of the SPSL and also to use his Israeli contacts over the Yugoslav 2.

After Hitler invaded the Soviet Union in June 1941, making it ideologically correct for communists to support the war effort, Engelbert became part of the government's secret 'Tube Alloys' team in Cambridge, to work on the creation of an atomic bomb in concert with the teams in Los Alamos in the United States. He was taken on against MI5's advice – they had suspicions of him, but no actual proof. His employers felt his value as a scientist outweighed his potential danger as a communist, but MI5 was assured that he would not have access to the most confidential materials. Paul Broda also notes,

> He did not get access, since famously by no means all the research done across the Atlantic came to Cambridge or indeed the British in Montreal. EB sent what he could, but how much that was is an open question, in spite of the Soviet boasts.

Esther had a hand in this move, having put him in touch with a boyhood friend from Vienna, now a research physicist in Cambridge. Hans von Halban, who would have been classified as Jewish by the Nazis, had fled Austria and become a French citizen in 1939. In 1940, he was in Paris working with the research team of Frédéric Joliot-Curie on creating nuclear chain reactions.

He enters the history books together with physicist Dr Lew Kowarski, who was Russian and also became a French citizen only in 1939, when, with the Germans at the gates of Paris, Joliot-Curie told them to take the global stock of rare heavy water to England lest it fall into German hands.

In her essay in *France and Nuclear Deterrence – A Spirit of Resistance*, Diane Dosso narrates how they sailed from Bassens near Bordeaux on a cargo ship, the *SS Broompark*, the precious cargo

> representing 26 canisters (185 kg) attached to a raft behind the cargo ship with the hope that it would resist a potential torpedo attack.

In Halban's 1964 obituary, the *New York Times* wrote,

> Many British scientists said after the war that the arrival in Britain of Drs. Halban and Kowalski was a decisive point in Britain's wartime nuclear research.

It was a decisive point for Engelbert Broda.

Having gained access to research being done across the Atlantic, from 1942 he voluntarily passed to the Soviets whatever work leading to the creation of the first nuclear weapon came to Cambridge.

MI5's reservations were well informed and well founded, though the ultimate proof had to wait until the KGB files were opened in 2004. Although Engelbert presented himself as a Jewish Viennese liberal, the Security Service knew in detail about his communist commitments and his relationship with the then-suspected Soviet agent Edith Tudor-Hart. (She confessed in 1947 to MI5, but only that she had worked for the Soviets pre-war.)

On his own initiative Engelbert had given Edith a detailed report for her to pass on to the Communist Party. After that first report, Edith was instructed to get him to agree to meet a comrade. He first met 'Glan', a Soviet intelligence officer, in January 1943. They then met every two to three weeks. By August he was Moscow's main source on the future bomb. His Soviet handlers code-named Engelbert 'Eric'.

Paul Broda quotes KGB files that describe Eric in 1943

> as the main source of information on work being done on Enormous
> [the prospective nuclear weapon] in England and in the USA.

He was using visits to Paul and to the Austrian Centre in London to cover his deliveries. The files also describe him as 'completely selfless in his work with us' and the information he delivered as 'exceptionally valuable'.

From the Soviet viewpoint, the decisive impact of this flow of secret information is beautifully caught by Vasily Grossman in the course of his Second World War masterpiece *Life and Fate*, at its heart the battle for Stalingrad. The significant moment is an unheralded phone call from Stalin to Viktor Shtrum, a leading nuclear physicist who has recently made a breakthrough in his work on the structure of the atom. Nonetheless, following an unguarded remark about the regime, Shtrum is being professionally and personally edged into the cold. That is until an unheralded, probably life-saving, telephone call:

> Good day, Comrade Shtrum.

Has he everything he needs to continue his research? asks Stalin.

As history tells us, Berti was far from the only Soviet source on the advance of Western nuclear research, nor the only one in Paul Broda's life. As he relates in his comprehensive and moving *Scientist Spies*, his mother married again in 1953 – to the British nuclear spy Alan Nunn May.

Hilde and Engelbert had separated in 1940, after Engelbert had been interned, and were divorced in 1946. Hilde was living and working as a doctor in London and Engelbert was in Cambridge, where Paul was also at school and, later, university.

Working for the SPSL in Cambridge until 1944, Esther formed a close relationship with Paul, which continued into later life. For instance, she attended his Cambridge graduation, and when Engelbert had returned to Austria in 1947, she used their extensive correspondence to report and comment on Paul's well-being.

Paul recalls,

> As Berti saw me and heard from me much less than he wanted, Tess was a surrogate who was fond of me from Cambridge days and who could sometimes tell him she had seen me.

As a teenager, Paul had also made occasional visits to the SVS when in London.

What was the nature of Esther's relationship to Berti? Paul has a pithy summing up:

> No letters between Berti and Tess exist from this period [1942–1944], but allusions to that time in later letters show their close but probably platonic friendship.

Indeed, Tess described herself as facilitating Berti's being given a visa for Italy in 1947 so that he could go to Rome to meet the woman who became his second wife, Ina Jun (1899/1900–1983), a Jewish Yugoslav poet and translator from Zagreb, a communist and former partisan, whom he had known before the war.

In *Refugee Scholars*, Esther says,

> We knew all the European science attachés and I was able to ask the one from Italy to see Broda. As a result Broda was enabled to go to Italy, and meet his friend. They subsequently married.

In fact, as she tells Engelbert in a 1947 letter, the visa on a travel document was collected by a mutual friend, Mrs Löw-Beer. Having seen him on his way through London, she wrote of sensing an evident inner core of unhappiness, of restlessness, dissatisfaction.

Engelbert had applied in 1946 for a permit to return to Austria. The British authorities were reluctant, but had no grounds to keep him in the country. By April 1947, he was back in Vienna working for the Federal Ministry for Electrification and Energy. (Of the hundreds of Austrians helped by the SPSL, only seven returned.) In 1948 he found a post at the university, managing his projects on so-called soft money until he was finally appointed a professor in 1964. He retired in 1980, nationally recognised for his contribution to Austrian science. The Americans remained suspicious of his possible continuing covert attachment to the Soviets when at the university.[49] The British authorities directed a special watch on him should he return to the UK.

Of course we ask if Esther had knowledge or suspicions of Engelbert's spying.

Some textual analysis might suggest she did. We might note the continuing use of 'Broda' in her *Refugee Scholars* account of him, after an initial 'He was Dr Engelbert Broda'. 'Broda himself eventually returned to Vienna . . .'

No single rule governs names in *Refugee Scholars*. Men can be surname only – 'Wittgenstein' – or first name 'Louis' [Rapkine]. Following her long and close relationship with Broda 'Berti' she called him 'Engelbert' might have been expected.

Also, given her closeness to Engelbert and his son Paul, and their years-long correspondence after he returned to Vienna, his one-paragraph mention in *Refugee Scholars* effectively puts him at a distance from her.

She begins with contact through the Society for Visiting Scientists, remarking that her

> contacts with refugee scholars and their British colleagues sometimes enabled me to help people in unexpected ways.

One such, the first, happened to be a refugee scientist who was a member of the SVS.

---

49 The FBI put together a massive file on him, which Covid made impossible to access in time for this book.

He was Dr Engelbert Broda who was a refugee from Austria who dearly loved his country and was determined to go back there at the earliest possible time. He first came to see me in 1938 immediately after Austria was invaded by the Nazis.

After the war, he was anxious to get to Rome to see a woman he admired very much. But he held only an Austrian passport and it was difficult for him to get an Italian visa. But, as we have seen, SVS contacts came to his rescue.

At the SVS we knew all the European science attachés and I was able to ask the one from Italy, who was a very charming helpful man, to see Broda. As a result Broda was enabled to go to Italy to meet his friend. They subsequently married.

A one-sentence mention of Paul as Professor of Applied Molecular Biology follows before she returns to Broda:

Broda himself eventually returned to Vienna, and became Professor at the University. He did some pioneer research and wrote a biography of the great Austrian scientist, Boltzmann. There was a great celebration at the University on Broda's seventieth birthday. He died not very long after.

This was a man whom she had known since 1938, whose son she was close to, and to whom she had written begging him to stay in Britain. Berti does not even qualify for 'friend' for her readers. It is interesting how she limits her relationship to 'Broda', the anecdote of assistance to people in unexpected ways to post-1944 – after his covert life as Eric. In *Scientist Spies*, Paul Broda notes their correspondence that started in 1947 included thirty-seven letters up to 1952.

Engelbert's second marriage to Ina Jun was not a success and Esther felt close enough to him to advise him on it. She never took up his constant invitations to Vienna, though recalling her earlier pleasure in the city, for instance writing in 1963 of the city in the spring

the Rathauspark that I went through every day with its magnificent chestnut tree, and the magnolias.

He paid a flying visit to Britain in 1948, but understandably did not return after that although, for her part, she constantly urged him to. They met only once after his return to Vienna, briefly in Yugoslavia in 1959 after his second marriage had broken down, and in a letter the same year she pressed him to come to England to find a wife – English or, she inserted, American.

Paul Broda, in reflecting how he went to Austria in the summer and usually at Easter to see his father – whose 'problems with visas and entry to the UK only gradually emerged' – says,

> When I saw Tess then and later, she never asked me the obvious question as to why he did not visit me, her or England.

The obvious question becomes, 'What did she know and when did she know it?' But while it might seem unlikely that she was not contacted by MI5's spy hunters, no evidence suggests that she was. Berti's caution is clear in a letter to Esther of June 1961 when he writes of pondering up to the last moment whether he should go to Paul's Cambridge graduation: 'whether I should go this time, but . . .'

This apparent recognition – shared recognition? – of the risk could have been intended as a reference to his previous contacts with Alan Nunn May, who was arrested in 1946.

In March 1949 she wrote:

> It was tantalizing to know that Berti was as near as Paris and yet couldn't hop over the Channel.

Couldn't?

Paul writes:

> Perhaps her friendship with him was too important for her to allow herself to think that Berti might also have been a spy. In my own friendship with Tess I always had to balance my appreciation of what she had done for Berti and her fondness and concern for me with my dislike of her antipathy to [Paul's mother] Hilde and Alan [Nunn May] and the thought she was applying double standards.

In nearly forty years of correspondence with Engelbert Broda, with descriptions of her life and living, she makes only two directly Jewish references, one in 1950 and one in 1951.

In December 1950 she ends a letter to Engelbert,

> Keep well, and write to me again – the sun hasn't set yet and there are still some Joshuas about.

If the reference is to the biblical Joshua as a spy – one of the twelve sent by Moses into the Promised Land – is she warning him that he is being investigated? Is that the significance of the strange remark, '– the sun hasn't set yet'? 1950 had already seen the arrest of Klaus Fuchs and the defection of Guido Pontecorvo. And, possibly in the light of what follows, that she has even been questioned about him?

> I value my personal friendships above anything else and shall not renounce them.

(Paul makes the point that his father would probably not have picked up the Joshua reference. However, the significance lies in Esther's making the reference.)

And in March 1951 – when she wrote apparently in praise of the Society for Visiting Scientists,

> It's been quite gratifying to see how high our little SVS stands in scientific esteem, and whereas some time ago I might have been inclined to add und damit kann man Schabbas [sic] machen [and you can make Shabbos with it] – I don't think so now.

– was this actually another attempted warning against their being able to get together? Esther favoured directness in her correspondence; it was not like her to be oblique.

Given the shortcomings of *Refugee Scholars* in offering any real insight into the person who was Esther Simpson, her letters to Berti are a potential source of such information. But a word of caution is still required. So often, Esther is writing not just *to* the recipient but *for* that recipient, as is clear from her letters to Berti, presenting herself as a woman with whom they would feel comfortable. (In the long correspondence with Berti, they both write in English.)

In summer 1959 Esther found time for a working holiday that took her to a meeting in Dubrovnik – 'it might revive my dormant wanderlust'. En route to Zagreb, in the Slovenian city of Celje, she finally met Engelbert, who had travelled from Austria to meet her. This was after the break-up of his second marriage, and she found that 'after all the years they could still speak freely'.

In a follow-up letter to Berti, we get a brief coded passage about her earlier private life that brings the reader up short.

Perhaps it was the long habit of advising exiles that led Esther into advising on others' personal problems of which she had no direct knowledge or experience – though authoritative statements on subjects or areas where she had no personal knowledge are frequent. For instance on Berti's going to Spain, which she had not visited,

> I wonder what you will make of Spain, though of course Barcelona is different.

On mutual friends in India,

> If one leaves out Calcutta and other centres of misery, there is so much that is beautiful and exciting, as [the friends] no doubt found.

Or on Israel, where

> German as a subject is very unpopular.

In this letter to Berti she analyses the failure of his marriage to Ina, whom she had just met for the first time. She seems to have written without much pause for reflection:

> When you told me about your mother, it seemed to me that the description you gave fitted Hilde. And today I saw Ina again, and understood better what you were talking about. In your life you have married two women, by which I mean extremely feminine wives. Ina has a completely feminine approach to problems, and when it comes to personal relationships you have a completely masculine one.

(Neither in its extreme is a good thing.) This morning there was lots of opportunity for Ina to talk – she knows that I saw you yesterday. One thing you didn't tell me, that Ina still loves you very much. Jealousy is an illness and its victims are to be pitied. Ina must have been jealous of your work, your friends, your interests, and what your reaction to that would be I know. On the other hand, Berti, there may be some ways of withdrawing from an intolerable situation that are less cruel than others. Ina had thought she was starting a new life with you. She took an interest in the entirely new world of science you revealed to her, and made your family – particularly Paul – hers. In the long run it was stifling for you and you acted accordingly. But from her point of view it was a brutal withdrawal by you of precious gifts you had given her, leaving her high and dry, and more desolate than before. I admit she does not seek the reasons why there was this withdrawal she finds so devastating. *For myself, when I made that break, it had to be complete forever – that was my bad character – but I'm grateful for it, even though the deadly sin of pride was at the bottom of it* [author's italics]. I'd like to say a lot more, though – to beg you not to invest people with qualities they haven't got and then be disappointed. With all love, dear Berti.

In his reply Berti ignored the feminine/masculine analysis and her reference to her too making a complete break. He implies that Esther does not know the real situation as he shrugs off her intervention:

I made my mistakes because I could not break in good time the circle into which faulty upbringing had locked me. It is a pity as I could have made a family happy, but I am afraid it is a not terribly interesting story objectively . . . Ina is a remarkable woman and has many fine qualities, and is indeed a great poet. But I fear that in her neighbourhood I shall never feel at my ease, and shall always be on my guard. The Ehrlich sisters [Ina's maiden name] like it if people are at their service. In the case of Ina, this applies not only to assistance in every step she takes, but more subtly to the things of the mind. She will always ask me to be at her disposal with what I think and feel and say. And she will always try and try and try to check. She does not understand that one

cannot order feelings and thoughts. I am afraid that there is no other
possibility than to stay away as far as possible.

In her response, Esther re-explains his situation to him, but also brings
herself into it:

> I realised very quickly that she was vastly different from the idea I had
> of her before I met her. That was based on your accounts of twelve
> years ago, on her letters to me and on my own incurable naïvete
> [sic] . . . There is an intolerance of another point of view which I find
> unsympathetic and alarming. As I now see it, the first mistake was
> yours, and a ghastly one. It is one I should have made myself in the
> naïvete I have mentioned. You were in love with an idea of Ina; you
> added to your recollections and your admiration, attributes that in
> your conception should have been there, but weren't . . .

She rhapsodises for six or more sentences on Berti's pre-marriage state of
mind in marrying Ina, and then turns her psychologising on to Paul, now
twenty:

> That Paul should have his difficulties is not surprising; indeed I have
> always thought it a miracle how free he is of them in view of all he has
> had to go through. It is vitally important for Paul to learn to be
> independent of mind. I was always afraid that he would be conditioned
> in his thinking.

Later, with Paul at Cambridge, Esther wrote:

> Paul and I had an evening together. I was tremendously relieved to
> find him relatively unaffected by the dark spots that could have led to
> emotional complications. He accepts his environment, but in a natural
> way, not aggressively, as might have been the case if he were
> consciously rejecting something else. By some miracle he has
> developed into a normally happy young man.

Berti rejoined that there were hidden difficulties in Paul which could be
traced to the events of his childhood but he hoped Paul would be able
to deal with the problems. He turned to his own absence and, though

knowing how unlikely this was after Nunn May's, Fuchs's and Pontecorvo's arrests, added,

> Certainly I shall come to London before long one day.

In *Scientist Spies* Paul adds,

> Perhaps his policy was to hold out to Tess the possibility of a visit rather than to risk a discussion or worse following a flat 'no'.

As already noted, when Paul graduated in 1961, Berti kept up the pretence (as it can only have been) of his going to England remaining a possibility – 'I pondered practically to the last moment', he wrote to Esther – and she represented him at the ceremony. Again, in his letter of thanks to her, he hoped they could have a good chat in London in the autumn.

The two sides of Esther's approach to life are clearly in view here. Her readiness actively to support her chosen friends on the one hand balanced by, or more likely as the expression of, her needing to be in charge on the other.

To return to Ina, after the break with Engelbert she lived largely in Zagreb, translating and writing poetry – her *The Poet in the Time of Barbarism* reflecting on her wartime experience – and literary criticism. She died in 1983, in the same year as Engelbert.

These exchanges are also notable for containing that rare, possibly unique, expression of Ether's own emotional history, when she writes to Berti:

> . . . I admit she does not seek the reasons why there was this withdrawal she finds so devastating. *For myself, when I made that break, it had to be complete forever – that was my bad character – but I'm grateful for it, even though the deadly sin of pride was at the bottom of it* [author's italics].

In the context of Berti's break from Ina, the reference to 'that break' seems plainly enough to be to 'the withdrawal [Ina] finds so devastating', though the association is with the withdrawing Berti not the consequently devastated Ina.

In Esther's case the parallel is incomplete: her 'break' cannot be from a marriage. She remained Sinovitch until her deed poll changed her name to her brother's choice Simpson.

We must also take account of the reference to her 'bad character' in making the break complete forever for which she is grateful – presumably as it allowed her freedom to pursue her own interests – even though this meant the 'deadly sin of pride' that was at the bottom of it. This reading assumes that 'the bad character' is a reference to 'the deadly sin of pride' that was responsible for her making the break complete forever.

Her 'own incurable naïvete' must be included in our analysis. Pride and incurable naïveté are far from incompatible; the former might be excused by the latter, though she does not claim this Austenian mitigation.

No direct evidence of that complete break presents itself, but circumstantially we might risk a bet, bearing in mind the requirement for pride at the bottom of it. Of what was she, could she have been, sufficiently proud?

Initially, I was drawn to the modernist portrait of Esther by the Leeds artist Jacob Kramer, with the inscription 'For Esther August 1929'. Esther had started work in Vienna with IFOR on 5 September 1928, and so must have returned to Leeds from the Austrian capital to sit – unless he painted it from memory – though she does not mention this in her account of her relationship with Kramer in *Refugee Scholars*.

Known as the 'Modigliani of the North', Kramer was a Jewish immigrant from Ukraine who had come to Leeds with his family at the beginning of the twentieth century, fleeing the pogroms. Jacob became an established artist, an Expressionist, and taught at the Leeds School of Art. He had a profound sense of being Jewish and his work was deeply involved with elucidating the meaning of Jewish life, but he also became well known as a portraitist; his sitters included Mahatma Gandhi, Frederick Delius and Lord Rothschild.

The frontispiece of *Refugee Scholars*, the portrait dedicated 'to Esther', is one of simplified geometric form, showing her with eyes closed, though not in tranquillity. It has presence, a certain force.

Although she mentions Kramer in *Refugee Scholars*, it is solely in the context of his hearing her play while she was at university and of his work being affected by music.

She relates how music had provided an introduction to Kramer through a pianist with whom she played in Leeds very often, Joe Williams:

> . . . and someone who came to listen to us as often as he could was the
> artist Jacob Kramer. The local college of art now bears his name. Jacob
> Kramer had no musical training at all, but he was very much affected
> by music, and the first time he heard Joe play Scriabin it had such an
> effect on him that he promptly went back home and painted a terrific
> picture. It was in thick oils like little mountains, the background being
> a kind of ochre colour, with vermilion and black streaks across. It was,
> of course, an abstract, but that was what he felt like after hearing Joe
> play Scriabin.

She does not say where she saw that picture or when.

Jacob Kramer died unmarried in 1962. Apart from a press cutting
from the *Daily Telegraph* 7 April 1973, relating to an exhibition of his work,
nothing from, to or about Kramer is listed in her extensive archive at Leeds
University.

The portrait might testify to a burgeoning relationship. That she had
journeyed to Leeds from Vienna to see him. As for a further conjecture on
what might then have driven a complete break initiated in retrospect by
her bad character, the sin of pride, the incurable naïveté (presumably still
early in life)? At the portrait's date she had not yet become a Quaker, but
the first stirrings of interest in Vienna come around this period.

Speculation shifts. 'That break' becomes an earlier rejection of her
inherited Judaism and her parents' traditional expectations that she – a
university graduate proud of her first-class degree – should conform to the
traditional role of the Dvinsk daughter: marriage, home, family.

In this version, her 'bad character' becomes a repeat of her parents' reproach
at her rejection of all they held dear as Russian Ashkenazic Jews. 'The deadly
sin of pride' becomes her sense of having risen above her unassimilated
family, the 'cosmopolitanism' of the home as she had termed it, to 'feel part
of England' – as she put it in a letter to Broda we will come to shortly.

Was her early departure from Breslau caused by the Weiss family's
expectation of her observing their conservative Jewish practice? (Hannah
Arendt has Rahel as a young girl making her first journey to Breslau 'to
those inescapable provincial Jewish relations through whom at the time
every assimilated Jew with a European cultural background was connected
to the Jewish people and the old manners and customs he had discarded'.)

All this is sheer conjecture, of course; we could stretch it to include a break too with Kramer.

At this point a passage comes to mind from a letter Esther wrote on 15 November 1983 three weeks after Engelbert's death. Paul Broda thought I should see it, saying, 'From your standpoint one letter stands out':

> The letter was in fact written from Tess to Gitta Deutsch, who was my father's companion (rather than partner) towards the end of his life. Gitta Deutsch was the thrice-married daughter of Otto Erich Deutsch, an SPSL grantee and the Deutsch of the Schubert catalogue, who lived in Cambridge when ES and EB were there in the War. EB also knew her then as a very attractive 16-year-old. She returned to Vienna in the late '70's.

The letter contains this significant memory, one with religious practice at its heart:

> When I was 17, in my last year at school, I heard a brilliant lecture on 'Brand' by Ibsen. That, I thought, was the right attitude, Brand's: [sic] stand on your own two feet, be independent of people and objects that remind you of them. When I was 26 [in 1929 Esther was in Vienna with IFOR and attracted to the Quakers] I realised that was all wrong.

This looks very much as if here we have the timeframe for our speculation.

Esther about to enter university with the determination to stand on her own two feet and be independent of people and objects that remind her of them – expressed in the break with her parents' *Yiddishkeit*. Then the later rejection of the belief in being independent of people, expressed not as a return to Ellis's and Sarah's unassimilated culture but in joining the Quakers.

So, was the 'Steingold' she gave to Swarthmore Penn as her mother's maiden name a gesture of continuing separation? Equally, was referring in 1933 to her brother and his non-Jewish wife in Newcastle as 'home' a signal of the continuing breach with her widowed father in Leeds? What of his missing headstone?

Contemplating all this as a possibility in that era, the early life of Dora Diament (1898–1952) offers an example. Five years older than Esther, daughter of a pious Hasidic Polish Jewish family, she ran away from home to Berlin rather than marry as tradition demanded of her. Her family turned their backs on her, reciting ritual mourning prayers.

In 1923 Dora entered history, becoming the lover of Franz Kafka in the year before his death. Escaping to England in 1939, she was interned as an enemy alien in Port Erin camp on the Isle of Man. After her release she devoted herself to the preservation of Yiddish.

It is tempting to add that Esther devoted herself to the preservation of mainly Jewish refugee academics.

54

Questions Remain

What did Esther believe? As a Quaker, pacifist, socialist – all or any of those? And what was the nature or basis of her relationship with Engelbert Broda?

No one has thought longer and harder about this than his son Paul, who can also bring memories of his own contacts to bear, as well as a detailed familiarity with her post-war letters to Vienna.

Paul directed me to her letter to Engelbert of 18 December 1950 marking out her concern for the individual,

> . . . to me human relationships are the most important, because the most [sic] constructively creative factors operating in this world of woe. The human individual is what matter to me, not 'humanity', and certainly not any Moloch of a 'state' which purports to speak for 'humanity' . . .

Later, [50] she reflected on her situation as a child of immigrant parents,

> . . . Don't mistake me; when I say I feel part of England, it isn't out of any chauvinism – it's a mixture of the consciousness of privileges enjoyed during my childhood that my parents never had, the real affection I bear for what is best in the English character and institutions – but I believe that I have to belong to the world too; I do not feel a citizen of the world. England so far allows me to be that – far too many countries would not.

---

50 Letter to Engelbert Broda, December 1950.

And the following summer (13 August 1951) she added:

> . . . my interest is in saving life and the preservation of what is best in
> the human spirit . . .

A Quaker pacifist but not an appeaser; but how to explain this letter to
Broda of 29 August 1952? Esther manages to condemn Chamberlain's
appeasement while she shudders over the current policy of joint defence
with the US:

> . . . Incidentally, without the Chamberlain policy before 1939 millions
> of people would be alive now who are dead. And as regards the present
> position, I cannot help viewing with a shudder the transformation of
> England into the main atom bomb base of America – perhaps very soon
> of Messrs Eisenhower and Nixon. No, I cannot share your optimism.
> Had the British [Ed: note not 'we'] pursued a more independent policy,
> the world would not be in the sorry state in which it is now.

Paul also wrote to me with the letter already partly quoted, dated
15 November 1983, three weeks after his father's death, written to Gitta
Deutsch.

> I think all the time of Berti, and try not to let my desolating sense of
> loss overcome my gratitude for Berti's life and work, and for his
> enduring friendship.

She knew exactly how Gitta felt, wanting to be worthy of Berti's ideal,
trying to follow 'his behest not to cleave too strongly to any individual'.
She herself had known and admired what she described in the letter as 'a
puritanical almost calvinistic [sic] streak' in Berti. At 17, in her last year at
school, a brilliant lecture on Ibsen's *Brand* had taught her to be independent
of people; to stand on your own two feet. But since she had worked in
Vienna, at 26, she saw that was not the way we were made. 'We are fellows
one of another.' Mourn the lost, yes, but not to the point where we spurn
what still exists of life and fellowship, and being there for those who seek
our help or support.

> Cherish your years of friendship with Berti. They have enriched your
> life, so you can't deny them. Berti remains part of you; through

knowing him you became a different Gitta from the earlier one. That
is his immortality: in his descendants, and his influence on others who
in their turn will propagate that influence. There are so many of us
who loved him and who are different and better for having known
him. Let us acknowledge this proudly.

Not everyone would agree with that version of the message of Ibsen's verse
drama as recollected by Esther from her school days, though standing on
her own two feet, independent of family and friends was certainly her way
in the years after leaving university.

Whether or not Esther's description of Berti's ideal – not cleaving too
strongly to any individual – is an accurate representation of Engelbert's own
communist outlook, her insistence on keeping hold of life and on fellowship
towards those who might need our help sound a good representation of
what motivated Esther's own life's work, and perhaps of her envisaging her
FRSs as her children and as a family from their uprooted, unassimilated
emigrant days.

Her stance has a strong biblical ring to it (in the King James version): ' . . .
not to cleave too strongly . . .', *cf.* ' . . . ye that did cleave unto the Lord . . .'
Deuteronomy 4, 'We are fellows one of another'/ *cf.* 'We have fellowship one
with another' – I John 1:7. 'World of woe' *cf. Revelation*.
    One other sentence calls for our attention:

> There are so many of us who loved him and who are different and
> better for having known him. Let us acknowledge this proudly.

Proudly? One would expect such a qualifier where the person praised has
engaged in otherwise dubious or shaming activities, not died esteemed for
his scientific work. What could Esther have had in mind? Had she let slip
'proudly' (in spite of his spying for the Soviets)?
    Not every refugee initiative met with her approval. In 1965 Jewish
refugees, including some of her 'children', launched the 'Thank You
Britain' appeal to express refugees' gratitude to Britain for giving them
sanctuary, the proceeds to go towards a fellowship and lectures under
the auspices of the British Academy. In a letter to Engelbert she tore into
the idea.

She was very critical of Thank You Britain, she wrote. The appeal letter was very badly framed – most un-English; the target too low; another fellowship when this field came already well provided. She didn't doubt the goodwill, only the wisdom; it was probably not too well handled. She first heard of it on one of those magazine programmes on the wireless. 'If, after all this, you and your friends feel like contributing, do not hesitate to express your own opinions.' Hans Krebs had wanted a list of the scholars in Britain from her, 'and I had not reason to withhold it from him'.

In 1991 Esther suffered an accident involving a car. She noted to Cooper that the driver was Polish, 'insured with a Baltic company'. And while she sustained no permanent injury, the accident and the pursuit of compensation plainly took their toll. She became increasingly deaf, finding it hard to follow the proceedings at SPSL Council meetings.

She remained busy, telling Cooper in July 1991 of having to deal with a grant for a Somalian. In the same letter she records attending the Harveian Dinner at the Royal College of Physicians where the oration was given by a member of the SPSL Council, Sir Raymond Hoffenberg KBE MD FRCP.

And on 2 August 1991 Cooper wrote to congratulate her on becoming one of the first Honorary Fellows of the Royal College of Physicians.

He was also consulting her on the ordering of the book, her list of distinctions, distinguishing between first- and second-generation scholars, refugees' war service. Distinctions first, war service last would complete her story very nicely.

He was still struggling to encourage her to include something about her background and early days in Leeds. That, he assured her fruitlessly, was what made her great achievements so interesting.

What is of interest is why Tess Simpson was so resistant to recapitulating the early days of Esther Sinovitch – when Esther Sinovitch had done so well – and even 'Esther' was to be pushed away. The subject of *Refugee Scholars* is given as Tess Simpson. But just as she turned her back on her own start in life as a child of refugees, always to be assimilated but never native, so she insisted on her 'children's' retention of their restart in life as refugees, her true connection with them.

As for the outlook driving her life's work, the comment that seemed to the author to get closest was made by someone who had worked with her:

> Essentially, she was people led, uninterested in the issues that had brought them to her door.

That seems true enough, even on the gravest issue of her century. Yet even that insight in all its brevity needs qualification.

The word 'friends' comes to mind. People led and friendship led. Esther's insistence on displaced scholars for whom she opened the way to safety becoming her friends, or at least, and on the evidence of *Refugee Scholars*, those belonging to the category of mainly-Jewish German-speakers. Then, in a decolonising, post-colonial, Cold War world, between working to secure a future for global academic refugees and playing chamber music, perhaps too little time remained for any active campaigning, even on academic freedom.

This is not to diminish her commitment. As Henry James is quoted as assuring us, 'Excellence does not require perfection.'

55
Envoi

Esther Simpson died in hospital on 19 November 1996. A memorial gathering was held for her at the Royal Society on 14 April 1997. A pleasing conceit, the tributes were divided into four 'movements' of which the first was a performance of Haydn's string quartet No. 4 in D Major (opus 20). The programme recorded that:

> Family, friends and colleagues are coming together today to celebrate Tess Simpson's long, rich and generous life. This she tirelessly dedicated to the cause of academic freedom, to the free exchange of knowledge, and to the support of many hundreds of academic refugees who were the victims of racial, political or religious intolerance and repression.
>
> Tess is also remembered tonight for her gifts for music and friendship, and as a pacifist and Quaker.

Six years earlier, she had been present at the Royal Society Anniversary Meeting at which the departing president, Lord Porter, a Nobel laureate in Chemistry, had made his closing address. Later, she wrote to Ray Cooper that in the course of his speech Lord Porter had asked her to stand up. (She was not caught by surprise as she had been alerted to his intention.)

In response, Cooper came clean. He had prompted it in a roundabout way, to make up for an earlier failure by the Imperial War Museum to include Esther in a meeting to mark internment.

But let us leave Dr Simpson as perhaps she would have liked to be remembered – and was by 'Jack' Costello:

Father John E. Costello SJ of Regis College in the University of Toronto met Esther when researching his biography of the philosopher John Macmurray, a friend of Esther's who had also been an adviser to the AAC/SPSL.

Father Costello described her in a letter to the present author,

> In her own way – and in God's way, I believe – she was a saint – plain and simple. No worldly category fits.

She had invited him to lunch at the Royal Society, he remembers:

> I was waiting on the sidewalk corner not far from Trafalgar Square/St. James Park—where we had agreed on the phone to meet. It was a cool but very pleasant day. Then, precisely at the time designated, I saw a small elderly lady walking crisply in my direction. She was wearing a 1940s herring-bone grey coat with an equally worn hat from those years . . . but as I looked at her I remember saying to myself: that woman looks just like Mom did when she took me as a 3-4-year-old in our small Quebec town to pick up a new booklet of wartime ration coupons before going shopping.
>
> When this woman approached me – and I knew for certain just by looking at her and from what I had heard, that this was Esther Simpson – she looked straight into my face and, as though names didn't matter, and who I was was obvious and beyond question, said: 'We're having lunch at the Royal Society and you look just like John Macmurray.' Not even 'Hello' Then she started walking . . . and I had to catch up to her, meet her pace, and absorb the news of where we were headed.
>
> As we approached the Royal Society I was relieved that she was dressed so simply . . . so very 1940's 'simply' . . . mainly because it met the level of my rumpled jacket as well. But what suddenly struck me with such a sense of liberation was: What we're wearing doesn't matter! It doesn't matter to her at all! And it doesn't have to matter to me – As we went through the entrance door, Esther was greeted in a warm and familiar way by the doorman and she greeted him by name.

It was then that I began to understand that, in some way, she was at home here. And it all became crystal clear that as we headed down the corridor towards the Dining Room there was 'work' to do before the pleasures of lunch. The walls on both sides were lined with the portraits of world-class scientists, many of whom Esther had known, or knew yet. And she knew them as 'my boys' – namely, refugee-scholars whom she had welcomed and helped decisively to find their way into a new life after escaping the snares of the Nazi regime. As we walked, she pointed them out, named them by name, and at the end of the corridor recalled there were 14 of 'her boys' honoured there for their contributions to science and the world.

She happily accepted, in her own fashion, the role of being their 'mother' as they learned to walk and talk and live in the new world into which they had come. She also insisted, in her obvious poverty, on taking the bill; leaving the president of a theology college at the University of Toronto squirming, and barely self-possessed enough to murmur: Thank you . . .

Jack Costello added,

Esther reflected on her life journey in a May 21, 1993 letter to me . . . After a short introduction referring to a letter I had written to her, she reflects. . .

'I don't deserve the generous things you have written. As I told you, I am very conscious of being myself a nobody, who has had the immense privilege of knowing and making friends with outstanding people, and my work has enriched my life immeasurably. You can imagine how I feel about our refugee scholars . . .'

What is most significant I feel is the brave, forthright manner she had, and the encouragement she gave to anyone who was among those most in need. And the way she gave herself to those who were in great need. This has been noted so often, that I don't want to overplay the obvious.

In her own way – and in God's way, I believe – she was a saint – plain and simple. No worldly category fits.

In the May 1993 letter to Fr Costello, in which she described her consciousness of being a nobody privileged to know outstanding people, Esther had shown how the historical fate of displaced German scholars lived on for her from the first days of the AAC,

> 'They arrived in 1933, onwards, from Hitler's Germany, a fine academic future destroyed, colleagues who crossed the road to avoid looking them in the face, arrival in a new country, with a new language, no funds, no future. Then I saw them gradually settle in, make their mark, their children go to our schools and develop into British citizens. The rest is history, as portrayed in Ray Cooper's book. And our Society helped them on their way, and I shared their triumphs, and rejoice in their children and grandchildren, who are contributing so much to the countries of their adoption . . .

Yet the very last word must go to Engelbert Broda.

Engelbert Broda – the Soviets' 'Eric' – died in October 1983. His son Paul reflected to me that:

> For the first half of his post-war life he was an outsider, and discriminated against professionally, but from the mid-sixties on he gradually became accepted and then esteemed.

Four months before his death he had written,

> Dearest Tess, I do not have the date of your birthday and so I am writing to you in the blue now. Many, many happy returns among all the scientists, many of them eminent, whom you gave such decisive help, and their children and grandchildren. To paraphrase Winston Churchill (but let's not diminish his memory by the present PM) Never in history has so much help been given to so many with so little material basis!
>
> Well, some will be just grateful, and some jolly well they ought to be, but some will always love you, we among them. I do so much hope your birthday will be happy.

Acknowledgements

This project started with my friend and co-author of three books David Edmonds. He discovered Miss Simpson while researching his study of the Vienna Circle, *The Murder of Professor Schlick*. The discovery prompted his compelling 2018 BBC Radio 4 documentary *Miss Simpson's Children* and an ensuing 5,500-word *Jewish Chronicle* article. They then sparked interest in a possible book. At that time, David did not want to undertake it, but suggested I should. He also shared with me his original research and was always available for discussion and to read drafts. Naturally, responsibility for the outcome is mine and mine alone.

That adjuration also extends to Paul Broda. Without the access he allowed me to the years-long correspondence between his father Engelbert Broda and Esther Simpson, this book would not have been possible. It also benefited hugely from his personal knowledge of Esther from his boyhood and his own service to the Society for the Protection of Science and Learning, both elaborated in fruitful interchanges and in his eagle-eyed readings of the emerging text. My gratitude is also to Liz Fraser, Esther's successor as SPSL Secretary. She could not have been more helpful in her recollections of working with Esther, making documents available and suggesting other contacts, as well as reading the text. My thanks go to Esther Saraga, whose sensitive account of her parents' emigration – *Berlin to London: An Emotional History of Two Refugees* – was essential reading. I learned much from her parents' correspondence that Esther kindly shared with me, and from her own perceptions.

The book *Refugee Scholars: Conversations with Tess Simpson*, recorded, compiled, edited and published by the late Ray Cooper, is central to our knowledge of Esther and her work, together with his follow-up book, *Retrospective Sympathetic Affection*. I am most grateful to his children, Hugh, Martin and Frances, for their cooperation with this project, their supply of documents, and their consent to my use of their father's work. Hugh's own memory of Esther as 'Redoubtable, clear-eyed, and determined' has been something of a lighthouse in darkness.

I also benefited from and am most grateful for enlightening conversations with Shula Marks, a former SPSL/CARA council member and chair of council; Alan Phillips, a former general secretary of WUS, managing refugee scholarship programmes including those for Chilean refugees; Anthony Grenville, the doyen of German-Jewish refugee studies; and, for her command of MI5's interest in German and Austrian political refugees, Charmian Brinson.

Alan Phillips, who also kindly read the text, sent me accounts of Esther that demanded to go verbatim into the text. So did Father John Costello SJ's vivid account of being lunched by Esther at the Royal Society as part of his research into his biography of John Macmurray. He also kindly retrieved pertinent documents from his own research.

In an epic misfortune of timing, most of the work for this study fell to be carried out during the Covid-19 pandemic and lockdown. Libraries and archives closed or limited access. Esther's personal archive is held in the Brotherton Library at Leeds University, which devised a form of virtual access to the holding during pandemic restrictions, of which I took vital advantage. The Brotherton staff could not have been more friendly, helpful and supportive in enabling me to view key documents. The AAC/SPSL archive is held by the Bodleian Library Oxford. I was immensely fortunate to have Beau Woodbury explore this for me, always with an unerring eye for the potentially significant. The executive director of the SPSL's successor, the Council for At-Risk Academics (CARA), Stephen Wordsworth, read the draft text; I am most grateful for his consent to use of AAC/SPSL documents held by the Bodleian and also of Esther's letters to

Engelbert Broda held in Vienna. I was able to visit the Library of the Society of Friends for archival insights into Esther *qua* Quaker. This was always something to be looked forward to for the friendly and pivotal assistance of the library staff. I would like particularly to thank Libby Adams and Lisa McQuillan for their help with my lines of enquiry. My initial contact with the Quaker Hampstead Meeting, of which Esther was a prominent member, was most generously responded to by Rod Harper; as well as with his own memories of her, he supplied me with essential contacts.

I owe The London Library and its dedicated staff, that essential resource for a writer at the best of times, profound gratitude for their exceptional service during the pandemic.

Further afield, I was fortunate to be in touch with Esther's Canadian family. Her second cousin Morty Wellen shared the extensive family tree he had created from its Latvian origins and his own memories of meeting Esther in London, as did Rochelle Shereff and Heidi Lack. I am most grateful to them.

I must also record my profound gratitude to Barbara Suchy for her unfailing help on all aspects of German-Jewish history touched on in this book. I want similarly to thank Diane Dosso in France for sharing with me her highly informative work on the preservation of French science during the Second World War, and in particular the role of Louis Rapkine, and also for her visits to the French government archives on my behalf.

Cyril Pearce generously shared his extensive research into First World War conscientious objectors from Leeds, including the military documentation for Esther's brother Israel.

I want to record my thanks to Judith Elam for her moving account of her grandfather's internment, and Rachel Pistol for her research into the official classification of aliens. These appeared on Tony Hausner's Isle of Man internment email group, interned-on-iom@googlegroups.com, required reading for current interest in and information on internment. I am grateful to Peter and Leni Gillman for approving my use of their *Guardian* letter on internment.

Very helpfully, June Jones recalled daily life in Crawford Street Leeds for me, and Hamdi Zanfahy shared his warm memories of Esther, whom he welcomed to the north London house where she acquired a flat on her eventual (but never complete) retirement. John Marshall Grant kindly passed me the transcript of his grandmother Irene Grant's BBC talk on her rescue of Bertolt Brecht's daughter Barbara from the Gestapo, and his sister Eleanor her memories from Esther's visits to Donald and Irene's London flat. Julia Simpson kindly gave permission for the use of Esther's family photograph.

A gallery of kind responders took an interest in my enquiries or appeals for information about Esther: her roots in Leeds, local Quaker membership, her brother Israel's teaching career in Newcastle, her contacts in Vienna and London. My thanks go to Richard Bourke, Jonathan Brown at Jesmond Park Academy, Jocelyn Campbell, David Cowans, Jeanne Damico at Swarthmore Pennsylvania, Madelaine Drohan, Helen Greaves, Jalka of *Konfliktkultur*, Daniel Kravetz, Charles Lewis of the Hampstead Music Club, Freda Matthews, Oliver Pickering, Genevieve Silvanus, John Veit-Wilson, Michael Yudkin, Trudy Zimmerman at the Wellcome Trust.

My understanding of Esther, for whom personal reticence was a way of life, benefited deeply from conversations with my wife Elisabeth and daughter Esther and their psychological insights.

At my publisher, Little, Brown, commissioning editor Tom Asker was a constant support. Writing in the 100th anniversary of *The Waste Land* I am prompted to say he was the Ezra Pound of this text. *Il miglior fabbro* no less.

I also felt privileged to work on the text with his Little, Brown colleagues Rebecca Sheppard and Alison Tulett.

I want to express my gratitude to my agent Veronique Baxter at David Higham, and to Sara Leighton.

Bibliography

Arendt, Hannah: 'We Refugees', Menorah Journal, 31, no. 1, 1943

    The Origins of Totalitarianism, New York, Schocken Books, 1951

    Rahel Varnhagen: The Life of a Jewish Woman, tr. Winston R. & C., New York, New York Review Book, 2022

Auerbach, Erich: *Scholarship in Times of Extremes: Letters of Erich Auerbach (1933–46), on the Fiftieth Anniversary of His Death*, Cambridge, Cambridge University Press online, 2020

Berghahn, Marion: *Continental Britons German-Jewish Refugees from Nazi Germany*, Oxford, Berg Publishers, 1988

Bentwich, Norman: *The Rescue and Achievement of Refugee Scholars: The Story of Displaced Scholars and Scientists 1933–1952*, The Hague, Martinus Nijhof, 1953

Beveridge, William: *A Defence of Free Learning*, London, Oxford University Press, 1959

Boonstra, Jensen, Kniesmeyer (eds): *Antisemitism: A History Portrayed*, Amsterdam, Anne Frank Foundation, 1993

Boyd, Julia: *Travellers in the Third Reich: The Rise of Fascism Through the Eyes of Everyday People*, London, Elliott & Thompson, 2017

Brecht, Bertolt: *Refugee Conversations,* ed. Tom Kuhn, tr. Romy Fursland, London, Methuen Drama, 2021

    Love Poems, tr. David Constantine and Tom Kuhn, foreword by Barbara Brecht-Schall, New York, WW Norton 2014

Briggs, Asa: *Victorian Things*, London, Penguin, 1988

Broda, Paul: *Scientist Spies: A Memoir of My Three Parents and the Atom Bomb*, Leicester, Matador, 2011

Cohen, Susan: 'The British Federation of University Women: Helping academic women refugees in the 1930s and 1940s', April 2010 Board of International Affairs of the Royal College of Psychiatrists, published online by Cambridge University Press, 2 January 2018

Cohn, Willy: *No Justice in Germany: The Breslau Diaries 1933-1931,* ed. Norbert Conrads, tr. Kronenberg, Stanford Studies in Jewish History and Culture, Stanford, 2012

Cooper, Ray (ed.): *Refugee Scholars: Conversations with Tess Simpson*, Leeds, Moorland Books, 1992

Retrospective Sympathetic Affection: A tribute to the academic community, Leeds, Moorland Books, 1996

Costello, John: *John Macmurray: A biography*, Edinburgh, Floris Books, 2002

Crawford, Ulmschneider, Elsner (eds): *Ark of Civilization: Refugee Scholars and Oxford University 1930-1945,* Oxford, Oxford University Press, 2017

Crowther, James: *Fifty Years with Science*, London, Barrie & Jenkins, 1970

Edmonds, David: *The Murder of Professor Schlick: The Rise and Fall of the Vienna Circle,* Princeton, Princeton University Press, 2020

Miss Simpson's Children, 2017 BBC Radio 4 Documentary www.bbc.co.uk

Engel, David: *The Holocaust: The Third Reich and the Jews*, Harlow, Pearson Education, 2000

Erbelding, Rebecca: *Rescue Board: The Untold Story of America's Efforts to Save the Jews of Europe,* New York, Anchor Books, 2019

Evans, Richard J.: *The Coming of the Third Reich*, London, Allen Lane, 2003

Fermi, Laura: *Illustrious Migrants: The Intellectual Migration from Europe 1930–41,* Chicago, University of Chicago Press, 1968

Friedländer, Saul: *Nazi Germany & The Jews The Years of Persecution 1933–39,* London, Weidenfeld & Nicolson, 1997

Fritzsche, Peter: *Hitler's First Hundred Days: When Germans Embraced the Third Reich*, New York, Basic Books, 2020

Golding, Louis: *The Jewish Problem*, London, Penguin, 1938

Grenville, Anthony: *Encounters with Albion: Britain and the British in Texts by Jewish Refugees from Nazism*, Cambridge, Legenda, 2018

Grossman, Vasily: *Life and Fate*, tr. Chandler, London, Collins Harvill, 1985

Haffner, Sebastian: *Defying Hitler: A Memoir*, tr. Pretzel, London, Weidenfeld & Nicolson, 2002

Hartshorne, Edward Y., *German Universities and National Socialism*, Cambridge Mass, Harvard University Press, 1937

Hawkins, Richard A.: 'The Dudley Refugee Committee and the Kindertransport 1938–1945', *Jewish Historical Studies* 51 (1), 2020

Hentschel, K. ed., Hentschel, A. tr., *Physics and National Socialism: An Anthology of Primary Sources*, Basel, Birkhäuser, 1996

Hirschfeld, Gerhard (ed.): *Exile in Great Britain Refugees from Hitler's Germany*, Oxford, Berg, 1984

Hughes, Jeff: *Doing Diaries: David Martin, the Royal Society and scientific London, 1947–1950*, London, Royal Society Publishing, 2012; https://doi.org/10.1098/rsnr.2012.0037

Imperial War Museum Sound Archive https://www.iwm.org.uk/collections/sound

Jewish Gen Jewish Families of Dvinsk, https://www.jewishgen.org/databases/Latvia/DvinskFamilies.htm

Jurgensen, Céline & Mongin, Dominique eds, *France and Nuclear Deterrence – A Spirit of Resistance*, la Fondation pour la Recherche Stratégique 75016 PARIS 2020. Originally published in France by Odile Jacob in August 2018

Kapp, Yvonne: *Time Will Tell: Memoirs*, London, Verso, 2003

Kapp, Yvonne & Mynatt, Margaret, *British Policy and the Refugees, 1933–41*, London, Frank Cass, 1997

Katz, Bernard: Obituary of A. V. Hill, Biographical Memoirs of Fellows
    of the Royal Society, Royal Society Publishing, November 1978,
    https://doi.org/10.1098/rsbm.1978.0005

Kent, Aaron M.: *Identity, Migration and Belonging: The Jewish Community
    of Leeds 1890–1920*, Newcastle upon Tyne, Cambridge Scholars
    Publishing, 2015

Klemperer, Victor: *I Shall Bear Witness: The Diaries of Victor Klemperer
    1933–1941*, ed. and tr. Chalmers, London, Weidenfeld & Nicolson, 1999

Kruger, Horst: *Growing Up Under Hitler*, tr. Shaun Whiteside, London,
    The Bodley Head, 2019

Lanouette, William: *Genius in the Shadows: Biography of Leo Szilard –
    The Man Behind the Bomb*, Chicago, University of Chicago Press, 1994

Lochner, Louis, ed. and tr.: *The Goebbels Diaries*, London, Hamish
    Hamilton, 1948

London, Louise: *Whitehall and the Jews 1933-1948: British Immigration Policy,
    Jewish Refugees and the Holocaust*, Cambridge, Cambridge University
    Press, 2000

Lorant, Stefan: *I Was Hitler's Prisoner*, London, Penguin, 1935

Marks, Weindling, Wintour (eds): *In Defence of Learning: The Plight,
    Persecution, and Placement of Academic Refugees 1933–1980s*, The British
    Academy/Oxford University Press, 2011

Oldfield, Sybil: *Doers of the Word: British Women Humanitarians 1900–1950*,
    London, Oldfield/Continuum, 2001

    The Black Book: The Britons on the Nazi Hit List, London, Profile Books,
    2020

Ory, Pascal; Blanc-Chaléard, Marie-Claude eds. *Dictionnaire des étrangers
    qui ont fait la France*, Paris, Robert Laffont, 2013

Peierls, Rudolf: *Bird of Passage: Recollections of a Physicist*, Princeton,
    Princeton Legacy Library, 1985

Rall, Jack A.: 'Nobel Laureate A. V. Hill and the refugee scholars, 1933–
    1945', *Advances in Physiology Education*, 25 April 2017,
    https://doi.org/10.1152/advan.00181.2016

Rathbone, Eleanor: 'Rescue the perishing: A summary of the position
    regarding the Nazi massacres of Jewish and other victims and of
    proposals for their rescue: an appeal, a programme and a challenge',
    London, The National Committee for Rescue from Nazi Terror, 1943
    'Continuing terror: How to rescue Hitler's victims, a survey and a
    programme', London, The National Committee for Rescue from
    Nazi Terror, 1944

Remarque, Erich Maria: *The Night in Lisbon*, tr. Manheim, New York,
    Random House, 2014

Robbins, Lionel: *Autobiography of an Economist*, London, Palgrave
    Macmillan, 1971

Robinson, Andrew: *Einstein on the Run: How Britain Saved the World's
    Greatest Scientist*, New Haven, Yale University Press, 2019

Roth, Joseph, *What I Saw: Reports from Berlin 1920–1933*, tr. Hofmann,
    New York, WW Norton, 2003

Saraga, Esther: *Berlin to London: An Emotional History of Two Refugees*,
    Elstree, Valentine Mitchell, 2019

Seabrook, Jeremy: *The Refuge and the Fortress: Britain and the Flight from
    Tyranny*, London, Palgrave Macmillan, 2009

Serge, Victor: *Last Times*, tr. Ralph Manheim, revised and foreword
    Richard Greeman, New York Review Books, 2022

Smith, Michael: *Six: A History of Britain's Secret Intelligence Service*,
    London, Biteback 2010; see also https://spartacus-educational.com/
    Frank_Foley.htm

Schweitzer, Bernard: 'Rebecca West and the Meaning of Exile', *Partial
    Answers: Journal of Literature and the History of* Ideas, Volume 8,
    Number 2, June 2010, pp. 389–407 (Article), published by Johns
    Hopkins University Press

Strauss, Herbert: Leo Baeck Institute Year Book XXV and XXVI
    1980/1981: *Jewish emigration from Germany*, Oxford Academic

Szilard, Leo, Weart & Szilard, Gertrud Weiss (eds): *Leo Szilard: His
    version of the facts: Selected recollections and correspondence*, Cambridge
    Mass, MIT Press, 1978

Wasserman, Jacob: *My Life as a German and a Jew*, London, Allen & Unwin, 1934

Webb, Stephanie: *Curtains Drawn: The Experience of Leeds in World War One*, Leeds Museums and Art Galleries, 2014

Weindling, Paul: 'Medical Refugees and the Modernisation of British Medicine 1930–1960', *Social History of Medicine*, 1 December 2009

Weitz, Eric D.: *Weimar Germany Promise and Tragedy*, Princeton, Princeton University Press 2018

Wharton, Edith: *The Custom of the Country*, New York, Scribner's, 1913/Bantam Classic, 2008

Wiener, Alfred: *The Fatherland and the Jews London*, Granta and the Wiener Holocaust Library, 2021

Woodbridge, Steven: 'Fifth Column Fears in Richmond 1939–1940: A Brief Survey', *Richmond History Journal*, no. 29, 2008

Zürndorfer, Hannele: *The Ninth of November*, London, Quartet, 1983

Index